Chinese Grammar 101

Book 10

Grammar, Phrases, Sentence Construction, Pinyin, Phonetics, Stroke Order, Radicals, Cursing, Other Stuff

大毛猴子
Dà Máo Hóuzi
Big Hairy Monkey
www.SpeakandWriteChinese.com

All rights reserved. No part of this publication may be reproduced, photocopied, stored in a retrieval system, and transmitted in any form or by any means, electronic, mechanical, recording or otherwise, without the prior written permission of the author and publisher. But really, I am pretty flexible on this. My goal is to provide information to learn the written Chinese language so if you need copies for educational purposes or you are really cheap you can e-mail me for consent.

Library and Archives Canada Cataloguing in Publication

Dà, Máo Hóuzi, 1969-

Title: Chinese Grammar 101
Grammar, Phrases, Sentence Construction, Pinyin, Phonetics, Stroke Order, Radicals, Cursing, Other Stuff / Dà, Máo Hóuzi

Subtitle: A Comprehensive Approach to Learning Chinese Language, Book 10
Includes index. Includes Some Text in Chinese.

ISBN 978-1-926564-20-3

Chinese Language-Grammar. 2. Chinese language--Textbooks for Second Language Learners--English speakers. I. Dà, Máo Hóuzi II. Title.

III. Series: A Comprehensive Approach to Learning Chinese Language, Book 10.

PL1171.D27 2011   495.1'5   C2010-906723-1

Author: Dà Máo Hóuzi
Editor-in-Chief: Dà Máo Hóuzi
Authentic Chinese Editor: Lu XueFeng
Copy Editor: Dà Máo Hóuzi
Graphics / Tables / Covers: Dà Máo Hóuzi

This is Book 10 in the Series,

A Comprehensive Approach to Learning Chinese Language

Monkey Monk Publications
Stoney Creek, Ontario, Canada

Copyright © 2011 Dà Máo Hóuzi

Published by Monkey Monk Publications

Book 1) Hanzi and the Kangxi Radicals

Book 1a) The Rules of Chinese Characters and Mandarin

Book 2) 425 Easy Chinese Characters

Book 2a) 101 Easy Chinese Characters

Book 2b) 300 Easy Chinese Characters

Book 3) 425 Intermediate Chinese Characters

Book 4) 425 Advanced Chinese Characters

Book 5) 425 Chinese Characters Using 1 to 5 Strokes

Book 6) The First 251 Most Common Chinese Characters

Book 7) The Second 251 Most Common Chinese Characters

Book 8) The Third 251 Most Common Chinese Characters

Book 9) The Fourth 251 Most Common Chinese Characters

Book 10) Chinese Grammar 101

Book 11) Chinese Grammar 201

Book 12) Chinese Grammar 301

Book 13) The First 500 Chinese Characters Practice Drills

Book 14) The Second 500 Chinese Characters Practice Drills

Book 15) The Third 500 Chinese Characters Practice Drills

Book 16) The Fourth 500 Chinese Characters Practice Drills

Book 17) The Fifth 500 Chinese Characters Practice Drills

Book 18) The Sixth 500 Chinese Characters Practice Drills

Book 19) The Seventh 500 Chinese Characters Practice Drills

Book 20) Rude, Ignorant, Derogatory and Insulting Mandarin Chinese

Preface to the General Introduction

Standard Mandarin is an official language of the United Nations. More people speak Mandarin than any other language. If you are a native English speaker you will need to turn on a part of your brain that is relatively dormant. This is the only language that exists that is not driven by a sound based signal system. A Chinese character is a logogram, a symbol. There are no consistent or reliable signals for meaning or sound in a character. After you learn a character you may be able to pick clues out of a small number of characters. If you never speak a word of Mandarin or travel to China you can still make a change in your brain that will open a whole new way to memorize.

The Chinese have always intrigued me. I was first exposed to them in university. I marvelled at how they could ace physics, math, chemistry, engineering and computer science yet barely speak English. It was not until I looked at their language that I began to understand. Their language is based on a system of a visual image representing meaning. Although each character has defined meanings, compiled together they may have totally different meanings. It would be nice if two characters beside each other as A and B equalled AB but in many situations it is more complex. $A + B = AB$ exists but so does $A + B = C$. If you learn 200 characters in a paragraph and write all their meanings in an English sentence format, the product may be incomprehensible.

Initially you will struggle with learning complex characters. But like all skills you will improve. Many people lament the difficulty to me but my response is always, ***2 billion people cannot be wrong***.

Other Useful Things in This Book

One of the reasons my books are all so big is that they have a huge appendix in the back of the book. The bookstores and internet sellers are pushing multitudes of crap quality books that do not provide the essentials of learning the language. I am not a linguist by training, far from it.

If you are considering buying a book that promises some new revolutionary approach, or a fast and easy way to learn this language, don't waste your money. I have them all and I took the useful parts out of them to write my books. I will give a list of useless books at the back of this book so that you don't waste you money on the books I have stacked up by my desk.

Included is a 176 page appendix that has the entire picture. This information did not come easily. The great white man always thinks he has a better way so it was difficult to find all the esssentials in English written language books.

A Chinese student takes years to master the essentials of the written language. You could work on this casually your entire life. One of the biggest walls in the progress of a Chinese student is a high school exit exam called the (高考, **gāokǎo**). This is actually an abbreviation for four words written with eight characters. On this exam they are still being tested on the basics of their language, after studying if for 12 years.

So, if you have not mastered the essentials of the language, detailed in the ***Table of Contents***, please very thoroughly read and understand the back of the book. You will not find this detail in another book.

Disclaimer

Observation and criticism, they are different. First, I love China. It has been a fascinating and rewarding experience to work and travel in China. If I extoll the virtues of China, you will take this in a positive light and the Chinese government and Chinese people will love me. If I told you that China is a dirty disgusting shit hole third world country riddled with massive corruption, toxic air, soil and food supply, you would think I was criticizing China. I have spent a lot of time in China, I have worked in 23 countries and travelled in perhaps 75. I think my observations are fairly astute. Notice I didn't indemnify the previous statement.

Somehow, China in various forms has survived 5000 years, says the Chinese. But this is not true either. Neither the geographic confines, the governance, the name of the country, nor the people have remained the same. The land mass is of course still there but has been reshaped, denuded of trees and grass, hunted to near extinction and abused beyond immediate repair in many areas. Large fertile farm areas are being covered with cities, dams and reservoirs. Currently one coal fired power plant is completed each week. Yet over a million people die each year from lung disease. Industrial accident deaths are abysmal. Last year, about 127,000 people in China died in workplace accidents and there were 17 incidents with death tolls over 30.

These are statistics from the Chinese embassy website. So I assure you that the numbers are much higher. China is not known to tell the truth when it comes to negative statistics. http://www.china-embassy.org/eng/gyzg/t269441.htm

The health care system in China is an unregulated nightmare where anyone can call themselves a ***Traditional Chinese Doctor*** and hang out a shingle and poison and mistreat the poorest people. Intravenous clinics are all over the place where you can sit in a window exposed to the street and get infused with bottles of coloured liquid. Mold, mildew, fungus, mushrooms, tree bark, fish bladders, ground finger and toe nails, just about anything goes into these medicines. Hepatitis A, B and C are rampant with 300,000 plus people dying from Hepatitis B annually. Vaccine programs are just beginning now, however, lack of public education and cost prevents more than one million babies from being vaccinated each year. Vaccines cost pennies.

Cancer, well, what a mess that is. There are areas with 100 times the incidence of gastrointestinal cancers as in the West. Gynecologic cancers are taking many young women. Liver cancer from chronic hepatitis is another killer. Unregulated use of pesticides, you buy them on the street, and unregulated use of industrial chemicals and their disposal is setting China up for cancer unlike the world has ever seen. With a health care system in shambles and unaffordable, the suffering will be immense.

The education system is an international embarrassment. Cheating, corruption, nepotism, a Chinese university degree can vary from useless, bought and not authentic, to the rare school that has international standing. There are signs in the Beijing Subway selling university diplomas and degrees. Illiteracy is rampant. Most people who are 50 years and older have almost no education. The era of Mao oversaw the execution of doctors, lawyers, teachers, accountants and the higher educated. China claims 85% literacy. I would say 25% are literate by UN standards.

China is on a collision course of its own greed with pressured resources of water, air, soil, food, electricity, health care, education, worker safety and public health. All are a mess. The only thing that works reliably is cell phones. The superpower, super economy, super military is a façade. Like all failing societies, they are their own worse enemy. You can look at their national debt, gross domestic product, or any form of financial success. But what you need to remember is that this is a communist country. The government does very little for the people. Money is to be horded and shared by the politicians. This happens on every level of government, of which there are seven levels.

My wife comes from a village of 1800 people near a city of just over 1 million. The city gives money to the mayor of her village for the school, road upkeep, cleaning, etc. But none of this gets spent on the village. The mayor and his friends spend the money at the best restaurants and hotels in town, and the brothels. To placate the villagers, he tells them that the government is building an entire new village for them. There are 900,000 similar villages in China. When I explain to my family that they need to see this on paper, all are afraid to get involved. So their village is piled high with garbage and the school is a wreck. When I offered money to rebuild the school, relatives told me that the teachers and principal would take it all.

China is a master of manipulating statistics. They brag about their average income doubling in 15 years, from 70 cents a day to about $1.40. But the cost of living has more than doubled. The standard of living for the 800 million peasants has not improved at all. The gap between the poor and the rich is widening. Tax evasion is the national sport. China is so huge and unorganized that it is a logistics nightmare to catalogue the people and collect tax. You will never see the real China in a movie or commercial. China projects their false success with the Olympics, their space program and shiny buildings.

If China was to build their country on the infrastructure model of successful countries, they would soon collapse. I love China, but they are in huge trouble.

Table of Contents

#	Chapter	Page
1.	Title Page	1
	Credits Page	2
2.	Published by Monkey Monk Publications	3
3.	Preface to the General Introduction	4
4.	Other Useful Things in This Book	5
5.	Disclaimer	6
6.	Table of Contents	9
7.	Introduction	13
8.	Using This Grammar Work Book	15
9.	Character Chapter Index	19
10.	What Lies Ahead	28
11.	First 25 Characters Chapters	29
1	(的, de, possessive particle)	29
2	(一, yī, one, a little)	57
3	(是, shì, is, to be)	65
4	(不, bù, no, not)	74
5	(了, le, completed verb action marker)	80
6	(有, yǒu, have)	97
7	(人, rén, person)	105
8	(我, wǒ, me / I)	117
9	(在, zài, at, be at, be in, be on)	124
10	(他, tā, he)	134
11	(这, zhè, this)	141
12	(中, zhōng, middle, centre, mid, interior)	148
13	(大, dà, big, huge, large, major, great, wide, deep)	159
14	(来, lái, come)	169
15	(上, shàng, on, up, on top, upon, upper, higher, over, to	186
16	(国, guó, country, state, nation, kingdom)	199
	Bill and His Authentic Chinese Experience	203
17	(个, gè, non-specific measure word)	208
18	(到, dào, to, to go to, towards, until, arrive, arrive at, reach)	228
19	(说, shuō, to speak)	244
20	(们, men, pluralizing suffix)	251

21	(为, wèi, stand for, support, for, on account of, on behalf of)	257
22	(子, zǐ, child, son)	271
23	(和, hé, and)	285
24	(你, nǐ, you)	292
25	(地, de, manner adverb forming particle, acts as -ly)	303
12.	Vietnamese Beef Noodle Soup January 22nd 2011	320
13.	The Book to Date	321
14.	Dumb Dumb Drills	324
15.	Numbers	330
16.	Numbers - Eleven to Twenty	334
17.	Numbers - Twenty to Thirty	335
18.	Numbers - Twenty to One Hundred	336
19.	Numbers - One Hundred and Beyond	337
20.	Ordinal Number Character	342
21.	Multiplier Character	343
22.	Ordinal Number and Multiplier	344
23.	Currency ¥	345
24.	Calendar Dates	350
35.	One to One Hundred Word Number Chart	352
36.	Cooking Lesson Number One	353
37.	悯农, Mǐn Nóng, Pity Farmer Poem	356
38.	Locative Particles	358
39.	Excellent Chinese Language Books	362
40.	Useless Terrible Chinese Language Books	363
41.	Colours (色, sè, colour)	364
42.	Survival Swearing in China	365
43.	Bonus Filth Section	378
44.	The Cursing Exam	380
45.	Language Lessons	381
46.	Conditional Sentences, Using *If*	390
47.	Sentence Parsing 1	394
48.	Comparative Grammatical Constructions	397
49.	Sentence Parsing 2	403
50.	The Subordinating Conjunctions	407
51.	Sentence Parsing 3	410
52.	Current Progressive or Continuous Tense	413
53.	Sentence Parsing 4	417

54.	Tips on Using 吃饭了吗	421
55.	Connecting Nouns and Pronouns with (和, hé, and)	421
56.	Sentence Parsing 5	427
57.	Acknowledge Previous Experience (过, guò, in the past)	431
58.	Parsing Sentences 6	434
59.	Grammatical Vague-alities	439
60.	Common Requests or Commands	445
61.	Adjectives in Mandarin Grammar	447
62.	Threateningly Big List of Adjectives	450
63.	The shì 是 ... de 的 Construction	463
64.	Expressing Distance with (离, lí, from)	467
65.	The Chinese Sense of Direction	470
66.	Guizhou Veh lee Dangerous!	471
67.	Descriptive Pairs	489
68.	Lists of Common Countable Noun Indicators	492
69.	Table of Nominal Classifier CNI's	493
70.	Table of Mass Grouping Classifiers	498
71.	Table of Time Unit CNI's	502
72.	Table of Mass and Volume CNI's	503
73.	Table of Distance CNI's	504
74.	Currency CNI's	505
75.	Sentence Building Constructions	506
76.	Sentence Building Vignettes	507
77.	Wang and Chang Meet	508
78.	Wang and Chang Get Stupid About a Picture Book	512
79.	Wang and Chang Talk Shit About School	519
80.	Wang Thinks Chang's Wife has a Big Ass	523
81.	Wang and Chang go to a Gay Bar	527
82.	Wang and Chang Compare Their Penises	534
83.	Kangxi Radicals	548
84.	List of the 214 Kangxi Radicals	556
85.	Written Variants	570
86.	Stroke Order	573
87.	Basic and Compound Strokes	574
88.	Development of Stroke Order Rules	575
89.	The Six Single Strokes	589
90.	Stroke Variations and Additives	590

91.	Compound Strokes	592
92.	Exercise for Individual Strokes	598
93.	Eight Principles of Yong	553
94.	Guide to Pronunciation	556
95.	Initials	660
96.	Finals	664
97.	Tones	671
98.	Tonal Shift Patterns, or Tone Sandhi	678
99.	Hanyu Pinyin	683
100.	Rules of Pinyin	686
100.	Chinese Learning Websites	717
101.	How to Find the Ultimate Tools	718
102.	My Personal Favourites	719
103.	Using a Computer in China	725
104.	How to Spend Your Money Wisely	726
105.	Finding a Chinese Language Partner	727
106.	Version of Original Stroke Order Rules	728
107.	Ending this Book	730
108.	Erratum?, Errors?, I don't think so!, Ideas?	731

Introduction

Chinese Grammar 101 is a thorough grammar study based on the statistically first 25 Chinese characters. These characters come from a list of the 3000 most common characters. This is list was compiled from a computer analysis of a recorded conversation database.

In writing this grammar book I have tried to make it a one stop book for everything you need to have the basics of writing, reading, speaking and understanding grammar. I put all the essentials, the basics, in the back of the book. There are over 175 pages of Chinese language fundamentals, strokes, stroke order, pronunciation, **Hanyu Pinyin** and a very thorough study of the 241 Kangxi Radicals. This appendix is in fact bigger than most of the introduction books on the market, in entirety.

Mandarin grammar has close parallels to English grammar. However, most people in Canada last took formal grammar in grade six or seven. To efficiently learn another language, you need to have a very thorough understanding of the named terms of grammar. English has eight categories, Mandarin has perhaps 20.

In learning grammar, look at sentence patterns, remember the construction and then substitute other words. If you can use *he*, you can use *she*. If you can use *want*, you can use *need*. Build a reportoire of portions of sentences and mix them around.

Most (外国人, **wài guó rén, outside country person**) or *foreigners* focus on phrase books and run around China saying; (你好,你好, **nǐ hǎo nǐ hǎo, you good you good**) the usual greeting, generally looking like idiots. Most give up on learning more than the common greetings and niceties. This is not because Mandarin is so difficult, it is because there are so many terrible introductory books that contaminate the learning curve and give learners a feeling of hopelessness.

China, and all things Chinese, is something you can study the rest of your life. Unlike your perception gained from television, most people in China have never seen or meet a foreigner. China is a fascinating place, a challenge for the experienced traveller, I hope this grammar book helps you with acquiring a functional strategy to learn the language and explore a fascinating society and culture.

大毛猴子

Dà Máo Hóuzi
Big Hairy Monkey
www.SpeakandWriteChinese.com

Using This Grammar Book

Grammar sucks. What lies ahead is surely to be grammatical chaos. 25 characters with associated common words with character writing practice and intensive grammar work. I have no idea how many total words I will have introduced, but I will count them before I send this for publishing. My promise in writing this book is that I would just heads-up do it with no real plan beyond picking 25 characters, so there is no going back. I also promise to entertain you, talk shit, and plain ramble all over the Mandarin grammatical world.

I have had great experiences in China, arrested for being white, twice, let off the train in the wrong city in the middle of the night, twice. This is so that they can sell my soft sleeper berth to someone else. Then there was the brawl with 11 youth in a Guizhou internet cafe. Canada 6 China 0. That's hospitalisations for the other team. As of June 2010, I have worked in 23 countries, and China has been the most amazing experience. I was put in jail in Guiyang for being mugged by three youth in the middle of the day, **you not allowed beat Chinese people**, said the police and government person. Yes, you can buy your way out of jail in China. The officials fully acknowledged the crime but apparently I was not allowed to lay a beating on the three hoodlums to get my back pack back.

But I continue to go back. Overall, it is safer than any other place I have worked, well, maybe Cuba was safer, and the balance of adventure and excitement is excellent. Plus, the people are among the nicest I have ever immersed in. I know, I know, you are thinking of the problems I had. If you take a city of 10 million people or more, and there are many in China, and 1% are naughty, that makes 100,000 bad guys and most are in the core of the city where you will probably be, and they are looking for the rare traveller. Compare this to some intercity areas in the USA where

85% of men 15 to 45 years of age have felony convictions. Anyway, I digress, I will use the character work sheets for character writing practice from my other books. They are simple to use. All you need to know on strokes, stroke order and such is in the 176 page appendix.

At the upper left of each table is a large Chinese character. This is of course the topic character for the work sheet. Immediately below the topic character is a small box with the alphabetic sound that represents the usual sound of this character. The method of representing the sound of the character is called (拼音, **Pīnyīn**, **spell sound**). This use of the Roman alphabet was developed and embraced by China so that school children across China would have a standardized sound for each character. China historically was unified by the written language. The spoken language had and has over 250 recognized very distinct variations. (拼音, **Pīnyīn**, **spell sound**) helped China develop a universal literacy of spoken language. At the back of this work book is a guide to pronunciation.

The third box, below the (拼音, **Pīnyīn**, **spell sound**) box, is the common or usual English translation. Like an English word, a Chinese character can have more than one meaning. To the right of these first three boxes is an area to write your own notes and also a brief explanation of the meaning of the character along with the character and the (拼音, **Pīnyīn**, **spell sound**). Below all of these, making the fourth row and crossing the page, is a long box in which the stroke order of the character is shown. As you move from left to right across the box, one extra stroke is added until finally the entire character is drawn.

Then come the practice boxes. Photocopy, overwrite or use a clear acetate with a wipe off marker and get to work using the correct stroke and stroke order. Chant the (拼音, **Pīnyīn**, **spell sound**) and the meaning. Pick about 10 lesson tables and do one character on each of all ten lessons and repeat this cycle. Then there is the grammar, haven't written it yet so not sure how I will do it.

In your pursuit to learn, avoid phrase books that do not give honest translations. There are many terrible ones that will delay you in your pursuit of increasing your languages skills. Avoid any books that offer *quick and easy*, *revolutionary* and other miraculous ways to learn the language . I always maintain that hundreds of billions of Chinese over thousands of years have probably distilled an effective way to learn the language.

Save yourself money by reading my book reviews. These are very thoroughly researched book reviews. Below are some of the worst books I have ever seen, irrespective of category. The problem with book buying is that you probably buy with the promises of an easier way to learn Mandarin, nice covers, and big promises. At least that is how I did it. **http://chineselanguagebookreview.blogspot.com/**

So here are some horrid books.

Chinese Through Tone and Color (Worst idea)
ISBN 978-0-7818-1204-7
by Nathan Dummit

Chinese For Dummies (Worst book in the known universe)
ISBN 978-0471788973
by Wendy Abraham

1400+ Chinese Conversational Phrases (Worst translations)
ISBN 978-1-4196-6583-7
by Ju Brown

1880+ Chinese Business and Trade Phrases (Worst translations part II)
ISBN 1-4392-0247-8
by Ju Brown

The First 100 Chinese Characters (There is no quick and easy method)
"**The Quick and Easy Method to Learn the 100 Most Basic Chinese Characters**"
ISBN 978-0-8048-3830-6
by Alison and Lawrence Mathews

The Second 100 Chinese Characters (There is no quick and easy method)
ISBN 978-0-8048-3831-3,
by Alison and Lawrence Matthews

Learning Chinese Characters (Using strategy of book is more effort than not)
A Revolutionary New Way to Learn and Remember the 800 Most Basic Chinese Characters
ISBN 978-0-8048-3816-0
by Alison and Lawrence Matthews

    The Matthews team, Alison and Lawrence, promise *quick*, *easy and revolutionary*. Nathan Dummit assigns colours to each character to learn tone, umm, Nathan, read about *Tone Sandhi*. He is mad at me. Doesn't like my online comments. Wendy Abraham's effort are stupid, pathetic and definitely the worst book in the market. Her book is the only book I have read in my life in which I actually feel insulted and uncomfortable. Now Ju Brown, claims to be a Ph.D. yet she spells it wrong. Then she spells *English* as *Engligh* on the first page of her book and spells *website* as *webstie* on the cover. Then she decorates her cover with marijuana leaves. Marijuana leaves, I know these things. You gotta love self publishing. She has the worst translations on the market for phrases. She is really mad at me. She made some nasty defensive comments on Amazon.com then deleted them. Anyway, lets get to it.

Character Chapter Index
Chinese Grammar 101

1	(的, de, possessive particle)	29
2	(一, yī, one, a little)	57
3	(是, shì, is, to be)	65
4	(不, bù, no, not)	74
5	(了, le, completed verb action marker) (了, le, sentence final particle indicating a new situation) (了, liǎo, to end, finish, settle, dispose of)	80
6	(有, yǒu, have)	97
7	(人, rén, person)	105
8	(我, wǒ, me / I)	117
9	(在, zài, at, be at, be in, be on) (在, zài, to exist, to live, to live at, exist at) (在, zài, to depend on, rest with)	124
10	(他, tā, he)	134
11	(这, zhè, this)	141
12	(中, zhōng, middle, centre, mid, interior)	148
13	(大, dà, big, huge, large, major, great, wide, deep)	159
14	(来, lái, come)	169
15	(上, shàng, on, up, on top, upon, upper, higher, over, to climb up, to go into, above, to go up, upward, mount, to board) (上, shàng, first of two parts, primary, before, previous, last) (上, shàng, higher, superior, better) (上, shàng, go to, leave for, to)	186
16	(国, guó, country, state, nation, kingdom)	199

17	(个, gè, non-specific measure word) (个, gè, an individual, a piece)	208
18	(到, dào, to, to go to, towards, until, arrive, arrive at, reach)	228
19	(说, shuō, to speak)	244
20	(们, men, pluralizing suffix)	251
21	(为, wèi, stand for, support, for, on account of, on behalf of) (为, wèi, for, for the sake of, in order to) (为, wéi, do, act, act as, be, become)	257
22	(子, zǐ, child, son) (子, zi, noun suffix)	271
23	(和, hé, and) (和, hé, together, with, union, harmony) (和, hé, gentle, mild, kind, peace)	285
24	(你, nǐ, you)	292
25	(地, de, manner adverb forming particle, acts as -ly) (地, dì, earth, ground, dirt, soil, fields) (地, dì, place, position, distance)	303

Chinese Grammar 201

26	(出, chū, go out, come out, exit, to go beyond, to put forth) (出, chū, to occur, to produce, to happen, to arise, to exceed) (出, chū, a measure word for dramas, plays, or operas) (出, chū, pay out, expend)	
27	(道, dào, a way, a method, a doctrine) (道, dào, a way, a path, a channel, a road, streak of light) (道, dào, classifier for rivers, topics) (道, dǎo, to lead)	
28	(也, yě, also, too, as well) (也, yě, either, even, more or less, by and large)	
29	(时, shí, period, season, o'clock, time, when, hour)	

30	(年, nián, year)
	(得, de, adverbial particle)
31	(得, dé, get, reach, achieve)
	(得, děi, should)
32	(就, jiù, just, simply, right away, at once, then, only)
	(就, jiù, to approach, to move towards, to undertake)
33	(那, nà, that)
	(要, yào, want)
34	(要, yào, to want, vital, will, shall, need, must)
	(要, yāo, demand, ask, request, coerce)
35	下, xià, below, under, go down, underneath
	(下, xià, to decline, to go down)
	(下, xià, second of two parts, next, latter)
	(面, miàn, noodle, flour)
	(面, miàn, face, side, surface, aspect, top)
	(面, miàn, classifier for mirrors, flags)
36	(以, yǐ, take, use)
	(以, yǐ, according to, because of, in order to, so as to)
	(以, yǐ, empty verb suffix)
37	(生, shēng, to bear)
	(生, shēng, give birth, to be born, life, to grow, to bear, to produce)
38	(会, huì, know how to, can, able)
	(会, huì, meet, meeting, society, union, party)
	(会, kuài, accounting)
	(会, huǐ, moment)
39	(自, zì, self)
	(自, zì, from, since, oneself, self)

40	(着, zhe, verb particle marking a continuing progress state) (着, zháo, touch) (着, zhuó, wear clothes, dress) (着, zhāo, put in, add)
41	(去, qù, go, to go, to leave, to depart) (去, qù, get rid of, remove, cast out) (去, qù, be apart)
42	(之, zhī, it) (之, zhī, subordinator similar to 的 de)
43	(过, guò, particle) (过, guò, pass, cross, go by, exceed) (过, guò, experiential verb particle)
44	(家, jiā, home, household, family) (家, Jiā, surname Jiā) (家, jiā, school of thought) (家, jiā, as a suffix to form Reflexive Personal Pronouns)
45	(学, xué, study, learn, knowledge) (学, xué, to imitate, to mimic) (学, xué, branch of study as –ology, subject of study) (学, xué, school, college, university)
46	(对, duì, answer, reply) (对, duì, correct, agree, right) (对, duì, mutual, pair)
47	(可, kě, able) (可, kě, -able, may, can)
48	(她, tā, she, her)
49	(里, lǐ, in, inside, lining) (里, lǐ, neighbourhood) (里, lǐ, half kilometre)

50	(后, hòu, after, behind) (后, hòu, queen)

Chinese Grammar 301

51	(小, xiǎo, small, tiny, few, young)
52	(么, me, grammatical particle) (么, me, interrogative suffix)
53	(心, xīn, heart)
54	(多, duō, many, much, more)
55	(天, tiān, day, sky) (天, tiān, heaven, god)
56	(而, ér, and, and yet) (而, ér, furthermore, as well as, but not, yet not) (而, ér, shows causal relation, shows change of state, shows contrast)
57	(能, néng, can) (能, néng, can, be able)
58	(好, hǎo, good) (好, hǎo, good, good to..., easy to…) (好, hào, to like) (好, hāo, in good condition)
59	(都, dōu, all, always) (都, dōu, even, already) (都, dū, capital city)
60	(然, rán, right) (然, rán, so, like that)
61	(没, méi, not) (没, mò, drown, sink, submerge, overflow) (没, mò, conceal, vanish, confiscate) (没, mò, die)
62	(日, rì, sun, day)

63	(于, yú, from) (于, yú, in, at, for, to, by, than)
64	(起, qǐ, to arise, get up, start) (起, qǐ, to unload, to remove) (起, qǐ, to raise, to build) (起, qi, when used as a verb complement)
65	(还, hái, still, yet, even, still more, also, too, as well as) (还, hái, passably, fairly) (还, huán, return, give back)
66	(发, fā, send out, deliver, distribute) (发, fā, to utter, express, shoot, emit, develop, expand) (发, fà, hair) (发, fà, to make a fortune (slang))
67	(成, chéng, become, finish, complete, succeed, accomplish) (成, chéng, win) (成, Chéng, surname Chéng) (成, chéng, one tenth)
68	(事, shì, matter) (事, shì, matter, affair, thing, event, accident, job, responsibility) (事, shì, job)
69	(只, zhǐ, only, single, one, just, merely) (只, zhī, measure word for one of a pair) (只, zhī, measure word, for birds and some animals)
70	(作, zuò, do, make) (作, zuó, spoil, waste, humiliate, insult) (作, zuó, humiliate, insult)
71	(当, dāng, accept, serve as) (当, dàng, proper, right, equal, at or in the very same..., to pawn, suitable, adequate, fitting, replace, represent)

72	(想, xiǎng, desire) (想, xiǎng, think, feel, consider, want, remember, desire)
73	(看, kàn, look) (看, kàn, see, look, look at, read, think, consider) (看, kān, look after, tend, take care of)
74	(文, wén, script) (文, wén, language, literature)
75	(无, wú, not) (无, wú, without, nothingness, have not)
76	(开, kāi, open, initiate, begin, start) (开, kāi, to operate a…, to start)
77	(手, shǒu, hand) (手, shǒu, a person skilled in something)
78	(十, shí, ten, 10)
79	(用, yòng, to use)
80	(主, zhǔ, master) (主, zhǔ, lord, master, host, god)
81	(所, suǒ, place)
82	(方, fāng, side, direction, place, region, position) (方, fāng, side, a carpenter's square) (方, fāng, prescription, recipe) (方, fāng, method, way)
83	(又, yòu, again) (又, yòu, again, both… and…)
84	(如, rú, like, similar, such as, as if, for example, measure up) (如, rú, as, as if) (如, rú, be in accord with, according to, in accordance with)
85	(前, qián, front, in front of, previous, ago, before, former, first, preceding, formerly, ahead)

86	(本, běn, basis)
	(本, běn, basis, origin, edition, foundation)
	(本, běn, classifier for books, periodicals, files)
87	(三, sān, three, 3)
	(三, sān, more than two, several, many)
88	(见, jiàn, meet)
	(见, jiàn, appear to be, meet with, call on)
	(见, jiàn, to show, appear, become visible)
89	(经, jīng, pass through, to undergo, to endure)
	(经, jīng, classics, sacred book, scripture, canon)
	(经, Jīng, surname Jīng)
90	(头, tóu, head, a head of)
	(头, tóu, top, first)
	(头, tóu, classifier for livestock, garlic)
91	(面, miàn, noodle, flour)
	(面, miàn, face, side, surface, aspect, top)
	(面, miàn, classifier for mirrors, flags)
92	(公, gōng, public affairs, official duties)
	(公, gōng, following a surname, a respectful form of address for an elderly or married man)
	(公, gōng, common, accepted)
93	(同, tóng, same, similar)
	(同, tóng, together, in common)
94	(已, yǐ, stop, cease, end, finish, complete)
	(已, yǐ, already, thereafter, afterward)
95	(行, xíng, okay, capable, competent, acceptable, all right)
	(行, xíng, go, walk, travel, circulate, prevail)
	(行, xíng, overflow, rise beyond)
	行, háng, héng, a line, a row)

	(老, lǎo, old, outdated)
96	(老, lǎo, venerable)
	(老, lǎo, always)
	(从, cóng, from, follow)
97	(从, cóng, from, through, join)
	(从, cóng, follower, secondary)
98	(动, dòng, to use)
	(动, dòng, to act, to move, to change)
	(两, liǎng, two)
99	(两, liǎng, both, some, a few)
	(两, liǎng, either side, both sides)
	(两, liǎng, measure word for tael weight)
	(长, cháng, long, lasting, length)
100	(长, zhǎng, grow up, chief, head, older, elder)
	(长, cháng, steadily, regularly)

What Lies Ahead

These chosen characters encompass the 25 most commonly used characters. As such, they have great utility and versatility. Obviously, Mandarin Chinese is not English. You will not see obvious parallels in some of the characters. I thought initially of given watered down descriptive uses for some of these characters, but there are too many books that are watered down and do not come close to covering the use of the characters that are the most significant to master.

Grammatical particles are initially difficult to use and understand. Chinese characters being invariant, that is, you cannot alter them to give different meaning, require other characters in other positions and roles to give increased versatility to the language.

Because some of these characters have complex and diverse use, I will present the most common uses first. I will mark the uses that have highest utility, somehow, you will figure it out when you get there. Once you get past the grammatical particles and characters that modify meaning, it is clear sailing.

Like all languages, there are numerous levels of success. With Mandarin Chinese you can communicate that which you want with several hundred characters, if they are well chosen. More difficult is understanding someone with a bigger repetoire of words and more complex sentence constructions.

To the best of my knowledge, there is no other book that tries to integrate writing Chinese characters with this degree of learning Mandarin grammar and speaking skills. My promise to you is that this book includes all that you need to know to master these skills with the most common Chinese Characters.

的

de — particle

Notes: Grammatical Particle

(的, **de**, **possessive particle**)

(的, **de**, **grammatical particle**), has numerous uses in **Hanyu**. It can be used to make a personal pronoun into the possessive form. The form is (personal pronoun) + 的 = possessive pronoun.

Example 我的, **wǒ de**, me + **possessive particle** = **my / mine**.

Stroke order: ′ 亻 冇 甪 白 白′ 的 的

的

1) Constructing the Possessive Form of a Noun or Pronoun

(的, **de**, **grammatical particle**) has numerous uses in **Hanzi**. It is used to make a *Proper Noun* or a *Common Noun* into the possessive form. Functionally, it acts as an *apostrophe s*. To create the English possessive form of a *Mr. King* we form *King's*. The equivalent construction for Chinese grammar is,

王 + 的 = 王的
Wáng + **de** = **Wáng de**
King + 's = King's

A *Direct Object Noun* can then be put immediately after this construction. As in English we would say, *King's car*, *car* being the *Direct Object*, in Mandarin Grammar, using (**car**, 车, **chē**), we form,

王的 + 车 = 王的车
Wáng de + **chē** = **Wáng de chē**
King's + car = King's car

Note that there is no spacing between the Chinese characters. Historically the characters were written top to bottom, right to left, with no spacing or punctuation. Most writing in mainland China is now left to right, top to bottom. Recently there is some use of punctuation, particularly with *periods* and *commas*, hopefully increasing.

The Romanized interface used to assign standardized sounds to Chinese characters is called **Hanyu Pinyin**. The rules for **Hanyu Pinyin** construction are at the back of this book.

A *Personal Pronoun* is a word that takes the place of a *Proper Noun* such as (王, **Wáng**, **King**), a family name. *Personal Pronouns* can be used when the *Proper Noun* is known or assumed by context. Using the example **King**, we can refer to *King* as *he* or *him*. *He* and *him* are *Personal Pronouns*. To form the *Possessive Personal Pronoun* in English we use *his*, meaning, *belonging to he*, and in this example *he* is *King*.

(他, **tā**, **he**) is the written Chinese character word for *he* or *him*. The *Possessive Personal Pronoun* is formed thus,

他	+	的	=	他的
tā	+	de	=	tā de
he			=	his

Using the above conventions we can then write,

他	的	车
Tā	de	chē
His		car

Grammatical convention calls the speakers perspective the *First Person*. The *Personal Pronoun* thus formed is called the *First Person Pronoun*. In English, this is the word *I* / *me*. Mr. King, in referring to himself or his possessed objects, can use the possessive grammatical form *mine* or *my*.

These words mean *belonging to me* or *of mine*. The Chinese character word for *me* is (我, wǒ, me / I). To form the possessive form the structure is thus,

我 + 的 = 我的
wǒ + de = wǒ de
me   = mine

And this of course can become,

我 的 车
wǒ de chē
my car

English recognizes a *Subjective* form of the *First Person Pronoun* and an *Objective* form. Acting as a *Subject* to a sentence is the word *I*, acting as an *Object* of the sentence is the word *me*. This is best demonstrated with simple sentence examples.

Me is Mr. King.
Mr. King is me.

If you substitute *me* for *I* in the second sentence and *I* for *me* in the first sentence, the sentences become awkward sounding. Chinese grammar does not recognize an *Objective* and *Subjective* **First Person Pronoun**. (我, wǒ, me / I) is used in all situations. I chose to use (我, wǒ, me) as it reminds me of people I know.

2) Modification of the Noun Phrase

(的, **de**, **marker of noun modification**) Modifiers coming before the modified forms the basis of Chinese grammar. Noun modifiers may be *Nouns*, *Pronouns*, *Verbs*, *Adjectives* or *Verb Phrases*.

The format is **modifier** + (**的**, **de**) + **head noun**.

Modifier	+ 的 +	Head Noun	=	Modifier +(的, **de**) + Head Noun
Noun	+ 的 +	Noun	=	Noun +(的, **de**) + Noun
Pronoun	+ 的 +	Noun	=	Pronoun +(的, **de**) + Noun
Adjective	+ 的 +	Noun	=	Adj. +(的, **de**) + Noun
Verb	+ 的 +	Noun	=	Verb +(的, **de**) + Noun
Verb Phrase	+ 的 +	Noun	=	Verb Phrase +(的, **de**) + Noun

The word or words that compose the main noun, called the *head noun*, and the associated words that modify it, create a *noun phrase*.

For the most simple sentence, there can be a *Subject Noun* or *Pronoun*, a *Verb*, and an *Object Noun*. Either of these nouns can exist as single nouns or can evolve into noun phrases with modification. Whether the nouns are *Proper Nouns*, *Common Nouns* or *Pronouns*, the grammatical construction is unchanged.

Subject Verb Object or **SVO** is an easy to work with and common sentence construction in Mandarin grammar. You can communicate anything you want with this construction. Unfortunately, that will not help you understand the other common sentence constructions used in Mandarin grammar.

Single Pronoun Subject, Verb, Single Noun Object

Pronoun	Verb	Noun
我	喜欢	苹果
Wǒ	xǐhuan	píngguǒ.
I	like	apple.
Subject	Verb	Object

Grammatical terms are at times imprecise. You will find books that will call a single noun the *Noun Phrase*. The definition of *Phrase* varies, but it must contain a noun if it is a *Noun Phrase* and there is no consensus beyond that.

For this book the **Subject** (**S**) and it's modifiers will be called the ***Subject Noun Phrase*** (**SNP**). The ***Verb*** (**V**) and it's modifiers will be called the ***Verb Phrase*** (**VP**). The ***Object*** (**O**) and it's modifiers will be called the ***Object Noun Phrase*** (**ONP**). In keeping with those who have gone before me, I may at times refer to a single word as a phrase in these situations.

In the above table there is no need to use (的, **de**) as the nouns are unmodified. However, the following example is more complex in structure.

Pronoun	Verb	Adjective		Adjective		Noun
我	喜欢	大	的	红	的	苹果
Wǒ	xǐhuan	dà	de	hóng	de	píngguǒ.
I	like	big		red		apple.
Subject	Verb	Adjective Phrase				Object

Although this construction is grammatically correct, it is in fact unusual and unlikely to be spoken. This is where the Chinese language gets more complicated. To entertain my wife, I ran it past her. Her explanation was typically Chinese. She noted it was,

> *"**Most correct but wrong**, Chinese people never say this. Chinese people feel very uncomfortable to say or hear so many the (的, de) They do not like too many the (的, de) in the same sentence. Throw away the (的, de)."*

The further explanation of this is long but important and again translated from my Chinese wife.

> *"**First**, most apples are red and it does not give added information to add the (的, de). The Chinese people know that apples are red so this does not help them. Also, red apple is almost a proper noun as it is so common. Therefore it does not need the (的, de). The (大, dà, big) sound is common and does not surprise the Chinese people. Therefore you do not need to add the (的, de). The Chinese people like the apple very much. So don't use too many the (的, de)."*

So there you go, makes sense right?. Irrespective of grammatical rules, understandability and simplicity prevail when the meaning is clear and the wording is common.

So when put to the question as to which construction is proper or understandable she gave these choices,

我	喜欢	大	的	红	的	苹果
Wǒ	xǐhuan	dà	de	hóng	de	píngguǒ.
Me	like	big		red		apples.

我	喜欢	大	的	红	苹果
Wǒ	xǐhuan	dà	de	hóng	píngguǒ.
Me	like	big		red	apples.

我	喜欢	大	红	的	苹果
Wǒ	xǐhuan	dà	hóng	de	píngguǒ.
Me	like	big	red		apples.

我	喜欢	大	红	苹果
Wǒ	xǐhuan	dà	hóng	píngguǒ.
Me	like	big	red	apples.

Or, all possible combinations. And this may vary throughout the country. When put to the question of which construction is most common she gave ,

我喜欢大红苹果,

that is, no (的, **de**), and

我喜欢大红的苹果

As confusing as this seems, this typifies the concept of *meaning having precedence over form and function*. Economy of words and effort is a hallmark of Mandarin grammar. Chinese grammar rules can always hold second place to convention, casual rules and attempts to generalize rules to all situations. As a student, it is best to be over correct and then modify your speaking by experience and watching Chinese people cringe with discomfort and correcting you when you use *too many the* (的, **de**).

It is obvious that *Adjective Phases* (**AP**) exist in Mandarin grammar. In keeping with the general format, an *Adjective Phrase* can be composed of more than one adjective and each adjective can be formed from one or more characters. Words are also compounded together in English to form new words that sometimes show dissociation from the meaning of the individual words.

However, it gets more complex yet. A Mandarin word can be one character, or it can be more than one character. This makes it necessary to be able to distinquish in the character string the position of the components of the sentence and their grammatical value. Although you will speak with the words you know, you will be constantly confronted with compounded characters you may or may not know.

If you work with the *SVO* construction, adjectives modifying the *Object* come before the **ONP**.

Adjective Rule #1

Adjective Phrases that are composed of one character do not need a (的, **de**) before the ***Head Noun***. You can use the (的, **de**) but it is not necessary. Either will be understood.

AP_1 +/- (的, **de**) + **Head Noun**

Adjective Rule #2

Serial one-character adjective words that are distinct and composed of one character each do not need a (的, **de**) before the ***Head Noun***. But you can use the (的, **de**). Either will be understood.

AP_1 +/- (的, **de**) + AP_2 +/- (的, **de**) + **Head Noun**

Adjective Rule #3

Single word adjectives composed of two or more characters forming each word use the (的, **de**) before the ***Head Noun***, unless the construction is well known and common.

$AP_{(a+b)}$ + (的, **de**) + **Head Noun**

Adjective Rule #4

Adjective phrases that include both single character words and multiple character words follow the rules for each individual adjective. The single character adjective word need not have the (的, **de**) and the multi-character adjective word must have the (的, **de**). This rule is irrespective of the order of the single character adjectives and multi-character adjectives.

AP_1 +/- (的, **de**) + $AP_{(a+b)}$ +(的, **de**) + **Head Noun**

$AP_{(a+b)}$ +(的, **de**) + AP_1 +/- (的, **de**) + **Head Noun**

As soon as you master these rules you will be confronted with apparent exceptions. My favorite example to put before Chinese people and then to ask for an explanation is this one, (中国人, **zhōngúo rén**, **Chinese person**). Grammatical convention says that there should be a (的, **de**), (中国的人, **zhōngúo de rén**, **Chinese person**). However, the familiarity of the phrase or word is such that it takes on status as an individual word and the **Pinyin** is often written **zhōngúorén**.

Rule #2 explains why the *Most Common* version of *I like big red apples* is 我喜欢大红苹果 with no (的, **de**). The (的, **de**) does remove grammatical ambiguity when added and indentifies the separation of the *Adjective* (*s*) and the *Head Noun*. However, both (大, **dà**, **big**) and (红, **hóng**, **red**) are single character adjectives and do not require (的, **de**).

These rules can be generalised to almost all situations. You also have to learn to construct sentences as you speak. Like English, you may not always know where you are going with your thinking as fast as you are talking. So if you use *too many the* (的, **de**) your efforts will be understood and Chinese people will correct you, I assure you.

3) Noun Modifying a Noun

Pronoun	Noun		Noun
我们的	孩子	的	衣服
Wǒmen de	háizi	de	yīfu...
Our	children	's	clothing...

Although the above construction may appear to have *too many the* (的, **de**), in this situation it is fixed as (我们的, **wǒmen de**, **our**) has distinct meaning from (我们, **wǒmen**, **we / us**). The (的, **de**) acts to change meaning and it creates a *Possessive Pronoun* while marking noun modification.

In this situation (孩子, **háizi**, **children**) modifies (衣服, **yīfu**, **clothing**). The character (的, **de**, **'s**) functionally acts like an *apostrophe s*.

In situations where one person references another and the social connection is immediate, (的, **de**) is often omitted after *Pronouns*. The use of (的, **de**) is *most correct*, understood, but unnecessary in spoken Chinese. This means an acceptable spoken form of the above sentence would include 我们 rather than 我们的.

Example: Most Correct

我的	妈妈
Wǒ de	māma
My	mother

Example: Most Common

我	妈妈
Wǒ	māma
Me	mother

Below is an example of a *Pronoun* modifying a noun. This forms a *Subject Noun Phrase* (**SNP**) when used in the context of a more complex sentence.

4) Pronoun Modifying a Noun

我的	车
Wǒ de	chē
My	car

This above example was also used at the beginning of this character chapter. In the first example I identified (的, **de**) as marking the possessive form of a *Pronoun*. This is what it appears to do when it stands alone such as (我的, **wǒ de**, **my**). It is functionally used however to show modification of a *Noun* as in the example immediately above and below.

我的	车	太老了
Wǒ de	chē	tài lǎo le.
My	vehicle	extreme old.
	SNP	Adjective Phrase

Note that the above example does not have any equivalent of the word *to be* or *is*. This is the **most correct** and **most common**. Chinese grammer does not generally use the verb *to be* or *is* when the **Subject Noun Phrase** is equated to an *Adjective* with no *Object*. The situations in which it does occur are when additional emphasis is needed or when showing surprise or resolving disbelief. Mandarin grammar has many idiosyncracies.

Note that there is no obvious verb in the above sentence. This leads some grammarians and authors to call the **AP** a *Stative Verb*. I think this is a narrow way to view another cultures grammar. There is simply no verb there and the sentence is understandable. So this does not follow **SVO** word order. An *Adjective Phrase* (**AP**) is an **AP**, I digress.

Don't ask about the (了, **le**), my wife told me it **has no meaning here but is necessary**. We will cover it in a latter pages.

Then there is also the issue of (了, **le**, **CRS**). This is explained in character #**5**. I have no idea which page it is on as I have not written it yet. If you are dying of curiousity take a look chapter 5.

If you want to construct this sentence in an **SVO** form and attempt to preserve the meaning, it gets slightly more complex. English has *Definite Articles* (**DA**) and *Indefinite Articles* (**IDA**). Mandarin grammar uses an alternate construction.

A **Definite Articles** (**DA**) marks that its *Noun* is a particular one identifiable to the reader or listener. It may be the same thing that the speaker has already mentioned, or it may be something uniquely specified. The definite article in English is *the*.

The man knew the fastest way to the bar.

In the above sentence the *man* the *bar* and the *fastest route* are specific. The **DA** acts to mark their specificity. This has markedly more specificity than,

A man knew a fast way to a bar.

Alternately, if you compare,

Give me the book,

to

*Give me **a** book*,

you can again see the specificity confered by the **DA** *the*.

An **Indefinite Articles (IDA)** marks that its ***Noun*** is a generic or a non-specific one identifiable to the reader or listener. It may be something that the speaker is mentioning for the first time, or its precise identity may be irrelevant or hypothetical, or the speaker may be making a general statement about any such thing. English uses *a* or *an*, depending on the initial sound of the next word, as its ***Indefinite Article***.

*She had **a** house so large that **an** elephant would get lost without **a** map.*

The word *a* or *an* introducing an unspecified noun or the name of a general category, ***a** dog*, ***an** apple*, ***an** orange*. *An* is used when the next word begins with a vowel or a silent unpronounced *h*, as in ***an** egg* or ***an** hour*.

Subject	Verb		Adjective Phrase				Object
我	有	一	辆	很	老	的	车
Wǒ	yǒu	yī	liáng	hěn	lǎo	de	chē.
Me	have	one / a		very	old		vehicle.
SNP	**VP**		**CNI**	**AP**			**ONP**

The below example shows the format in which you can use the copula verb (是, **shì**, **is / to be**) when equating a ***Subject Noun*** to an ***Object Noun*** modified with an ***Adjective***.

我的	车	是	一	辆	很	老	的	车
Wǒ de	chē	shì	yì	liǎng	hěn	lǎo	de	chē.
My	vehicle	is	one / a	(CNI)	very	old		vehicle.
Subject Noun Phrase		Verb	Object Noun Phrase					

The *AdjectivePhrase* is (很老, **hěn lǎo**, **very old**) and (的, **de**) marks modification of the *Object Noun* (车, **chē, vehicle**). The character (辆, **liǎng, CNI**) will be explained when we cover the character (个, **ge**) in chapter 17. The complete *Object Noun Phrase* is (一辆很老的, **yì liǎng hěn lǎo de chē**).

5) Adjective Modifying a Noun

红	苹果
hóng	píngguǒ
red	apple

This above example is the simple one word A*djective* (红, **hóng**, **red**) modifying the *Common Noun* (苹果, **píngguǒ, apple**). Again, no (的, **de**) is necessary as this follows the one character adjective modifying a noun rule.

Adjectives modifying a noun that are constructed of two or more characters are followed by (的, **de**). However, the example below is two single word *Adjectives* yet the noun is marked with (的, **de**) as it marks a *specific* car.

很	贵	的	车
Hěn	guì	de	chē.
Very	expensive		car.

In this above situation the overall construction adds specificity as to which car. It is difficult to assign an exact meaning to (的, **de**) in this situation other than it marks noun modification and *specificity* like a grammatical particle. This makes the grammatical construction somewhat idiomatic and it must be memorized rather than intuitive. Perhaps it is easier to memorize this construction if you think of the (的, **de**) marking a possessive state similar to an apostrophe *s* and belonging to a dropped *Personal Pronoun*. This is actually exactly what it is. The (的, **de**) belongs to a character that is not there, the *Dropped Pronoun*. Hip linguists actually use the term *Pro-drop* when referring to Mandarin Grammar. So, the most correct grammatical form is;

我	的	很	贵	的	车
Wǒ	de	hěn	guì	de	chē.
My		very	expensive		car.

So the (我, **wǒ**, **me**) and the (的, **de**) function together to mark a possessive state and the possessive state marks specificity like a *Definitive Article* (**DA**). The *Adjective Phrase* (**AP**) is actually inserted between the two.

In the below example, (的, **de**) can be interpreted to properly belong to the subject (我, **wǒ**, **me**) marking the possessive state with (喜欢, **xǐhuan**, **to like**) dropped in between. (的, **de**) is exactly where it should be. It is before the *Object Noun Phrase* that it modifies. The above and below examples are really the same concept. However, Mandarin Grammar favours not having the *Subject Pronoun*, it is assumed by context. It is not wrong to use it, however, it will seem over formal.

Subject	Verb		Object
我	喜欢	的	车
Wǒ	xǐhuan	de	chē.
Me	like		car.
	My liked		car.

The most correct English gloss would be a sentence that identifies a specific car that the speaker likes. Perhaps it is best to compare it to the construction in which (的, **de**) is omitted. Here the sentence becomes generic and loses specificity. Here, the most correct gloss would be a sentence that identifies that the speaker likes *cars*.

我	喜欢	车
Wǒ	xǐhuan	chē.
I	like	car.

6) Action Verb Modifying a Noun

In the below example, you can see that the second verb, (写, **xiě**, **write**) acts like an adjective to modify the Head Noun (字, **zì**, **character**).

这	是	写	的	字
Zhè	shì	xiě	de	zì.
This	is	write		character.
This	is	written		character.

The English equivalent would be ***This is a written character***. The two verbs, (是, **shi**, **is**) and (写, **xiě**, **write**), do not act as co-verbs with one modifying the other. The second verb, (写, **xiě**, **write**) is thus part of the **Object Noun Phrase** and it modifies (字, **zì**, **character**). Again, although very different than English grammar, the (的, **de**) is exactly where the rules put it, before the *Head Noun* of the *Object Noun Phrase* (ONP).

他们 是 来 的 人

Tāmen	shì	lái	de	rén.
They	is	come		person.
They	is	came		person.
Subject	Verb	Object Noun Phrase		

This above example identifies a group of people who have arrived. There are of course other ways to put the same information forth. But this grammar structure and use of (来, **lái**, **come**) is common. There is a tendency of people who write books to work *have* and *who* into these translations. This however is a disservice as the same meaning can be constructed integrating the Chinese equivalent of *have* and *who*.

Obviously, literal translations do not always make a clean translation. The meaning above is generally preserved and I would encourage you to *think Chinese* versus memorize vast numbers of more liberal and creative translations. Both of these above examples have (是, **shì**, **is**) as the principle verb of the sentence.

The verbs (写, **xǐe**, **write**) and (来, **laí**, **come**) do not act as co-verbs to the verb (是, **shì**, **is**). Rather they act to modify the **Object**. They are part of the **Object Noun Phrase**, not part of a **Verb Phrase**. You can see that the sentence divides nicely into understandable components.

7) Verb-Object Compounds Modifying a Noun

Chinese words can include more than one character to compose the word. One of the constructions not seen in English is the **Verb-Object Compound**.

When you see the below translations you will see that they make sense in translation and do not need non-literal glosses. However, many *Verb-Object Compounds* are idiomatic in that the sum meaning of the individual words is not a product of the individual words. This means they must be memorized.

In the following examples the *Verb-Object Compound* (**VOC**) acts to modify the *Noun* similar to the role of an *Adjective*. The verb is directly related to the noun of the *Verb-Object Compound* and together they modify the *Head Noun* of the *Object Noun Phrase*. Therefore they are separated by the (的, **de**) as the *Verb-Object Compound* modifies the *Head Noun*.

她	是	唱歌儿	的	女孩子
Tā	shì	chàng gē'r	de	nǚháizi.
She	is	song-sing		female child.
Subject	Verb	VOC		Object
Subject	Verb		Object Noun Phrase	

Roughly, this above sentence means ***She is the song singing girl***. When you separate the **ONP** out of the sentence, you can again see (的, **de**) before the *Head Noun* of the **ONP**. For some reason that us Westerners are unable to appreciate, the skill of singing is highly valued in China. It is the only place in the world where a guy can be popular based on his ping pong and singing skills.

他	是	买书	的	人
Tā	shì	mǎishū	de	rén
He	is	buy-book		person
Subject	Verb	VOC		Head Noun
Subject	Verb	Object Noun Phrase		

Roughly, this above sentence means *He is the book buying person*.

Other **Verb-Object Compounds** have their own story arising from the mists of history. (伤风, **shāngfēng**, **hurt wind**) has an idiomatic meaning of *catch cold*. I am sure someone has a Ph.D. in which they claim they know how this association came about with it's own cute story.

我	有	伤风	的	后遗症
Wǒ	yǒu	shāngfēng	de	hòuyízhèng.
Me	have	hurt wind		after-remain-disease.
Me	have	cold		after effects.

Chinese of course is not linguistically related to English so you can gloss (后遗症, **hòuyízhèng**, **after remain disease**) as *after-effects*, *sequelae* or *complications*. So a reasonable gloss is *I have cold after-effects*.

8) Prepositional Phrase plus a Verb Modifying a Noun Phrase

A **Prepositional Phrase** always occurs before the sentences main **Verb** and it's **Object**. Although this grammatical construction is initially clumsy to a native

English speaker, it nicely creates a setting in which the *Subject*, the **Prepositional Phrase** and the *Verb Action* are given in a very logical manner.

Subject + Prepositional Phrase + Verb + Object Noun Phrase

老	王	在	家	里边	喝	啤酒
Lǎo	Wáng	zài	jiā	lǐbian	hē	píjǐu.
Elder	Wang	at	house	inside	drink	beer.
Subject		Prepositional Phrase			Verb	Object

The *Prepositional Phrases* gives additional information to a sentence. If the *Prepositional Phrases* is removed, the remaining sentence stands on it's own, grammatically complete, but with less information.

A *Prepositional Phrase* creates a relationship with a *person*, *place or thing*, that is, a *Noun*, that is not the *Direct Object Noun*, for the *Subject*.

There are representative prepositions in **Hanyu Grammar** that mirror **English Prepositions**. The proper construction of a *Prepositional Phrase* has defined components. The easiest format to initially study is the *Locative Phrase* (LP). A LP of course defines a location.

This *Prepositional Phrase* (PP), coming immediately before the *Verb*, modifies the *Verb*. The PP is always started with (在, **zài, at**). This is a *Preposition* itself.

The first component of the *Locative Phrase* (LP) is the *Preposition* which leads all *Locative Preposition Phrases* being (在, **zai, at, located at / in / on**) In this book the use of (在, **zai, at**) will be called the *Locative Phrase Marker*. (LPM)

(在, **zai**, **at**) begins a phrase that acts as a *Co-Verb* to the main *Verb* of the sentence. The order of words after (在, **zai**, **at**) follows the usual biggest to smallest format of Mandarin Grammar.

The second component is the *Noun* or *Noun Phrase* which of course fulfills the noun definition of *person*, *place*, or *thing*. This can be a single noun or a phrase. This is the *Head Noun* (**HN**) of the *Prepositional Phrase* (**PP**).

The third component is variable, it can further define the relationship of the *Preposition Phrase Noun Phrase*. For examples of locations, this further narrows the location of the *Object* relative to the *Noun Phrase*, which is of course within the *Prepositional Phrase*. This comes at the end of the *Prepositional Phrase*. It can be a single character word or phrase composed of multiple characters. This third component is called the *Locative Particle* (**LP**). The **LP**'s are words that further define the location. If you look in the index you will find a page of *Locative Particles*.

The *Verb* connects the *Prepositional Phrase* to the *Object*. The *Object Noun Phrase* finishes the phrase. So you are probably wondering where the (的, **de**) comes into play.

在	公园	里边
Zài	gōngyuán	lǐbian
At	park	inside
LPM	Head Noun	Locative Particle
	Preposition Phrase	
	Locative Phrase	

As this can be part of a bigger sentence, (在, **zai**, **located at**) is always present. It is not uncommon to drop the (在, **zai**, **located at / in / on**) when it begins a sentence, this is not *correct* but it is *common*.

我	在	公园	里边	找	玩	的	人
Wǒ	zài	gōngyuán	lǐbian	zhǎo	wán	de	rén.
Me	at	park	inside	look for	play		person.
Subject	Prepositional Phrase			Verb			
Subject	Locative Phrase			Verb			ONP

You can see that the above **ONP** has a Verb modifying the Noun with (的, **de**) marking the *Head Noun* modification. As English favours the prepositional phrase at the end of the sentence, most would gloss it thus, however, the Chinese grammar preserves the meaning and I suggest you learn it this way.

The Hanging (的, de)

One of the confusing features to students are the apparent unexplained uses of (的, **de**) that follow no apparent rules. A sentence taken out of context may make no sense at all. The *Object Noun* may be left out of a sentence when it has been previously introduced. This is typical of the Chinese language which when spoken may variably delete the subject, verb, and pronouns. There are other situations when there is no rational explanation and these situations must be memorized. The (的, **de**) may in fact belong to a part of the sentence that is not readily recognised.

An example is the sentence 多大的鞋子. The literal translation is *Much big of shoes*. First, there is nothing to identify that it is a question, which it is. There are not any of the three common grammatical structures that are question forming structures. You must simply know that to a Chinese speaker (多大的, dūo dà de) asks, *what size*?

This is a very useful expression in the market while shopping. The sentence is thus functionally partitioned as such.

多大的	鞋子	
Duōda de	xiězi	?
Much big of	shoes	?
Size of	shoes	?

In keeping with the overall theme of Chinese being a constantly reducing language, (的, de) can be dropped in some situations. There is no pattern to these structures, it is just a matter of common usage. Again this falls into the category of most common versus most correct. Some learners want to sound local versus proper. The difficulty is that even if you want to speak formal grammar, you need to understand what others are saying.

你	多大	岁数	
Nǐ	duōdà	suìshù	?
You	much big	years number	?

So this is common but not formal. The correct grammar is,

你	多大的	岁数	
Nǐ	duōdà de	suìshù	?
You	much big of	years number	?

Not having anything to do with our (的, **de**) theme, this can be further reduced to simply,

多大	了	?
Duōdà	**le**	?
Much big	CRS	?

This is also a structure to ask age. However, in keeping with the complexity of Chinese, this is a little rude to ask of someone older than yourself. Go figure. There are in fact different question formats used for different age groups and different levels of respect. However, they cut us foreigners a break on these complexities.

The character (了, **le**, CRS) acts as a grammatical particle and marks the **Current Relevant State**. Again, there are idiomatic exceptions that just are and they defy explanation. It can also mark verb completion, known in English as the **Present Perfect Tense** (了, **le**, VC). In the above example, it marks neither, it just is.

Here is an example of the *hanging* (的, **de**).

这儿	有	两个	苹果
Zhè'r	**yǒu**	**liǎng ge**	**píngguǒ**.
This place	have	two piece	apple.

No (的, **de**) here right, however,

你	吃	大	的	我	吃	小	的
Nǐ	**chī**	**dà**	**de**.	**Wǒ**	**chī**	**xiǎo**	**de**.
You	eat	big.		Me	eat	small.	

The complete form is,

你	吃	大	的	苹果	我	吃	小	的	苹果
Nǐ	chī	dà	de	píngguǒ.	Wǒ	chī	xiǎo	de	píngguǒ.
You	eat	big		apple.	Me	eat	small		apple.

Missing, is the **Object Noun** (苹果, **píngguǒ**, **apple**). Now, as we covered on page, **Adjective Rule #1**,

Adjectives that are composed of one character do not need a (的, de). You can use the (的, de) but it is not necessary.

So, if you are using this *hanging* (的, **de**) construction you need to plan ahead and implement the optional (的, **de**) rule before you drop the **Object Noun Phrase**. Well, that's all I know about (的, **de**).

The character 的 is a composite character composed of the character for *white* (白, **bái**, **white**) and the character for *spoon* (勺, **sháo**, **spoon**). Hence 白勺 becomes 的.

I am leaving this big space here as I am sure I must have left out something.

Notes:

| 一 yī one | Notes: Quantitative Adjective

(一, **yī, one, a little**) is the number one. It can also be used to indicate a small amount.

(一, **yī, diminutive verb prefix**) 一 can act to diminish verb intensity. The grammatical form is *verb 一 verb*. A typical example is (看一看, **kàn yī kàn, look little / quick look**). |

一

(一, **yī, yí, yì, one**) is much simpler than the first character (的, **de**), but not much. You can see that there are three tone pronunciations. The simpliest usage is when (一, **yī, one**) numbers are being serially spoken and it is pronounced in the first tone.

(一, **yī, one**) is the number one. As in English it can be used to identify the quantity of a countable noun. Chinese grammar however uses various characters to mark countable nouns . These characters come between the number and the countable noun. This class of characters is variably called measure words or classifiers and in this book will be called *Countable Noun Indicators* (**CNI**). They measure nothing and are sometimes classfiers but this is a secondary role.

一	个	车
yī	ge	chē
one / a	piece	vehicle
Number	CNI	Countable Noun

(个, **gè,**) is the *Countable Noun Indicator* (**CNI**) in this example. The meaning is somewhat fluid and (个, **gè, piece**) is generic whereas there are many specific **CNI** that to a degree create classes of the target *Object Noun*. This is where the term *classifier* comes from. The specific **CNI** for (车, **chē, vehicle**) is (辆, **liàng,**). This can be used for any vehicle except boats. If you look in a reference to find the meaning of (辆, **liàng, CNI vehicles**), you will find none, only that it is a **CNI** for vehicles.

You can also see that this structure acts like *a*, in English, this is an ***Indefinite Article***. (一个, **yīgè**, **a / one piece**) does not specify a specific car, but only *a car*.

一	辆	车
Yī	liàng	chē
One / a	of	vehicle
Number	CNI	Countable Noun

(一, **yí**, **one**) is the grammatical form when used before another word that is written with the fourth tone. There are no other rules to this simple rule. So the tone goes up, then down. Why?, Who knows? Which incidently you write like this.

为什么	谁	知道
Wèishénme?,	Shéi	zhīdao?
For what?,	Who	know?
Why?,	Who	know?

(为什么, **wèishénme**, **for what**, **why**) makes reasonable sense as a compound construction. (为, **wèi**, **for**, **on account of**, **on behalf of**) is used very similar to the English word *for*. (什么, **shénme**, **what**) can be used with no other question forming particles or constructions to signal a question. ***For what***, and ***why***, seem interchangeable to me.

(谁, **shuí**, **shéi**, **who**) is another question forming word. In fact, ***what***, ***where***, ***how***, ***who***, ***when and why*** all act as question forming words, as in English.(谁, **shéi**, **who**) is more common in casual conversation and (谁, **shuí**, **who**) is more formal.

To further confuse, (谁, **shuí**, **who**) is also the written form. Now given that the character is of course written the same, and Chinese people do not use **Pinyin** to write, it seems apparent from my wife that when you are silently reading to yourself in Chinese, you silently speak (谁, **shuí**, **who**), or she is messing with me.

(知, **zhī**, **to know, to realize, to sense**) is compounded with (道, **dào**, **road, path, way**) to form (知道, **zhīdao**, **to know**). This is an example of a *Verb Object Compound* (**VOC**). Literally, the Chinese word means ***to know the way***. This is a great starter word when learning Mandarin. You can fool a lot of people by nodding your head and saying, (知道, **zhīdao**, **know**)

我	知道
Wǒ	zhīdao.
Me	know.

or

我	不	知道
Wǒ	bù	zhīdao.
Me	not	know.

or

你	知道	吗
Nǐ	zhīdao	ma?
You	know	?

This (道, **dào**, **the path**), is the path of *Taoism* or *Daoism*. *Tao* is the older pre-*Hanyu Pinyin Wade-Giles Romanisation* pronunciation and spelling. *Daoism* forms part of the moral construct of *Confucian* thought.

Remember the television show <u>**Kungfu**</u> (1972 to 1975) with David Carradine? He was my model of Asian philosophy. I watched the re-runs for years as a child. This sparked my interest in China, Asian philosophy, Kung fu and Chinese food. June 4th 2009 he was found hanging in a Bangkok hotel room closest. He died from auto erotic asphyxiation. That is, he tied himself up, including a noose around his neck and his ballsac. I guess he slipped off of the chair (一点, **yī diǎn**, **a little bit**) Strange way to get off. So much for childhood heroes. I still have Wayne Gretzky.

This is not the second chapter that I wrote in this book. So, you are probably wondering what this story has to do with (一, **yī**, **one**). The answer, nothing. It is just that (一, **yī**, **one**) is not so interesting and I tend to digress.

(一, **yī**, **one, a little, a small amount**) is used to identify diminution or a small amount of something. There are several common forms.

一	点
yī	**diǎn**
one	**drop**
a little	

(一点, **yī diǎn**, **a little bit**)
(一点点, **yī diǎn diǎn**, **a little bit**)
(一点儿, **yī diǎn'r**, **a little bit**)

are all common character forms of diminution using (一, **yī**, **one**, **a little**).

你	要	吃	一点	米饭	吗
Nǐ	yào	chī	yīdiǎn	mǐfàn	ma?
You	want	eat	a little	rice meal	?

As (一点, **yī diǎn**, **a drop**) modifies a *Noun* and answers the question *how much*, it acts as an **Quantitative Adjective**.

(一, **yī**, **diminutive verb prefix**) In addition to acting as a number it also acts to diminish verb intensity. The grammatical form is *verb* (一, **yī**, **one**) *verb*. The character (一, **yī**, **one**, **a little**) is interposed between the duplicated verb. A typical example is,

看	一	看
kàn	yī	kàn
look	one	look
	a little look	

It is used in the context of have a *little look* or have a *quick look*. Other common examples are,

尝	一	尝
Cháng	yī	cháng.
Taste	one	taste.
	a little taste	

听	一	听
Tīng	yī	tīng.
Listen to	one	listen to.
	a little listen	

(一, **yī, verb immediacy prefix**) can be used before a *Verb* to indicate immediacy. The construction can indicate that the verb was enacted immediately and quickly.

我	就是	那么	一看
Wǒ	jiùshì	nàme	yīkān.
Me	just is	like that	one look.

Me just is like that quickly look.

(一, **yī, noun entirety prefix**) can be used to indicate entirety of a *Noun*. This works particularly good for nouns that have duration.

一	天	到	晚	我	工作
Yī	tiān	dào	wǎn	wǒ	gōngzuò.
One	day	to	night	me	work.
All day		to	night	me	work.

(个, gè, piece of)

(车, chē, vehicle)

(辆, liàng, CNI vehicles)

(一个, yīgè, one piece of, a)

(为, wèi, for)

(什么, shénme, what)

(为什么, wèishénme, for what, why)

(谁, shuí, who)

(谁, shéi, who)

(知, zhī, to know, to realize, to sense)

(道, dào, road, path, way)

(知道, zhīdao, to know)

(点, diǎn, a drop)

(尝, cháng, taste)

(听, tīng, listen to)

(一点, yī diǎn, a little bit)

(一点点, yī diǎn diǎn, a little bit)

(一点儿, yī diǎn'r, a little bit)

(车, chē, vehicle)

(个, ge, piece)

(为什么, wèishénme, for what?)

(为什么, wèishénme, why)

(要, yào, want)

(什么, shénme, what)

(一点, yī diǎn, a little bit)

(一, yī, one, a little, a small amount)

(一点, yī diǎn, a little bit),

(一点点, yī diǎn diǎn, a little bit)

(一点儿, yī diǎn'r, a little bit)

(为, wèi, for)

(为, wèi, on account of, on behalf of)

(为, wèi, on behalf of)

(一, yī, yí, yì, one)

(的, de)

(吃, chì, eat)

(就是, jiùshì, just is)

(那么, nàme like, that)

是	Notes: Verb
shì is	(是, **shì**, **is**, **to be**) (是, **shì**, **is**) is the equivalent of the English verb *to be*. Its use is near the same except that it is not often used when the **Topic - Subject** is equated with an adjective and no target **Object – Noun**.

丨 冂 冃 日 旦 早 早 昱 是

是 是 是 是 是 是 是 是

是	是	是	是	是	是	是	是	是	是
shì is	shì is	shì is	shì is	shì is	shì is	shì is	shì is	shì is	shì is
是	是	是	是	是	是	是	是	是	是
shì is	shì is	shì is	shì is	shì is	shì is	shì is	shì is	shì is	shì is
是	是	是	是	是	是	是	是	是	是
是	是	是	是	是	是	是	是	是	是
是	是	是	是	是	是	是	是	是	是
是	是	是	是	是	是	是	是	是	是
是	是	是	是	是	是	是	是	是	是
是	是	是	是	是	是	是	是	是	是
是	是	是	是	是	是	是	是	是	是

是

(是, **shì**, **is**, **to be**) is the most common verb. It is used very similar to the English equivalent. (是, **shì**, **is**, **to be**) creates a sentence like a math equation, similar to the function of the (=, *equal sign*). That is, it equates the *Subject* of the sentence with its direct *Object*. Mandarin grammar favours this construction when the *Object* is a noun, such as in the example below. It is often called the *equational verb* or *copula verb*. I have no idea what *copula* means..

Subject	Verb	Object
他	是	王
Tā	shì	Wáng
He	=	Wang
He	is	Wang

Less common, but grammatically correct, is the use of (是, **shì**, **is**, **to be**) to equate an adjective to the *Subject*. You will read books that say that his construction is not used, but it is. It is used to overcome disbelief or to add emphasis to the statement. *Adjectives* that describe a feature or quality are referred to as *attributive adjectives*. The below statement would be emphatically stated. So if the chic was thought to be nasty looking this would be an appropriate way to express surprise.

Subject	Verb	Adjective
她	是	美丽
Tā	shì	měilì !
She	is	beautiful !

(是, **shì**, **is**, **to be**) is also used to answer affirmatively to the questions that use (是, **shì**, **is**) in the construction. So, if your name is Wang and you are asked if you are Wang, one correct way to answer is simply to say (是, **shì**, **is**). The usual affirmative responses that function the same include,

(是的, **shìde**, **is**, **yes**)

(是, **shì**, **is**, **yes**)

(是啊, **shì'a**, **yes!**)

The character (是, **shì**, **is**, **to be**) is composed of the *Kangxi Radical* number 72 (日, **rì**, **sun**), and the bottom is just a variant of writing (正, **zhèng**, **correct**).

Common words with (是, **shì**, **is**, **yes**)

(可是, **kěshì**, **but**, **yet**) from (可, **kě**, **can**, **may**) and (是, **shì**, **is**, **yes**). This word is often used as a conjunction to join two phrases as in English.

他	是	我	的	朋友	可是	我	也	爱	你
Tā	shì	wǒ	de	péngyou	kěshì	wǒ	yě	ài	nǐ.
He	is	mine		friend	but	me	also	love	you.

(但是, **dànshì**, **but**, **yet**) from (但, **dàn**, **but**, **yet**) and (是, **shì**, **is**, **yes**). This word is also a conjunction and can be used interchangeably with (可是, **kěshì**, **but**, **yet**).

(可是, **kěshì**, **but**, **yet**) and (但是, **dànshì**, **but**, **yet**) can be used to begin sentences, but only in a response to a statement.

王:	我	要	这个,	好	不	好?
Wáng:	Wǒ	yào	zhèige,	hǎo	bu	hǎo?
Wang:	Me	want	this one,	good	not	good?

张:	但是	我	要	那个,	不	好	啊
Zhāng:	Dànshì	wǒ	yào	nàge!	bù	hǎo	ā.
Zhang:	But	me	want	that one!	Not	good	!

(好不好, **hǎo bù hǎo**, **good not good**) has a common and special significance. It is often used at the end of a sentence to seek agreement to the person being addressed. If the listener agrees, he / she will say (好, **hǎo**, **good**). If the listener disagrees, he / she will say (不好, **bù hǎo**, **not good**).

(是的, **shìde**, **is**, **yes**) as mentioned earlier, (是的, **shìde**, **is**, **yes**) can be used as an affirmative reply.

王:	你	是	张	吗
Wáng:	Nǐ	shì	Zhāng	ma.
Wang:	You	is	Zhang	?

(吗, **ma**, **question particle**, ?) acts to mark a statement as a question. Functionally, it acts as a question mark.

张:	是的
Zhāng:	Shì de.
Zhang:	Is.

The negative response is, (不是, **bú shì**, **not is**).

张:	不是
Zhāng:	**Bú shì**.
Zhang:	Not is.

(不是吗, **bú shì ma**, **not is**?) is used to question the correctness of the negative response. The expression is used similar to *is that not so*? seeking agreement on a negative response.

(不是, **búshì**, **not is**) can be used to construct a sentence similar to the use of *isn't*.

这	不是	你	要	的	书	吗
Zhè	búshì	nǐ	yào	de	shū	ma.
This	not is	you	want		book	?
This	isn't	your	wanted		book	?
Subject	Verb Phrase	Object Noun Phrase				

This above sentence is interesting as the *Object Phrase* (**OP**) contains (的, **de**). The most formal correct grammar would give the choice of using (你的, **nǐde**, **your**) rather than (你, **nǐ**, **you**), but this is *too many the* (的, **de**). Also, (的, **de**) can be omitted as the construction is *close and personal*. The sentence tells you that the book does not belong to (你, **nǐ**, **you**) but that he wanted to own the book and is being questioned about it. Perhaps the most understandable translation would be, ***Is this not the book you wanted***?

This is where the grammatical term *Nominalization* comes in. **Book** is modified with ***your wanted***, hence, the use of (的, **de**) properly placed immediately before the *Head Noun* of the *Object Noun Phrase* (**ONP**) and immediately after the modifiers.

(还是, **háishi**, **or**) from (还, **hái**, **still, yet**) and (是, **shì**, **is**).

去	还是	不	去	
Qù	háishi	bú	qù	?
Go	or	not	go	?

(就是, **jiùshì**, **just is, exactly, precisely**) from (就, **jiù**, **just**) and (是, **shì**, **is**). This word can be used to add precision or emphasis to a statement or can be used like *just*.

现在	就是	八	点	半
Xiànzài	jiùshì	bā	diǎn	bàn.
Now	just is	eight	o'clock	half.

This sentence construction is often used in response to being asked as to what time it is. (就是, **jiùshì**, **just is**) is usually used in time answers.

我们	就是	两	位	人
Wǒmen	jiùshì	liǎng	wèi	rén.
We	just is	two	person	person.
			CNI	

This is something that you would want to tell the greeter or hostess at a restaurant when there are several hundred other parties waiting with numerous guests and you spy a table for two.

CNI or *Countable Noun Indicator* is a concept partially evolved in English. It is however fully evolved in Mandarin grammar and is *velly intelesting*.

One way to classify nouns is by separating them into countable and non-countable categories. In Mandarin grammar, countable nouns are marked by a character that is specific to a collection of nouns. These nouns often share physical characteristics.

At some point in this book I will explain this in greater detail but I am losing enthusiasm already. Not for writing the book but for explaining **CNI's**. Chinese grammar books are divided between using the term *measure word* or *classifiers*.

Suffice to say, there is a simple format. In the character string you must first have a number, then the specific **CNI**, then the target *Countable Noun* (**CN**).

(要是, **yàoshi**, **if**) from (要, **yào**, **want**) and (是, **shì**, **is**).

要是	下雨	我们	就	不	去	游泳	了
Yàoshi	xiàyǔ	wǒmen	jiù	bú	qù	yóuyǒng	le.
If	down rain	we	just	not	go	swim	.

Always, (老是, **lǎoshi**, **always**) can be expressed with several different constructions. (总是, **zǒngshì**, **always**) can be used interchangeably. (老, **lǎo**, **old**) and (总, **zǒng**, **generally**) somehow individually combine with (是, **shì**, **is, yes**) to create the meaning *always*.

You will often read that Mandarin is evolving into a language in which *words* are becoming disyllabic, that is, they are composed of two characters. If you look at a word frequency list (**Wenlin**) you will find out that this is not true. The most common words used remain monosyllabic.

You can see from the above examples that these are disyllabic words. However, both the monosyllabic characters (老, **lǎo, always**) and (总, **zǒng, always**) exist to share the same meaning with their disyllabic mates.

These single syllable forms are common and casual. However, the daily speech of China is also casual. So there are four common *Words* to express *always*. Only the word (总, **zǒng, generally**) and it's compound make any immediate sense.

我们	总是	去	那	家	饭店	吃饭
Wǒmen	zǒngshì	qù	nà	jiā	fàndiàn	chīfàn.
We	always is	go	that	family	restaurant	eat meal.

(老, **lǎo, always**)

(老是, **lǎoshì, always**)

(总, **zǒng, always**)

(总是, **zǒngshì, always**)

Generally, they can be used interchangeabley.

The simpliest sentence using Mandarin grammar need only have a *Subject*, a *Verb* and an *Object*. It is very useful to make tall skinny lists of *Verbs*, *Pronouns* and *Nouns* and stick the *Verb* list in the middle and the *Pronouns* on the left and the *Nouns* on the right. This is a great way to practice all the skills, character recognition, phonetics, and sentence construction.

(是的, shìde, is)

(是, shì, is, yes)

(是啊, shì'a, yes!)

(是, shì, is, to be)

(王, wáng, king, sovereign, prince)

(王, wáng, king, Surname Wang)

(丽, lì, beautiful)

(美, měi, beautiful)

(的, de, grammatical particle)

(日, rì, sun)

(正, zhèng, correct)

(吗, ma, question particle?)

(不是吗, bú shì ma, not is?)

(但是, dànshì, but, yet)

(但, dàn, but, yet)

(还是, háishi, or)

(还, hái, still, yet)

(就, jiù, just)

(好, hǎo, good)

(不, bù, not, no)

(可是, kěshì, but, yet)

(位, wèi, CNI for people)

(可, kě, can, may)

(我们, wǒmen, we, us)

(就是, jiùshì, just, exactly, precisely)

(半, bàn, half)

(二, èr, two)

(人, rén, person)

(两, liǎng, two)

(现在, xiànzài, now)

(点, diǎn, drop, dot)

(八, bā, eight)

(那个, nàge, that one)

(这个, zhèige, this one)

(老, lǎo, old)

(要, yào, want)

(也, yě, also)

(爱, ài, love)

(去, qù, go)

(总, zǒng, generally)

(老是, lǎoshi, always)

(总是, zǒngshì, always)

(啊, ā, elation interjection)

不	Notes: Adverb
bù not	(不, **bù**, **bú**, **no**, **not**) (不, **bù**, **not**) is most commonly used to negate a verb. All **Hanzi** / **Hanyu** verbs except (有, **yǒu**, **have**) are negated in the form of (不, **bù**, **not**) preceding the verb.

一 丁 不 不

不 不 不 不 不 不 不 不 不

不	不	不	不	不	不	不	不	不	不
bù	bù	bù	bù	bù	bù	bù	bù	bù	bù
not	not	not	not	not	not	not	not	not	not
不	不	不	不	不	不	不	不	不	不
bù	bù	bù	bù	bù	bù	bù	bù	bù	bù
not	not	not	not	not	not	not	not	not	not

不

(不, **bù**, **no, not**) is most commonly used in front of a verb to negate the verb action. Grammatically, it is an *Adverb*.

(要, **yào**, **want**) translates exactly like it's English equivalent and negates as such (不要, **búyào**, **not want**).

我	不要	这个
Wǒ	búyào	zhèige.
Me	not want	this one.

(能, **néng**, **can**) translates exactly like it's English equivalent and negates as such (不能, **bùnéng**, **not can**).

她	不能	来	了
Tā	bùnéng	lái	le.
She	not can	come	CRS.

(给, **gěi**, **give**) translates exactly like it's English equivalent and negates as such (不给, **bùgěi**, **not give**).

你	没有	给	我	很	多
Nǐ	méiyǒu	gěi	wǒ	hěn	duō.
You	not have	give	me	very	much.

他	不是	我的	爸爸
Tā	bú shì	wǒde	bàba.
He	not is	my	papa.

(不是, **bú shì**, **not is**) is the most commmon form of saying *no* to a question whereas (不是吗, **bú shì ma**, **not is**?) asks for agreement with the negative response to a question.

Questions can be formed in Mandarin grammar by making the statement and then adding a sentence final particle that marks a question. (吗, **ma**, **question particle**,?)

This leaves the listener waiting for the end of the sentence to know if it is a question or not. An alternate form that gives an early signal to note that the spoken expression is a question, is to construct the possible answers to the question in the verb phrase of the sentence.

王:	你	是不是	张
Wáng:	Nǐ	shì bú shì	Zhāng.
Wang:	You	is not is	Zhang.
	Subject	Verb Phrase	Object

The term *phrase* is vaguely defined to those who fancy themselves grammarians and authors. One of the more common forms of sentence construction in Mandarin grammar is **Subject Verb Object**, also known as **SVO**. This is demonstrated in the above example.

The possible answers, embedded into the question, are (是, **shì**, **is**) and (不是, **bú shì**, **not is**).

The person asking the question, showing some degree of disbelief or surprise at hearing (不是, **bú shì**, **not is**) can say (不是吗, **bú shì ma?**, **not is?**)

It is not necessary to use the question particle (吗, **ma**, **question particle**,?) at the end of a sentence in which you use a ***Question Asking Verb Phrase Construction***. This character, used only in a sentence final position, is generally spoken in a neutral tone. Please see the chapter on tones at the back of the book.

However, occassionally it is used after a pause, notably more so by young girls than males. In this situation it is used with a rising tone. Question final particles are otherwise spoken in a neutral tone. With internet chatting, it is common to see *ma?*, *ma?*, *ma?* while she is waiting for a reply, and you are busy chatting with 6 other girls.

你	是	不	是	我的	男	朋友	吗	吗
Nǐ	shì	bú	shì	wǒde	nán	péngyou?	ma?	ma?
You	is	not	is	me	male	friend?	ma?	ma?
You	is	not	is	my		boyfriend?	?	?

(是不是吗, **shì bú shì ma**, **is not is?**) is particularilly sloppy street grammar but is nevertheless used. However, guys, in China it is deemed *girly* and *whiney*. If you use it you will be deemed (奶油, **nǎiyóu**, **cream, butter**) from (奶, **nǎi**, **milk**) and (油, **yóu**, **oil**). (奶油, **nǎiyóu**, **cream butter**) is a euphamism for effeminate or gay.

You will note that (朋友, **péngyou**, **friend**) does not preserve the third tone of (友, **yǒu**, **friend**) in the *Hanyu Pinyin*. When characters that are nouns share similar meaning are compiled together to form a compound character word, the second character is spoken in the neutral tone, usually.

(不, bù, not, no) also has specific tone change rules. When it is used before a character spoken with the fourth tone, (不, bù, not, no) is then spoken with a second tone as such (不, bú, not, no). When (不, bù, not, no) appears between verbs to construct a question format verb phrase, it is correctly spoken with a neutral tone. (不, bu, not, no).

That is all I know about (不, bú, not, no).

(是, shì, is, to be)
(不好, bùhǎo, not good)
(不是吗, bú shì ma, not is?)
(好, hǎo, good)
(不, bù, not, no)
(是, shì, is, to be, yes)
(是的, shìde, is) yes)
(是, shì, is, yes)
(是啊, shì'a, yes!)
(王, wáng, king, sovereign, prince)
(王, Wáng, King, Surname Wang)
(啊, ā, indicating elation)
(的, de, grammatical particle)
(可是, kěshì, but, yet)

(但是, dànshì, but, yet)
(但, dàn, but, yet)
(好, hǎo, good)
(不好, bù hǎo, not good)
(吗, ma, question particle,?)
(不是, bú shì, not is)
(还是, háishi, or)
(还, hái, still, yet)
(就是, jiùshì, just, exactly, precisely)
(就, jiù, just)
(有, yǒu, have)
(可, kě, can, may)
(是不是, shì bú shì, is not is?)
(男, nán, man, male)

(朋, péng, friend)

(友, yǒu, friend)

(朋友, péngyou, friend)

(丽, lì, beautiful)

(是不是吗, shì bú shì ma, is not is?)

(奶油, nǎiyóu, cream, butter)

(好不好, hǎo bu hǎo?, good not good?)

(美, měi, beautiful)

(美丽, měili, beautiful)

(奶, nǎi, milk)

(油, yóu, oil)

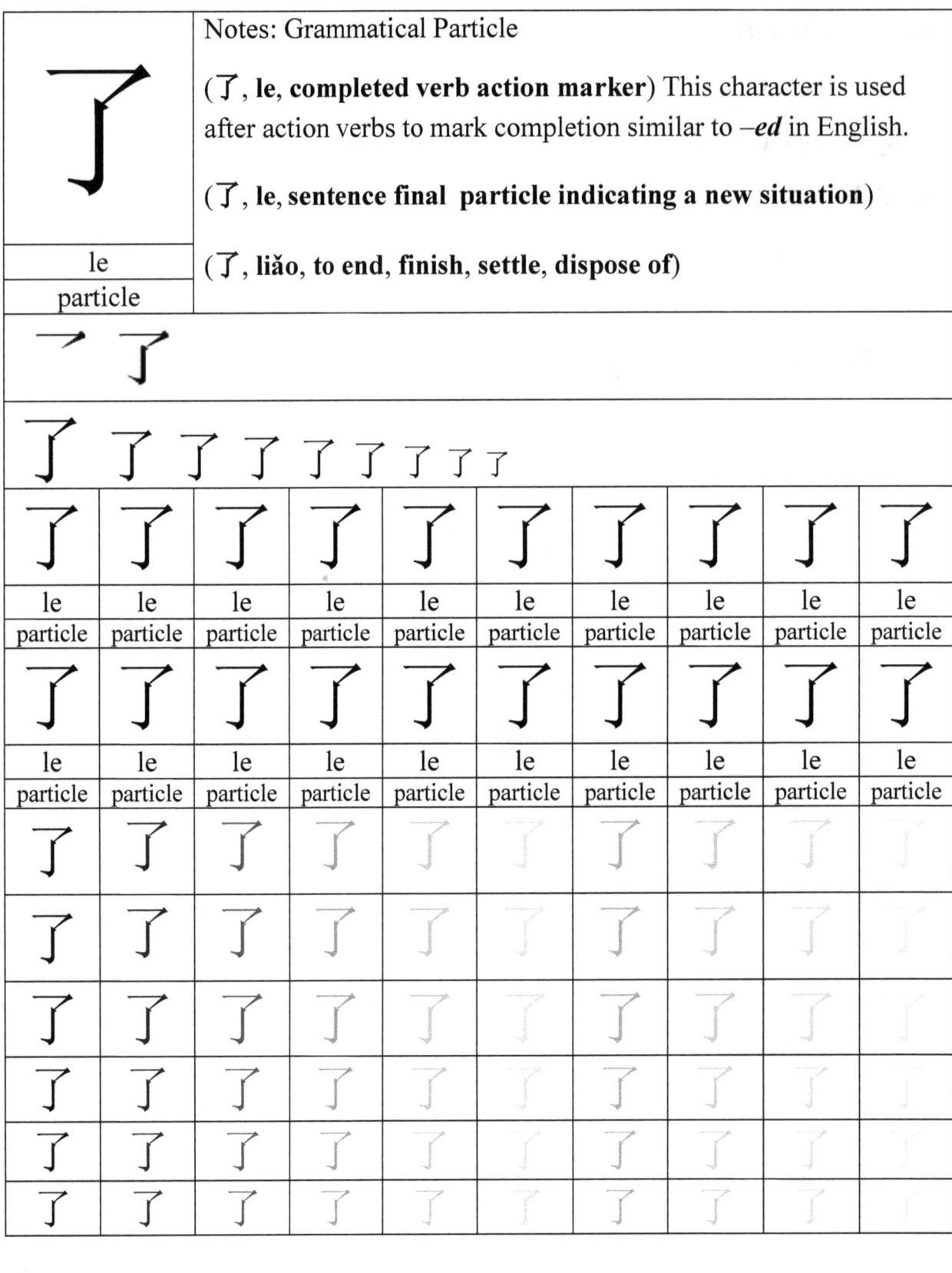

了

There are different common uses of the character (了, **le**). It can act both as a grammatical particle or a component of compound characters. Chinese characters are invariant, that is, they cannot be changed as they stand to alter meaning. However, other characters are used in the character string sentence to create verb tense or otherwise modify meaning.

While it is true that verb tense is invariant for any given character, it is not true that *Chinese* language does not have verb tense. Verb tense is constructed by the use of additional characters, placed at specific places in the character string to mark tense or by creating a setting that clearly defines the degree of *Verb Action*.

(了, **le, completed action verb marker**) is placed immediately after *Action Verbs* (**AV**) to show completion of verb action. Functionally, it acts as *–ed*. Not all English verbs are conjugated in a predictable pattern and are marked with *–ed* as a form of completion. When writing in *Hanyu Pinyin*, the (了, **le, -ed**) is attached directly to the completed verb.

Marking a verb action as completed is called the *Perfect Tense* in English Grammar. Interestly, the most common verb (是, **shì, is**) is not completed with (了, **le, -ed**). The closest equivalent to the *Perfect Tense* is (是的, **shì de, is**)

(来, **lái, come**)	(来了, **láile, came**)
(给, **gěi, give**)	(给了, **gěile, gave**)
(吃, **chī, eat**)	(吃了, **chīle, ate**)

(跳, tiào, jump)	(跳, tiàole, jumped)
(放屁, fàngpì, fart)	(放屁了, fàngpìle, farted)
(叫, jiào, call)	(叫了, jiàole, called)

You can see from the example below, (昨天, zuótiān, previous day) establishes past tense in the sentence. (给了, gěile, gave) also signals past tense through verb completion. So, you can see the three character word below. Eager? The literal translation is **three horn pants**. Go figure that one out.

昨天	我	给了	她	新	红	三角裤
Zuótiān,	wǒ	gěile	tā	xīn	hóng	sānjiǎokù.
Previous day,	me	gave	her	new	red	panties.

Have you read in other books that crap about the right sided Radical of a character giving phonetic clues. This is generally untrue. There are true examples but they are uncommon. The phonetic clue of (昨, zuó, previous day) is (乍, zhà, **phonetic**). You can see how (昨, zuó) sounds like (乍, zhà) right. That's a phonetic clue right? It is also used in other characters and pronounced (乍, zhà, zuò, zuó, zhǎi, zhà, zǎ).

Now, I am trying to inject some Chinese cultural stuff. Red is a happy and lucky colour in China. A girl wanting to find a man to marry will wear red in her attire. Now that is a subtle signal, right? The first Valentines day in China I spent with the girl I eventually married, she told me the custom of buying your girlfriend clothing for Chinese New Year. Valentines Day and New Years were almost on the same date. So she wanted a bra and underwear. So I am thinking, *this is good, finally*!. It took three attempts for her to be bold enough to go into a lingerie store. The first store she wouldn't go in, shy, the second she ran out of as there was a male attendant. The third one we succeeded. The panties cost $1.42, the bra $3.00. So to look like a big shot Western rich guy I bought her doubles. I was never to see those panties or bras again until after we got married. Althought she was always quick to tell me when she was wearing them. I later learned that these four pieces of lingerie doubled her collection.

Red, is the traditional colour for brides. When her younger sister got married, at minus 10 degrees, outside, she wore head to toe red, I froze my nutbag off but a good times was had by all.

Here is another example of (了, **le**) showing **Verb Completion**. There is where Mandarin gets interesting. If you had wanted to invite five guests and you changed it to one guest, then the correct (了, **le**) is to show a change in **Current Relevant State**. (了, **le, CRS**). This would change the *Pinyin* to **qǐng le** versus **qǐngle**. This of course does not change the **Hanzi**. Chinese of course do not use **Pinyin** in their day to day life. So, often you will see the (了, **le, CRS**) at the end of the sentence floating free written as 我只请一位客人了

我	只	请了	一	位	客人
Wǒ	zhǐ	qǐngle	yī	wèi	kèren.
Me	only	invited	one		guest.

(请, qǐng, request, invite)   (客人, kèren, guest)

(请了, qǐngle, invited)   (了, le)

Here is an example using (了, **le**) twice. Both are different, the second shows ***Verb Completion*** (**VC**). The first marks a mood. This mood of course depends on how the speaker expresses the sentence.

太	臭	了	你	放屁了	吗
Tài	chòu	le.	Nǐ	fàngpìle	ma.
Extreme	stink.		You	farted	?

You can see the ***Verb Completion*** (**VC**) marked in (放屁了, **fàngpìle**, **farted**) the incompleted form being of course (放屁, **fàngpì**, **fart**). Maybe this above example is not the best choice. (了, **le**) appears twice and they are grammatically different. The first (了, **le**) marks a ***Bounded Event*** (**BE**). Without getting a Ph.D. in Mandarin grammar, this is a complicated concept and appears idiomatic until the day when you have sudden understanding of this concept, which has not happened to me yet. Some books say that this use of (了, **le**) acts to diminish the intensity of the statement and prevent offending the listener. If that was true, you simply would not use (太, **tài**, **extremely**). There is a heirarchy of ***Superlatives*** similar to English. So for now, until you reach Mandarin enlightenment, just remember that if a short statement starts with (太, **tài**, **extremely**) has an *Adjective* next, then stick (了, **le**) at the end.

Probably the most important phrase in this form that you will initially need to use is (太贵了, **tài gùi le**, **extreme expensive**). You will get cheated in the market. You can inject some humour in the situation by saying (太贵了, **tài gùi le**, **extreme expensive**), maybe throw a (啊, **ǎ**, **interjection indicating puzzled surprise**) at the end. (太贵了啊, **tài gùi le ǎ**, **extreme expensive!**), maybe the merchant will have mercy on you and only charge you five times as much as the locals.

(来了, láile, came) is the *Perfected* form of (来, lái, come).

来了	吗
Láile	ma.
Came	?

(来了吗, láile ma, came?) asks if someone has arrived. Functionally, it has the same meaning as (到了吗, dàole ma, arrived?), from (到, dào, arrive).

(叫了, jiàole, called) specifically refers to calling out by voice.

你	的	太太	你	叫了	吗
Nǐ	de	tàitài,	nǐ	jiàole	ma.
Your		wife,	you	called	?

(太太, tàitai, wife), somewhere in this book I mentioned that compound characters can take the form of A+B=C, that is, the sum of each pays no relation to the final meaning. (太, tài, extremely) and (太太, tàitai, wife) are a fine example of the profound cleverness of Mandarin grammar.

(太太, tàitai, wife)

(叫了, jiàole, called)

(到, dào, arrive)

(到了吗, dàole ma, arrived?)

(来, lái, come)

(来了, láile, came)

(了, le)

(放屁, fàngpì, fart)

(放屁了, fàngpìle, farted)

(臭, chòu, stink)

(太, tài, extremely)

(三角裤, sānjiǎokù, panties)

(新, xīn, new)

(红, hóng, red)

(角, jiǎo, horn)

(裤, kù, pants)

(昨, zuó, previous day)

(昨天, zuótiān, previous day)

(今天, jīntiān, today)

(明天, míngtiān, tomorrow)

(昨晚, zuówǎn, yesterday evening)

(昨天, zuótiān, yesterday)

(昨夜, zuóyè, last night)

(请, qǐng, request, invite)

(请了, qǐngle, invited)

(客人, kèren, guest)

(了, le)

(前天, qíantīan, day before yesterday)

了

(了, **le, sentence final particle indicating a new situation**) is used at the end of a sentence to mark a change in information. **CRS** or **Current Relevant State** is a term used in formal grammar books, hence (了, **le, CRS**). Many of the uses seem idiomatic, that is, they do not apparently follow rules and they stand out as unexplainable.

Using *Hanyu Pinyin*, which is relatively useless to write sentences with, the syllable *le* is not joined to but is written separate from any other word. This differs from the (了, **le, completed verb action marker**) which is attached directly to the *Verb* it marks to complete.

(了, **le, CRS**) signals that the particular sentence is the most current version of events. This may mean that other sentences or statements have been made that differed from the most current one. This also makes it difficult to give a good example without giving previous sentences.

If there is no other situation, (了, **le,**) then acts to mark the sentence behind it as the most current situation. As Mandarin Verbs can occur at the end of the sentence, the only clue in **Hanyu Pinyin** as to the function of (了, **le,**) is its relationship to the preceding word. Attached, it is *Verb Completion* (**VC**), unattached, it marks **CRS**. But then **Pinyin** is not used very much in China.

The change in relevant state can mark completion of an act or change to an ongoing act.

他	最	变	胖	了
Tā	zuìjìn	biàn	pàng	le.
He	recent	change	fat.	

The above example of (了, **le**,) marks a change creating a new state. This example the change is completed but the *Verb* is not marked as thus.

(胖, **pàng**, **fat**)   (近, **jìn**, **near, close**)

(变, **biàn**, **change**)   (最近, **zuìjìn**, **recent**)

(最, **zuì**, **most**)

电影	已经	开始	了
Diànyǐng	yǐjīng	kāishǐ	le.
Electric shadow	stop constant	operate start.	
Movie	already	start.	

The above example of (了, **le**,) marks a change to an ongoing state.

(已, **yǐ**, **stop, cease, end**)

(经, **jīng**, **longitude**)

(已经, **yǐjing**, **already**)

(电, **diàn**, **electric**)

(影, **yǐng**, **shadow**)

(开, **kāi**, **open**)

(始, **shǐ**, **begin, start**)

了

Modal Particles mark mood. (了, **le**,), as previously noted has uses that are less clear. The below example shows the use. There are many examples and some are unpredictable. In a language where tone can change meaning *Modal Particles* evolved to mark emphasis or de-emphasis or unexpected results irrespective of voice changes. There is no consensus on absolute use of this form of (了, **le**,). Note the use of (是, **shì**, **is**, **to be**) to mark emphasis.

这	真	是	太	好	了
Zhè	zhēn	shì	tài	hǎo	le!
This	real	is	extreme	good	!

Modal Particle

In linguistics, **Modal Particles** are always uninflected words, and are a type of grammatical particle. Their function is that of reflecting the mood or attitude of the speaker or narrator, in that they are not reflexive but change the mood of the verb. The translation is often not straightforward and depends on the context. Mandarin Chinese depends highly on the use of modal particles. Changing the pitch of the word or phrase would make the meaning of the sentence different, so many particles have been developed to add to the end of the sentence to express emotion.

From Wikipedia, the free encyclopedia

http://en.wikipedia.org/wiki/Modal_particle

了

(了, liǎo, to end, finish, settle, dispose of)

赶快	把	这	件	事儿	了	了
Gǎnkuài	bǎ	zhè	jiàn	shì'r	liǎo	le.
Pursue quick	grasp	this	CNI	matter	finish.	
Quickly	grasp	this		matter	finish.	

In this above example you can see the double (了).

(快, kuài, quick) (赶, gǎn, pursue)

(赶快, gǎnkuài, quickly) (把, bǎ, grasp)

(事, shì, matter, issue) (件, jiàn, CNI matters)

(办得了, bàndeliǎo, do achieve finish) works for *it can be done* or *accomplish*.

这	件	事儿	办得了	我	没有	问题
Zhè	jiàn	shì'r	bàndeliǎo,	wǒ	méiyǒu	wèntí.
This	CNI	matter	accomplish,	me	not have	problem.

In the above example, (我, wǒ, me) and (有, yǒu, have) are optional.

(问题, wèntí, problem) (得, de, achieve)

(办, bàn, do) (没有, méiyǒu, not have)

Compound Words

(了, **le**,) and (了, **liǎo**,) can be used to create compound words in which neither adds any apparent meaning to the word. Nor do you intuitively know the correct pronunciation without previous familiarity to the word. And there are a shit load of them.

(为了, **wèile**, **for**, **for the sake of**, **in order to**) is the simpliest way to express *for*. Mandarin grammar does not make a great attempt to use this word and in situations that you would think that if fit nicely, Mandarin just does not use it. This gets back to the theme of **understandable** but ***not necessary***. This is a typical construction below.

我	为了	你	生了	这个	孩子
Wǒ	wèile	nǐ	shēngle	zhèige	háizi.
Me	for	you	born	this	child.

(孩子, **háizi**, child)　　　　　　　　(这个, **zhèige**, this one)

(生, **shēng**, to give birth to)　　　(为了, **wèile**, for)

你	了解	她	吗
Nǐ	liǎojiě	tā	ma.
You	understand	her	?

(解, **jiě**, explain)　　　　　　　　(了解, **liǎojiě**, to understand)

(了, **liǎo**, to end, finish)

Although modifiers come before that modified in Mandarin grammar, (极了, **jíle**, **extremely**) comes after the word it modifies.

她	聪明	极了
Tā	cōngming	jíle.
She	intelligent	extremely.

(极, **jí**, **extremely**)　　　　　　　　(明, **míng**, **clear**)

(聪明, **cōngming**, **intelligent**)　　　(聪, **cōng**, **intelligent**)

(算了, **suànle**, **forget about it**)

你	不要	去	就	算了
Nǐ	búyào	qù	jiù	suànle.
You	not want	go	just	forget it.

(算, **suàn**, **to calculate, compute**)　　(要, **yào**, **want**)

(对了, **duìle**, **correct**) from (对, **duì**, **correct**).

你	猜	对了
Nǐ	cāi	duìle.
You	guess	correct.

(猜, **cāi**, **guess**)

(对了, **duìle**, **correct**)

对了	你	还	没有	吃药	呢
Duìle,	nǐ	hái	méiyǒu	chīyào	ne.
Correct,	you	still	not have	eat drug	.

(吃, **chī**, eat) (呢, **ne**, affirmation particle)

(药, **yào**, drug) (对, **duì**, correct)

(吃药, **chīyào**, eat drug) (对了, **duìle**, correct)

(不, **bù**, not) (不要, **búyào**, not want)

(完了, **wánliǎo**, finish) and (完了, **wánle**, finish) are spoken expresssions of the same meaning and different pronunciation.

我	完了,	老婆	打死了	我
Wǒ	wánle,	lǎopo	dǎsǐle	wǒ.
Me	finished,	wife	beat dead	me.

(婆, **pó**, woman) (打, **dǎ**, beat) (打死, **dǎsǐ**, beat dead)

(老, **lǎo**, old) (死, **sǐ**, death)

(老婆, **lǎopo**, wife) (我, **wǒ**, me)

(得了, **déle**, achieved) is used to acknowledge and act that is finished or enough of an act. *Stop it*! *Hold it*! *Enough*!

饭	得了
Fàn	déle.
Meal	achieved.

(饭, **fàn**, meal)

(得, **dé**, get, reach, achieve)

(好了, **hǎole**, **good**) indicates that (好, **hǎo**, **good**) has occurred and (了, **le**) marks the new state, the *Current Relevant State*.

他	的	病,	好了
Tā	de	bìng,	hǎole.
His		illness,	good.
			CRS

(病, **bìng**, **disease**)

(罢了, **bàle**, **indicating limitation**) acts like a *Sentence Final Particle* and it marks that the topic is finished, no more discussion. In the below example, buddy may not want to buy his wife or mistress these shoes. The expression creates finality.

这	双	鞋	不过	十	块	钱	罢了
Zhè	shuāng	xié	búguò	shí	kuài	qián,	bàle!
This	pair	shoe	however	ten	piece	money,	cease!
CNI			Conjunction	CNI			

(过, **guò**, **pass, cross**)   (钱, **qián**, **money**)

(不, **bù**, **not**)   (双, **shuāng**, **pair**)

(不过, **búguò**, **but, however**)   (这, **zhè**, **this**)

(鞋, **xié**, **shoe**)   (十, **shì**, **ten**)

(块, **kuài**, **piece**)   (罢, **bà**, **cease**)

Here are some more common (了, **liào**) and (了, **le**) words.

(就, **jiù**, **just**)

(是, **shì**, **is**)

(就是了, **jiùshìle**, **just is**)

(除, **chú**, **except**)

(了 **chúle**, **except**)

(起, **qǐ**, **to rise**)

(了不起, **liǎobuqǐ**, **amazing, terrific, extraordinary**)

(了得, **liǎode**, **outrageous, terrible**)

(临, **lín**, **to face**)

(临了, **línliǎo**, **finally, in the end**)

(望, **wàng**, **observe**)

(了望, **liàowàng**, **watch, keep a lookout**)

(不得了, **bùdéliǎo**, **terrible, awful**)

(免, **miǎn**, **exempt, excuse**)

(免不了, **miǎnbuliǎo**, **be unavoidable**)

(末, **mò**, **end**)

(末了, **mòliǎo**, **finally, in the end**)

(大, **dà**, **big**)

(大不了, **dàbuliǎo**, **at the worst**)

(少, **shǎo**, **little, small, less**)

(少不了, **shǎobuliǎo**, **be indispensable, be unavoidable**)

(来, lái, come)

(来了, láile, came)

(给, gěi, give)

(给了, gěile, gave)

(吃, chī, eat)

(了, chīle, ate)

(跳, tiào, jump)

(跳, tiàole, jumped)

(放屁, fàngpì, fart)

(放屁了, fàngpìle, farted)

(叫, jiào, call)

(叫了, jiàole, called)

(已, yǐ, stop, cease, end)

(经, jīng, longitude)

(已经, yǐjing, already)

(电, diàn, electric)

(影, yǐng, shadow)

(开, kāi, open)

(始, shǐ, begin, start)

(胖, pàng, fat)

(变, biàn, change)

(最, zuì, most)

(近, jìn, near, close)

(最近, zuìjìn, recent)

(过, guò, pass, cross)

(不, bù, not)

(不过, búguò, but, however)

(鞋, xié, shoe)

(块, kuài, piece)

(钱, qián, money)

(双, shuāng, pair)

(这, zhè, this)

(十, shì, ten)

(罢, bà, cease)

(病, bìng, disease)

(婆, pó, woman)

(老, lǎo, old)

(老婆, lǎopo, wife)

(打, dǎ, beat)

(死, sǐ, death)

(我, wǒ, me)

(打死, dǎsǐ, beat to death)

(饭, fàn, meal)

(得, dé, get, reach, achieve)

(了, liǎo, to end, finish)

(了, le, completed action)

(了, le, SFP new situation)

有	Notes: Verb
yǒu have	(有, **yǒu**, **have**) is the common **Hanzi / Hanyu** possessive verb. It can be used to form a question in the verb negation format by stating thus, (有没有, **yǒu méiyǒu**, **have not have**). (有, **yǒu**, **have**) is the only **Hanzi / Hanyu** verb not negated with the adverb (不, **bù**, **not**) but is negated with (没, **méi**, **not**).

一 ナ 冇 冇 有 有

有 有 有 有 有 有 有 有 有

有

(有, yǒu, have) is unique as it is the only verb that is not negated with the *Adverb* (不, bù, not) but rather with (没, méi, not). Its use is near identical with the English equivalent. Verb constructions are very easy to use with this character.

你	有	西瓜	吗
Nǐ	yǒu	xīguā	ma.
You	have	west melon	?

Incidently, (西瓜, xīguā, west melon) is what us *foreigner* call *watermelon*. An alternate question format the gives an early signal as to that you are asking a question is;

你	有	没有	西瓜
Nǐ	yǒu	méiyǒu	xīguā?
You	have	not have	west melon?

So, if you do have some west melon, you can say (有, yǒu, have) or (有的, yǒu de, have). If you try and figure out how the (的, de) gets involved, well, send me an email. (的, de) often gets tacked onto the end of short expressions without a defined grammatical explanation.

If you do not have any *west melon*, you can say (没有, méi yǒu, not have). Now, if you have only a little supply of melon, or you do not want to brag, you can invoke the very common term, (一点, **yīdiǎn, a little**) and say (有一点, **yǒu yīdiǎn, have a little**). This can further be abbreviated to (有点, **yǒudiǎn, have a little**).

(西瓜, **xīguǎ, west melon**), our *watermelon*, seems to have some mystical value in China. They go crazy for that stuff. God forbid if I should buy one out of season for my mother-in-law. First she will scold me for paying 3.5 kuai a pound, about 49 cents. She always figures that she can get a better price. Then she will scold me for buying it out of season as the flavour is (不好, **bù hǎo, not good**). Then comes the (谢谢你, **xièxie nǐ, thank thank you**). Finally comes the gold toothed smile and the (大刀, **dàdāo, big knife**) as she shaves it into slices that you can see through.

Now, to further confuse you, in the north of China and in the Beijing area, there is a phonetic accessory called (儿化, **érhuà**). Note that I have not included an English translation for meaning. (儿化, **érhuà**) is the addition of a retroflexive *r* sound to the end of certain words. This adds no meaning to the word other than identifying that you are from the north area around Beijing. So then, (一点, **yīdiǎn, a little**) becomes (一点儿, **yīdiǎn'r, a little**) and the letter *n* becomes silent.

This then leads to (有一点儿, **yǒu yīdiǎn'r, have a little**) and then to (有点儿, **yǒudiǎn'r, have a little**), simple, right?

This is as such not proper Mandarin but is becoming common in China as people move around more.

哎,	师傅,	你	有	没有	苹果
Āi!,	shīfu!,	Nǐ	yǒu	méiyǒu	píngguǒ?
Heh!,	master!,	You	have	not have	apple?

Now, if you note a loudish interjective quality to the above example, welcome to China. Throw a hip check in and an elbow shot and push right to the front of the line in the outdoor market. Commonly, the (你, nǐ, you) would be dropped. ***Personal Pronouns***, if obvious, are often dropped.

当然,	有的
Dāngrán,	yǒu de.
Of course,	have.

In the above example, (有, **yǒu**, **have**) and (有的, **yǒu de**, **have**) can be used interchangeably.

Some of the uses of (有, **yǒu**, **have**) are grammatically different but understandable.

我	没有	你	高
Wǒ	méiyǒu	nǐ	gāo.
Me	not have	you	tall.

Now, my wife and I just had a long conversation, half in Mandarin and half in English as to how to explain what happens next. The above example is commenting on personal height. Now compare it to this example below which is more correct.

我	没有	你 的	高
Wǒ	méiyǒu	nǐ de	gāo
Me	not have	your	tall
SPrP	VP		Adj.

This grammatical structure is not commenting on personal height. This is commenting on objects of different heights in which the *Subject* speaker's *Object* is not as tall as the *Indirect Objects* (**IO**) *Object*. (我, **wǒ**, **me**) is the *Subject Pronoun Phrase* (**SPrP**) and (高, **gāo**, **tall**, **high**) acts as the *Direct Object* (**DO**)

To further confuse you, the most correct form of the above example has *too many the* (的, **de**).

我 的	没有	你 的	高
Wǒ de	méiyǒu	nǐ de	gāo.
Mine	not have	your	tall.
SPrP	VP		Adj.

This example is *most correct* but uncommon.

The below example typifies the simplicity of Mandarin grammar. If you **English-ify** the verb (吃, **chī**, **eat**) and change it to (吃, **chī**, **to eat**) the translation makes more sense.

家里	有的	吃	没有的	吃
Jiālǐ	yǒude	chī	méi yǒude	chī?
House inside	some	eat	not some	eat?
House inside	some	to eat	not some	to eat?

Buried inside this above example is (有没有, yǒu méiyǒu, have not have) marking the question construction.

If you try and apply the conventional 8 categories of English grammar words to this above example, you run into problems. (有的, yǒu de, have, some, have some) acts as a *Verb-Object Compound* (**VOC**). Overall the **VOC** probably best translates to *have something*. If you look at the conventional *Subject Verb Object* (**SVO**) sentence construction, you get this;

家里	有的	吃	没有的	吃
Jiālǐ	yǒude	chī	méi yǒude	chī?
House inside	have some	eat	not have some	eat?
House inside	have something	to eat	not have something	to eat?
Topic				

The *Subject*, which is also the *Topic*, is a *Prepositional Phrase*, that is, it describes a location. The format of Mandarin grammar places the *Locative Phrase Particle* (**LPP**) after the *Head Noun* of the *Noun Phrase*. The **LPP** answers the question of *where* of the *Head Noun*.

(些, xiē, some, few) combines with (有, yǒu, have) to form the compound character (有些, yǒuxiē, some).

有些	难	有些	不	难	懂	吗
Yǒuxiē	nán,	yǒuxiē	bù	nán,	dǒng	ma.
Some	difficult,	some	not	difficult,	understand	?

(只, **zhǐ**, **only**) and (有, **yǒu**, **have**) combine to form (只有, **zhǐyǒu**, **only have**). The use is reasonably the same. In English *only have* and *have only* can generally be used interchangeably. (只有, **zhǐyǒu**, **only have**) can be used in some Mandarin constructions to represent what in English would be ***only*** alone.

我	只有	六	本	书
Wǒ	zhǐyǒu	liù	běn	shū.
Me	only have	six	volume	book.

(时, **shí**, **time interval**) a noun, combines with (有, **yǒu**, **have**), a verb to make a *Temporal Adverb* (有时, **yǒushí**, **some time**) or (有时候, **yǒushíhou**, **sometimes**).

有时	我们	去	北京	有时	去	上海
Yǒushí	wǒmen	qù	Běijīng,	yǒushí	qù	Shànghǎi.
Sometime	we	go	Beijing,	sometime	go	Shanghai.

or,

有时候	我们	去	北京	有时候	去	上海
Yǒushíhou	wǒmen	qù	Běijīng,	yǒushíhou	qù	Shànghǎi.
Sometime	we	go	Beijing,	sometime	go	Shanghai.

(上海, Shànghǎi, Shanghai)

(北京, Běijīng, Beijing)

(去, qù, go)

(六, liù, six)

(书, shū, book)

(有些, yǒuxiē, some)

(难, nán, difficult)

(懂, dǒng, understand)

(师傅, shīfu, master worker)

(哎, āi, hey!, ah!)

(有没有, yǒu méiyǒu, have not have)

(苹果, píngguǒ, apple)

(一定, yīdìng, certain)

(有, yǒu, have)

(有的, yǒu de, have some)

(没有, méi yǒu, not have)

(没, méi, not)

(不, bù, not)

(一点, yīdiǎn, a little)

(儿化, érhuà)

(有一点, yǒu yīdiǎn, have a little)

(有点, yǒudiǎn, have a little)

(西瓜, xī gǔa, west melon)

(儿, ér, child)

(有没有, yǒu méiyǒu, have not have)

(化, huà, change)

(一点儿, yǒu yīdiǎn'r, have a little)

(高, gāo, tall, high)

(高, gāo, above average)

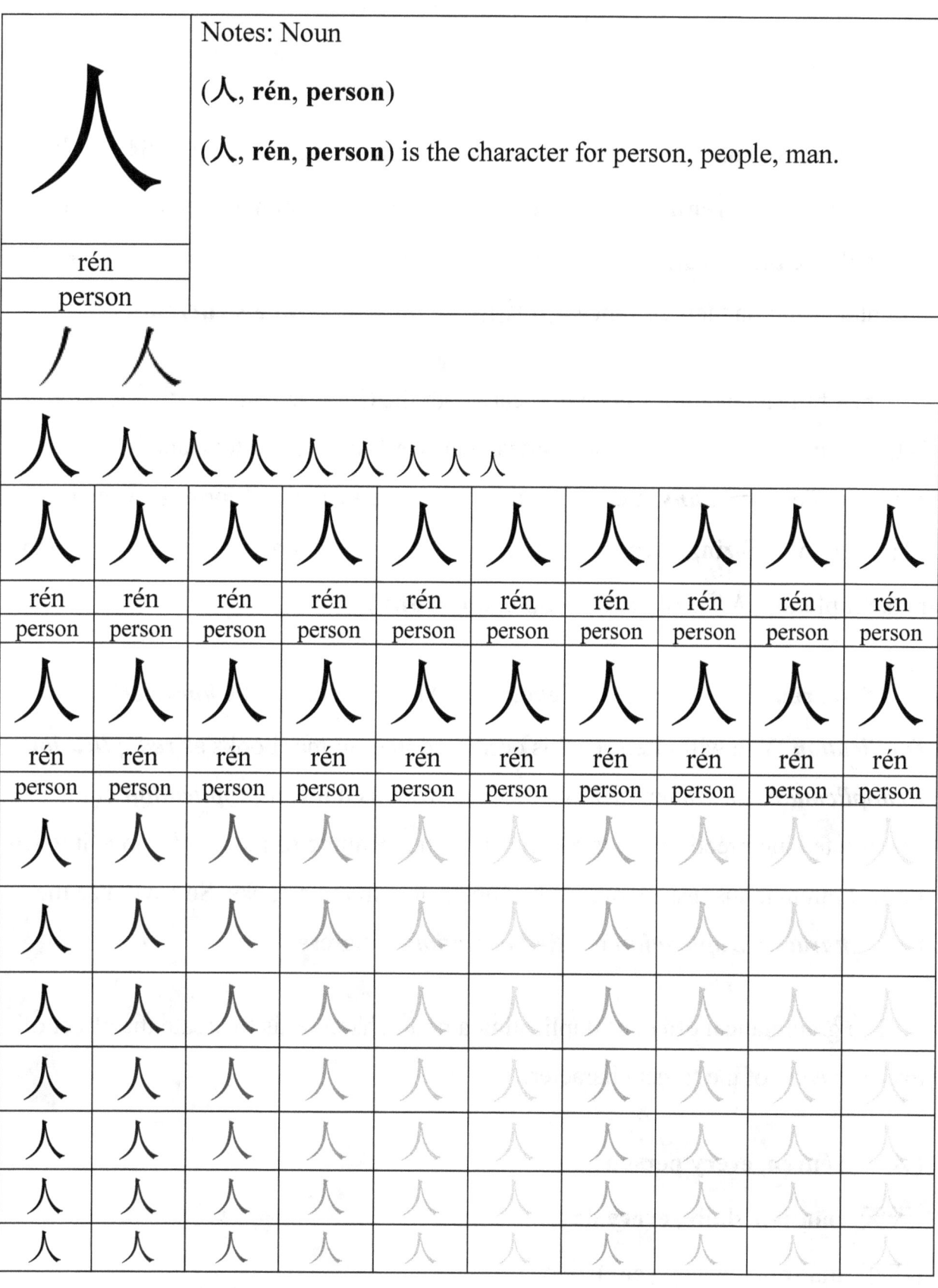

(人, **rén**, **person**) is a common noun that matches readily to its English equivalent. (人民, **rénmín**, **the people**) is a strong and common theme in China. You will see these characters on public buildings, parks, monuments, the sides of mountains and on their currency. (人民币, **rénmínbì**, **People's currency**)

One of the many things you will hear about the Chinese language that is not true, is that plural forms do not exist. That is, that words and characters, and in this example, *Person Nouns*, are invariant and do not take a plural form. However (们, **men**, **pluralizing suffix**) is a character that goes after a **Person Noun (PN)** to make it plural. (人们, **rénmen**, **people**, **humanity**)

(人人, **rénrén**, **every person**, **every one**) is an example of *Character Duplication*. You will often see this described in grammar books as *reduplication*. *Reduplication* is a grammatically awkward word as it means *duplication* but is constructed incorrectly as *re* is redundant in the meaning of the word. I love it when Ph.D. grammarians use a word of the uneducated in their books. So I will use the term *Character Duplication* not *Reduplication*, I digress.

The grammatical effect of duplicating a noun character is to create the effect of *every* or *each* of the target character.

(人人, **rénrén**, **every person**)
(天天, **tiāntiān**, **daily**, **every day**)
(年年, **niánnián**, **every year**)

The *People's* is a strong theme in Chinese signage, songs and thinking. You will see (人民, **rénmín**, **the people**) on propaganda signs on mountainsides, schools, government building, billboards, really, anywhere.

(别, **bié**, **separate**, **other**) combines with (人, **rén**, **person**) to create the compound (别人, **biéren**, **other people**). Also (别, **bié**, **do not**).

你	不要	告诉	别人
Nǐ	búyào	gàosù	biéren.
You	not want	tell	other person.

Overall, the above sentence is an instruction telling a person to not tell another.

I don't really need another example of (别人, **biéren**, **other people**) but the below example includes one of the most unlikely compound words.

别	动	别人	的	东西
Bié	dòng	biéren	de	dōngxi.
Do not	move	other people's		east west.
Do not	move	other people's		thing.

It is hard to imagine how (东西, **dōngxi**, **east west**, **thing**) came to be.

上海	有	多少	人口
Shànghǎi	yǒu	duōshǎo	rénkǒu?
Shanghai	have	much little	person mouth?
Shanghai	have	how much	population?

(人口, **rénkǒu**, **population**) or *people mouth* echoes the thinking in the use of (口人, **kǒu rén**, **mouth people**). The latter term is a marker for the number of people in a household in which (口, **kǒu**, **mouth**) is the **CNI** for (人, **rén**, **people**). (多少, **duōshǎo**, **much little**, **how much**) is a question forming word.

(才, **cái**) is another character with a host of unrelated meanings. It can act like a *Temporal Adverb* (**TA**) marking an immediacy of time. It is often glossed as *just then*, *then and only then* or *just now*. (才, **cái**, **just now**) *Temporal Adverbs* come in the *Sentence Initial* position in Mandarin grammar, or, immediately after the *Subject*.

Before a number it can mean *just*, setting limits on the number. But for the sake of this example, it means (才, **cái**, **talent**, **ability**).

(才, **réncái**, **a person of talent**) is an unusual compound word as the modifier is after the modified.

他	是	一	个	人才
Tā	shì	yī	ge	réncái.
He	is	a		person of talent.
He	is	a		expert.

As you can see, most of the words in the list below are Noun compounds that have to do with people. Placing nouns is perhaps the easiest part of Mandarin grammar. This list is rather extensive and most of the characters are simple to draw, learn, and are common. You have looked at the **Rules of Stroke Order** in the back of the book, right?

(众, zhòng, many people)
(众人, zhòngrén, everybody)
(工, gōng, work)
(工人, gōngrén, worker)
(女, nǚ, female)
(女人, nǚrén, woman)
(个, gè, a, an)
(个人, gèrén, an individual)
(老, lǎo, old)
(老人, lǎorén, old man, old woman)
(口, kǒu, mouth)
(人口, rénkǒu, population)
(客, kè, visitor, guest)
(客人, kèren, visitor, guest)
(主, zhǔ, master)
(主人, zhǔrén, master, host, owner)
(才, cái, ability, talent)
(人才, réncái, a person of talent)
(男人, nánrén, male)
(男人, nánrén, male person, men)
(老, lǎo, old)
(家, jia, home)
(老人家, lǎorenjia, old person)

(工, gōng, work)
(人工, réngōng, man work, labour)
(体, tǐ, body)
(人体, réntǐ, person body)
(大, dà, big)
(大人, dàren, big person, adult)
(家, jia, home)
(人家, rénjiā, dwelling)
(群, qún, crowd)
(群, qún, group, swarm, flock)
(人群, rénqún, crowd)
(爱, ài, love)
(爱人, àiren, spouse)
(妇, fù, woman)
(妇人, fùrén, wife)
(亲, qīn, kin, kiss)
(亲人, qīnrén, close relatives)
(士, shì, scholar)
(人士, rénshì, personage)
(本, běn, basis, foundation)
(本人, běnrén, I, me, myself, oneself)
(商, shāng, merchant)
(商人, shāngrén, businessman)

(行, xíng, go)

(行人, xíngrén, pedestrian)

(新, xīn, new)

(新人, xīnrén, people of a new type)

(古, gǔ, ancient)

(古人, gǔrén, ancient people)

(夫, fū, man)

(夫人, fūren, wife)

(前, qián, before, front)

(前人, qiánrén, forefathers)

(身, shēn, body)

(人身, rénshēn, human body)

(洋, yáng, ocean)

(洋人, yángrén, foreigner)

(友, yǒu, friend)

(友人, yǒurén, friend)

(手, shǒu, hand)

(人手, rénshǒu, manpower)

(狂, kuáng, crazy)

(狂人, kuángrén, madman)

(丛, cóng, crowd)

(人丛, réncóng, retinue, crowd)

Here is one of my all time favourites (人行道, rénxíngdào, sidewalk). The literal and correct translation is *person walk path*. Sidewalks in huge Chinese cities can be 10 metres or more wide. This gives room for cars and motorcycles to drive on them. Some of these sidewalks will be miles of beautiful polished granite. This does not stop a huge truck from driving on it and crushing the beautiful stone. I always get this overall feeling that the rank and file person in China does not care about the infrastructure of their country. As fast as the country improves China, the Chinese destroy the country.

China is a country of unregulated personal behaviour, as long as it does not directly offend the state. It is common for businesses to extend their manufacturing onto the sidewalk. The sidewalks then become precarious to walk on so people walk on the service road for bicycles and motorbikes, amongst the vehicles. The roads are often divided so that cars are kept off the bike and motorcycle road. Then there will be a divider in the middle of the road to stop pedestrians from crossing. But none of this works. You can be driving your motorcycle down the motorcycle road and a family of 4, 5, whatever, will be walking abreast and not move. Then a dump truck will be driving the wrong way up the street. There are over 75,000 road deaths in China each year, 1% of the worlds vehicles and 25% of the worlds motor vehicular deaths. This will get much worse. However impractical, the aspiring Chinese wants a car. The cities evolved without parking lots so sidewalks have become the parking lots of China. A car is power in China and a driver will plough his way through the pedestrian walkways turning right, entirely ignoring the law and peoples safety. So keep your head up. So are Chinese drivers 25 times worst than the world average?

(**人道, réndào, humanity, human sympathy, humanitarianism**) is a pretty optomistic way to look at mankind. (**道, dào, path**) can mean a physical *route*, *road* or *way*, or it can mean a more esoteric spiritual route. To make a compound that implicates the ***way of people to be humane*** is hardly Chinese. China has the lowest charitable giving of any country in the world. It also has one of the lowest levels of people volunteering to help others.

I was sleeping in Chengdu during the horrible earthquake in 2008, didn't wake up. It was felt in India but not in my bedroom. It is said that this event was the awakening of Chinese people to give to help others. Massive numbers of citizens mobilized to bring water, food and tents to Sichuan province. This was huge news in China as groups of car owners convoyed to deliver. What shocked me and awoke me to this attitude was the Chinese media's surprise at their own people helping. So here is an example of how wordy translations can get and why students never learn Mandarin grammar from many sources.

见死不救	不	人道
Jiànsǐbújiù	bù	réndào.
Look at death not save	not	person way.

The source I *borrowed* this sentence from gave this translation.

> *It's inhuman to see someone in a life-and-death situation without trying to help.*

Now that is wordy and explains why students *give up*. 16 words to explain three. But what a masterpiece of a compound word, (见死不救, **jiànsǐbújiù**, **look at death not save**). I have often read online blogs where Chinese bloggers spew on about how us foreign folk will never understand their language and how a single word can be like an entire sentence. This rather supports the one word one sentence argument.

(见, **jiàn, look at, see**)

(死, **sǐ, die, death**)

(不, **bù, not**)

(救, **jiù, rescue, save**)

   (人为, **rénwéi, man-made**) from (为, **wéi, do, make accomplish**). (为, **wéi**) is another character with myriad meanings.

(为, **wèi, for, on account of**)

(为, **wéi, be, become**)

(为, **wèi, stand for, support**)

(为, **wéi, do, accomplish**)

(为, **wéi, act, serve as**)

这	是	人为	的	事故
Zhè	shì	rénwéi	de	shìgù.
This	is	man do		mishap.
This	is	man made		mishap.

(为, **wéi, do, make accomplish**)

(事, **shì, issue matter**)

(故, **gù, reason, cause**)

(事故, **shìgù, accident mishap**)

There are books that give lame ass explanations as to the pictographic meaning of characters. (间, **jiān, room, between**) I have read 间 described as a (日, **rì, sun**) shining throught a door (门, **mén, door**) which means (间, **jiān, room**). 间 is also used as a **CNI** for the number of rooms. However, (间, **jiān, room**) seldom is used alone as a single character word. If you look at the words it holds second character to, it defines a space more like *do you have room* rather than *you two should get a room*. That is, it defines a domain or area. (人间, **rénjiān, person space**) defines the physical realm of mankind, that is the human world. (人间, **rénjiān, human world**)

人间	的	事	是	难	料
Rénjiān	de	shì	shì	nán	liào.
Human world		matter	is	difficult	anticipate.

(事, **shì, matter, issue, matter**)   (难, **nán, difficult**)

(料, **liào, anticipate**)

(生, **shēng**, **to birth**, **to live**) is a character that has a perplexing number of meanings, most having to do with some phase of the early growth cycle of life. Here is one of my favorite bad translations, leaves the role of the wife out completely. The translation in the book I used is *When is the baby due*?

你	的	太太	哪	天	生
Nǐ	de	tàitai	nǎ	tiān	shēng.
Your		wife	which	day	give birth.

(人生, **rénshēng**, **person life**) refers to the lifespan of humans.

人生	是	短暂	的	旅程
Rénshēng	shì	duǎnzàn	de	lǚchéng.
Person life	is	brief		journey.

(短, **duǎn**, **short time**)

(暂, **zàn**, **temporarily**)

(短暂, **duǎnzàn**, **brief**)

(旅, **lǚ**, **travel**)

(程, **chéng**, **rule**, **regulation**)

(旅程, **lǚchéng**, **route**, **itinerary**)

Here are a few more words that are not *Person Nouns*.

(心, **xīn**, **heart**)

(人心, **rénxīn**, **popular feeling**)

(力, lì, strength, force)
(人力, rénlì, manpower)
(动, dòng, move)
(动人, dòngrén, moving, touching)
(性, xìng, nature of)
(人性, rénxìng, human nature)

(人, rén, person, people)
(人民, rénmín, the people)
(们, men, pluralizing suffix)
(人们, rénmen, people, humanity)
(人人, rénrén, everyone)
(天天, tiāntiān, daily, every day)
(别, bié, separate, other)
(别, bié, do not)
(别人, biéren, other people)
(他人, tārén, another person, others)
(工人, gōngrén, worker)
(人家, rénjia, somebody else)
(人口, rénkǒu, population)
(口, kǒu, mouth)
(别, bié, separate, other, don't)
(动, dòng, move)
(东西, dōngxi, thing)

(才, cái, talent, ability)
(人才, réncái, a person of talent)
(人情, rénqíng, human feelings)
(人事, rénshì, person matters)
(人行道, rénxíngdào, sidewalk)
(见, jiàn, look at, see)
(死, sǐ, die, death)
(不, bù, not)
(救, jiù, rescue, save)
(日, rì, sun)
(门, mén, door)
(生, shēng, to birth)
(间, jiān, room)
(人生, rénshēng, person life)
(短, duǎn, short time)
(暂, zàn, temporarily)
(短暂, duǎnzàn, brief)

116

(旅程, lǚchéng, route, itinerary)

(旅, lǚ, travel)

(程, chéng, rule, regulation)

(心, xīn, heart)

(人心, rénxīn, popular feeling)

(力, lì, strength, force)

(人力, rénlì, manpower)

(动, dòng, move)

(动人, dòngrén, moving, touching)

(性, xìng, nature of)

(人性, rénxìng, human nature)

(为, wéi, do, make accomplish)

(事, shì, issue matter)

(故, gù, reason, cause)

(事故, shìgù, accident mishap)

(为, wèi, for, on account of)

(为, wéi, be, become)

(为, wèi, stand for, support)

(为, wéi, do, accomplish)

(为, wéi, act, serve as)

(见, jiàn, look at, see)

(死, sǐ, die, death)

(不, bù, not)

(救, jiù, rescue, save)

(事, shì, matter, issue, matter)

(难, nán, difficult)

(料, liào, anticipate)

(短, duǎn, short time)

(暂, zàn, temporarily)

(短暂, duǎnzàn, brief)

(旅, lǚ, travel)

(程, chéng, rule, regulation)

(旅程, lǚchéng, route, itinerary)

(人民币, rénmínbì, People's currency)

我	Notes: Singular First Person Pronoun (我, wǒ, me) 　(我, wǒ, me / I) is the character for the *First Personal Pronoun me / I*.
wǒ	
me	

丿 亠 千 手 扌 我 我

我 我 我 我 我 我 我 我 我

我	我	我	我	我	我	我	我	我	我
wǒ	wǒ	wǒ	wǒ	wǒ	wǒ	wǒ	wǒ	wǒ	wǒ
me	me	me	me	me	me	me	me	me	me
我	我	我	我	我	我	我	我	我	我
wǒ	wǒ	wǒ	wǒ	wǒ	wǒ	wǒ	wǒ	wǒ	wǒ
me	me	me	me	me	me	me	me	me	me

我

(我, wǒ, me / I) is the *First Person Pronoun* that functions exactly as it's English equivalent. (们, **men, pluralizing suffix**) is used to form plural forms of human nouns and pronouns. (的, **de, possessive particle**) is a character used to form the posseessive form of animate nouns, that is persons and animals. Together these characters form,

(我, wǒ, me / I)

我	喜欢	这个
Wǒ	xǐhuan	zhèige.
Me	like	this one.

(我的, wǒ de, my / mine)

我的	老婆,	太	便宜	啦
Wǒ de	lǎopo	tài	piányi	la.
My	wife	extreme	cheap!	

(啦, **la, sentence final exclamatory particle**) is said to be a hybrid particle phonetically combining (了, **le, Current Relevant State**) and the exclamatory particle (啊, **ā, ah!, sentence final elation particle**). The (的, **de**) is optional as the relationship is close and personal.

(我们, wǒmen, we / us)

我们	能	不能	帮助	你
Wǒmen	néng	bùnéng	bāngzhù	nǐ?
We	can	not can	help	you?

(我们的, wǒmen de, our)

你	要	用	我们的	车	吗
Nǐ	yào	yòng	wǒmen de	chē	ma.
You	want	use	our	vehicle	?

(自, zì, self) and (己, jǐ, oneself) are combined to form (自己, zìjǐ, oneself). This is an example of **A+B=AB**. Characters are not always combined logically to make a word that is a product of the meaning of each individual character / word. Often when the combination is based on two words that have similar meaning, the second syllable is spoken in the neutral tone. Apparently not true in this case.

An example would be *friend* (朋友, péngyou, friend) composed of the characters (朋, péng, friend) and (友, yǒu, friend). A simple **A+B=AB** combination in which the second syllable is spoken in the neutral tone. This is more common with *Nouns* than other parts of grammar.

(我自己, wǒzìjǐ, I myself) and (自我 zìwǒ, self, oneself) are logical relatives. (自己, zìjǐ, oneself) can also be tacked on to the other common **Personal Pronouns** (她, tā, she), (他, tā, he), (你, nǐ, you) and (妳, nǐ, you (f)). This in term forms (她自己, tāzìjǐ, she self), (他自己, tāzìjǐ, he self), (你自己, nǐzìjǐ, you self) and (妳自己, nǐzìjǐ, you self).

You can see that the verbal expression of *you* and *he* and *she* are not gender marked and made distinguishable by distinct sounds. **Tā** in fact represents the above forms of *he* and *she* plus both forms of *it*. (它, **tā**, **it**) represents the inanimate form of *it*, that is, things like cars and non-living objects. Chinese scholars are always extoling the cleverness of their 5000 year old language and embellishing the reliability of all the clues in the characters. So I guess (匕, **bǐ**, **an ancient type of spoon**) is the inanimate clue in the character.

(牠, **tā**, **it**) is the animate form of *it*. That is, it represents living things. There is legitably a clue in this character with (牛, **niú**, **cow**) squished into the left side of the character (它, **tā**, **it**).

我自己	认为	这	是	一个	好	主意
Wǒzìjǐ	rénwéi	zhè	shì	yīge	hǎo	zhǔyì.
Me self	think	this	is	one of	good	idea.

(我国, **wǒguó**, **our country**) comes from (我, **wǒ**, **me**) and (国, **guó**, **country**). It is specifically used to refer to China. (非常, **fēicháng**, **not common**) is a common superlative used to mark the positive uniqueness of the modified word.

我国	非常	漂亮
Wǒguó	fēicháng	piàoliang.
Our country	not common	beautiful.
Our country	uncommonly	beautiful.

A common negating *Adverb* is (非, **fēi**, **not, non**). (常, **cháng**, **common, often**) is another common word. I think I exposed you to character duplication elsewhere in these lessons. (常常, **cháng cháng**, **frequently**, **often**, **usually**) is duplicated to give the same meaning. Now, to show you the utility of Mandarin, (往, **wǎng**, **to go toward**) is a verb and it's compound duplicated form is (往往, **wǎngwǎng**, **often**), a *Temporal Adverb*. That makes sense right?

So for a lark, I just asked my wife if I can say

王　　往往　　往　　王后　　看望
Wáng　wǎngwǎng　wǎng　wánghòu　kànwàng.
King　often　to　Queen　visit.

"Of course you can say this, but the Chinese people do not understand this. First, there is too many the wang. So many the wang make the Chinese people a little uncomfortable. They not understand. Chose the many the other word without the wang."

Usually duplication acts to diminish the intensity of verbs and to accentuate the quality of adjectives. (看, **kān**, **look at**) differs from the duplicated form (看看, **kànkàn**, **look at look at**) as the former is a serious look at something and the latter is a quick look at something. Where is this going, oh right, so (常常, **chángcháng**, **frequently**, **often**, **usually**) should mean more often than (常, **cháng**, **common**, **often**).

(我家, **wǒjiā**, **my home**, **my family**) is compiled from (我, **wǒ**, **me**) and from (家, **jiā**, **home**, **family**).

我家 有 五 口 人

Wǒjiā yǒu wǔ kǒu rén.
Me family have five mouth person.

Here are some other common (我, **wǒ**, **me / I**) compounds. These actually make sense in the A + B = AB sort of way.

(我见, **wǒjiàn, my opinion**) compounded with (见, **jiàn, to perceive**)

(忘我, **wàngwǒ, oblivious of self, selfless**) compounded with (忘, **wàng, forget**)

(我方, **wǒfāng, our side, we**) compounded with (方, **fāng, side**)

(我们俩, **wǒmenliǎng, we two**) compounded with (俩, **liǎng, two, both**)

(我侬, **wǒnóng, me**) compounded with (侬, **nóng, you**)

(我人, **wǒrén, we, us**) compounded with (人, **rén, person**)

And here is the usual list of words used in this chapter.

(我, **wǒ, me / I**)

(我的, **wǒ de, my / mine**)

(我们, **wǒmen, we / us**)

(我们的, **wǒmen de, our**)

(的, **de, possessive particle**)

(们, **men, pluralizing suffix**)

(用, **yòng, use**)

(喜欢, **xǐhuan, like**)

(车, **chē, vehicle**)

(能, **néng, can**)

(帮助, **bāngzhù, help**)

(老婆, **lǎopo, wife**)

(便宜, **piányi, cheap**)

(自, **zì, self**)

(己, **jǐ, oneself**)

(自己, **zìjǐ, oneself**)

(我自己, **wǒzìjǐ, I / me self**)

(自我 **zìwǒ, self, oneself**)

(朋, **péng, friend**)

(友, **yǒu, friend**)

(朋友, péngyou, friend)

(她, tā, she)

(他, tā, he)

(你, nǐ, you)

(她, tā, she)

(她, tā, she)

(他, tā, he)

(你, nǐ, you)

(妳, nǐ, you)

(她自己, tāzìjǐ, she self)

(他自己, tāzìjǐ, he self)

(你自己, nǐzìjǐ, you self)

(妳自己, nǐzìjǐ, you self)

(它, tā, it)

(匕, bǐ, an ancient type of spoon)

(牠, tā, it)

(牛, niú, cow)

(主, zhǔ, master)

(意, yì, meaning, idea)

(主意, zhǔyì, idea)

(我家, wǒjiā, my home, my family)

(啊, ā, interjection indicating elation)

(非, fēi, not, non)

(常, cháng, common, general)

(非常, fēicháng, not common)

(漂亮, piàoliang, beautiful)

(常常, chángcháng, often)

(看, kān, look at)

(看看, kànkàn, take a look at)

(往, wǎng, to go toward)

(往往, wǎngwǎng, often)

(我国, wǒguó, our country)

(我国, wǒguó, our country)

(我家, wǒjiā, my home, my family)

(王后, wánghòu, queen)

(看望, kànwàng, visit)

(往往, wǎngwǎng, often)

(漂, piāo, drift, float about)

(亮, liàng, bright, light)

(啦, la, final exclamatory particle)

(了, le, Current Relevant State)

(啊, ā, ah!, final elation particle)

在	Notes: Verb
zài at	(在, **zài**, **at**, **be at**, **be in**, **be on**) is a character that is used to precede a noun phrase that gives a location in a sentence. (在, **zài**, **to exist**, **to live**, **to live at**, **exist at**) (在, **zài**, **to depend on**, **rest with**)

一 ナ 广 尤 在 在

在 在 在 在 在 在 在 在 在

在

(在, zài, at) in the simpliest form mirrors the English word *at*.

我	在	北京	住
Wǒ	zài	Běijīng	zhù.
Me	at	Beijing	live.

You will see creative translations of the role of (在, zài, at). This often occurs with (在, zài, at) occurring at the end of a sentence. Inaccurate translations occur because dropping words is so common that native speakers forget the dropped word and accept the truncated form as full form.

请问	老	王	在	吗
Qǐngwèn,	Lǎo	Wáng	zài	ma.
Please ask,	Old	Wang	at	?

What is missing is (这儿, zhè'r, this place). The full form of the sentence is;

请问	老	王	在	这儿	吗
Qǐngwèn,	Lǎo	Wáng	zài	zhè'r	ma.
Please ask,	Old	Wang	at	this place	?

This sentence below has authors to claim (在, zài, at) means *exist*.

我	爸爸	已经	不在	了
Wǒ	bàba	yǐjīng	búzài	le.
Me	father	already	not exist.	
Me	father	already	dead.	

However, (不在, **búzài**, **not exist**) and (不在, **bú zài**, **not at**) have different meanings. Although this can be discerned in *Hanyu Pinyin*, Chinese characters are not written with spaces between words. You noticed the difference, right? You can see that they are different in the character string?

The below example (在, **zài**, **at**) introduces a *Preposition Phrase* (**PP**) preceding the *Verb Phrase* 干. Mandarin grammar places the **PP** before the **Verb Phrase** (**VP**).

你	在	这里	干	什么
Nǐ	zài	zhèlǐ	gān	shénme?
You	at	this place	do	what?

(正在, **zhèngzài**, **straight at**) is a verb phrase that signals an ongoing verb process. For the sake of making my work easier, I cut and pasted this from another chapter in this book. You will see **VP**'s marked with (正在, **zhèngzài**, **straight at**) acting as a co-verb.

(呢, **ne**, **continuing verb action particle**) can also be part of a frequently bastardized grammatical construction that creates the *Current Continuous Verb Tense*. This is a good example between formal Mandarin grammar and colloquial grammar. This also explains as to why you may read about or see (在, **zài**, **at**) alone before a verb. The most complete and formal construction is interesting. The verb phrase begins with (正在, **zhèngzài**, **straight at**). (正, **zhèng**, **right**, **straight**, **correct**) and (在, **zài**, **at**) compounded to create this word. If you look in a dictionary, you will not see a word attributed to this compound character, rather you will see some variation of (正在, **zhèngzài**, **marks a verb phrase meaning to be in the process of**).

However, if you ask yourself as to what a native Chinese speaker reads when he sees these characters, *straight at* does a pretty good job of introducing a continuous verb action. Certainly I have seen much worse translations. (着, **zhe**, **indicating continuing progressive state**) is the immediate post-verb continuous activity marker. Functionally, it acts like *–ing*. But, we are not finished. Then the sentence can be finished off with (呢, **ne**, **indicating continued state or action**). In a language that is typified by simplicity in grammar, this is a construction that marks the verb action three times. So here it is in entirety.

Subject	Co-Verb	Verb	Noun	Other Verb	
她	正在	迈着	步子	走	呢
Tā	zhèngzài	màizhe	bùzi	zǒu	ne.
She	straight at	stepping	step	going forth.	
She	is	stepping	a step	going forth.	

I asked my wife what Chinese people, compare (正在, **zhèngzài**, **straight at**) to, she said (是, **shì**, **is**). This makes absolute sense. In English, *is* marks the *Current Continuous Verb Tense* with *Action Verbs*. So, of the 35 plus books I have on Mandarin, I have never seen this. But it works. So, you first read it here, (正在, **zhèngzài**, **is**). She also looked at me like I was mentally retarded.

So you are thinking, okay, a little complex but I can get that. But here is the catch, most of that construction is optional. In fact you will often hear the (正, **zhèng**, **straight**), the (着, **zhe**, **-ing**) and the (呢, **ne-ing**) excluded. Really, a real linguist would have problems with the previous sentence. I am not sure that you can hear something that is excluded. So, for the purests, in fact, you will often hear only the (在, **zài**, **at**) used. I always use the long form, the reason that I do that is Chinese people look shocked and say something like. **You glamma velly goo de**. That alone is worth it.

(着, **zhe**, **-ing**) and (呢, **ne**, **-ing**) are often paired together without (在, **zài**, **at**) or (正在, **zhèngzài**, **is**).

她	睡着	呢
Tā	shuìzhe	ne.
She	sleeping	-ing.
She	sleeping	.

Now here is a ringer, kind of like a review.

你	要	找	的	人	他	正在	开会
Nǐ	yào	zhǎo	de	rén,	tā	zhèngzài	kàihuì.
You	want	looking for		person,	he	is	attend meeting.

(正在, **zhèngzài**, **is**) marks that the person looked for is presently attending a meeting. (他, **tā**, **he**) is optional. (找的人, **zhǎo de rén**, **looking for person**) is the **Object Noun Phrase**. *You want the person you are looking for*, *he is attending a meeting* would be the correct translation.

(做, **zuò**, **do**, **make**) (作, **zuò**, **do**, **make**) are both *Verbs* that share similar meaning but slightly different use. If you are really clever you can see how this only matters in writing, not speaking. This is an example in which (正在, **zhèngzài**, is) is shortened to (在, **zài**, at).

你	在	做	什么
Nǐ	zài	zuò	shénme?
You	at	do	what?

(目前, **mùqián**, now) and (现在, **xiànzài**, now) are the most common forms of *now*.

现在	几	点	了
Xiànzài,	jǐ	diǎn	le?
Now,	how many	of the clock?	

So, what is it like having a Chinese wife? I just went to the kitchen for a snack. There is no Coke, no chips, no cookies, no cake. So I had some dried micro shrimps, picked turnip, seaweed salad, cold rice and cold tea. I have lost 12 kilograms. My blood pressure has dropped 15 points top and bottom. She picks grapes, apples and pears from relatives abandoned orchards. My grocery bill is one quarter what it used to be. A one kilogram bag of sugar lasted over one year. And I eat like a king. I just got her a bread maker so all or our bread is now hand made. She hates spending $3.89 for a loaf of bread. Each night she makes me 2 litres of tea with ginger, jasmine tea, cinnamon, dried orange peel, green tea and lord knows what else. She cannot understand how I can drink cold beverages. But she accepts it. If a leaf of lettuce goes bad in the fridge she has a meltdown and needs supportive psychotherapy.

(实, shí, true, real) forms (实在, shízài, really).

我	实在	太	忙	了
Wǒ	shízài	tài	máng	le.
Me	really	extreme	busy	

Again you see that typical use of (了, le) mated with (太, tài, extreme) and an adjective stuck between them.

(乎, hū, to, at, with, than) lends no meaning to (在乎, zàihu, care about).

你	在乎	不	在乎	我	用	你的	电脑
Nǐ	zàihu	bú	zàihu	wǒ	yòng	nǐ de	diànnǎo?
You	care	not	care	me	use	your	computer.

(所在, suǒzài, place, location) literally *place at*.

这	就是	问题	的	所在
Zhè	jiùshì	wèntí	de	suǒzài.
This	just is	question		place.
Subject	Verb	Object Noun Phrase		

The gloss that was given for this sentence is; ***That's where the question arises***. The words *question* and *problem* are used somewhat interchangeably in Mandarin. Obviously this is a sentence that requires context. The literal translation would thus work.

(内, **nèi**, **inside**) is often used on signs in China as it is a one character word and saves space over the other usual words that are two characters, (里边, **lǐbian**, **inside**), (里面, **lǐmian**, **inside**) and (里头, **lǐtou**, **inside**).

(在内, **zàinèi**, **include**)

这个	组	包括	你	在内	共	十	个	人
Zhèige	zǔ	bāokuò	nǐ	zàinèi	gòng	shí	ge	rén.
This one	group	include	you	include	total	ten	of	people.

(包括…在内共…, **bāokuò… zàinèi gòng…**, **include…include total…**) is a common grammar construction. Insert your favorite *Object* in the middle and number phrase on the end.

(组, **zǔ**, **group**) (包括, **bāokuò**, **include**)

(包, **bāo**, **wrap**) (共, **gòng**, **total**)

(括, **kuò**, **include**)

(场, **chǎng**, **site**) can also mean *field* or *court*. (在场, **zàichǎng**, **be on the scene**) literally means *at the site*. I think I cursed (当, **dāng**, **accept**) at another chapter.

当时	我	也	在场
Dāngshí	wǒ	yě	zàichǎng.
Then	me	also	at site.

I was on the spot then was the gloss given for this sentence.

(时, shí, time) (在场, zàichǎng, be on the scene)

(当, dāng, accept) (当时, dāngshí, then)

(场, chǎng, site)

(好在, hǎozài, fortunately, luckily) from (好, hǎo, good).

好在	她	没有	受伤
Hǎozài	tā	méiyǒu	shòushāng.
Good at	she	not have	receive suffer.
Lucky	she	not have	injury.

(受, shòu, accept)

(伤, shāng, injure)

(受伤, shòushāng, be injured)

(存, cún, store, keep, preserve) forms (存在, cúnzài, exist).

英雄	的	形象	总是	存在	于	人们	的	心中
Yīngxióng	de	xíngxiàng	zǒngshì	cúnzài	yú	rénmen	de	xīnzhōng.
Hero		image	always	exist	in	people		heart.

(心中, xīnzhōng, in the heart) (总是, zǒngshì, always)

(英雄, yīngxióng, hero) (存在, cúnzài, exist)

(形象, xíngxiàng, image)

(于, yú, in)

(请问, qǐngwèn, please ask)
(干, gān, do)
(这儿, zhè'r, this place)
(目, mù, eye)
(前, qián, front of)
(目前, mùqián, now)
(现, xiàn, appear)
(现在, xiànzài, now, at present)
(里边, lǐbian, inside)
(里面, lǐmian, inside)
(里头, lǐtou, inside)
(问题, wèntí, question, problem)
(乎, hū, to, at, with, than)
(在乎, zàihu, care about)
(不在乎, bú zàihu, not care about)
(场, chǎng, site, field, court)
(好在, hǎozài, fortunately, luckily)
(时, shí, time)
(当, dāng, accept)
(场, chǎng, site)
(在场, zàichǎng, be on the scene)
(当时, dāngshí, then)
(受, shòu, accept)

(伤, shāng, injure)
(受伤, shòushāng, be injured)
(好在, hǎozài, fortunately, luckily)
(好, hǎo, good)
(组, zǔ, group)
(包, bāo, wrap)
(括, kuò, include)
(包括, bāokuò, include)
(共, gòng, total)
(心中, xīnzhōng, in the heart)
(英雄, yīngxióng, hero)
(形象, xíngxiàng, image)
(总是, zǒngshì, always)
(存在, cúnzài, exist)
(于, yú, in)
(乌, wū, crow)
(有, yǒu, have)
(没有, méiyǒu, not have)
(没有东西, méiyǒu dōngxi, nothing)
(东西, dōngxi, thing)
(东, dōng, east)
(西, xi, west)
(乌有, wūyǒu, crow have, nothing)

134

他 (tā, he)

Notes: Singular Third Person Pronoun

(他, **tā**, **he**)

(他, **tā**, **he**) is functionally the masculine Third Person Singular Pronoun. Although it is pronounced the same as (她, **tā**, **she**, **her**) the gender is preserved in the written character with the left sided gender specific Radical (亻, **rén**, **male**).

Stroke order: 丿 亻 仂 仦 他

他

(他, tā, he) is the masculine **Second Person Pronoun**. Its use is exactly the same as in English. However, China, being a very male dominated society, also uses (他, tā, he) to represent females. Many references list (他, tā, he) as also meaning (他, tā, he, him, she, her, it). The situation is not improved by the fact that the spoken syllable is the same for all common forms of *he*, *she* and *it*.

There is a proper form of the female version of the feminine **Second Person Pronoun**, (她, tā, she). Oddly, it is not favoured by most women in China. In fact, it is not on many electronic forms of character selection. Hopefully this will change in the future. For the sake of grammatical clarity and the woman of China, in this book and my writings I will preserve the gender specificity of the characters.

Like (我, wǒ, me / I), the derivative character words can be constructed thus;

(们, men, pluralizing suffix)
(的, de, possessive particle)
(他, tā, he)
(他的, tā de, his)
(他们, tāmen, they)
(他们的, tāmen de, theirs)
(他自己, tā zìjǐ, him self)

他们	怎么	先	到	了
Tāmen	zěnme	xiān	dào	le?
They	how	first	arrived?	

(怎么, **zěnme**, **how**) is a question forming word. Its presence signals a question. There is no need for the question forming particle (吗, **ma**, **question particle**) or the *Verb Phrase* constructions that utilize negation.

There are not a lot of common words that utilize (他, **tā**, **he**) as a component. Somewhat expectedly they form pronouns. (其, **qí**, **his**, **her**, **its**, **their**, **he**, **she**, **it**) is a character that is used to mark or form *Personal Pronouns*. It is not used in modern grammar by itself. (其他, **qítā**, **others**, **the rest of**) is a *Collective Personal Pronoun*.

It is interesting, well, I find it interesting, that the meaning of both characters is relatively the same, the compounded structure is a form of synonym duplication. However, the tones are preserved and particularily the second component does not have a neutral tone. Then, the compound meaning is not the sum of the individual characters. Note I do not use the word reduplication.

其他	的	香蕉	都	坏	了
Qítā	de	xiāngjiāo	dōu	huài	le.
Other		banana	all	bad.	

If you like bananas you will love the varieties in China. In the west we have such a small profile of bananas. The bananas we get are designed for green picking and ease of transport. In China, I favour the tiny ones with a lemony flavour. The component characters are (香, **xiāng**, **fragrant**) and (蕉, **jiāo**, **plantain**, **banana**) forming (香蕉, **xiāngjiāo**, **banana**).

Nothing puts a smile on my mother-in-laws face like fresh fruit. Now guys, a little cultural tip. If you are visiting a girl in China and get invited to her home, this is a very serious step. Make sure you buy some fresh fruit for the mother and some liquor or cigarettes for the father. If there is a brother or sister bring them some vacuum packed spiced boiled chicken feet for snacks, they love that shit.

My wife in one year can carry on a conversation in English with no limits. She had years of theory in school but no English speaking teacher. I really don't want her to learn more as her grammar is so cute, but that would be wrong. So we are at a party last Friday and we are in a group talking about our pets. She pipes in a story about her dog when she was six years old. She tells how the dog was pregnant and would go through a small animal passway arch in their family compound wall. The dog went out and then got stuck returning home and died struggling to get through the arch. So her punch line,

"*O my gaw, in the morning, the dog my pet, at night, the dog my dinner*".

You got to love China. Then while everyones jaw dropped, she explained how her father and uncle prepped the dog. No one asked about the unborn puppies. People slowly drifted away from the conversation.

Interestingly, (都, **dōu**, **all**) can be used for (都, **dōu**, **both**), it is an *Adverb* that does not differentiate above two. There are other characters that are used to represent *two* or a *couple*. Most confusing is that (都, **dōu**, **all**) is also used in city forming names and is pronounced (都, **dū**, **capital**, **metropolis**).

(他人, **tārén**, **another person, others**) is the only other word I can think of that has any immediate use . (人, **rén**, **person**) we have covered. I hope that you have determined by now that compound character words often do not take the form of **A+B=AB**. It is two pronouns making a third but there is no elegance to the addition.

不是	我	我	觉得	是	其他	的	他
Búshì	wǒ,	wǒ	juéde	shì	qítā	de	rén.
Not is	me,	me	think	is	other	of	person.

The above is like the *fart in the elevator* comment.

(觉得, **juéde**, **think**) can be used interchangeably with (以为, **yǐwéi**, **think**). (其, **qí**, **it**) is entirely optional. As I have probably mentioned, **Personal Pronouns** are often dropped if their use is obvious. There are always options in grammatical construction. You could also use (其他, **qítā**, **others**) and (人, **rén**, **person**) forming the short phrase pronoun phrase (其他人, **qítā rén**, **other person**). Note that the characters and **Pinyin** syllables are identical. But, the rhythmn of speech is not. This is difficult for the learner to perceive. (其他人, **qítā rén**, **other person**) has a slight pause after (其他, **qítā**, **others**) and before the 人, **rén**, **person**). Similarily, you can anticipate the pattern in the example in the table above. These pauses are created by very small changes in the consistency of air flow coming out of your speech apparatus. Simply, the two syllable words flow more fluidly and there is a small diminution of airflow between the individual words.

(其, **qí**, **his, her, its, their, he, she, it**) acts to mark that a human noun is involved. It acts like a **Personal Pronoun** specifically marking human involvement.

Eventually you are going to have to learn to curse while you are in China, or take anger management classes. (他妈的, **tāmā de**, **his mother**) is used similar to the ghetto *yo mama* or *your mother*. It is an interjection, a vulgarity. Its' severity depends on usage, if you use it on a stranger, run, if your girlfriend says it, laugh.

Now get a load of this, I have a program called ***Wenlin***. It is a fantastic reference for Chinese characters. I can search the most common words by frequency. The word (安非他命, **ānfēitāmìng**, **amphetamine**) is the seventh most common word with (他, **tā**, **he**) as part of the compound. What is that about? This is a phonetic loan word. A word composed of characters that bear some resemblance to the phonetics of the English word. The component characters do not add meaning, only a vague phonetic similarity. Like, why say *Toronto* when you can say (多伦多, **Duōlúnduō**, **Toronto**)

(他, **tā**, **he**)
(她, **tā**, **she**)
(我, **wǒ**, **me / I**)
(们, **men**, **pluralizing suffix**)
(的, **de**, **possessive particle**)
(他的, **tā de**, **his**)
(他们, **tāmen**, **they**)
(他们的, **tāmen de**, **theirs**)
(怎么, **zěnme**, **how**)
(到, **dào**, **arrive, reach, go to**)
(了, **le**, **completed verb action**)

(吗, **ma**, **question particle**)
(其, **qí**, **his, her, its, their, he, she, it**)
(其他, **qítā**, **others, the rest**)
(他人, **tārén**, **other person**)
(香, **xiāng**, **fragrant**)
(蕉, **jiāo**, **plantain, banana**)
(香蕉, **xiāngjiāo**, **banana**)
(都, **dōu**, **all**)
(坏, **huài**, **bad**)
(人, **rén**, **person**)
(他妈的, **tāmā de**, **his mother**)

(都, dū, capital, metropolis)

(觉得, juéde, think)

(以为, yǐwéi, think)

(认为, rénwéi, think)

(先, xiān, before, earlier, first)

(自己, zìjǐ, self)

这 zhè this	Notes: Demonstrative Pronoun (这, zhè, this) (这, zhè, this) is a **Demonstrative Pronoun** that is used in the same way that the English *this* is used. The pronunciation is changed when it is used before a **CNI**. (这个, zhèige, this one)

丶 亠 丆 文 ʼ文 讠文 这

这 这 这 这 这 这 这 这 这

这	这	这	这	这	这	这	这	这	这
zhè	zhè	zhè	zhè	zhè	zhè	zhè	zhè	zhè	zhè
this	this	this	this	this	this	this	this	this	this
这	这	这	这	这	这	这	这	这	这
zhè	zhè	zhè	zhè	zhè	zhè	zhè	zhè	zhè	zhè
this	this	this	this	this	this	this	this	this	this
这	这	这	这	这	这	这	这	这	这
这	这	这	这	这	这	这	这	这	这
这	这	这	这	这	这	这	这	这	这
这	这	这	这	这	这	这	这	这	这
这	这	这	这	这	这	这	这	这	这
这	这	这	这	这	这	这	这	这	这
这	这	这	这	这	这	这	这	这	这

这

(这, zhè, this) works like the English equivalent. It acts to point out or *Demonstrate*, hence the grammatical term *Demonstrative Pronoun*. In English, *this*, *that*, *these*, *those* are the *Demonstrative Pronouns*. A Pronoun acts to take the place of a noun that is understood, inferred, or previously referenced.

(这, zhè, this) is also expressed as (这, zhèi, this) when it preceeds a *Countable Noun*. Either form can be used before a *Countable Noun* (**CN**) but the *Countable Noun Indicator* (**CNI**) must be used.

这个	人	真	好
Zhèige	rén	zhēn	hǎo.
This one	person	real	good.

(这个, zhège, this one) or alternately (这个, zhèige, this one) can be used in the above example. The plural form (这些, zhèxiē, these) can be formed thus,

这些	人	真	好
Zhèxiē	rén	zhēn	hǎo.
This some	person	real	good.
These	person	real	good.

(些, xiē, some) acts as a pluralizing **CNI**. It nevers occurs as a stand alone character.

(这里, **zhèlǐ**, **this place**, **here**) and (这儿, **zhèr**, **this place**, **here**) are two common derivative words that share the same meaning. (这儿, **zhèr**, **here**) is more common in North China and (这里, **zhèlǐ**, **here**) is more common in South China, apparently, I have never appreciated this. Influx of internal immigrate labour to big cities has homogenized the language to some degree. (里, **lǐ**,) and (儿, **ér**,) act to mean *place* when forming these compound characters. The stand alone meanings are (里, **lǐ**, **inside**) and (儿, **ér**, **child**). You can see the common sense of the language.

今天	我们	来	这儿,	然后,	我们	去	那儿
Jīntiān	wǒmen	lái	zhè'r,	ránhòu,	wǒmen	qù	nà'r.
Today	we	come	here,	then,	we	go	there.

I use the above sentence near daily when my mother-in-law asks what we are doing for the day. For some reason this sends her into gales of laughter, flashing her gold incisor at me, but it is grammatically correct. For emphasis I will point to obscure places on the 50 year old map on the wall, which of course shows Tibet and Taiwan as part of China. Maybe I shouldn't get into that.

钱包	在	这里
Qiánbāo	**zài**	**zhèlǐ**.
Money bag	at	this place.
Purse	at	here.
Subject	Verb	Object
	Location Phrase	

The construction of preposition phrases is slightly different in Mandarin grammar. All *Location Phrases* (**LP**) or *Preposition Phrases* (**PP**) are initiated by

(在, **zài**, **at**). This makes it easy to pull the location out of a character string. (在, **zài, at**) can also be glossed as (在,**zài, to be at, to be in, to be on**). I just realized that two lessons back is the chapter on (在, **zài, at**). But I have not done it yet. So I will go and polish it up and then you can look back there. Plus, this is the (这, **zhè, this**) chapter.

So, continued, (样, **yàng, manner, appearance, shape, form**) mates nicely with (这, **zhè, this**) to form (这样, **zhèyàng, this manner, like so, as such, like this, this way**). This is a very common word in a society in which everyone thinks that they are an expert and are continually showing others the correct way.

我	这样	地	开车
Wǒ	zhèyàng	de	kāichē.
Me	this manner		operate car.
Subject	Adverb Phrase	Adverb Marker	VOC

Now, as I am writing this I am passing these sentences past my wife, who is shaving potatoes at the kitchen sink, while singing some patriotic communist tune. Her comment,

"As I stand here by the sink, I feel uncomfortable when you say this, there is too many the de".

Canada offers free fulltime school to immigrants. So this week her class is working on creating a setting for a sentence, hence the *As I stand here by the sink*. So, once again we have the **too many the de** issue. But this is a different *de* than the lesson one (的, **de, marker of noun modification**). This current *de* acts as a grammatical particle to mark an *Adverb* or *Adverb Phrase* (**AdvP**). After a phone call to her Mandarin teacher in China, (**Skype**), she conceded that her choice of *de* (的, **de**) was wrong and my *de* (地, **de**, **-ly**) was correct.

I don't point this out to gloat, which I often do anyways, but amongst the numerous Chinese nationals I know in Canada, their understanding of Mandarin grammar is very basic. This of course does not limit their speaking or comprehension. I note this to point out the huge gap between formal grammar and colloquial grammar. Another format would be,

我	开车	是	这样	地
Wǒ	kāichē	shì	zhèyàng	de
Me	operate car	is	this manner	
Subject	VOC	Verb	Adverb Phrase	

Anyways, (开车, **kāichē**, **operate vehicle**) is a word that opens the door to an interesting family of **Verb-Object Compounds** (**VOC**). The verb (开, **kāi**, **to operate**, **to enact**) is used to signal the natural and expected operation of the **VOC Object**. You will often see it incorrectly translated to mean *to open*, *to drive*. In many situations it indicates the beginning and continuation of an expected action.

When my wife came to Canada, (这样, **zhèyàng**, **this manner**) was a useful word.

这样	做
Zhèyàng	**zuò**.
This manner	**do.**

(做, **zuò**, **do**, **make**) is a common form of the English verb *to make* or *to do*. Another form of the verb is (干, **gān**, **do**).

干	这个
Gān	**zhèige**.
Do	**this one**.

(这么, **zhème**, **so**, **such**, **this way**, **like this**) is an adverb hence is acts to modify a verb. (么, **me**, **adverb suffix**) is also the same character used to mark interrogation. (么, **me**, **interrogative suffix**). How these differing uses evolved is lost in the opium smoke of time. (办, **bàn**, **do**) is another form of the English verb *to do*.

这么	办
Zhème	**bàn**.
This way	**do**.

(这边, **zhèbian**, **this side**)

到	这边	来
Dào	**zhèbian**	**lái**.
Toward	**this side**	**come**.

(这, **zhè**, **this**)　　　　　　　　　(这个, **zhèige**, **this one**)

(这, **zhèi**, **this**)　　　　　　　　　(些, **xiē**, **few**, **some**)

(个, **ge**, **non-specific CNI**)　　　　(这些, **zhèxiē**, **these few**)

(这个, **zhège**, **this one**)　　　　　(这里, **zhèlǐ**, **here**)

(这里, zhèlǐ, this place)

(这儿, zhèr, here)

(这儿, zhèr, this place)

(里, lǐ, inside)

(儿, ér, child)

(我, wǒ, me)

(来, lái, come)

(钱, qián, money)

(包, bāo, bag, sack)

(包, qiánbāo, purse)

(在, zài, at)

(样, yàng, manner)

(样, yàng, appearance)

(这么, zhème, so, such, this way, like this)

(样, yàng, shape)

(样, yàng, form)

(这样, zhèyàng, this manner)

(这样, zhèyàng, this way)

(这样, zhèyàng, like this)

(开, kāi, to operate, to enact)

(做, zuò, do, make)

(干, gān, do)

(么, me, adverb suffix)

(么, me, interrogative suffix)

(办, bàn, do)

(这边, zhèbiān, this side)

(地, de, -ly, adverbial particle)

中	Notes: Adjective
zhōng	(中, **zhōng**, **middle**, **centre**, **mid**, **interior**) The most common use of this word comes from its association with the characters that we know as *China*. (中国, **zhōngguó**, **middle kingdom**).
middle	(中, **zhǒng**, **to hit**, **to suffer**, **to sustain**)

丨 冂 口 中

中 中 中 中 中 中 中 中

中	中	中	中	中	中	中	中	中	中
zhōng	zhōng	zhōng	zhōng	zhōng	zhōng	zhōng	zhōng	zhōng	zhōng
middle	middle	middle	middle	middle	middle	middle	middle	middle	middle
中	中	中	中	中	中	中	中	中	中
zhōng	zhōng	zhōng	zhōng	zhōng	zhōng	zhōng	zhōng	zhōng	zhōng
middle	middle	middle	middle	middle	middle	middle	middle	middle	middle

(中, **zhōng**, **middle**) is of course the word that forms the root of the Chinese version for the word China, (中国, **Zhōngguó**, **Middle Kingdom**). The word (国, **guó**, **kingdom, country**) is used to form compounds for many other countries as well. The word *China* actually derives from the *Qing Dynasty*. My guess is that a combination of (清, **qīng**, **purge**) combined with (啊, **ā**, **elation interjection**) formed (清啊, **qīng ā**) as a phonetic for *China*.

Given that the tone deaf foreigners heard *Canton* when the Chinese said *Guangzhou*, it seems reasonable. The *Qing Dynasty* was the realm of the *Manchu* from 1644 to 1911. Execution, torture and serfdom was refined to a murderous art. This is when the **Death of a Thousand Cuts** was perfected in which a person was skinned alive for a long list of crimes. China often glorifies its history, but most of it is thousands of years of oppression of peasants and cruel imperialism. Those nice outfits and trippy hats were only for the elite ultra priviledged.

http://en.wikipedia.org/wiki/Slow_slicing

The Chinese written language is known as (汉字, **Hànzì**, **Han character**) or (汉字, (中文, **Zhōngwén**, **Middle Script**). To inquire about the ability to use it, you must use the verb (会, **huì**, **able to, know how to**) rather than the verb (能, **néng**, **can**). 会 concerns a learned skill whereas 能 concerns possiblity of an act. Both of these verbs often act as co-verbs modifying another verb. They may also be referred to as *Auxillary Verbs*.

(中, **Zhōng**, **middle**) is often used as an abbreviation for the country name of (中国, **Zhōngguó**, **Middle Kingdom**).

你	会	不	会	写	中文
Nǐ	huì	bú	huì	xiě	Zhōngwén.
You	know how to	not	know how to	write	Chinese script.

It has become fashionable to use **TCM**, (中药, **Zhōngyào**, **Chinese medicine**) or **Traditional Chinese Medicine**. Even in Western countries this is an unregulated mess of variably qualified practitioners giving out concoctions of nebulous efficacy. Toronto Ontario has a **TCM** college. After you pay your tuition and attend for 4 years they give you a diploma that gives you no regulated authority. Studies have shown that 93% of the medications have no active ingredients, that is, there is no evidence that they work. This is perhaps is why the Chinese are always defending their medicine as *slow acting with no side effects*. Most afflictions, particularily when you are young, resolve on their own. If there are not biologically active components, you will not have side effects. If you cough, sneeze or fart in China your friends will pull out two or three little boxes of capsules to try and doctor you up with **TCM**.

My (功夫, **gōngfu**, **skill**) *kungfu* teacher in **Hanyuan, Sichuan** province has no training in any type of health care. Yet he also uses the address of (大夫, **dàifu**, **doctor**). He has little boxes of capsules on his desk along with a shelf of antibiotics and typical Western medicine. He hands them out indiscriminately to his students.

Whatever **TCM** once was, the diseases have changed and the medicines have changed. China is now entrenched in the diseases of modern society and the West.

Cancer, diabetes, heart attack and stroke are now rearing their ugly heads. The **TCM** doctors no longer collect, prepare and preserve their own *medications*. I am sure the toxic air, water and soil does not help. So the **TCM** doctors in China also give out all the Western medications that you can buy with no prescription in China, with no training in the use of these drugs.

The **TCM** doctor is the (中医, **Zhōngyī, doctor of TCM**), from (医, **yī, doctor**). The pharmacy is the (药店, **yàodiàn, medicine store**), from (店, **diàn, store**) and (药, **yào, medicine, drug, remedy**).

A word of advice, when you go to China, get boosters for all your vaccinations. Especially hepatitis A and B. Rabies from rabid dogs is also a big problem with thousands of people dying each month. Some provinces have ordered all the dogs executed to solve the problem locally. Efficient right? I am not sure if you can eat a rabid dog, but I am sure they try.

(中央, **zhōngyāng**), (中间, **zhōngjiān**), (当中, **dāngzhōng**) and (中部, **zhōngbù**) all represent forms of *Middle* or *Centre*. All can be used interchangably. According to the Mrs.;

> *Use the* (中央, **zhōngyāng**) *if you want to make the pretty sentence or the poem. Use* (中部, **zhōngbù**) *for the middle of the very big thing like Sichuan province, the centre area not so specific. The* (中间, **zhōngjiān**) *is the common form of the speak. Use the* (当中, **dāngzhōng**) *to include things mixed together near the middle.*

She just finished grade 12 English and received a final mark of 84%. You will note at the front of my book that she is my *Authentic Chinese Editor*. You can see how she helps to clarify things with her extensive knowledge of Mandarin and English.

(中央, **zhōngyāng**, **center, middle**)　　(当中, **dāngzhōng**, **middle, center**)

(中间, **zhōngjiān**, **center, middle**)　　(中部, **zhōngbù**, **middle**)

舌头	在	嘴	中间
Shétou	**zài**	**zuǐ**	**zhōngjiān.**
Tongue	at	mouth	middle.

(中心, **zhōngxīn**, **center, hub**) is a word that you will see all over China. China has 120 million people in the public pay including 50 million retired military servicemen and 30 million public institution employees. (中心, **zhōngxīn**, **center**) refers typically to an administrative centre or meeting place, they are everywhere. (心, **xīn**, **heart**) and (中, **zhōng**, **center**) both lend meaning to the compound word.

北京	大学	有	一个	学生	中心
Běijīng	**dàxué**	**yǒu**	**yīge**	**xuésheng**	**zhōngxīn.**
North Capital	big school	have	one of	student	centre.
Beijing	university	have	one of / a	student	centre.

Properly, (北京, **Běijīng**, **Beijing**) means *North Capital*.

(北, **Běi**, **North**)　　　　　　　　(学, **xué**, **to study**)

(京, **jīng**, **Capital**)　　　　　　　(生, **shēng**, **to give birth to, to bear**)

(北京, **Běijīng**, **Beijing**)　　　　(学生, **xuésheng**, **student**)

Education is revered in all societies. In China the success of children in school can define the families social status in a community and the ultimate financial success of the family. Entire extended families and often villages will sponsor a child for higher education. The separation of ages in similar to the British model of school. This is probably modeled on Hong Kong's history with the British. The youngest go to (幼儿园, **yòu'éryuán**, **kindergarten**) at 4 or 5 years of age. Then comes (小学, **xiǎoxué**, **primary school**) for grades 1 to 6. After you have completed this there is (中学, **zhōngxué**, **middle school**) for grades 7 to 12. This can be split into (初中, **chūzhōng**, **junior middle school**) and (高中, **gāozhōng**, **high school**). The former is grades 7 to 10 and the latter grades 11 and 12. Then if your family has enough money, or you win a scholarship or you pay off the correct official, it is off to (大学, **dàxué**, **university**). Most correctly, any of the terms that describe a school should in long form be (学校, **xuéxiào**, **school**).

我的	同学	上	高中	学校
Wǒ de	tóngxué	shāng	gāozhōng	xuéxiào.
My	same study	go to	high school	school.
My	classmate	go to	high school	school.

This is an example in which the usual translation loses meaning and changes grammar construction. (同学, **tóngxué**, **classmate**) infers *together* without using any form of *together*. (同, **tóng**, **same**) defines the togetherness of the relationship. It is not necessary to define that they go to the same high school because this is covered with (同学, **tóngxué**, **classmate**, **same study**).

(校, xiào, school)

(学校, xuéxiào, school)

(幼, yòu, young)

(儿, ér, child)

(园, yuán, garden)

(幼儿园, yòu'éryuán, kindergarten)

(小, xiǎo, small)

(学, xué, to study)

(初中, chūzhōng, junior middle school)

(小学, xiǎoxué, primary school)

(初, chū, beginning of)

(高, gāo, tall, high)

(高中, gāozhōng, high school)

(中学, zhōngxué, middle school)

(大, dà, big)

(大学, dàxué, university)

我们	都	已经	到了	中年
Wǒmen	dōu	yǐjīng	dàole	zhōngnián.
We	all / both	already	arrived	middle year.
We	all / both	already	arrived	middle age.

(经, jīng,) is another of those *choke-on-your-eggroll* words that has so many different meanings that you will never unravel the etymology of the compound word (已经, yǐjing, already). *Menstrual period*, *classics of literature*, *to endure*, *constant*, it is a real linguistic mess.

(已, yǐ, stop, cease, end) is a character that is a Radical that has three different ways to write it that all have different meanings. Note the subtle differences.

(已, yǐ, stop, cease, end)　　　　　(己, jǐ, 6th of the 10 Heavenly Stems)

(己, jǐ, oneself)

(巳, sì, 6th of the 12 Earthly Branches)

(午, **wǔ**, **noon time period**) is not specifically noon but is the interval around and including the Western concept of high noon, 12 o'clock. Most of the Chinese time words are not clock time as they evolved from a time before clocks were invented. Although I am sure China claims they invented the clock.

(中午, **zhōngwǔ**, **noon, midday**) comes the closest to being 12 noon. In chapter 15 you will see that (上, **shang**, **above**) also can mean (上, **shang**, **before**). The latter part of the morning is (上午, **shàngwǔ**, **before noon, forenoon**). The earliest part of the morning is (早上, **zǎoshang**, **morning**) and (早, **zǎo**, **morning**) can also mean (早, **zǎo**, **early**). As (上, **shang**, **above**) can mean *before*, (下, **xià**, **under**) can also mean (下, **xià**, **after**) (下午, **xiàwǔ**, **afternoon**) then becomes the afternoon time period.

(晚, **wǎn**, **late**) is an adjective. Rather vague in terms of time but the compound word (晚上, **wǎnshang**, **evening**) has come to mean any time of the night. Literally it means *late before* and includes that latest part of the afternoon even before the sun goes down. A common greeting is (晚上好, **wǎnshang hǎo**, **late before good**) which is roughly equivalent to *good evening*.

(夜, **yè**, **night**) refers to a time of the night that is dark. You can see all the word derivatives below. (夜里, **yèlǐ**, **night inside**) is used similar to *during the night*.

明天	中午	我们	到	定州	去
Míngtiān	zhōngwǔ	wǒmen	dào	Dìngzhōu	qù.
Next day	middle noon	we	to	Dingzhou	go.

(其, qí, his, her, its, their, he, she, it)

(其中, qízhōng, which)

(空, kōng, sky)

(空中, kōngzhōng, in the sky)

(途, tú, route)

(途中, túzhōng, en route)

(断, duàn, break)

(中断, zhōngduàn, suspend)

(外, wài, outside)

(之, zhī, classical pronoun)

(之中, zhīzhōng, within)

(农, nóng, peasant)

(中农, zhōngnóng, middle peasant)

(旬, xún, period of 10 days)

(从, cóng, from)

(从中, cóngzhōng, from the inside)

(途, tú, route)

(中途, zhōngtú, halfway)

(中午, zhōngwǔ, noon)

(我们, wǒmen, we)

(到, dào, to)

(定州, Dìngzhōu, Dingzhou)

(去, qǔ, go)

(明天, míngtiān, next day)

(早, zǎo, morning, early)

(早上, zǎoshang, morning)

(早晨, zǎochen, early morning)

(午, wǔ, noon time period)

(上, shang, before)

(上午, shàngwǔ, before noon)

(中午, zhōngwǔ, noon, midday)

(下, xià, after)

(下午, xiàwǔ, afternoon)

(晚, wǎn, late)

(晚上, wǎnshang, evening)

(夜, yè, night)

(半夜, bànyè, midnight)

(半, bàn, half)

(夜晚, yèwǎn, night)

(午夜, wǔyè, midnight)

(夜里, yèlǐ, at night, during night)

(啊, ā, elation interjection)

(中国, Zhōngguó, Middle Kingdom)

(清, qīng, purge)

(中, zhōng, middle)

(国, guó, kingdom, country)

(朝, cháo, dynasty)

(文, wén, script)

(写, xiě, write)　(功夫, gōngfu, skill)

(汉字, Hànzì, Han character)　(心, xīn, heart)

(会, huì, able to, know how to)　(校, xiào, school)

(药, yào, medicine, drug, remedy)　(学校, xuéxiào, school)

(医, yī, doctor)　(幼, yòu, young)

(中央, zhōngyāng, center, middle)　(儿, ér, child)

(中间, zhōngjiān, center, middle)　(园, yuán, garden)

(当中, dāngzhōng, middle, center)　(幼儿园, yòu'éryuán, kindergarten)

(中部, zhōngbù, middle)　(小, xiǎo, small)

(药, yào, medicine, drug, remedy)　(学, xué, to study)

(医, yī, doctor)　(小学, xiǎoxué, primary school)

(药店, yàodiàn, medicine store)　(初, chū, beginning of)

(店, diàn, store)　(高, gāo, tall, high)

(中央, zhōngyāng, center, middle)　(高中, gāozhōng, high school)

(中间, zhōngjiān, center, middle)　(中学, zhōngxué, middle school)

(当中, dāngzhōng, middle, center)　(大, dà, big)

(汉字, Hànzì, Han character)　(大学, dàxué, university)

(会, huì, able to, know how to)　(中年, zhōngnián, middle age)

(汉字, Hànzì, Han character)　(北, Běi, North)

(会, huì, able to, know how to)　(京, jīng, Capital)

(舌, shé, tongue)　(北京, Běijīng, Beijing)

(头, tou, head)　(学, xué, to study)

(舌头, shétou, tongue)　(生, shēng, to give birth to, to bear)

(嘴, zuǐ, mouth)　(学生, xuésheng, student)

158

(同学, tóngxué, classmate)　　(中年, zhōngnián, middle age)

(同, tóng, same)　　(已, yǐ, stop, cease, end)

(已经, yǐjīng, already)　　(年, nián, year)

(中药, Zhōngyào, Traditional Chinese medicine)

(中医, Zhōngyī, doctor of Traditional Chinese medicine)

(初中, chūzhōng, junior middle school)

(清朝, Qīngcháo, Qing dynasty, 1644-1911)

(中文, Zhōngwén, Chinese written language)

(中外, Zhōng-wài, China and foreign countries)

(上旬, shāngxún, middle ten days of month)

(中旬, zhōngxún, middle 10 days of month)

(下旬, xiàxún, last ten days of month)

大	Notes: Quantitative Adjective (大, dà, big, huge, large, major, great, wide, deep) (大, dà, oldest, eldest, elder)
dà	
big	

一 ナ 大

大 大 大 大 大 大 大 大 大

大	大	大	大	大	大	大	大	大	大
dà	dà	dà	dà	dà	dà	dà	dà	dà	dà
big	big	big	big	big	big	big	big	big	big
大	大	大	大	大	大	大	大	大	大
dà	dà	dà	dà	dà	dà	dà	dà	dà	dà
big	big	big	big	big	big	big	big	big	big
大	大	大	大	大	大	大	大	大	大
大	大	大	大	大	大	大	大	大	大
大	大	大	大	大	大	大	大	大	大
大	大	大	大	大	大	大	大	大	大
大	大	大	大	大	大	大	大	大	大
大	大	大	大	大	大	大	大	大	大
大	大	大	大	大	大	大	大	大	大

1. (大, dà, big) is an *Adjective* of quantity. *Quantitative Adjectives* can be *absolute*, such as numbers, or they can be *relative*, such as size markers. Using English we can say *big*, *bigger*, *biggest*. In Hamilton, Ontario they say *good*, *gooder* and *goodest*. Mandarin does not have this so they modify by using other words to describe the degree of big. These rules can of course be applied to words other than (大, dà, big).

2. (大, dà, big) can also mark position in a heirarchy or family position. It does not mean *old* or *senior* as some books note, it means *big*. Other than the word for adult, (大人, dàren, adult), the second character of these words cannot be explained with one word, they are what they are.

(大人, dàren, adult)

(大哥, dàgē, eldest brother)

(大伯, dàbó, father's elder brother)

(大姐, dàjiě, eldest elder sister)

(大娘, dàniáng, wife of father's elder brother)

(大嫂, dàsǎo, wife of one's eldest brother)

3. (大, dà, big) is also used in words of large scale.

(高大, gāodà, tall and big)　　(高, gāo, tall, high)

(大大, dàdà, great, enormously)　(大, dà, big)

(伟大, wěidà, great, mighty)　　(伟, wěi, great, imposing)

(广大, guǎngdà, vast, wide)　　(广, guǎng, wide, vast)

4. (大, **dài**) can also mark a person of importance.

(大夫, **dàifu, doctor**)   (夫, **fū, man**)

(大王, **dàiwáng, king**)   (王, **wáng, king**)

And for some reason rhubarb.

(大黄, **dàihuáng, rhubarb**)   (黄, **huáng, yellow**)

The common group greeting (大家好, **dàjiā hǎo, big family good**) comes from (大家, **dàjiā, everyone**) which really means *big family* and the pattern of greetings which stick (好, **hǎo, good**) at the end of greetings.

大家好	欢迎	来	北京	参加	这次	大会
Dàjiā hǎo!	Huānyíng	lái	Běijīng	cānjiā	zhècì	dàhuì.
Big family good!	Welcome	come	Beijing	attend	this time	big meeting.

Note how I worked (大会, **dàhuì, big meeting**) in there for another 大 word.

(会, **huì, to meet**)   (大会, **dàhuì, big meeting**)

(欢, **huān, happy**)   (参, **cān, join**)

(迎, **yíng, receive**)   (加, **jiā, to add**)

(欢迎, **huānyíng, welcome**)   (参加, **cānjiā, to attend**)

(来, **lái, come**)   (这次, **zhècì, this time**)

(北, **běi, north**)   (这, **zhè, this**)

(京, **jīng, capital**)   (次, **cì, time**)

(北京, **Běijīng, Beijing**)   (家, **jiā, family**)

(会, **huì, to meet**)   (大家好, **dàjiā hǎo, big family good**)

5. (大半, **dàbàn**, **big half, greater half**) functions as a meaning that is greater than a half so it is glossed as *likely* or *probably*.

这	件	事儿	大半	成不了
Zhè	jiàn	shì'r	dàbàn	chéngbuliǎo.
This		matter	big half	succeed not finish.
This		matter	likely	pointless.

(成不了, **chéngbuliǎo**, **pointless**)   (不, **bu**, **not**)

(事儿, **shì'r**, **matter**)   (了, **liǎo**, **to finish**)

(这, **zhè**, **this**)   (半, **bàn**, **half**)

(成, **chéng**, **succeed**)   (大半, **dàbàn**, **big half, likely**)

6. *Big school*, that is what the Chinese call institutes of higher education. The verb (学, **xué**, **to study, learn**) forms (大学, **dàxué**, **university, college**).

明年	我	到	大学	去
Míngnián	wǒ	dào	dàxué	qù.
Next year	me	to	big school	go.

(学, **xué**, **study, learn**)   (到, **dào**, **to**)

(明年, **míngnián**, **next year**)   (去, **qù**, **go**)

7. The (大跃进, **Dàyuèjìn**, **Great Leap Forward**) is one of China's embarrassing eras that was an attempt at reform from 1958 to 1961. *Mao's* great idea was to transform the country from an agrarian economy to a modern communist society through the process of agriculturalization, industrialization, and collectivization. His

brilliant idea was to copy the amazing success of communism in the USSR and Chinese-ify it. Clever right, the USSR was doing well. So he ordered kilns make in rural villages using coal to fire them and had everyone throw whatever metal they had into the kilns, pots, pans, farm tools, bikes….. In the process, up to forty-five million people were killed or died of starvation or worked to death. **Mao Zedong** led the campaign based on the **Theory of Productive Force**s, and intensified it after being informed of the impending disaster from grain shortages. In short, the more the project failed, the harder he pushed it forward, clever. Never occurred to him that everyone was starving as their farm tools were melted into low grade pig iron. **Chairman Mao**, the great helmsman, hero of modern day China, mass murderer.

The **Great Leap Forward** ended in catastrophe, triggering a widespread famine that resulted in possibly more than 20 million deaths. **Mao** was criticized by the party. Party members less economically left-wing like **Liu Shaoqi** and **Deng Xiaoping** rose to power, and **Mao** was marginalized within the party, leading him to initiate the **Cultural Revolution** in 1966. You can fool some of the people some of the time….Then they set out to destroying their 5000 year cultural heritage.

8. Gotta go?, (大便, **dàbiàn**, **defecate**) is the word. Take the **Big Convenient**, almost anywhere really. Little kids squat right on the sidewalk with their split ass pants and dump a load. Now how convenient is that? (便, **biàn**, **convenient**) So, what is urinate, **Little Convenient** of course. (小便, **xiǎobiàn**, **urinate**)

9. Going shopping? Want some of those fake **Coach** bags and some **DG** boots? Maybe a **Rolex** watch for $10 and some **Versace**? You need to know the size and the cost. **Big little** or (大小, **dàxiǎo**, **size**) is the common term for *size*. **Much little**, or (多少, **duōshao**, **how much**) asks the price. The below asks the price for one of ?

多少	钱	一	个
Duōshao	qián	yī	gè...?
Much little	money	one	of...?

10. The price of something is the (价, **jià**, **price**). To ask the *price* is *much big price*? (多大价, **duōda jià**, **much big price**?)

An example of price asking is the sentence 多大的鞋子. The literal translation is ***Much big of shoes***. First, there is nothing to identify that it is a question, which it is. There are not any of the three common grammatical structures that are question forming structures. You must simply know that to a Chinese speaker (多大的, **duō dà de**) asks, *what size*?

This is a very useful expression in the market while shopping. The sentence is thus functionally partitioned as such.

多大的	鞋子	
Duōda de	xiězi	?
Much big of	shoes	?
Size of	shoes	?

In keeping with the overall theme of Chinese being a constantly reducing language, (的, **de**) can be dropped in some situations. There is no pattern to these structures, it is just a matter of common usage. Again this falls into the category of most common versus most correct. Some learners want to sound local versus proper. The difficulty is that even if you want to speak formal grammar, you need to understand what others are saying.

你	多大	岁数	
Nǐ	duōdà	suìshù	?
You	much big	years number	?

So this is common but not formal. The correct grammar is,

你	多大的	岁数	
Nǐ	duōdà de	suìshù	?
You	much big of	years number	?

Not having anything to do with our (的, de) theme, this can be further reduced to simply;

多大	了	?
Duōdà	le	?
Much big	CRS	?

This is also a structure to ask age. However, in keeping with the complexity of Chinese, this is a little rude to ask of someone older than yourself. Go figure. There are in fact different question formats used for different age groups and different levels of respect. However, they cut us foreigners a break on these complexities.

11. (大概, dàgài, general idea) from (概, gài, general, approximate).

那	件	事儿	我	只	知道	一	个	大概
Nà	jiàn	shì'r	wǒ	zhǐ	zhīdao	yī	ge	dàgài.
That	CNI	matter	me	only	know	a		general idea.

Big much number (大多数, **dàduōshù**, **great majority**) is composed of the characters (大, **dà**, **big**), (多, **duō**, **much**) and (数, **shù**, **number**). It makes reference to the greater majority of people.

大多数	人	不	吸烟
Dàduōshù	rén	bù	xīyān.
Majority number	people	not	smoke.

(吸, **xī**, **inhale**) (吸烟, **xīyān**, **smoke**)

(烟, **yān**, **smoke**) (数, **shù**, **number**)

12.   (不大, **búdà**, **not big**, **not often**) serves to signal decreased frequency of an event. If functions similar to *I am not big on*……

我	不大	去	他	的	那儿
Wǒ	búdà	qù	tā	de	nà'r.
Me	not big	go	his		that place.

Alright, this chapter has gone on long enough, here are more commons words taken from the *Wenlin CD*.

(多大, **duōdà**, **much big**)   (大众, **dàzhòng**, **big crowd**)

(扩, **kuò**, **enlarge**)   (陆, **lù**, **land**)

(扩大, **kuòdà**, **enlarge big**)   (大陆, **dàlù**, **big land, PRC**)

(量, **liàng**, **quantity, amount**)   (方, **fāng**, **side**)

(大量, **dàliàng**, **big amount**)   (大方, **dàfang**, **generous**)

(众, **zhòng**, **crowd**)

(大, dà, big)　　　　　　　　　　(大约, dàyuē, about, around)

(多, duō, much)　　　　　　　　　(多大价, duōda jià, much big price?)

(数, shù, number)　　　　　　　　(大米, dàmǐ, white rice)

(重大, zhòngdà, great, major)　　　(大便, dàbiàn, defecate, night soil)

(大道, dàdào, wide road)　　　　　(私, sī, personal)

(道, dào, road)　　　　　　　　　(大多, dàduō, mostly)

(大街, dàjiē, main street)　　　　　(局, jú, situation)

(街, jiē, street)　　　　　　　　　(大局, dàjú, big situation)

(大门, dàmén, big door entrance)　(吸, xī, inhale)

(大门, dàmén, main entrance)　　 (烟, yān, smoke)

(巨大, jùdà, huge)　　　　　　　　(吸烟, xīyān, smoke)

(大夫, dàifu, doctor)　　　　　　　(数, shù, number)

(大学, dàxué, university)　　　　　(学, xué, study, learn)

(学, xué, study, learn)　　　　　　(明年, míngnián, next year)

(大会, dàhuì, big meeting)　　　　 (到, dào, to)

(巨大, jùdà, huge)　　　　　　　　(去, qù, go)

(概, general, approximate)　　　　(大气, dàqì, atmosphere)

(大车, dàchē, cart)　　　　　　　 (大肠, dàcháng, big intestine)

(大都, dàdū, for the most part)　　(大力, dàlì, vigorously)

(方, fāng, direction, place)　　　　(大力, dàlì, energetically)

(大地, dàdì, the world)　　　　　　(大自然, dàzìrán, nature)

(价, jià, price)

(大大小小, dàdàxiǎoxiǎo, big and small)

(大大, 洋洋, dàdàyángyáng, innocent and straightforward)

来

lái
come

Notes: Verb

(来, **lái**, **come**) is the verb *to come*.

一 ㄧ ㄗ 于 平 来 来

来 来 来 来 来 来 来 来 来

来	来	来	来	来	来	来	来	来	来
lái	lái	lái	lái	lái	lái	lái	lái	lái	lái
come	come	come	come	come	come	come	come	come	come
来	来	来	来	来	来	来	来	来	来
lái	lái	lái	lái	lái	lái	lái	lái	lái	lái
come	come	come	come	come	come	come	come	come	come
来	来	来	来	来	来	来	来	来	来
来	来	来	来	来	来	来	来	来	来
来	来	来	来	来	来	来	来	来	来
来	来	来	来	来	来	来	来	来	来
来	来	来	来	来	来	来	来	来	来
来	来	来	来	来	来	来	来	来	来
来	来	来	来	来	来	来	来	来	来

来

(来, **lái**, **come**) can be used to mark the direction of movement towards the speaker. In most of these constructions, (去, **qù**, **go**) can be substituted for a request away from the speaker. In the below example you would use (那, **nà**, **that**) to form (那边, **nàbiān**, **that side**) to go with (去, **qù**, **go**). As in English, *this* is considered closer in distance and time than *that*.

到	这边	来
Dào	**zhèbiān**	**lái**.
To	this side	come.

(到, **dào**, **toward**)   (边, **biān**, **side**)

(这, **zhè**, **this**)   (这边, **zhèbiān**, **this side**)

Another way to express *to* or *toward* is (向, **xiàng**, **to**, **toward**). (到, **dào**, **to**, **toward**) and (向, **xiàng**, **to**, **toward**) are generally matched with specific destinations or (去, **qù**, **go**).

向	那边	去
Xiàng	**nàbiān**	**qù**.
Toward	that side	go.

(那, **nà**, **that**)   (去, **qù**, **go**)

(那边, **nàbiān**, **that side**)   (向, **xiàng**, **toward**)

To pass by, (走过, **zǒuguò**, **pass by**) is composed from (走, **zǒu**, **go forth**) and (过, **guò**, **cross, cross over, pass**). To call someone over who is passing by you say;

走过	来	吧
Zǒuguò	**lái**	**ba**.
Go forth cross over	come	!
Come here !		

This construction functions very similar to *come here*. Another equivalent construction is;

过来	吧
Guòlái	**ba**.
Cross come	!
Come here !	

(走, **zǒu**, **go forth**) (走过, **zǒuguò**, **cross come**)

(过, **guò**, **cross, pass**) (吧, **ba**, **expectation particle**)

When I first meet my wife and we were working on shared communication phrases I said to her one day, *come to daddy* in a malevolent voice. After the usual dictionary interpretation she gave me this odd look like I was a pervert. I tried to further explain the reference to **Butt Head** and **Bevice** and that this was an affectionate phrase and funny, which of course fell on deaf ears and she taught me;

到	老外	这儿	来
Dào	**lǎowài**	**zhè'r**	**lái**.
To	foreigner	this place	come.

到	老外	这儿	来
Dào	lǎowài	zhè'r	lái.
To	old outsider	this place	come.

To foreigner this place come.

So this above is how I call my wife over when I am at her families home in China. Now, for some reason, this still gives her and her family, three years later, uncontrolled laughing. On *International Talk Like a Pirate Day*, September 19th, I did my best pirate voice and despite explanations, again, Chinese pirates do not talk English like our pirates, they speak Cantonese, so it again fell on *deaf ears* and I get the *my strange husband* look.

www.internationaltalklikeapirateday.com

(老, lǎo, old, venerable)   (这边, zhèbiān, this side)

(外, wài, outside)   (那边, nàbīan, that side)

As (这儿, zhè'r, this place), (这边, zhèbiān, this side) are a near location and are paired with (来, lái, come). (那边, nàbīan, that side) and (那儿, nà'r, that place) are a further away location and are paired with (去, qù, go).

到	那儿	去
Dào	nà'r	qù.
To	that place	go.

(这儿, zhè'r, this place)   (那儿, nà'r, that place)

(那边, nàbīan, that side)   (去, qù, go)

(起来, qǐlái, rise come, arise, begin) can mark the beginning of an activity. The use of this is generic and can be applied to various situations.

冷 起来 了
Lěng qǐlái le.
Cold rise come.
Cold beginning.

(了, le, CRS) (起来, qǐlái, rise come, arise, begin)

(起 qǐ, rise, rise up) (冷, lěng, cold)

Mandarin grammar compounds words with verbs to show action completion. This is aptly demonstrated with (来, lai, come) in *change of location* compounds.

(上, shàng, up)	+ (来, lái, come)	(上来, shànglái, up come)
(下, xià, down)	+ (来, lái, come)	(下来, xiàlái, down come)
(进, jìn, enter)	+ (来, lái, come)	(进来, jìnlái, enter come)
(出, chū, exit)	+ (来, lái, come)	(出来, chūlái, exit come)
(回, huí, return)	+ (来, lái, come)	(来, huílái, return come)
(走, zǒu, go forth)	+ (来, lái, come)	(走来, zǒulái, go forth come)
(过, guò, cross, pass)	+ (来, lái, come)	(过来, guòlái, cross come)

You can turn these short phrases into polite requests by sticking something nice in front of them like (请你, qǐng nǐ, please you) and adding expectation to the ending such as (吧, ba, marking mild imperative).

请你,	进来	吧
Qǐng nǐ	jìnlái	ba.
Please you	enter come	!

(出来, chūlái, exit come) is that which you say to someone when you want them to pass through typically a doorway and come outside and toward the speaker. Its partner tongue stumbler is (出去, chūqù, exit go), this time away from the speaker.

快点儿	出来	吧
Kuàidian'r,	chūlái	ba!
Quick a little,	exit come	!

(下来, xiàlái, down come) or *to come down*.

猴子	从	树	上面	下来	了
Hóuzi	cóng	shù	shángmian	xiàlái	le.
Monkey	from	tree	top surface	down come.	

(猴子, hóuzi, monkey) (树, shù, tree)

(从, cóng, from) (上面, shángmian, top surface)

你	上来	看一看
Nǐ	shànglái	kànyikàn.
You	up come	look one look.
You	come up	take a look.

You can turn this into a question by sticking (吗, **ma**, ?) at the end or adding slight urgency or expectation by adding (吧, **ba, marking mild imperative**) at the end of the sentence.

(上来, **shànglai, up come, come up**) (吗, **ma**, ?)
(看看, **kànkan, look**) (请你, **qǐng nǐ, please you**)
(吧, **ba, marking mild imperative**)

Farm crops harvested are *taken down* and are also (下来, **xiàlái, down come**).

Okay, so where are we, right, we have covered the words that show movement completion toward a speaker using compound words with (来, **lái, come**), we have covered the usual meaning of *come*, that is an act toward a destination. There is also a more formal way to express *come*. (来到, **láidào, come**) is functionally the same but more formal.

如果	你	来到	我的	村	你	可以	见	我	妹妹
Rúguǒ	nǐ	láidào	wǒde	cūn,	nǐ	kěyǐ	jiàn	wǒ	mèimei.
If	you	come	my	village	you	can	meet	me	sister.

(如果, **rúguǒ, if**) (可以, **kěyǐ, can, may**)
(来到, **láidào, come**) (见, **jiàn, meet**)
(村, **cūn, village**) (妹妹, **mèimei, younger sister**)

Now, words or phrases that answer the question **when** are *Time Adverbs* or *Temporal Adverbs* (**TA**). These play a prominent role in the Mandarin sentence and do not show the placement variety as in English grammar. The typical Mandarin sentence is constructed *Subject Verb Object*. When a *Temporal Adverbal Phrase* is inserted the order can only be **TA** *Subject Verb Object* or *Subject* **TA** *Verb Object*.

明天	我	去	北海
Míngtiān	wǒ	qù	Běihǎi.
Tomorrow	me	go	North Sea.
Temporal Adverb	Subject	Verb	Object

or

我	明天	去	北海
Wǒ	míngtiān	qù	Běihǎi.
Me	tomorrow	go	North Sea.
Subject	Temporal Adverb	Verb	Object

Sticking the **TA** in the *Sentence Initial* position *Topicalizes* it and makes it the *Topic* of the sentence. Mandarin grammar is often noted to be a *Topic – Comment* style of construction. Books vary as to how dominant this style of grammar is but given that most people in China do not speak Mandarin and that written and spoken language varies dramatically, I would pay little heed to believing this to be the basis of Mandarin grammar construction. It is however a simple and predictable format and works as a great basis of learning the language.

(北, **běi**, north)   (明, **míng**, bright)

(海, **hǎi**, sea)   (天, **tiān**, day)

(北海, **Běihǎi**, North Sea)   (明天, **míngtiān**, tomorrow)

Here are some *Temporal Adverbs* and sentence constructions using them.

后来	怎么样
Hòulái,	zěnmeyàng?
Behind come,	how appear?
Afterward,	what happened?

(后, hòu, behind)

(后来, hòulái, afterward, later)

(怎, zěn, how)

(怎么, zěnme, how?)

(样, yàng, appearance)

(怎么样, zěnmeyàng, how appear)

(怎么样, zěnmeyàng, how what appear?) is a catch all phrase that asks about a current state of affairs. Equivalents in the English language vary across countries, cultures and race. *What's up*, *how is it going*, *wuz up*, *sup*, *howze it goin*. You can throw it after any phrase to question the current state of affairs.

(怎么了, zěnme le, how what?) is another common (么, me, what?) phrase that questions a problem or difficult situation. Equivalents in the English language would include, *problem?*, *what's wrong*, *what has happened?* So when your girl comes crying to you or your Chinese made car catches on fire, (怎么了, zěnme le?).

她	怎么	了	病	了	吗
Tā	zěnme	le,	bìng	le	ma?
She	how what	?	sick		?
She	what's wrong	?	sick?		

(病, bìng, disease, fall sick)

你	将来	有	什么	计划
Nǐ	jiānglái	yǒu	shénme	jìhuà?
You	take come	have	what	plan?
You	future	have	what	plan?

(将, jiāng, take) (划, huà, mark)

(将来, jiānglái, in the future) (划, huà, character stroke)

(计, jì, count, compute, calculate) (计划, jìhuà, a plan)

你	近来	身体	好	吗
Nǐ	jìnlái	shēntǐ	hǎo	ma?
You	near come	body	good	?
You	recently	body	good	?

(近, jìn, near, close) (体, tǐ, body)

(近来, jìnlái, recently, lately) (身体, shēntǐ, body, health)

(身, shēn, body)

毕业	以来	我	没有	工作
Bìyè	yǐlái	wǒ	méiyǒu	gōngzuò.
Graduate	taking come	me	not have	work.
Graduate	since	me	not have	work.

(以, yǐ, using, taking) (毕, bì, finish)

(以来, yǐlái, since) (业, line of business, endeavour)

(毕业, bìyè, graduate, finish school)　　(工作, gōngzuò, work)

(工, gōng, work)　　(没, méi, not)

(作, zuò, make, do)　　(没有, méiyǒu, not have)

(向来, xiànglái, always, all along, hitherto, up to now) marks continuity from a past time to the current time and is often glossed as *always*. (向, xiàng, toward) can also be glossed as *formerly*. (向, xiàng, formerly) works better to define the relationship with the past as (向来, xiànglái, formerly come).

我	向来	不	喜欢	跳舞
Wǒ	xiànglái	bù	xǐhuan	tiàowǔ.
Me	toward come	not	like	jump up dance.
Me	formerly	not	like	dance.

(跳, tiào, jump, jump up)　　(欢, huān, happy)

(舞, wǔ, dance)　　(喜欢, xǐhuan, to like)

(跳舞, tiàowǔ, dance)　　(向, xiàng, toward)

(喜, xǐ, happiness)　　(向, xiàng, formerly)

(来自, láizì, come self, come from) is used to refer to a source of origin for the *Object* of the *Verb*. The reason I chose (巴黎, Bālí, Paris) as the destination is to demonstrate the lame ass thinking of whoever made these *Phonetic Loan Names*.

我们	来自	巴黎
Wǒmen	láizì	Bālí.
We	come self	Paris.

All the phonetics exist in Mandarin to put together a near identical sounding word for *Paris*. You first heard it here, (怕日死, **pàrìsǐ**, **fear sun dead**). So what do they do for the island of *Bali*, (巴厘岛, **Bālí dǎo**, **Bali Island**). Exact same phonetic.

(日, **rì**, **sun, day**)　　　　　　　　(岛, **dǎo**, **island**)

(死, **sǐ**, **die**)　　　　　　　　　　(怕, **pà**, **fear**)

(巴, **bā**, **hope for**)　　　　　　　(厘, **lí**, **1/3 millimeter**)

Paris, incidently is the most over rated city in the world. Really, the *French* have very little left to be proud of so they rant on about *Paris*. Chinese girls have this delusion that *French* and *Italian* men are the most romantic in the world. Yah, right. If France would give up on the French language and speak English they might get somewhere.

Grammar Snippet of the Day
December 11th 2010

So, I am grocery shopping with my wife yesterday. Of course, we go to an Asian grocer. Hamilton is not big enough to have dedicated Chinese grocers like Toronto which is great because the food, sauce, vegetable etc. selection represents all of South East Asia and China. Having a Chinese wife can mean that each bean is individually checked before it goes into the bag so if you are in a hurry,.... Anyways, at the end of my peering at unknown fish species, marvelling at blue chickens and picking up a free ranging crab off the floor and a snail making an escape on the outside of the tank, she says, 你 **done** 了吗, or *you finished*?

This is in fact perfect grammar construction mixing two languages. (吗, **ma**, ?) marks that it is a question and always goes in the *Sentence Final* position. The character (了, **le**, **CRS**) marks the current state of activity. *Done* is her word substitution for (完, **wán**, **finished**, **complete**). This is a Mandarin word that exists in the *Past Perfect Tense*. (**PPT**) This of course raises the question as to why the *Particle* (了, **le**, **CRS**) is attached so commonly to (完, **wán**, **done**) if the word on its own represents a completed act.

(完了, **wánle**, **finished**, **done**) in fact exists as a discrete word and has exactly the same meaning and if you want to make an educated Chinese person squirm and look confused, ask them as to why you cannot just say (完, **wán**, **done**) instead of using (完了, **wánle**, **done**). I perpetually ask Chinese educated people these questions and in keeping with a society in which questioning is oppressed, they have no idea and are not taught this in school. But it is done to provide a sound and rhythm balance and not for a grammatical distinction. So, for this vignette, (我完了, **wǒ wánle**, **me done**).

(完, **wán**, **exhaust**, **finish**, **complete**)

这	支	笔	你	用完	了	吗
Zhè	zhī	bǐ	nǐ	yòngwán	le	ma.
This	branch	brush	you	use finish		?
DP	CNI	Object		Verb Phrase		
	Topic		Subject	Verb Phrase		

(支, **zhī**, **branch**, **support**) is the **CNI** for slender objects, military contingents, songs, wattage, *etc*. Can you believe that *?*, *etc*., the reference I used actually gave *etc*. like you can intuitively guess the other *Countable Nouns*, wattage, wtf?

(前来, **qiánlái**, **come**) literally translates as *before come* or *in front of come*.

我	前来	向	您	请教
Wǒ	qiánlái	xiàng	nín	qǐngjiào.
Me	before come	toward	you	invite advice.

(向, xiàng, to face, toward) (请教, qǐngjiào, seek advice)

(请, qǐng, please, invite) (前, qián, before)

(教, jiāo, teach) (来, lái, come)

The character (越, **yuè**) includes glosses of *get over*, *jump over*, *exceed*, and *overstep*. The phrase construction 越, **yuè**……越, **yuè**…… is usually interpreted as *the more…. the more*….(越, **yuè**, **the more**). As (来, **lái**, **come**) can mark verb completion (越来越, **yuèláiyuè**) is glossed as *more and more*.

天气	越来越	热	了
Tiānqì	yuèláiyuè	rè	le.
Weather	more and more	hot.	

(越来越, yuèláiyuè, more and more) (天气, tiānqì, weather)

(热, rè, hot) (越, yuè, exceed)

(到来, dàolái, arrive come, arrive)

versus

(来到, láidào, arrive, come)

For (到来, dàolái, arrive come, arrive) the character word (来, lái, come) acts to show completion of the act of arriving. That is, it marks current, complete verb action and may be glossed as *arrived*. Whereas for (来到, láidào, arrive, come) the character word (到, dào, arrive) marks verb action completion for (来, lái, come). From the perspective of the person at the train station platform, their guest has (来到, láidào, arrive, come) whereas the train guest has (到来, dàolái, arrived).

(来说, láishuō, concerning, about)

versus

(说来, shuōlái, having brought this up...)

For (说来, shuōlái, having brought this up...) the word (来, lái, come) acts to mark verb completion for (说, shuō, speak) and can gloss as *spoken* or *stated*. It can act as a *Speakers Perspective* and function similar to *as I said* or *as I spoke*.

说来	我	还	觉得	你	是	一	个	呆子
Shuōlái,	wǒ	hái	juéde	nǐ	shì	yī	ge	dāizi.
Spoken,	me	still	think	you	is	one of / a		idiot.

As I stated, I still think you are an idiot.

(还, hái, still)　　　　　　　　　　(说来, shuōlái, stated)

(觉得, juéde, think)　　　　　　　(来说, láishuō, concerning, about)

(呆子, dāizi, idiot)

来说	德国	人	他们	常常	有	平方	头
Láishuō	Déguó	rén,	tāmen	chángcháng	yǒu	píngfāng	tóu.
Come say	German	people,	they	often	have	square	head.
About	German	people,	they	often	have	square	head.

(德国, Déguó, German)

(常, cháng, often, common)

(常常, chángcháng, often)

(经常, jīngcháng, often)

(往, wǎng, toward)

(往往, wǎngwǎng, often)

(时, shí, time)

(时时, shíshí, often)

(时常, shícháng, often)

(每, měi, each, every)

(每每, měiměi, often)

(胖, pàng, fat)

(有, yǒu, have)

(平, píng, level, even)

(方, fāng, side)

(平方, píngfāng, square)

(头, tóu, head)

(看来, kànlai, look at come, it seems, it looks as if)

看来	要	下雨	了
Kànlái	yào	xiàyǔ	le.
Look at come	want to	down rain	.

The above is an interesting construction. Whereas (来, **lai**, **come**) can mark verb action completion, the event referenced is a future event. (看来, **kànlai**, **look at come**) references a future event. The overall construction creates an expectation of an event. That is, it predicts an event. (要, **yào**, **want to**) agrees with a possible future event. (下雨, **xiàyǔ**, **down rain**) is a continuous tense verb, that is, it is ongoing. The economy of Mandarin grammar becomes apparent as to fully translate this would be something like; *look at what is coming it wants to be raining down*, that is, it is a prediction that it is going to be raining.

(来不及, **láibují**, **come not reach**) is used to mark that it is *too late to do something*. (及, **jí**, **reach**)

已经	来不及	说	再见	了
Yǐjīng	láibují	shuō	zàijiàn	le.
Stop endure	come not reach	say	again meet	.
Already	too late	say	good-bye	.

(及, **jí**, **reach**)　　　　　　　　　(再, **zài**, **again**)

(已, **yǐ**, **stop, cease, end**)　　　　(见, **jiàn**, **meet**)

(经, **jīng**, **endure**)　　　　　　　(再见, **zàijiàn**, **again meet**)

(已经, **yǐjīng**, **already**)

It is enticing to think that the Chinese take their words and translate them into something more understandable but they do not. But line three in the above paragraph is exactly what goes on inside their heads. You will oft hear the term *The Inscrutable Chinese*, which means *incomprehensible*, *mysterious* or *enigmatic*.

http://www.thefreedictionary.com/inscrutable

(过来, guòlái, cross over come) is used similar to *come here*. You can call someone over by calling (过来吧, guòlái ba, cross over come!)

你	过来	一下
Nǐ	guòlái	yīxià.
You	cross over come	one down.
You	cross come	at once.

(一下, yīxià, once, soon, all at once)

(过, guò, pass, go by, exceed, cross over)

I love this term, (过马路, guò mǎlù, cross the street, cross horse path).

(马, mǎ, horse)   (马路, mǎlù, horse path)

(路, lù, road, path, way)   (过马路, guò mǎlù, cross the street)

Here are some more common and useful words using (来, lái, come).

(本来, běnlái, originally, at first)   (未, wèi, have not, did not, not yet)

(原, yuán, primary, original)   (未来, wèilái, future, time to come)

(原来, yuánlái, originally, formerly)   (往, wǎng, toward)

(原来, yuánlái, as a matter of fact)   (来往, láiwǎng, come and go)

(来源, láiyuán, source, origin)   (回来, huílái, return come)

(来回, láihuí, come return, make a round trip)

| 上 shàng on | Notes: Preposition

(上, **shàng, on, up, on top, upon, upper, higher, over, to climb up, to go into, above, to go up, upward, mount, to board**)

(上, **shàng, first of two parts, primary, before, previous, last**)

(上, **shàng, higher, superior, better**)

(上, **shàng, go to, leave for, to**) |

丨 卜 上

上 上 上 上 上 上 上 上

上	上	上	上	上	上	上	上	上	上
shàng	shàng	shàng	shàng	shàng	shàng	shàng	shàng	shàng	shàng
on	on	on	on	on	on	on	on	on	on
上	上	上	上	上	上	上	上	上	上
shàng	shàng	shàng	shàng	shàng	shàng	shàng	shàng	shàng	shàng
on	on	on	on	on	on	on	on	on	on

上

(上, **shàng**, **up**) generally refers to things that are higher in position, status or order of appearance. (上, **shàng**, **up**, **over**, **top**) is mated to other characters as a prefix to describe the overall activity. These characters are called *Nominal Localizers* (**NL**) and are used to form position words, or *Prepositions*. These suffix characters are;

(面, **miàn**, **face**, **aspect**, **surface**)

(边, **biān**, **side**, **edge**, **rim**)

(头, **tóu**, **head**)

These all combine with (上, **shàng**, **up**) to form;

(上面, **shàngmian**, **on**, **above**, **on the top of**)

(上边, **shàngbian**, **on**, **above**, **on the top of**)

(上头, **shàngtou**, **on**, **above**, **on the top of**)

Location phrases have a defined word order in Mandarin grammar. The *Locative* word comes before the *Verb*. The *Topic* is in the *Sentence Initial* position. The **ONP** is in the *Sentence Final* position.

桌子	上面	有	一	碗	米饭
Zhuōzi	shàngmian	yǒu	yī	wǎn	mǐfàn.
Table	on	have	one	bowl	rice.
Topic	Locative	Verb	Object Noun Phrase		

(上, **shàng**, **go to, toward, attend**) can act as a verb to form *Verb Object Compounds* (**VOC**).

每天	我	上班	然后	回家
Měitiān	wǒ	shàngbān,	ránhòu	huíjiā.
Each day	me	go to work shift,	then	return home.

Some other common **Verb Object Compounds** are;

(学, **xué**, **school**)   (秤, **chèng**, **balance scale**)

(上学, **shàngxué**, **go to school**)   (上秤, **shàngchèng**, **on weigh scale**)

(厕, **cè**, **toilet**)   (岸, **àn**, **shore**)

(所, **suǒ**, **place**)   (上岸, **shàng'àn**, **go to shore**)

(厕所, **cèsuǒ**, **lavatory, toilet**)   (当, **dàng**, **proper, appropriate**)

(上厕, **shàng cèsuǒ**, **go to toilet**) (上当, **shàngdàng**, **to be tricked**)

(车, **chē**, **vehicle**)   (地, **dì**, **earth, fields**)

(上车, **shàngchē**, **up onto vehicle**) (上地, **shàngdì**, **go to field**)

Perception of time varies across cultures. The Western spatial concept of time follows the direction of reading a book. Most Western people think of the future as being to the right and the past being to the left with the current time being straight ahead. This is not reflected in the grammatical construction of our language however.

The Chinese concept of time follows their historic method of reading. That is, from top to bottom. The past is at the top and is often integrated with the character

(上, **shàng**, **up**). The usual translation of (上, **shàng**, **up**) is words related to a higher position. A more extensive translation includes;

(上, **shàng**, **on, up, on top, upon, upper, higher, above, to climb**)

(上, **shàng**, **to go into, to go to**)

(上, **shàng**, **previous, last, past, before**)

(上, **shàng**, **previous**) or (上个, **shàng gè**, **previous**) is integrated into many **Hanyu** words that deal with events in the past. This makes the grammatical use of it much easier to understand. The past is *above* henceforth (上, **shàng**, **previous**).

上	个	星期
Shàng gè		**xīngqī**
Above / previous		week

(星, **xīng**, **star**)　　　　　　　　　　(星期, **xīngqī**, **week**)

(期 **qī**, **time period**)

(上个月, **shànggeyuè**, **previous month**) all make more sense in light of this understanding. (月, **yuè**, **month**)

(上午, **shàngwǔ**, **previous to noon**) is slightly more complex. (午, **wǔ**, **11 a.m.-1 p.m, noon**) is time measured about the noon hour. So, (上午, **shàng wǔ**, **previous to noon**) is above that hence in the past therefore earlier in time and therefore morning. This is complex, but very Chinese. (午, **wǔ**, **noon**)

So, here below are three of the most common (上, **shàng**, **on**, **previous**, **go to**) words. Knock yourself out figuring out how the Chinese came to be put them together this way. (上午, **shàngwǔ**, **forenoon**) is morning but after school and work start. Which of course is vague.

(早, **zǎo**, **early**)　　　　　　　　　(上午, **shàngwǔ**, **forenoon**)

(早上, **zǎoshang**, **morning**)　　　　(晚, **wǎn**, **late**)

(午, **wǔ**, **noon**)　　　　　　　　　(晚上, **wǎnshang**, **evening**)

(马上, **mǎshàng**, **immediately**, **at once**, **right away**) is a common idiomatic expression composed of (马, **mǎ**, **horse**) and (上, **shàng**, **up on**). It can be used as an interjection to mark immediacy.

马上	走	吧
Mǎshàng,	zǒu	ba.
Horse upon,	go forth	!
Immediately,	go forth	!

(马上, **mǎshàng**, **immediately**) can also be used as a *Temporal Adverb*.

你	必须	马上	上学
Nǐ	bìxū	mǎshàng	shàngxué.
You	must	immediately	go to school.

(上来, **shànglai**, **up come**) is a simple *Verb Compound* (**VC**) that can be a polite invitation for a guest to come up the stairs to your house. So I amuse my multitudes of Chinese relatives at Chinese New Year by standing at the top of my in-laws stairs and saying; (上来上来, **shànglái shànglái**, **up come!**, **up come!**). Then they marvel at my Mandarin skills.

If you want the entire *impress the Chinaman* package to get them in the door and not insult anyone, here it is.

您	好	新	年	好	上来	上来	进去	好	吗
Nín	hǎo,	xīn	nián	hǎo,	shànglái	shànglái,	jìnqu,	hǎo	ma.
You	good,	New	Year	good,	up come	up come,	enter go,	good	?

(上, **shàng**, **up to**) can be used to mark upper limits of numbers.

上	一千	人
Shàng	yīqiān	rén.
Up to	one thousand	person.

Conversely, (以上, **yǐshàng**, **more than**) marks the lower limits of numbers.

这个	西瓜	有	十	斤	以上
Zhèige	xīguā	yǒu	shí	jīn	yǐshàng.
This one	west melon	have	ten	pound	take above.
This one	water melon	have	ten	pound	more than.

(上下, **shàng xià**, **above below**) indicates approximation.

这	辆	车	在	一千	块	钱	上下
Zhèi	liàng	chē	zài	yīqiān	kuài	qián	shàng-xià.
This	CNI	vehicle	at	1000	piece	money	above below.
This	CNI	vehicle	at	1000	piece	money	more or less.

As a suffix after a verb, (上, **shang**, **up**) generally contributes an upward moving component. As a suffix after a noun, (上, **shang**, **on**, **in**) generally contributes a *Preposition* like meaning noting position *on* or *in* an *Object*.

(不上不下, **búshàngbúxià**, **not up not down**, **so so**) is an idiomatic expression that denotes *indecision* or *mediocrity*.

大毛猴子	的	中文	成绩	不上不下
Dà Máo Hóuzi		Zhōngwén	chéngjì	búshàngbúxià.
Big Hairy Monkey	's	Middle Script	achieve grade	not up not down.
Big Hairy Monkey's		Chinese writing	success	so so.

The above sentence came about by a deal my wife and I made. I proofed some of her English homework and I heard giggling and this is what she wrote. This is the first time I let her add to the written component of this book. Strange irony to this. I polish her English and she laughs at my *Chinese*. Anyway, a new word. Remember the rules for tone for (不上不下, **búshàngbúxià**, **not up not down**, **so so**). Although (不 **bù**, **not**) is sometimes marked with the fourth tone, it is spoken with the second tone before fourth tone character words.

(成, **chéng**, **to achieve**)

(绩, **jì**, **grade**, **achievement**)

(成绩, **chéngjì**, **result**, **achievement**, **success**)

Have you used other Chinese language books?, I hope so. I have never seen another book that actually explains and provides the contributing characters on an ongoing basis. Really, it is not difficult. I use *Wenlin*, an excellent program. I just cut and paste and import. If you are serious about learning this language, *Wenlin* is an excellent program. Hopefully this plug will decrease my update fees. Actually, updates are free.

http://www.wenlin.com/

(中, **Zhōng**, **middle**)

(文, **wén**, **script**)

(中文, **Zhōngwén**, **Chinese written language**)

(上当, **shàngdàng**, **to be tricked**) is a word whose meaning is not equal to the sum of the individual characters. (当, **dàng**, **proper, appropriate**) represents one of the variations of an irritating character that is difficult to master and has numerous tones and meanings. (当, **dāng**, **to serve as**), (当, **dāng**, **undertake, accept**), (当, **dàng**, **proper, appropriate**) and then there is (当, **dǎng**) which has no defined meaning but is used to form (当戗, **dǎngqiàng**, **useful**).

小兔子	上当	受	了	猴子	的	骗
Xiǎotùzi	shàngdàng	shòu	le	hóuzi		piàn.
Little Rabbit	tricked	accept		monkey		deceive.

(小, **xiǎo**, **small**)　　　　　　　　　　(受, **shòu**, **accept**)

(兔, **tù**, **rabbit, hare**)　　　　　　　(骗, **piàn**, **deceive**)

(子, **zi**, **noun forming suffix**)　　(当, **dāng**, **accept**)

(兔子, **tùzi**, **rabbit**)　　　　　　　(猴, **hóu**, **monkey**)

(受, **shòu**, **suffer**)　　　　　　　　(上当, **shàngdàng**, **to be tricked**)

Forming *Time When* Words

(晚上, **wǎnshang**, **evening**) is the portion of the night before midnight and translates literally as (晚上, **wǎnshang**, **late before**), from (晚, **wǎn**, **late**).

(马上, **mǎshàng**, **at once, right away**) is one of the thousands of idiomatic cutisms that has some variant of a lame ass story entrenched in a historical setting. (马, **mǎ**, **horse**) supposedly was once a fast way to get around. The expression (马上, **mǎshàng**, **horse upon**) has come to mark immediacy.

(上午, **shàngwǔ**, **morning, forenoon**) is the late morning in contrast to the earlier (早上, **zǎoshang**, **morning, earlier**). For (上午, **shàngwǔ**, **forenoon**) the literal translation is (上午, **shàngwǔ**, **before noon**).

(晚, **wǎn**, **late**)

(马, **mǎ**, **horse**)

(早, **zǎo**, **early**)

(上, **shàng**, **before**)

(午, **wǔ**, **noon**)

(上午, **shàngwǔ**, **forenoon**)

(早上, **zǎoshang**, **forenoon**)

(马上, **mǎshàng**, **at once, right away**)

别	催	我	我	马上	就	做	完	了
Bié	cuī	wǒ,	wǒ	mǎshàng	jiù	zuò	wán	le.
Do not	rush	me,	me	immediately	just	make	finish.	

(别, **bié**, **do not**)

(催, **cuī**, **urge, hurry, rush**)

(马上, **mǎshàng**, **at once**)

(就, **jiù**, **just**)

(做, **zuò**, **make**)

(完, **wán**, **finished**)

Forming Location Words

(上面, **shàngmian**, above, on the top, surface of)

(上边, **shàngbian**, above, on the surface of)

(上头, **shàngtou**, above, over, on)

(面, **miàn**, face, surface), (边, **biān**, side, edge, rim) and (头, **tóu**, head) vary little in usage. There are subtle differences in describing faces of a cube and edges of a cube and beside a cube. However, for common use, they are interchangeable.

(以上, **yǐshàng**, use above) means *more than*. (以, **yǐ**, using, taking)

这个	西瓜	有	十	斤	以上
Zhège	xīgua	yǒu	shí	jīn	yǐshàng.
This one	west melon	have	ten	pound	more than.

(这, zhè, this)   (有, yǒu, have)

(这个, zhège, this one)   (十, shí, ten)

(西, xī, west)   (斤, jīn, pound)

(瓜, gua, melon)   (以, yǐ, using, taking)

(西瓜, xīgua, west melon)   (以上, yǐshàng, more than)

And here are a few bizarro words;

(上上下下, **shàngshàngxiàxià**, high and low, old and young, everybody)

(上上星期, **shàngshàng xīngqī**, the week before last)

(上上月, **shàngshàngyuè**, the month before last)

I asked my wife if you could say (上上上月, **shàngshàngshàngyuè**) to mark the month before the month before last, three months ago. Her reply, *that sounds dumb dumb, too many the* (上, **shàng**, on), *Chinese people going to laugh*.

Verb Object Compounds

(上, **shàng**) can also mean *go to* or *to attend*.

(上学, **shàngxué**, attend school, be at school)

(上班, **shàngbān**, go to work shift)

Okay, here are the usual extra words at the end of the chapter.

(上下, **shàng-xià**, above and below)

(上下, **shàng-xià**, more or less)

(天, **tiān**, day)

(天上, **tiānshàng**, sky)

(空, **kōng**, empty)

(上空, **shàngkōng**, in the sky)

(上空, **shàngkōng**, overhead)

(路, **lù**, path)

(一路上, **yīlùshàng**, all the way)

(之, **zhī**, it)

(之上, **zhīshàng**, on, above, over)

(进, **jìn**, enter)

(上进, **shàngjìn**, go forward)

(上进, **shàngjìn**, make progress)

(世, **shì**, world)

(世上, **shìshàng**, on earth)

(西, xī, west)

(瓜, guā, melon)

(西瓜, xīguā, west melon)

(以, yǐ, using, taking)

(以上, yǐshàng, more than)

(千, qiān, thousand)

(进, jìn, enter)

(去, qu, go)

(进去, jìnqu, enter go)

(年, nián, year)

(新, xīn, new)

(您, nín, you)

(必, bì, must)

(须, xū, must)

(必须, bìxū, must)

(走, zǒu, go forth)

(上, shàng, previous, before)

(早, zǎo, early)

(早上, zǎoshang, morning)

(午, wǔ, noon)

(上午, shàngwǔ, forenoon)

(晚, wǎn, late)

(晚上, wǎnshang, evening)

(星, xīng, star)

(期 qī, time period)

(星期, xīngqī, week)

(学, xué, school)

(上学, shàngxué, go to school)

(厕, cè, toilet)

(所, suǒ, place)

(厕所, cèsuǒ, lavatory, toilet)

(上厕, shàng cèsuǒ, go to toilet)

(车, chē, vehicle)

(上车, shàngchē, up onto vehicle)

(秤, chèng, balance scale)

(上秤, shàngchèng, on weigh scale)

(岸, àn, shore)

(上岸, shàng'àn, go to shore)

(当, dàng, proper, appropriate)

(上当, shàngdàng, to be tricked)

(地, dì, earth, fields)

(上地, shàngdì, go to field)

(面, miàn, face, aspect, surface)

(边, biān, side, edge, rim)

(头, tóu, head)

(每天, měitiān, every day)

(回家, huíjiā, return home)

(然后, ránhòu, then)

(上班, shàngbān, go to work shift)

(上, shàng, previous, before)

(上, shàng, go to)

(晚上, wǎnshang, evening)

(上午, shàngwǔ, forenoon)

(早上, zǎoshang, morning)

(马上, mǎshàng, immediately)

(上学, shàngxué, go to school)

(面, miàn, face, surface)

(边, biān, side, margin, edge, rim)

(头, tóu, head, first)

(桌子, zhuōzi, table)

(中, Zhōng, middle)

(文, wén, script)

(成绩, chéngjì, result, achievement, success)

(中文, Zhōngwén, Chinese written language)

(碗, wǎn, bowl)

(米, mǐ, rice)

(饭, fàn, meal)

(米饭, mǐfàn, cooked rice)

(回, huí, return)

(家, jiā, home)

(回家, huíjiā, return home)

(然, rán, correct)

(后, hòu, behind)

(然后, ránhòu, then)

(成, chéng, achieve)

(绩, jì, grade)

国

Notes: Common Noun

(国, **guó**, **kingdom**)

(国, **guó**, **country, state, nation**)

guó — kingdom

丨 冂 冂 尸 尹 囯 国 国

国

(国, **guó**, **country**) and (中, **zhōng**, **middle**) are of course the words that form the root of the Chinese word China, (中国, **Zhōngguó**, **Middle Kingdom**). The word (国, **guó**, **kingdom**, **country**) is used to form compounds for many other countries as well. The word *China* actually derives from the ***Qing Dynasty***. My guess is that a combination of (清, **qīng**, **purge**) combined with (啊, **ā**, **elation interjection**) formed (清啊, **qīng ā**) as a phonetic for *China*.

(中国, **Zhōngguó**, **Middle Kingdom**) comes from a different time when China thought it was between heaven and earth. China does not so much differentiate other countries taxonomy of name so (国, **guó**, **country**) can mean **country**, **state**, **nation** or **kingdom**. In casual conversation the Chinese will often refer to their country simply as (中, **Zhōng**, **Middle**)

Properly, (国家, **guójiā**, **country**, **state**, **nation**) is the term to apply to an independent country state. (家, **jiā**, **family**)

你	来自	哪个	国家
Nǐ	láizì	nǎge	guójiā.
You	come self	which	country.
You	come from	which	country.

(来, **lái**, **come**) (来自, **láizì**, **come from**)

(自, **zì**, **self**) (哪个, **nǎge**, **which**)

From (祖, zǔ, ancestor) comes (祖国, zǔguó, ancestor land, homeland).

A term you will often hear is (国民党, Guómíndǎng, Kuomintang). I always marvel at how non-English countries use English to manipulate their politics. Muslim countries use English protest signs. Anytime there is an opportunity for international exposure, they use English. Years ago I watched big fat Russian women protesting with English signs that they did not get enough food. This is the ***Chinese Nationalist Party***, but not the China you are thinking. This is Taiwan, or the **ROC**, the ***Republic of China***. Seems the boys who crossed the pond running from Mao and the 8th army still think they are China. The GMD or KMT considers themselves the legal government of Mainland China, the PRC, the People's Republic of China. Funny right, you can see how Beijing is listening to this. One day they will nuke their yellow asses. (民, **mín**, **people**) (党, **dǎng**, **political party**)

http://en.wikipedia.org/wiki/Kuomintang

(际, jì, border)

(国际, guójì, international)

(外, wài, outside)

(外国, wàiguó, foreign country)

(民, mín, the people)

(国民, guómín, citizens)

(家, jiā, family)

(国家, guójiā, country)

(天国, tiānguó, sky, heaven)

(爱, ài, love)

(爱国, àiguó, love country, patriotic)

(国, guó, country)

(中, zhōng, middle)

(清, qīng, purge)

(啊, ā, elation interjection)

(清啊, qīng ā)

Bill and His Authentic Chinese Experience

November 3rd 2010

So I go to Beijing to a medical conference, which registered a day late then started a day later yet. With me are two candy ass doctors, a surgeon and an anesthetist. Two pampered ass lily lappers that wear $300 shoes, $600 coats, $20 socks and expect to have single malt scotch and a Cuban cigar after a meal of Beijing roast duck, really, this happened. We went to medical school together. This sounds like the joke about the three doctors, which you probably do not know if you are not a doctor, anyhow. One friend, who will remain nameless, Bill, has only been to Florida as the great adventure of his life, the other has travelled the world extensively.

Beijing was a little bit of a shock to them, neither has had people cluster around them and stare and take pictures of them before. Neither had ever had the **Brad Pitt** experience where suddenly girls stare, giggle and ask if you have children, a polite way for a Chinese girl to ask if you are married. Mostly because both of them are hideously unattractive with the social skills of a turnip.

So then we hop on the local train and go to Baoding 保定, a prefecture level city of 10,890,000 that you have never heard of. Baoding was a whole new level of culture shock. Filthy air, filthy streets, raw sewage dumping into man made rivers downtown. I love Baoding, best donkey meat sandwiches in China. After some desensitization therapy there we then went by high speed reckless taxi to Dingzhou 定州, the *town* of my wife and her family. Actually, Dingzhou is no longer a town as there are now 1,140,000 people. Apparently they did a census and found out that their previous estimates were wrong. Under one million is a town, over, a city.

This was my two friends first visit to rural China. They were shocked at the poverty of the country people. This is about half the population of the real China, the 800 million peasants. I walked them through my wife's village, we hung out at the in-laws and generally ate a lot of street food BBQ. One of the more memorable experiences was buying a round of street beers for our new Muslim buddies. We had no problem getting them to drink but they wouldn't eat BBQ pork or dog on a skewer, they are funny like that. (干杯, **gān bēi**, **dry glass**) my Uigher buddies.

But all of this has little to do with this story. The real adventure in China is a long train ride. So we saw Brian off at the local post apocalyptic wreck of a train station to return to Beijing, and then we got 38 hour hard bed sleepers to Chengdu. Not because it is considered the city with the most beautiful women in the world, but because of Sichuan spicy food and tourist stuff. *my wife will read this*

So now that Bill had perused the Hutongs of Beijing, the brothels of Baoding, and the rural villages of Dingzhou, he thinks he is a hard core expeditionist. 38 hours on a Chinese train is a conditioning exercise. Privacy, clean food, toilet paper, are non-existent. No smoking, no spitting signs are ignored. Like, why the fuck do you have to put up *no spitting* signs on a train? Nothing like having a neighbour lay down a big green atoll of gob at the foot of your bed while he blows smoke rings and blasts garlic farts at your head. Incidently, farting is considered a normal public body function but god forbid if you should blow you nose in public. To make it really authentic for my friend I got him the top of three bunk beds.

No showers, floor level squat toilets piled high with shit and flooded with urine, mothers holding their babies over the sinks to piss and shit, pretty waitresses pushing open slop trays of food through the train, drunks vomiting in the aisles, this is the real Chinese train ride. Oh, and one seat per six beds should you decide to sit, bring your own toilet paper. And this is first class. Lower bunks end up being public seats.

Eventually we arrive in sub-tropical Chengdu, a nice change from freeze-your-ass-off Beijing. We take the local bus from the train station and get off in a location I am familiar with looking for a hotel. This is where the story goes for a shit.

Bill decides that he wants go looking for a hotel on the back of a bicycle powered three wheeled open cart taxi. I had previously warned him about this gig. First, the driver is 76 years old, or so he told me, and coughing like he has tuberculosis. Like most taxi drivers the world over, he is operating a taxi for a reason. He cannot read Chinese characters, he does not speak Mandarin but I can speak some of the local language. I give him a map with a destination hotel on it and he holds it upside down. I ask him to point to north and he points east. So I know we are fucked. But I know where the hotel is and Bill wants this authentic Chinese experience, how lame.

The old man struggles to lift our bags and lash them to the back of the trike taxi with a grody old rope. Numb nuts, my travel companion, not clever enough to have learned by observation, climbs onto the passenger seat and tips the cart over backwards and is suspended with the front wheel of the bicycle about 4 feet in the air. Now, he has an undergrad in nuclear engineering physics, a Masters degree from M.I.T., medical school and five years of post graduate surgical / medical training. But a dork wad could see that the rear wheels are in front of the passenger seat and the bags and that the rotation axis was in front of him when he sat down. So now he is screaming like a bitch, masses of Chinese sheeple are laughing at him so I let him hang there for a humiliating and embarrassing interlude.

Eventually I pull the thing down, get the old man to sit on the front seat and we head off. Bill says, *"now this is an authentic Chinese experience, this is what I came to China for"*, what a nimrod, it's a fucking taxi ride. He has no idea how authentic this is going to get. The old man makes an acute left turn in front of a bus, weaves through the masses of sheeple, and hits someone as he mounts the sidewalk driving through the food vendors. Then it is into the traffic weaving the wrong way up a one way divided street. Now Bill is screaming like his mangina is flapping in the wind. He is yelling in English telling the driver to stop and let him off. I tell him that the man does not understand so yell louder, and he does, what a dicksmack.

Then Bill starts yelling at me to tell the driver to stop and let us off. I am having a blast watching **Mr. Control Freak** lose it. This goes on with the driver going all over the place in a random manner shouting out direction requests to other drivers. He does not want to stop as he does not want to end his pre-negotiated fare of 20 kuai, three dollars, which is extravagant, but Bill offered to pay. 38 minutes later my joy ride ended, almost in a complete rectangular circuit to return to the Hotel 100 metres from where we started. Bill is an emotional wreck. I asked him how he liked his authentic Chinese experience. He is pissed at me now. But the story is not over.

I have never ridden on one of these where there was not cheating, an argument or some trouble. Now the driver wants 40 kuai as it took him so long to go net 100 metres. I offer him his negotiated 20 kuai, he will not take it. So I set it on his bike and start to walk away. A crowd has gathered and the old man starts screaming. The cell phone cameras start shooting and people start phoning, this is China. I stand and watch as I am as curious as they are. A young punk with a faggy hairdo says some very derogatory things about foreigners to the crowd but calls me American. This is a huge insult to a Canadian, anybody really. I surprise him by repeating the exact thing in perfect Mandarin but reference it to his mother and ask if he is Japanese. He is stunned for a moment then flies into a rage, this always works. The old man is still screaming for his 40 kuai and I explain to the crowd what transpired and our negotiated price, this is how it works in China. Then I hear, *beat the foreigner*.

Then **Hairdo Han** is in my face with two of his buddies and gives me a shove. Street brawls are common in China. He yells out that *foreigner take all our job and our girl*. I tell him that if the male youth of China were not such lazy non-productive workers and lousy in bed with small penises they would have both a job and a girl. I am marvelling at my Mandarin. The setting is perfect for him and his buddies to launch an assault. In 4 years I have been jumped three times, once at night by three men on a motorcycle, once by 11 punks in an internet café, once I was jumped in mid-day on a main street by three punks trying to rob me, so I have rather had it.

Fighting in China is like going 5 pin bowling with a 10 pin ball. The average weight of a Chinese man is less than 50 kilograms. I weigh 100 kilograms. The average 20 year old Chinese young is the size of a 13 year old Western youth. **Howling Han** lets out a combat yell and comes at me. The element of surprise is a huge advantage in a fight, especially when your travel partner is cowering behind the bike taxi and I am facing a crowd and three angry punks. So I surprise them. When a fight is inevitable, it is best to make a pre-emptive strike, my karate instructor told me this. I have meet numerous white and black travellers that have been beat by groups of Chinese male youth, never less than three. One Canadian boy I meet was in a coma in a hospital in Chengdu in 2007 from beer bottles to the head, for taking a Chinese girl to a night club. I have seen crowds beat people in traffic accidents. The uninvolved getting involved, a nation of people oppressed striking out with anger.

I side kicked this guy so hard as he came at me that he was horizontal to the ground at chest height. I grab his arm as he crashes to the ground, pull him sitting and I kick him in the face so hard that his nose explodes. Then I kick him in the balls as he is lying on the ground. While I am doing this I let out terrifying yalps, none of that pussifying Bruce Lee cat cry shit, who incidently was American, which really pisses off Chinese men when you tell them this.

One of my martial arts instructors also told me that when the odds are poor and you are out numbered, it is better to lay a severe beating on one person than try and fight several as the severe ongoing beating will terrify and defeat the others and they will hope another will go in second. This has always worked for me. I turn to face the crowd, take off my hoodie and calmly ask who is next, again in perfect Mandarin.

With 30 million police in China they are always close at hand. They always seem wimpy, effeminate and afraid. Five have amassed around the about 300 people watching this go down. I walk right up to them and give them shit for not helping me while I am being robbed by three (坏蛋, **huàidàn**, **bad egg**). I tell them that they are an embarrassment to their country and the Han people. They hang their heads in shame and I open my wallet and give them a fake professional card that I always carry, tell them I am a police officer from Canada and tell them that I am staying at the Mix Hostel, give them a Mix Hostel card that I got at a hostel in Beijing and I walk off collecting my travel mate who is speechless.

Bullshit baffles brains, China is predictable but not always in a positive way. Never been to the Mix Hostel in my life, but I hear it is a great place to stay in Chengdu.

www.mixhostel.com

http://en.wikipedia.org/wiki/Baoding

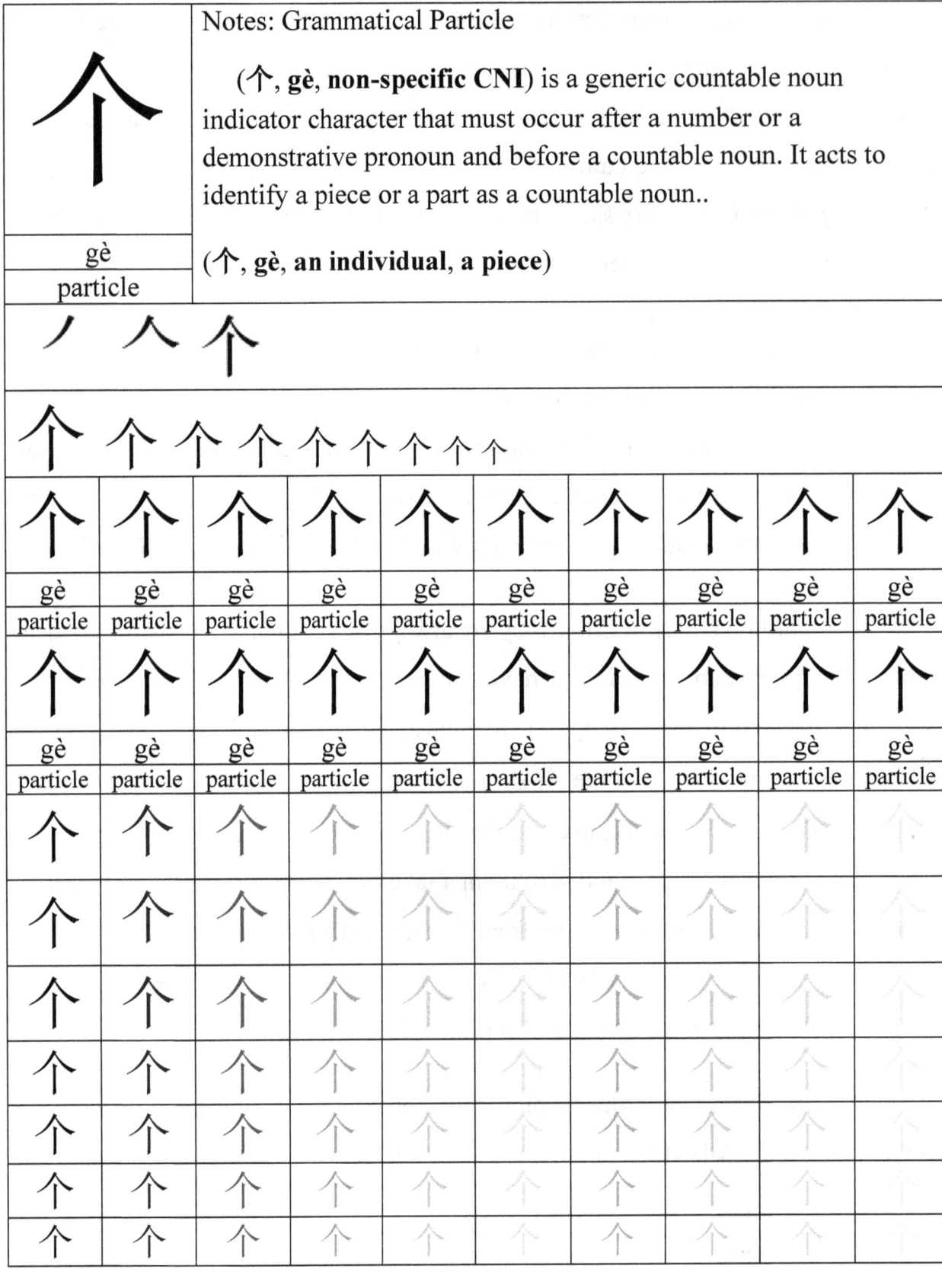

Notes: Grammatical Particle

(个, gè, **non-specific CNI**) is a generic countable noun indicator character that must occur after a number or a demonstrative pronoun and before a countable noun. It acts to identify a piece or a part as a countable noun..

(个, gè, **an individual, a piece**)

(个, gè, **non-specific Countable Noun Indicator**) is a concept that is not fully represented in English grammar. There are various terms used to describe the category of characters in which (个, **gè**, **an individual**, **a piece**) is the most common and most generic of the class. *Measure Word* and *Classifier*, are two of the descriptive words. However, neither adequately describes this class of characters. Some of them do vaguely classify the nouns that they mark into broad categories. I have never been able to figure out how the term *Measure Word* came into being.

Mandarin grammar marks *Countable Nouns* (**CN**) with specific characters. *Countable Nouns* are simply nouns that can be serially counted. They therefore much be objective and discrete. These characters provide an audible marker for nouns in a language that has very few distinct sounds. *Standard Mandarin* has 409 syllables spoken in up to 5 tones. The spoken understanding is much more difficult than that read. English has about 648,000 distinct sounds.

In this book the term *Countable Noun Indicator* (**CNI**) will be used. Other **CNI's** will be introduced as appropriate.

CNI's also act to visually mark the noun in a string of characters which helps decipher the grammar part. There are countable nouns marked by dozens of specific characters in this family. (个, **gè**, **an individual**, **a piece**) is the most common and the evolution of Mandarin grammar shows that there is a tendency to simplify the language further by use of (个, **gè**, **an individual**, **a piece**) rather than the dozens of other **CNIs**. The term for this is (个话, **gè huà**). (话, **huà**, **speech**) is a noun, meaning *a talk*, *a speech*, *a conversation*.

It took me a long time to figure out how to use (说, **shuō**, **to speak**, **to talk**) and (话, **huà**, **a talk**) not realizing one was a verb and one was a noun, or that *Verb Object Compounds* (**VOCs**) existed. (说话, **shuōhuà**, **speak**, **talk**, **say**, **chat**) is a **VOC**.

Perhaps a good way to demonstrate the difference is this example.

说	哪里	话
Shuō	nǎlǐ	huà?
Speak	which place	talk?
Speak	where	talk?

This is a question as it has a question forming word. (哪里, **nǎlǐ**, **which place**) formed from (哪, **nǎ**, **which**) and (里, **lǐ**, **inside**). When matched with a pronoun, such as (哪, **nǎ**, **which**) the reasonable meaning of (里, **lǐ**, **inside**) is (里, **lǐ**, **place**). You won't see that in any other book because I figured it out. *Which place* is of course *where*. (哪里, **nǎlǐ**, **which place**, **where**)

Other examples, being *Demonstrative Pronouns*, are;

(这, **zhè**, **this**)
(这里, **zhèlǐ**, **this place**, **here**)
(那, **nà**, **that**)
(那里, **nàli**, **that place**, **there**)

Because I have no idea which chapters I did first or what I have covered, I need to introduce the concept of **Pronoun Dropped** grammar. Which, I may have already covered, before or after this point, but not yet written. One of the great things about writing and publishing your own book is that you can do whatever you want, when you want.

Although English has some **Pronoun Dropped** characteristics, Mandarin relies extensively on it. The below example, which is functionally the same as the above example, is more readily understood in this format. Below, the **Personal Pronoun** (你, **nǐ**, **you**) is not dropped.

你	说	哪里	话
Nǐ	shuō	nǎlǐ	huà?
You	speak	which place	talk?
You	speak	where	talk?

Mandarin can be cut to the most rudimentary phrases. Once in **Hebei, Dingzhou**, a small town of one million people, not big enough to be on the country map, I was asked in a monster size store, (哪儿的, **nǎ'r de?**, **which of?**). (哪儿, **nǎ'r?**, **which?**) is a colloquial term using (儿化, **érhuà**, **suffixed non-syllabic retroflexing r**). The expression (哪儿的, **nǎ'r de?**, **which?**) is the most rudimentary way to ask someone where they are from. (化, **huà**, **to change**) is a verb and (儿, **ér**, **child**) acts as a phonetic with no intended meaning.

What that means is that it has no meaning, the *r* sound. It is added to words as a regional specific suffix, usually in the Beijing area. (哪儿, **nǎ'r?**, **which?**) has the same meaning as (哪里, **nǎli**, **where**). You will often here that (哪儿, **nǎ'r?**, **which?**) is Northern Mandarin and (哪里, **nǎli**, **where**) is Southern Mandarin.

So what does the (的, **de**) added to (哪儿, **nǎ'r?**, **which?**) Sometimes (的, **de**) appears to be hanging with no grammatical function. It is, cut to near nothing, an abbreviation for another abbreviated sentence (哪儿的人, **nǎ'r de rén?**, **which place person?**), the full proper grammer form of which is yet another sentence,

你	是	哪儿	的	人
Nǐ	shì	nǎ'r	de	rén?
You	is	which place	of	person?

China is no longer the regionally isolated place it was 25 years ago, The internal migrant population numbers in excess of 100 million as people travel to find work. Regional variants of Mandarin are gradually merging into what the Chinese government planned, that is, a national language, Standard Mandarin. Yet when my wife got off her first plane ride on our honeymoon in (广州, **Guǎngzhōu**), on the south coast of China, she automatically switched to saying (哪里, **nǎli**, **where**). Like she had been waiting to try it out, or it was programmed into her.

Incidentally, (广州, **Guǎngzhōu**) is *Canton*, from whence the extremely confusing language *Cantonese* originates. Now, apparently the British hearing the *Cantonese* people saying (广州, **Guǎngzhōu**), heard *Canton*. Does this surprise you? This is a group of people who think *fish and chips* is dining and they call the truck of a car *the boot*.

Now getting back to **CNIs**, (种, **zhǒng**, **type**, **kind**, **species**) is another **CNI**. *Demonstrative Pronouns* and *Interrogative Pronouns* also require a **CNI** when preceding a *Countable Noun*. (种, **zhǒng**, **type**, **kind**, **species**) is a **CNI** for objects that have multiple species. *Fish*, *trees*, *ethnic groups*, anything that has different subtypes. It too is somewhat generic and like many **CNIs**, is has overlap with more specific ones.

你	说	哪	种	语言
Nǐ	shuō	nǎ	zhǒng	yǔyán?
You	speak	which	type	language?

I suppose it does no great justice to give numerous examples of **CNIs**. Somewhere in the book I will make a list. Their use is simple. They are inserted between a number, a *Demonstrative Pronoun* or *Interrogative Pronoun* and their countable target *Object Noun*.

(哪个, **něige**, **which one**) can be used as an **Object** such as this example.

你	要	哪个
Nǐ	yào	něige?
You	want	which one?
Subject	Verb	Object

(个, **gè**, **an individual**, **a piece**) is also used to mark *Demonstrative Pronouns*. (这个, **zhèige**, **this one**) and (那个, **nàge**, **that one**) are the two common *Demonstrative Pronouns*. One of the first sentences I learned was,

我	不	喜欢	那个	我	喜欢	这个
Wǒ	bú	xǐhuan	nàge,	wǒ	xǐhuan	zhèige.
Me	not	like	that one,	me	like	this one.

I learned that sentence off of Benny, the self proclaimed words most famous Mandarin teacher, online. Benny used to be free online but now he is a capitalist.

http://www.askbennychinese.com/

Whereas English has *a* or *one* to mark non-specific selection of nouns, Mandarin uses (一个, **yī ge**, **a**, **one of**). This construction is a phrase, not a word.

她	要	一	个	狗肉	的	三明治
Tā	yào	yī	ge	gǒuròu	de	sānmíngzhì.
She	want	one	of	dog meat		sandwich.

(一个, **yī ge**, **a**, **one of**) functions to mark nouns as above, often it is simply abbreviated in conversation to (个, **ge**, **a**, **one of**). However, this confers further non-specifity of number to the sentence.

You may note that (三明治, **sānmíngzhì**, **sandwich**) is another example of a **Phonetic Loan Character (PLC)**. The individual characters give no meaning to the compound character word, they simply *loan* syllables to roughly *sound out* the word of another language.

Sandwiches are not part of traditional Chinese cuisine. So a word did not evolve to mark the meaning. I spent three years in China before I saw a loaf of bread. And good luck on finding butter. And if you do find a sandwich, make sure you look inside to see what is there. The donkey meat sandwiches (驴肉, **lǘròu**, **donkey meat**) in (保定, **Bǎodìng**) are tasty, or as the Chinese say, *dericious*.

When you get out the front door of the train station in **Baoding** just keep walking straight down the street in front of you. You will see six to eight traffic police sleeping, smoking, eating or playing games inside their all glass kiosk on the right side. The intersection will be a chaotic nightmare but the police will play on. Walk about one half kilometre and you will see three small restaurants on the right at an intersection, the farthest on the right is the locally famous (老驴头, **Lǎolǘ Tóu**, **Old Donkey Head**). Kind of has that British pub name appeal to it.

可能	我	有	个	猪鼻子
Kěnéng	**wǒ**	**yǒu**	**gè**	**zhūbízǐ**.
May possible	me	have	piece	pig nose.
Perhaps	me	have	piece	pig nose.

So in the above example, the merchant does not know how many pig noses he has, or if he has any. He cannot assign a specific number. Mandarin uses a ***single signal system*** for marking number. So, whereas we say, *six cars*, the Mandarin equivalent is *six car*. Whereas we say *these apples*, Mandarin says *this few apple*. Mandarin does not use the plurality in number markers that English uses.

Nothing is wasted in China, I have no idea what the usual use of a pig's head is but I have seen them roasted adorning large platters of (猪肉, **zhūròu**, **pig meat**). The tips of the ears and the nostrils get all blackened and burnt and it looks rather demonic.

(几个, **jǐ gè**, **how many piece**?) can be a question construction or a statement. This depends on the grammatical position and choice of *Verbs* and *Pronouns*. The first example asks as to number. The presence of this word signals that the sentence is a question. Like (一个, **yī ge**, **one of**) it is a phrase, not a word.

请问	你	想	要	几	个	孩子
Qǐngwèn,	nǐ	xiǎng	yào	jǐ	gè	háizi?
Please ask,	you	desire	want	how many	of	children?

(几个, **jǐ gè**, **some**, **few**) can also act as a *Quantitative Adjective* to the *Direct Object*. That is, it modifies the *Object* by varying quantity.

我	必须	有	几	个	鸡	蛋
Wǒ	bìxū	yǒu	jǐ	gè	jī	dàn.
Me	must	have	some	piece	chicken	egg.

Verbs can be serially stacked in Mandarin grammar, as in English. (必须, **bìxū**, **must**) can be used the same as *must* in English. (蛋, **dàn**, **egg**) is part of many compounded words that are insults, swear words. (王八, **wángba**, **tortoise**) and (蛋, **dàn**, **egg**) are combined to form (王八蛋, **wángbadàn**, **turtle egg**).

I have been told that this is a very serious insult in China, that the use of it will send a man into a rage and he will attack you uncontrolled. I use it all the time. I am not sure if the locals are shocked that I can speak Mandarin, that I know colloquial curses, or that I am twice their size, and look like a gorilla.

The history of it, apparently, is that tortoises and turtles do not know who their father is, therefore, you are telling the man that his wife is having sex with another man. That is a logical derivation, right? (滚, **gǔn**, **roll**, **turn**) and (蛋, **dàn**, **egg**) are combined to form (滚蛋, **gǔndàn**, **roll egg**). This is roughly equivalent to *Beat it*! *Scram*!, serious curses, right?

A Shanghai television personality recently caused great controversy in China by telling a *write-in* show watcher to (滚蛋, **gǔndàn**, **roll egg**). This was over the suggestion that the he speak Mandarin rather than the local Shanghai language. The rest of China thinks that Shanghai has its own arrogant attitude.

Shanghai's attitude comes from centuries of exposure and business with the West, and a feeling that they are their own unique country within China. The punishment for talking about splitting off from China includes execution so it is a silent movement.

Whereas (一个, **yīge**, **a**, **one of**) marks non-specific nouns, specificity can be marked with (这, **zhè**, **zhèi**, **this**) or (这个, **zhè**, **zhèige**, **this one**). This differs from (那, **nà**, **that**) (那个, **nàge**, **that one**) with the same reasoning as in English. Like English (这, **zhè**, **zhèi**, **this**) is closer in distance or time than (那, **nà**, **that**).

这个	吗	她	不要	这个	啊
Zhèige	ma.	Tā	búyào	zhèige	ă.
This one	?	She	not want	this one	ah!

The use of (啊, ā, á, ǎ, à, **interjection**) is an art all of its own. I always use it incorrectly to great amusement of the locals. Rather than a few extra pages on this, I will list it here.

(啊, ā, interjection indicating elation)

(啊, ǎ, interjection indicating puzzled surprise)

(啊, á, interjection indicating doubt or questioning)

(啊, à, interjection indicating agreement or approval)

Note the different tone assigned to (不, **bú**, **not**). Usually, it is spoken in the fourth tone. You will find a chapter on this in the back section of the book, which really, perhaps you should read that entire section first. In short, when (不, **bú**, **not**) occurs before a word that is spoken in the fourth tone, it changes to a second tone.

(个, **ge**, **a piece**, **individual**) you have some familiarity with. As noted previously, there is overlap in the useof **CNI's**. You have covered enough to know that making sense and speaking Mandarin can be mutually exclusive. Presented below are some common **CNI's**.

(名, **míng**, **name**) also acts as a **CNI**. Your (名字, **míngzi**, **name**) is your or anothers personal name.

我的	名字	叫	大	毛	猴子
Wǒ de	míngzi	jìao	Dà	Máo	Hóuzi.
My	name	called	Big	Hairy	Monkey.

My Chinese name came with a lot of forethought and alcohol. Immmediately before I went to China the first time, in November 2006, I meet with some Chinese friends in Toronto for some *tips*. Chinese people have no alcohol dehydrogenase. This is the enzymne that metabolizes alcohol. The smallest amounts can put the casual drinker into a stupor. They all agreed that the most important thing was that I carry some toilet paper and napkins in my pocket at all times and get a Chinese name.

The toilet paper advise turned out to be true. As they drank more and more they thought I should use (大, **dà**, **big**) as I was, relative to the rank and file Chinese comrade, huge. More alcohol and gales of laughter and they thought my body hair should fit into my name, so (毛, **máo**, **hair**). Then by the time they had drank the equivalent of about one beer and could barely stand, one friend suggested (猴子, **hóuzi**, **monkey**). This brought laughing until the point of the inability to breath, for them.

At first I was slightly hurt, but then they explained that the character of the Chinese monkey was highly praised and loved by the Chinese people. So when I compiled and put together (大毛猴子, **Dà Máo Hóuzi**, **Big Hairy Monkey**) they paused, jaws dropped with incredulous looks on their faces. A very serious talk ensued that I could never use a name like that as I would *lose face*, people would laugh at me and no one would take me serious, perfect. I am Canadian, I have no idea what *face* is and breaking-the-ice with people laughing sounded perfect for me.

Despite their dire warnings, I went to China with that name. I registered it with the **PSB**, the ***Public Security Burea***, i.e. ***Big Brother*** is watching your foreign ass presence. The look on their faces was priceless. I have been told many times by

Chinese officials that I cannot use that name, not for any reason other than it is funny, when I insist, they comply and that is now my official name on visas, hotel registrations, most wanted posters and such.

It is an ice breaker, when I meet the girl I was to marry, she warned me to never use it in front of her family as they would not *take me seriously*. So to her family, I am know as (大毛, **Dà Máo**), a *strong name*, as there is an affiliation with the great Chairman Mao, the Butcher of Beijing, the most prolific mass murderer of the 20th century. Variably attributed to have overseen the deaths of 35 to 72 million dead under his watch. Now her family thinks I am a Maoist. Yah, that's the association I want.

Last Chinese New Year, 2010, my mother-in-law commented that my antics are like the Chinese Monkey, and she laughed, and praised the Monkey Monk, her favorite televison show. My wife laughed so hard that she just about blew the meal out of her rice bowl. My publishing company is called **Monkey Monk Publications**. I digress;

Acting as a **CNI** (名, **míng**, **CNI for people**) works thus;

我	看见	三	名	美女
Wǒ	kànjian	sān	míng	měinǚ.
Me	look at perceive	three	of	beautiful girl.

(看, **kàn**, **to look at**) is often used as an incomplete *Verb Phrase*, that is, it requires another verb to determine the outcome of the attempt *to look at*. There are numerous Mandarin verbs with this *left-in-outcome-limbo* tense.

(见, **jiàn**, **perceive**) is used in these **Verb Verb Completion Compounds**, **VVCC's**, to specifically mark the completion of sensory experiences. (见, **jiàn**, **perceive**) marks the successful completion of an attempt to use your senses to perceive something appropriate to that sense. The compound forms a *Verb Phrase* that functionally acts as a completed *Verb Tense*.

This concept is perhaps more understandable when you look at the near necessity of compounded verbs that exist to mark degree of completion. One of the more common expressions you will learn to pick out and use is;
(听不懂, **tīngbudǒng**, **listen to not understand**). Simply, it means that there is an attempt to listen, and success was not achieved. (懂, **dǒng**, **understand**) is the verb used to complete the attempt *to listen* to. So the entire repetoire is;

我	听不懂
Wǒ	tīngbudǒng.
Me	listen to not understand.

You can see from the **Hanyu Pinyin** construction that **tīngbudǒng** is one word. This brings an interesting grammer construction into discussion, *Verb Completion Interruption*, or **VCI**. You will not find this term in even the most advanced grammar books as I made it up just now. However, this phrase demonstrates the necessity of creating verb tense using the various *Action Completion Verbs*. **ACV's**.

Like **CNI's**, some **ACV's** are generic and some are more specific. The verb (懂, **dǒng**, **understand**) makes complete sense as an **ACV** to complete the tense for (听, **tīng**, **hear**). So (听懂, **tīngdǒng**, **listen to understand**) is the *Perfected* form of *Verb Completion*. In English grammar, this represents the *Present Perfect* verb tense. This is another example of destroying the myths of Mandarin grammar in which one grammarian quotes after another the lack of verb tenses in Mandarin. A *word* in Mandarin can be one or more characters. The fact that one word can be encompassed within another does not make the word with less characters more or less of a word.

Suffix to say, Mandarin words can have verb tense. Mandarin verbs are not all in a neutral *untensed* form in their unmodified presentation. There are numerous examples, (找, zhǎo, to look for) is in the **Current Continuous** tense. I could go on, but now I am ranting.

Okay, where were we, so verbs of perception, (听, **tīng, to listen to**), (看, **kàn, to look at**) and (闻, **wén, to smell**) can all have their efforts to be enacted and completed modified with (见, **jiàn, perceive**). They can all have these efforts interrupted with (不, **bu, not**). So, therefore, all these forms exist;

(看, **kàn, to look at**)

(看见, **kànjiàn, look at perceive**)

(看不见, **kànbujiàn, look at not perceive**)

(听, **tīng, listen to**)

(听懂, **tīngdǒng, listen to understand**)

(听不懂, **tīngbudǒng, listen to not understand**)

(听见, **tīngjiàn, listen to perceive**)

(听不见, **tīngbujiàn, listen to not perceive**)

(闻, **wén, to smell**)

(闻不见, **wénjiàn, to smell perceive**)

(闻不见, **wénbujiàn**, **to smell not perceive**)

Yah, this is all coming together nicely, this chapter on **CNI's**. A polite **CNI** for people is (位, **wèi**, **polite CNI for people**). When you are at a nice restaurant in China, note I didn't say a clean one with toilet paper and towels to wipe the tables with and no chicken bones under the table, you can toss this one out to the amazement of all. Here is how you get seating for five.

请问	她们	是	那	五	位	客人	吗
Qǐngwèn,	tāmen	shì	nà	wǔ	wèi	kèren	ma.
Please ask,	they	is	that	five		guest person	?

(口, **kǒu**, **mouth**) is a **CNI** that can be used only for family members.

我	家	有	七	口	人
Wǒ	jiā	yǒu	qī	kǒu	rén.
Me	family	have	seven	mouth	person.

(口, **kǒu**, **mouth**) is also a **CNI** for *wells* and some *animals*.

一	口	井
Yī	kǒu	jǐng.
One	mouth	well.
#	CNI	CN

Pigs, for some reason use (头, **tóu**, **head**) for a **CNI**.

三	头	小	猪
Sān	tóu	xiǎo	zhū.
Three	head	little	pig.

(只, **zhī**,) acts as a **CNI** for some other animals. It also acts as a **CNI** for *vessels*, *some utensils* and *one of a pair of things*. You are probably wondering what these things have in common, nothing.

一	只	猫
Yī	zhī	māo.
One	of	cat.

Now, if you are a white guy like me and chopsticks still fall from your hands, you may want to know how to ask for one, the **CNI** is (支, **zhī, branch**).

服务员,	请	给	我	一	支	筷子
Fúwùyuán,	qǐng	gěi	wǒ	yī	zhī	kuàizi.
Service member,	request	give	me	one	branch	chopstick.

Now, (双, **shuāng, pair, twin, double, both, dual**) is a **CNI** works for things like shoes, trousers, eyes, but not for twins.

我	买了	一	双	鞋
Wǒ	mǎile	yī	shuāng	xié.
Me	bought	one	pair	shoe.

For twins, you know, those Korean twins with high heel shoes and red latex hot pants, the **CNI** is (对, **duì**, **pair**).

我	要	一	对	韩国	的	女孩儿	双胞胎
Wǒ	yào	yī	duì	Hánguó	de	nǚhái'r	shuāngbāotāi.
Me	want	one	pair	Han country	of	female	twins.

The Chinese Han (汉, **Hàn**) are always quick to point out that the Korean Han (韩, **Hán**) are different and use a different character and tone. Be particularly careful to get the tones right on these two as the Chinese feel insulted to be called Korean and Korean feel insulted to be called Chinese. Now the Japanese, they feel insulted that other people even exist.

(头, **tóu**, **head**) is the final **CNI** that I will cover, this chapter is going on way to long. Curiously, it is a **CNI** for *bulbs of garlic* and *head of cattle*. Not likely that you will be negotiating for a cow in the market but garlic is common.

师傅	你	有	没有	十	头	蒜
Shīfu,	nǐ	yǒu	méiyǒu	shí	tóu	suàn?
Master,	you	have	not have	ten	head	garlic?

(师傅, **shīfu**, **master**) was once a term of respectful address. It is now used generically to address anybody that you want something from. You can use it for either males of females but it is more commonly used for males.

(蒜, **suàn**, **garlic**)   (师傅, **shīfu**, **master**)

(没有, méiyǒu, not have)
(头, tóu, head)
(汉, Hàn ethnic Chinese)
(女孩儿, nǚhái'r, girl)
(双胞胎, shuāngbāotāi, twins)
(韩, Hán, Hán ethnic Korean)
(鞋, xié, shoe)
(只, zhǐ, only)
(服务员, fúwùyuán, attendant)
(服务, fúwù, to serve)
(服, fú, to serve)
(务, wù, affair, business)
(请, qǐng, to request)
(给, gěi, give, give to)
(员, yuán, member)
(筷子, kuàizi, chopsticks)
(对, duì, pair)
(猫, māo, cat)
(只, zhī, CNI certain animals)
(只, zhī, CNI for vessels)
(只, zhī, CNI for some utensils)
(只, zhī, CNI for one of a pair)
(只, zhǐ, only)
(猪, zhū, pig)

(井, jǐng, well)
(请问, qǐngwèn, request ask)
(她们, tāmen, they)
(是, shì, is, to be)
(那, nà, that)
(五, wǔ, five)
(位, wèi, polite CNI for people)
(客, kè, visitor, guest)
(客人, kèren, visitor, guest)
(口, kǒu, CNI for wells)
(口, kǒu, CNI for certain animals)
(口, kǒu, CNI for family members)
(家, jiā, family)
(只, zhī, CNI certain animals)
(只, zhǐ, only)
(双, shuāng, pair, twin, both)
(听, tīng, to listen to)
(听见, tīngjiàn, hear)
(美女, měinǚ, beautiful woman)
(看见, kànjian, to look at perceive)
(见, jiàn, perceive)
(闻见, wénjiàn, to smell)
(名, míng, CNI for people)
(个, gè, an individual, a piece)

(一个, yī ge, one of, one piece)

(不要, búyào, not want)

(猪肉, zhūròu, pork)

(几, jǐ, how many)

(几个, jǐ gè, a few, several)

(请问, qǐngwèn, please ask)

(可, kě, can, may)

(能, néng, can)

(可能, kěnéng, possible)

(子, zǐ, child)

(孩子, háizi, child)

(猪鼻, zhūbí, hog nose)

(驴肉, lǘròu, donkey meat)

(狗肉, gǒuròu, dog meat)

(三明治, sānmíngzhì, sandwhich)

(给, gěi, give)

(种, zhǒng, type, kind, species)

(这个, zhèige, this one)

(语, yǔ, language)

(言, yán, language)

(语言, yǔyán, language)

(听不见, tīngbujiàn, listen to not perceive)

(听懂, tīngdǒng, listen to understand)

(看不见, kànbujiàn, look at not perceive)

(化, huà, change)

(哪里, nǎli, where)

(哪里, nǎli, where)

(那里, nàli, that place, over there)

(里面, lǐmiàn, inside)

(哪里, nǎli, where)

(哪儿的, nǎ'r de?, which?)

(哪儿, nǎ'r?, which?)

(儿化, érhuà, suffixed retroflexing r)

(哪儿的, nǎ'r de?, which?)

(化, huà, to change)

(儿, ér, child)

(头, tóu, head)

(个, gè, an individual, a piece)

(滚蛋, gǔndàn, roll egg)

(猴子, hóuzi, monkey)

(蛋, dàn, egg)

(鸡, jī, chicken)

(找, zhǎo, to look for)

(支, zhī, branch)

到	Notes: Verb
	(到, **dào**, to, to go to, toward, until)
	(到, **dào**, arrive, arrive at, reach)
dào	(到, **dào**, verb action completion marker)
to	

一 乙 云 丕 至 至 到 到

到 到 到 到 到 到 到 到 到

(practice grid of 到 characters with dào / to labels)

到

(到, **dào**, to) when used to refer to the direction that something or someone is heading exists in several forms.

今天	我	从	北京	到	上海	去
Jīntiān,	wǒ	cóng	Běijīng	dào	Shànghǎi	qù.
Present day,	me	from	Beijing	to	Shanghai	go.

The above is clear and obvious and represents the common directional usage. There is an interesting and common construction that uses (上, **shàng**, go to). The usual meaning is (上, **shàng**, up). It is difficult to know if this meaning is preserved as unrelated languages are compared to each other by making a list of words and then writing a list of translations beside them. We say *up north*, *down south*. I have used electronic dictionaries in China that have absolutely wrong translations of English words. This is why websites such as **http://www.engrish.com/** exist.

It is interesting having arguments with Chinese people who have never met or spoken to a native English speaker before, about the meaning of English words. The construction (上... 去, **shàng...qù**, toward...go) is used thus,

明天	我们	上	广州	去
Míngtiān	wǒmen	shàng	Guǎngzhōu	qù.
Tomorrow	we	toward	Guangzhou	go.

Apparently this is formal. (往, **wǎng, go toward**) is often seen on subway lines in China. From the time your foot leaves the edge of the sidewalk until it gets on the subway can be one or two kilometer of stairs and underground hallways. I am most familiar with the subway in Toronto, Ontario, Canada. The distance between stops in Toronto can be shorter than the distance from the ticket wicket to the platform in China. So while you are walking with a few thousand people rushing madly from one subway line to another, at a transfer point, you will see a (往, **wǎng, go toward**) sign guiding you toward the next numbered subway platform.

(到, **dào, arrive, arrive at**) can exist as the expected form or the completed form. The following is the *Expected* verb form. (什么, **shénme, what**) is composed of the characters (什, **shén, what**) and the grammatical particle that acts as an interrogative suffix (么, **me, interrogative suffix**).

(时候, **shíhou, time**) is composed of (时, **shí, time**), as in an interval of time, and (候, **hòu, wait, await**). (什么时候, **shénme shíhou, what time**) elegantly compounds to mean *when*. Occassionally, Mandarin makes sense.

什么	时候	你	到
Shénme	shíhou	nǐ	dào?
What	time	you	arrive?
When		you	arrive?

Below is what I say when I roll into a train station and and the surge of people awaken me or someone elbows me in the head as they go by or smash my head with their suitcase.

到	了	吗
Dào	le	ma.
Arrive	-ed	?
Verb	VCM	QP
Arrived		?

(了, **le**, **Verb Completion Marker**) **VCM** functionally acts as *–ed* to mark completion of a verb action. Grammatical particles and suffixes can be serially stacked. (吗, **ma**, **question particle**) **QP** always comes last.

Mandarin grammar makes use of several verbs used in a suffix position to mark the tense of the verb. (到, **dào**, **achieved verb action**) does what many books say does not exist in Mandarin grammar, that is, it creates verb tense. Really, it is an argument of semantics. (看, **kàn**, **a look**) and (看, **kàn**, **to look at**) are amendable to modification. (看到了, **kàndào le**, **to look at achieved**) makes use of (到, **dào**, **-ed**) to create the *Current Completed* verb tense. There are two forms of (了, **le**). Apparently their history and derivation are both different, but the same character. (了, **le**, **CRS**) can mark the *Current Relevant State*. (看到了, **kàndào le**, **looked at**) represents the *Current Completed* verb state of *looking at*.

你	看一看	这个	看到	了	吗
Nǐ	kànyīkàn	zhèige,	kàndào	le	ma?
You	look one look	this one,	looked at	CRS	?
You	take a look	this one,	looked at	CRS	?

(看一看, **kànyīkàn**, **take a look**) and similar constructions are demonstrated in Chapter 2.

China loves idiomatic expressions and axioms. To give you an idea how poorly translation occurs, read the book translation of this expression under the example. This is a very famous common expression.

不到	长城	非	好汉
Búdào	Chángchéng	fēi	Hǎohàn.
Not arrive	Long wall	not	good Han.
Not arrive	Great Wall	not	good Han.

So the book translation is *one must reach one's goal*. You can see how this completely strips the cultural and ethnic racist overtones from the original. The *Han* are the ethnic majority of China, an overwhelming majority. China is chronically troubled with ethnic disparity and oppression of ethnic minorities. The overall message is that you are not truly *Chinese Han* until you pilgrimage to the *Great Wall*. From the perspective of the *Han* majority, this means you are not *Chinese* until you trek to the *Great Wall*. From the perspective of the ethnic minorities, China is defined by the *Han*, which is exactly how the *Han* feel. Most Chinese have a National Identity Card. That is, if their birth was legal and their parents registered them. On this card is one of fifty six ethnic group designations. This can determine your entire career success. Success being more readily available if you are *Han*.

For (到来, **láidào**, **come arrive**, **came**), (到, **dào**, **-ed**) is used to mark the successful attempt at coming. Interestingly, (来, **lái**, **come**) is also used in a suffix position to mark verb completion. There are no rules to determine which verb completion character is used to complete which verb. I have some lists somewhere which I will include if this book doesn't get too big. (到来, **dàolái**, **arrive come**, **arrival**, **arrived**) has similar meaning noting successful arrival.

她	来到	我们	的	家
Tā	láidào	wǒmen	de	jiā.
She	come arrive		our	house.
She	came		our	house

You can see the simple comparison to *came* in the above example.

我们	欢迎	他的	到来
Wǒmen	huānyíng	tā de	dàolái.
We	welcome	his	arrive come.
We	welcome	his	arrival.

You can see in my clever sentence below, different uses of (到, **dào**)

到	现在	为止	咱们	来到	中国	明天	到	都
Dào	xiànzài	wéizhǐ,	zánmen	láidào	Zhōngguó,	míngtiān	dào	Dū.
To	now	until,	we	came	China,	next day	arrive	Du.

Dū is a colloquial expression for (成都 **Chéngdū**, **Chengdu**). This is truly one of the great cities of China. Tea houses, historic sites, geography, Panda bears, and (美女, **měinǚ**, **beautiful woman**). This city is considered one of the four top cities in the world for girl watching. I have accidentally been in two of the others. If you like girls with long shiny black hair to the waist, long thin legs, flawless complexions and angelic dispositions, this is heaven. (成, **chéng**, **become, accomplish, succeed**) combines with (都, **dū**, **capital**) to become the *accomplished capital*.

(美, měi, beautiful) gets a lot of use in China. (女, nǚ, woman, female) forms compound characters for numerous feminine words. A common address for a young woman is (美女, měinǚ, beautiful woman). (小姐, xiǎojie, miss, young sister) is another. However, in some parts of China, (小姐, xiǎojie, miss, young sister) is also a form of address for prostitutes so you may not earn many points if you use this term for your girlfriend's younger sister.

In the chapter on (个, gè, an individual, a piece) I introduced **CNI's**. The **CNI** for (美女, měinǚ, beautiful woman) and (小姐, xiǎojie, miss, young sister) include (个, ge, individual), (名, míng, name) and (位, wèi, CNI people).

Other common words and phrases that use (到, dào, to) include these below. Most of these characters will be covered in the book as these are common characters. You will see that in some of the below examples (到, dào, **verb completion**) acts to mark verb completion. Compounds that use (到, dào, **verb completion**) can be split with (不, bù, not) to mark lack of verb completion.

(办, bàn, do)
(办到, bàndào, do achieve, done, accomplish)
(办不到, bànbudào, do not achieve)

这	件	事儿	不	容易	办到
Zhè	jiàn	shì'r	bù	róngyì	bàndào.
This		matter	not	easy	do achieve.
DP	CNI	Subject	Adverb Phrase		VP
Subject Noun Phrase			Adverb Phrase		Verb Phrase

(一天到晚, **yī tiān dào wǎn**, **day to night**, **all day long**) is easily understood. Mandarin grammar apparently favours loading a time phrase at the beginning of a sentence. This is one of the reasons that Mandarin is often defined as *Topic Prominent* grammar. A word or phrase that answers the question **when** is a *Temporal Adverb* (**TA**). Placing the **TA** at the beginning nicely creates a setting for the sentence. Simply stated, the *Topic* is what the sentence is about. (一, **yī**, **noun entirety prefix**) can be used to indicate entirety of a noun. This works particularily good for nouns that have duration.

一	天	到	晚	我	工作
Yī	tiān	dào	wǎn,	wǒ	gōngzuò.
One	day	to	night,	me	work.
All day		to	night,	me	work.

In this example above, (一, **yī**, **noun entirety prefix**) marks the entirety of the noun (天, **tiān**, **day**). I chose the word *all* to indicate the entire duration. It does not in fact mean *all*, it means *one*. However, in this context before a noun it marks the entirety of the noun.

我	想到	了	一个	主意
Wǒ	xiǎngdào	le	yīge	zhǔyi.
Me	think achieve		one of	idea.
Me	thought		one of	idea.

(想 **xiǎng**, **to think of**, **to desire**) combines with (到, **dào**, **VCM**) to create the completed form of the verb *to think*, that is, the *Perfect Tense* (**PT**). Big deal right?

So what is the meaning of (了, **le**)? Does it mark *Action Verb Completion* (**AVC**), does it mark *Current Relevant State* (**CRS**)? Do you feel the suspense building?

Really, I have no idea. I have petitioned 4 Chinese born people and they all give me different answers. Given that it is mid sentence and does not occur after a functionally complete sentence, it is not sentence final **CRS**. Given that Mandarin is a language of great economy, that is, it removes whatever it can when possible, it is not **VCM** as (到, **dào**) marks *Verb Completion* creating the *Perfect Tense*.

There are books of all different levels of analysis of Mandarin. It is difficult to assign *correct* to any one author when others have a different and conflicting perspectives. So when I ask my in-house Chinese editor, my wife, she says;

Really not that important, forget the (了, le). Make the sentence a little difference but not so important.

Then she says;

用	不用	都	没事儿
Yòng	búyòng,	dōu	méishì'r.
Use	not use	all	not issue.

The (儿, **ér**, child) as probably mentioned earlier is a phonetic additive without meaning that is used in the **North China Beijing** area. (没事, **méishì**, not matter) is actually a contraction for (没有事, **méiyǒu shì**, not have matter). In fact, any time you see (没, **méi**, not) not in front of (有, **yǒu**, have) the construction represents a grammatical contraction and the proper form is (没有, **méiyǒu**, not have). Although, it seems to irritate Chinese people when I use it even when they admit that it is correct. So I use it.

(了, **le**) can also mark **Bounded Events** where events are expressed in entirity. These are referred to as **Perfectivizing Expressions**. Some words lend themselves to explaining this better than others. (死, **sǐ**, **die**) only exists as a completed action in Mandarin grammar and it is almost always marked with (了, **le**), that is, it exists in the **Perfective State**, the act is complete with the use of the word, usually. So why is the translation not *dead* versus *die*? I think that this is because it includes the process of dying. Anyways, so much for theory.

我	的	老婆,	打死	了	我
Wǒ	de	lǎopo,	dǎsǐ	le	wǒ.
My		old lady,	beat to die		me.
My		wife,	beat to dead		me.

You can also create a **Future Perfect Tense** (**FPT**) without the use of (了, **le**). In this expression the construction is not bounded as it is in the future and may not happen. If you add the (了, **le**) it makes the sentence more threatening, says my wife. I guess it is that threat of **Verb Completion**.

你	要	死	吗
Nǐ	yào	sǐ	ma.
You	want	die	?

(忘, **wàng**, **forget**) is another example of a verb that exists in Mandarin grammar in the completed form hence the construction is usually (忘了, **wàngle**, **forgot**). Again, in the future tense it can be used without (了, **le**). Incidently, one of the many names my wife has for me is (忘了先生, **wàngle xiānsheng**, **forgot Mr.**) Mr. Forgot.

别	忘了	我
Bié	wàngle	wǒ.
Do not	forgot	me.

Here is another one of my favorite horrid translations.

不	到	黄	河	心	不	死
Bú	dào	Huáng	Hé	xīn	bù	sǐ.
Not	arrive	Yellow	River	heart	not	dead.

This of course means that if you do not reach your goal, you heart need not die. The source I referenced gave the translation *refuse to give up*, I think it is important to know the real translation. Rather **Chinese-ifies** it.

So my wife just called me to the desktop computer and said this. Incidently, this does not involve (到, **dào**, **to**).

我想干这个我想干那个但是我们只有两个 USB hole.

This is a reasonably easy sentence actually. China could help us all if the would put spaces between words. You need to learn to recognize characters that cluster to form words versus serial single characters. So we have to parse the sentence a little to make it understandable. Context of course is important. She was looking for a USB port and was blindly trying to plug a USB cable into any available hole.

我 想干 这个, 我 想干 那个, 但是, 我们 只有 两个 USB hole.

我	想	干	这个
Wǒ	xiǎng	gān	zhèige,
Me	desire	do	this,

As she demonstrated trying to push the USB stick into the printer port, and then;

我	想	干	那个
Wǒ	xiǎng	gān	nàge,
Me	desire	do	that,

while she is trying to push the USB stick into the network port.

但是
Dānshì,
But,

This is of course a conjunction, joining two phrases. The literal translation is *only is*. There are various Mandarin words that are glossed as *but*. They all have subtle difference in meaning. *Only is* sets limits on a future quantity.

我 想干 这个, 我 想干 那个, 但是, 我们 只有 两个 USB hole.

我们	只有	两	个	USB hole
wǒmen	zhīyǒu	liǎng	ge	USB hole.
We	only have	two	of	USB hole.

(只有, **zhǐyǒu**, **only have**) is a adverb verb compound word. I have no idea how some words evolved to be a compound versus just serial words combined to represent the same meanings as if they were compounded.

So, the overall meaning;

Me desire do this, me desire do that, but we only have two USB holes.

Cute as hell when she speaks part Mandarin and part English.

January 30th 2011

I love watching military shows. So I am watching **Dogfights** which highlights aerial dogfights of the various wars. This show is showing the air superiority of the Americans in the Vietnam war. I am pointing out the kill ratios of the American versus Vietnamese fighter planes, greater than 25 to 1. To her, she was taught that the Korean, Vietnam and Second World War were won by the Chinese, that is what they are taught, and there is some truth to it. Her response, *always the American is the great warrior, always wins, nobody shows the Chinese put the bamboo spear through their neck or cut off their head with the* (大刀, **dàdāo**, **big knife**). *America lose the war, never learn the lesson.* A little Chinese philosophy.

(别, bié, separate, other, do not)
(先生, xiānsheng, Mister)
(要, yào, want)
(老婆, lǎopo, old woman)
(打死, dǎsǐ, beat to death)
(死, sǐ, die)
(忘, wàng, forget)
(忘了, wàng le, forgot)
(用, yòng, use)
(不用, bùyòng, not use)
(都, dōu, all)
(儿, ér, child)
(有, yǒu, have)
(没, méi, not)
(事 shì, issue, matter)
(没有, méiyǒu, not have)
(没事, méishì, not matter)
(想到, xiǎngdào, thought of)
(儿, ér, child)
(主意, zhǔyi, idea)
(黄河, Huáng Hé, Yellow River)
(得, dé, get, reach, achieve)
(得到, dédào, get)
(达, dá, reach, arrive)

(达到, dádào, achieve)
(处, chù, place)
(到处, dàochù, everywhere)
(迟, chí, tardy, late)
(迟到, chídào, arrive late)
(天, tiān, day)
(晚, wǎn, late)
(想不到, xiǎngbudào, not anticipate)
(巴, bā, hope)
(巴不到, bābudào, anticipate)
(打不到的, dǎbudào, not achieved)
(办, bàn, do)
(办不到, bànbudào, not accomplish)
(办到, bàndào, accomplish)
(个, ge, individual)
(名, míng, name)
(位, wèi, CNI for people).
(美女, měinǚ, beautiful woman)
(小姐, xiǎojie, miss, young sister)
(成, chéng, accomplish)
(成都, Chéngdū, Chengdu)
(都, dū, capital, metropolis)
(明天, míngtiān, tomorrow)
(为止, wéizhǐ, up to, till)

(咱们, zánmen, we)
(中国, Zhōngguó, China)
(美, měi, beautiful)
(美女, měinǚ, beautiful woman)
(止, zhǐ, stop)
(到, dào, completion of verb action)
(什么, shénme, what)
(什, shén, what)
(时候, shíhou, time)
(时, shí, time)
(了, le, Verb Completion Marker)
(吗, ma, question particle)
(候, hòu, wait, await)
(你, nǐ, you)
(么, me, interrogative suffix)
(到, dào, to, to go to, towards)
(到, dào, arrive, arrive at)
(到, dào, verb completion marker)
(往, wǎng, go toward)
(上, shàng, go to)
(从, cóng, from)
(北京, Běijīng, Beijing)
(上海, Shànghǎi, Shanghai)
(去, qù, go)

(上… 去, shàng…qù, toward…go)
(广州, Guǎngzhōu, Canton)
(看一看, kànyīkàn, take a look)
(不到, bùdào, not arrive)
(到, dào, achieve)
(来, lái, come)
(到来, dàolái, arrive come)
(来到, láidào, come arrive)
(欢迎, huānyíng, welcome, greet)
(容易, róngyì, easy)
(吃, chī, eat)
(吃到, chīdào, eat achieve)
(吃不到, chībudào, eat not achieve)
(件, jiàn, CNI articles, issues, items)
(得, dé, get, reach, achieve)
(得到, dédào, succeed in obtaining)
(得到, dédào, gain, receive, got)
(达, dá, reach, arrive)
(达到, dádào, achieve, reach, attain)
(到达, dàodá, reach, arrive)
(处, chù, place)
(到处, dàochù, everywhere)
(直, zhí, straight, directly)
(直到, zhídào, until)

(等, děng, wait)

(迟, chí, late)

(迟到, chídào, arrive late)

(想 xiǎng, to think of, to desire)

(想到, xiǎngdào, thought of)

(没有事, méiyǒu shì, not have matter)

(没有事儿, méiyǒu shì'r, not have matter)

(等到, děngdào, by the time, when, wait until)

(想不到, xiǎngbudào, unable to anticipate)

(巴, bā, hope for)

(巴不到, bābudào, can't wait)

(巴到, bādào, anxiously until)

(才到, cái dào, just arrived)

说	Notes: Verb
shuō speak	(说, **shuō, to speak, to say**) (说, **shuō, act as a matchmaker**) (说, **shuō, refer to, to indicate**) (说, **shuì, to persuade, to win over, to convince**)

丶 讠 讠 讠ˊ 讠ˊˊ 讠⊓ 说 说 说

说 说 说 说 说 说 说 说 说

说	说	说	说	说	说	说	说	说	说
shuō speak	shuō speak	shuō speak	shuō speak	shuō speak	shuō speak	shuō speak	shuō speak	shuō speak	shuō speak
说	说	说	说	说	说	说	说	说	说
shuō speak	shuō speak	shuō speak	shuō speak	shuō speak	shuō speak	shuō speak	shuō speak	shuō speak	shuō speak
说	说	说	说	说	说	说	说	说	说
说	说	说	说	说	说	说	说	说	说
说	说	说	说	说	说	说	说	说	说
说	说	说	说	说	说	说	说	说	说
说	说	说	说	说	说	说	说	说	说
说	说	说	说	说	说	说	说	说	说
说	说	说	说	说	说	说	说	说	说

说

(说, **shuō**, **to say**, **to speak**) is a verb. When I began to study Mandarin every phrase book I used seemed to dwell on this verb. Some authors seem to have an obsession of teaching a person to ask or tell someone if they can or cannot speak English or Mandarin. To me, this is like flying to Nigeria and asking a Nigerian if they are black. Some things are self evident. If you are in China and you see a person with black hair, Asian type skin, almond shaped eyes, typically shorter than you and they look local, probably no point in asking them if they *speak Chinese*. Anyway, here goes;

你	会	不	会	说	中文
Nǐ	huì	bú	huì	shuō	Zhōngwén?
You	able to	not	able to	speak	Middle Language.

(会, **huì**, **able to**) is a verb that is used to qualify a skill that is learned. Functionally, it is used to represent *know how to*. (不会, **bú huì**, **not able to**) is an auxillary verb phrase, note that the *Hanyu Pinyin* separates the two syllables.

When I first began to study Mandarin, my book buying process was rather random. **Read and Speak Chinese for Beginners** , ISBN 0-07-141218-2 was one of the particularly pathetic books I bought. In the entire book there were only 12 verbs and an obsession to teaching students some generally not immediately useful things. At the back of the book are postage stamp sized cutout flash cards and for some reason a collection of flags. Perhaps the most striking thing about this book is that there is no *Hanyu Pinyin* at all, in the entire book, and the notation that *most dictionaries do not show these accents*, on page 5 of that book.

(听说, **tīngshuō**, **hear say**) can act like a *Noun* or a *Verb Verb Completion Compound*. As a noun, it is similar to the English noun **hearsay**.

这	只	是	听说	罢了
Zhè	zhǐ	shì	tīngshuō,	bàle.
This	only	is	hearsay,	stopped.

(罢, **bà**, **stop, cease**) is combined with (了, **le**, **CRS**) forming a sentence final verb phrase (罢了, **bàle**, **stopped**) that acts like a sentence final particle. It creates a rhetoric *final statement*. Some books use the translation, *that's all*.

As a verb, (听说, **tīngshuō**, **hear say**) can be used like this.

我	听说	她	到	了
Wǒ	tīngshuō	tā	dào	le.
Me	hear say	she	arrive	
Me	hear say	she	arrived.	

(明, **míng**, **bright**) signals clarity or brightness. (说明, **shuōmíng**, **say clear, explain**) is a verb that signals clear explanation.

你	能	说明	这	件	事	吗
Nǐ	néng	shuōmíng	zhè	jiàn	shì	ma?
You	can	say clear	this	CNI	matter?	

As mentioned elsewhere in the book, *Demonstrative Pronouns* require a **CNI** between them and the *Countable Noun*. (件, **jiàn**, **CNI for matters**)

There are two common forms of *again* in Mandarin. (再, **zài**, **again**) is used in the present time or future. (又, **yòu**, **again**) makes reference to events in the past. (再说, **zàishuō**, **again say**) is a verb phrase marking spoken repetition.

师傅,	再说	一边	多少	钱
Shīfu,	**zài shuō**	**yībiān,**	**duōshao**	**qían?**
Master Worker,	again say	one side,	much little	money?
Master Worker,	again say	one time,	how much	money?

You can agonize for eternity as to how two simple words, (多, **duō**, **many, much**) and (少, **shao**, **little, few**) combine together to form (多少, **duōshao**, **much little**) and then to mean *how much*. Better yet, figure out how (边, **biān**, **a side**) came to mean *a time*. (一边, **yībiān**, **one time**) can be used in many constructions to signal *one time* or *one attempt*. E-mail me when you figure it out, I used to agonize over these issues thinking that there was some logical explanation. damaohouzi@yahoo.com

(再说, **zàishuō**, **further say**) is a *Conjunction* used to join two phrases. Words like this provide a *Speaker's Perspective*. Note that the *Hanyu Pinyin* is joined, two syllables forming one word, which is different from the format of (再说, **zài shuō**, **again say**) in which the **Pinyin** is not joined. China and Chinese people do not use **Pinyin** except while learning the language and typing on computers. Character strings are unpunctuated with no spaces. So the use and meaning of the two similar structures is determined by sentence position and what preceeds and postcedes it, as you will not be seeing any **Pinyin** in China.

我	是	加拿大	人	再说	我	喜欢	啤酒
Wǒ	shì	Jiānádà	rén,	zàishuō	wǒ	xǐhuan	píjiǔ.
Me	is	Canada	person,	again say	me	like	beer.
Me	is	Canada	person,	further say	me	like	beer.

One of the several forms of *perhaps* is (说不定, **shuōbudìng**, **perhaps**, **maybe**) using (定, **dìng**, **decide**, **certain**) in the compound.

说不定	我	也	去
Shuōbudìng	wǒ	yě	qù.
Say not certain,	me	also	go.
Perhaps	me	also	go.

(说是, **shuōshì**, **say is**) declares the speakers perception of something heard.

说是	她	有	大	屁股
Shuōshì,	tā	yǒu	dà	pìgu.
Say is,	she	you	big	ass.
Is said,	she	have	big	ass.

(说来, **shuōlái**, **said**) is a compound using (来, **lái**, **come**) as a verb completion. The meaning of *come* is not part of the meaning. Effectively, the construction forms the completed tense of the verb (说, **shuō**, **say**). There are an assortment of verbs used to complete the action of other verbs. The pattern of use is irregular and not predictable by any rules.

说来	现在	你	必须	回家
Shuōlái	xiànzài	nǐ	bìxū	huíjiā.
Said,	now	you	must	return home.

(说话, shuōhuà, to converse) combines the noun (话, huà, a talk) to create a VOC that implies a longer-in-duration talk.

每天	她们	说话	像	老婆儿	一样
Měitiān	tāmen	shuōhuà	xiàng	lǎopó'r	yīyàng.
Every day	they	converse	resemble	old woman	same.

(说, shuō, to say, to speak), (话, huà, a speech, a talk) and (语, yǔ, language, words) are good characters to practice writing and using together. The share some common character components and usage. Hopefully you have found and used the appendix at the back of the book to learn stroke order and named strokes.

(喜欢, xǐhuan, like)

(啤酒, píjiǔ, beer)

(加拿大, Jiānádà, Canada)

(会, huì, able to)

(不会, bù huì, not able to)

(多少, duōshao, much little)

(多, duō, many, much)

(少, shao, little, few)

(多少, duōshao, how many)

(师傅, shīfu, master worker)

(钱, qián, cash)

(边, biān, a side)

(一边, yībiān, one time)

(再, zài, again)

(说明, shuōmíng, say clear, explain)

(听说, tīngshuō, hear say)

(说明, shuōmíng, say clear, explain)

(明, míng, bright)

(明白, míngbai, clear, understand)

(又, yòu, again)

(定, dìng, decide)

(说不定, shuōbudìng, perhaps)

(是, shì, is)

(屁股, pìgu, buttocks, ass)

(说是, shuōshì, say is)

(文, wén, language)

(必须, bìxū, must)

(回家, huíjiā, return home)

(罢了, bàle, verb phrase indicating limitation)

(再说一边, zàishuō yībiān, again say one side / time)

(件, jiàn, CNI for matters, issues, articles, items)

(中文, Zhōngwén, Chinese language)

(现在, xiànzài, now)

(话, huà, a speech, a talk)

(说话, shuōhuà, to converse)

(说, shuō, to say, to speak)

(罢了, bàliǎo, stop)

(像, xiàng, resemble)

(老婆, lǎopó, old lady)

(一样, yīyàng, the same)

(每天, měitiān, every day)

们	Notes: Grammatical Particle (们, **men**, **grammatical particle**) (们, **men**, **pluralizing suffix**) for *Personal Pronouns* and *Person Nouns*.
men particle	

丿 亻 𠂉 仁 们

们

(们, **men**, **noun pluralizing suffix**) has very defined and limited use. The only role it plays in Mandarin grammar is to form plural forms of ***Pronouns*** and ***Personal Human Nouns***. Perhaps you have read that plural forms do not exist in Mandarin. Most limiting statements you have read about the language are not true. Why they get perpetuated, I do not know. You will get many examples of these words in this work book so I will not belabour the issue now. I will put a chapter on family members name nouns later in the book, maybe. Actually, I will put a chapter on the most immediate family members name nouns. There are dozens of identifiers. We have aunt, uncle, cousin, brother, sister, etc. Mandarin has a unique name for the position and side of the family for each relative.

Anyhow, I will pick a couple of less common ones here to explain the use.

(咱们, **zánmen**, **we**, **you and I**) took me like three years to figure out the meaning. It is often described as the ***inclusive we***. I was always thinking, like, ***we is always inclusive***. But the inclusiveness is not only the speaker and others, it is to the person being addressed. So if you are in a conversation and being addressed directly using (咱们, **zánmen**, **we**, **you and I**) the speaker is including you. Conversely, if you are addressing someone, (咱们, **zánmen**, **we**, **you and I**) includes you, the addressee and whoever else you intend.

Us white folk will never know exactly what the Chinese are thinking. If you ask them the English meaning of a Mandarin word they will tell you the example they were taught in school or use their cellphone with it's integrated dictionary. This however does not tell you which images go on in their head. One of my first rewarding words was (火车站, **huǒchēzhàn**, **fire cart stand**). I travel all over China by train. This is the best way to meet the real Chinese people and see the real China.

A Chinese person does not translate Chinese characters into English word concepts when they use a Chinese word. When they use (火车站, **huǒchēzhàn**, **fire cart stand**), what they conceptualize is exactly what the words assemble. They do not think *train station,* as they cannot. Here are the characters and component words that create (火车站, **huǒchēzhàn**, **fire cart stand**).

(火, **huǒ**, **fire**)
(车, **chē**, **vehicle**)
(站, **zhàn**, **stand**)
(火车, **huǒchē**, **fire cart, train**)
(火车站, **huǒchēzhàn**, **railway station**)
(火车站, **huǒchēzhàn**, **fire cart stand**)

The name goes back to fire and smoke belching trains. (车, **chē**, **cart**, **vehicle**) covers every vehicle with four wheels. So (火车, **huǒchē**, **fire cart**) is what the word visualizes to them.

明天	咱们	去	火车站
Míngtiān	zánmen	qù	huǒchēzhàn.
Tomorrow	we	go	fire cart stand.

Strange language, right?

你们	怎么	先	到,	了	孩子们	呢
Nǐmen	zěnme	xiān	dào	le?,	háizimen	ne.
You	how	first	arrive?,		children	?
You	how	first	arrived?,		children	?
Subject						

(呢, **ne**, **repeat question particle**) is a handy particle. It acts to repeat the entire previous question but functionally inserts the word before it for the **Subject** of the previous sentence. Sort of a lazy linquistic question repeating particle. In the above sentence, it acts to ask how the **children** first arrived. Looking back, I am not sure the sentence makes much sense but I hope you get the idea.

(呢, **ne**, **continuing verb action particle**) can also be part of a frequently bastardized grammatical construction that creates the ***Current Continuous Verb Tense***. This is a good example between formal Mandarin grammar and colloquial grammar. This also explains as to why you may read about or see (在, **zài**, **at**) before a verb. The most complete and formal construction is interesting. The verb phrase begins with (正在, **zhèngzài**, **straight at**). (正, **zhèng**, **right**, **straight**, **correct**) and (在, **zài**, **at**) compound to create this word. If you look in a dictionary, you will not see a word attributed to this compound character, rather you will see some variation of (正在, **zhèngzài**, **marks a verb phrase meaning to be in the process of**).

However, if you ask yourself as to what a native Chinese speaker reads when he sees these characters, ***straight at*** does a pretty good job of introducing a continuous verb action. Certainly I have seen much worse translations. (着, **zhe**, **indicating continuing progressive state**) is the immediate post-verb continuous activity marker. Functionally, it acts like *–ing*. But, we are not finished. Then the sentence can be finished off with (呢, **ne**, **indicating continued state or action**). In a language that is typified by simplicity in grammar, this is a construction that marks the verb action three times. So here it is in entirety.

Subject		Verb	Noun	Other Verb	
她	正在	迈着	步子	走	呢
Tā	zhèngzài	màizhe	bùzi	zǒu	ne.
She	straight at	stepping	step	going forth.	
She	is	stepping	a step	going forth.	

When I asked my wife what Chinese people, who have not studied English, compare (正在, **zhèngzài**, **straight at**) to, she said (是, **shì**, **is**). This makes absolute sense. In English, *is* marks the **Current Continuous Verb Tense** as a *Co-Verb*. So, of the 35 plus books I have on Mandarin, I have never seen this. But it works. So, you first read it here, (正在, **zhèngzài**, **is**).

So you are thinking, okay, a little complex but I can get that. But here is the catch, most of that construction is optional. In fact you will often hear the (正, **zhèng**, **straight**), the (着, **zhe**, **-ing**) and the (呢, **ne-ing**) excluded. Really, a real linguist would have problems with the previous sentence. I am not sure that you can hear something that is excluded. So, for the purests, in fact, you will often hear only the (在, **zài**, **at**) used. I always use the long form, the reason that I do that is Chinese people look shocked and say something like. *You glama velly goo de*. That alone is worth it.

(着, zhe, -ing) and (呢, ne, -ing) are often paired together without (在, zài, at) or (正在, zhèngzài, is).

她	睡着	呢
Tā	shuìzhe	ne.
She	sleeping	-ing.
She	sleeping.	

(我们, wǒmen, we)

(人们, rénmen, people)

(他们, tāmen, they)

(你们, nǐmen, you)

(人们, rénmen, people, public)

(咱们, zánmen, we, you and I)

(它们, tāmen, they)

(她们, tāmen, they)

(哥, gē, elder brother)

(哥儿们, gē'rmen, brothers, pals)

(弟, dì, younger brother)

(兄, xiōng, elder brother)

(弟兄们, dìxiongmen, brothers)

(孩子, háizi, child)

(孩子们, háizimen, children)

(姐, jiě, elder sister)

(妹, mèi, younger sister)

(姐妹们, jiěmèimen, sisters)

(步子, bùzi, a step, pace)

(迈, mài, step)

(正在, zhèngzài, straight at)

(正, zhèng, right, straight, correct)

(在, zài, at)

(呢, ne, indicating continued action)

为	Notes: Preposition
	(为, wèi, stand for, support, for, on account of, on behalf of)
	(为, wèi, for, for the sake of, in order to)
	(为, wéi, do, act, act as, be, become)
wèi	
for	

丶 ⺈ 为 为

为 为 为 为 为 为 为 为 为

为	为	为	为	为	为	为	为	为	为
wèi	wèi	wèi	wèi	wèi	wèi	wèi	wèi	wèi	wèi
for	for	for	for	for	for	for	for	for	for
为	为	为	为	为	为	为	为	为	为
wèi	wèi	wèi	wèi	wèi	wèi	wèi	wèi	wèi	wèi
for	for	for	for	for	for	for	for	for	for

为

(为, wèi, for) readily glosses as *on account of*, *on behalf of*, or *for*.

你	这样	做	为	谁
Nǐ	zhèyàng	zuò	wèi	shéi.
You	this manner	do	for	who.
You	like this	do	for	who.

(这样, zhèyàng, this manner)   (样, yàng, manner)

(这样, zhèyàng, like this)   (谁, shuí, shéi, who)

(做, zuò, do, make)   (为, wèi, for)

(样, yàng, appearance, shape, form)

(因为, yīnwèi, because) can be used for *on account of* or *because*.

他	没有	回家	是	因为	你
Tā	méiyǒu	huíjiā	shì	yīnwèi	nǐ.
He	not have	return home	is	because	you.

(因, yīn, cause)   (回家, huíjiā, return home)

(为, wèi, for)   (没, méi, not)

(因为, yīnwèi, because)   (有, yǒu, have)

(回, huí, return)   (没有, méiyǒu, not have)

(家, jiā, home)   (是, shì, is)

(因为, yīnwèi, because) is often paired with (所以, suǒyǐ, therefore), joining two phrases.

因为	天	快	黑	了	所以	我	要	走	了
Yīnwèi	tiān	kuài	hēi	le,	suǒyǐ	wǒ	yào	zǒu	le.
Because	sky	quick	black,		therefore	me	want	go forth	!

(所, suǒ, place)　　　　　　　　　(黑, hēi, black)

(以, yǐ, using)　　　　　　　　　(天, tiān, sky)

(快, kuài, fast, quick)　　　　　　(走, zǒu, go forth)

(为什么, wèishénme, for what, why)

你	为什么	不	说话
Nǐ	wèishénme	bù	shuōhuà.
You	for what	not	speak talk.
You	why	not	converse.

(为, wèi, for)　　　　　　　　　(说, shuō, speak)

(什么, shénme, what)　　　　　　(话, huà, a talk)

(为什么, wèishénme, for what, why)　　(说话, shuōhuà, converse, talk)

(为了, wèile, for) is the closest Mandarin grammar has for a generic English equivalent. It is often glossed as *for*, *for the sake of*, *in order to*.

为了	前途	而	努力
Wèile	qiántú	ér	nǔlì.
For	future	and	work hard.

(前, qián, front)

(途, tú, road)

(前途, qiántú, future)

(而, ér, and)

(努, nǔ, put forth strength)

(力, lì, force)

(努力, nǔlì, work hard)

(认为, rènwéi, to think), see below for other grammatical forms of *think*. The below sentence is glossed as *What do you think about it*?

你	认为	怎样
Nǐ	rènwéi	zěnyàng?
You	think	how?

(认, rèn, recognize, know)

(想, xiǎng, think)

(觉得, juéde, think)

(以为, yǐwéi, think)

(想想, xiǎngxiang, think)

(怎, zěn, how)

(样, yàng, appear)

(怎样, zěnyàng, how)

(以为, yǐwéi, think) is another form of *think*.

人们	以为	我	迷路	
Rénmen	yǐwéi	wǒ	mílù	le.
People	think	me	lose path.	

(迷, mí, lost)

(路, lù, path)

(迷路, mílù, lose way, lost)

(以, yǐ, use, take)

(人, rén, person)

(们, men, pluralizer)

(人们, rénmen, people)

(以为, yǐwéi, think)

(成为, chéngwéi, become, turn into)

梦想	终于	成为	现实
Mèngxiǎng	zhōngyú	chéngwéi	xiànshí.
Dream think	finish from	become do	now true.
Dream	finally	become	reality.

(梦, mèng, dream)

(想, xiǎng, think)

(梦想, mèngxiǎng, dream of)

(终, zhōng, end, finish)

(于, yú, in, at, to, from, out of, by)

(终于, zhōngyú, at last, finally)

(现, xiàn, present, current)

(现实, xiànshí, reality, actuality)

(实, shí, true, real)

(成, chéng, become, turn into)

(为, wéi, do)

(成为, chéngwéi, become, turn into)

(为, wéi, do, accomplish, be become) spoken with the second tone acts as a verb of action.

他	左右	为难
Tā	zuǒyòu	wéinán.
He	left right	become disaster.
He	repeatedly	create difficulties.

This sentence incidently was glossed as *He found himself in a bind*.

(他, tā, he)

(为, wéi, do, accomplish)

(为, wéi, be, become)

(难, nán, difficult, disaster)

(难, nán, hard, troublesome)

(左, zuǒ, left)

(右, yòu, right)

(左右, zuǒ-yòu, left right)

(左右, zuǒ-yòu, repeatedly)

(左右 zuǒyòu, control, influence)

Whereas (为难, **wéinán, create difficulties**) is an act that creates problems for the **Subject** or the **Object** person, (难为, **nánwéi, difficult to perform**) is a struggle to perform an act. Literally, the gloss is (为难, **wéinán, become difficult**) versus (难为, **nánwéi, difficult to become**).

他	觉得	很		难为情
Tā	juéde	hěn		nánwéiqíng.
He	feel	very	difficult	become emotion.
He	feel	very		embarrass.

(他, tā, he) (难为, nánwéi, difficult to become)

(觉, jué, perceive) (情, qíng, feeling, emotion)

(觉, jiào, sleep) (情, qíng, sentiment, sensibility)

(觉得, juéde, feel, think) (难为情, nánwéiqíng, ashamed)

(很, hěn, very) (难为情, nánwéiqíng, embarrassed)

I know you are thinking **wtf, the author made a mistake** for the above example. But, note the word list above. Note (觉, **jué, perceive**) and (觉, **jiào, sleep**). Here are two totally unrelated meanings for the same character.

The example below was borrowed from a source that probably borrowed it from somewhere else. I have a huge pile of grammar books and I have traced the misuse of a single English word back through three books to the source author in 1968. All the sequential authors just copied his error without checking out the meaning of a bizarre English word. The original author was a Hong Kong born Chinese. I have issues with this as phrase books and many dictionaries use examples that are entirely inaccurate. The translation given below is *Let's call it a day*. First the Mandarin sentence makes no reference to plural subjects, *Let's* in the gloss is of course *let us*, obviously plural. (就, **jiù**, **just**) marks immediacy and / or sets limits on the verb, this is not included in the translation.

今天	的	工作	就	到此为止
Jīntiān	de	gōngzuò	jiù	dàocǐwéizhǐ.
Present day	's	work make	just	arrive this become stop.
Today's		work	just	stop here.

(今, **jīn**, **the present**)

(天 **tiān**, **day**)

(今天, **jīntiān**, **present day**)

(工, **gōng**, **work**)

(作, **zuò**, **make**)

(工作, **gōngzuò**, **work**)

(就, **jiù**, **just**)

(到, **dào**, **arrive**)

(此, **cǐ**, **this**)

(为, **wéi**, **become**)

(止, **zhǐ**, **stop, halt, arrive at**)

(为止, **wéizhǐ**, **become stop**)

(为止, **wéizhǐ**, **until**)

(到此为止, **dàocǐwéizhǐ**, **stop here**)

(无为, **wúwéi**) and the Doctrine of Non-Interference

Now here is something interesting. (无为, **wúwéi**, **nothing do**) is one of the principles of Chinese society. It arises from Taosim or Daoism, whichever you prefer. Basically it is the ***I don't give a shit about your problems*** philosophy. It is interesting as to how it can be presented palatably to sound like an approach to let people and society evolve without interference. Kind of like the ***Prime Directive*** on ***Star Trek***. But I have seen both James T. Kirk and Catherine Janeway interpret the ***Prime Directive*** on the fly. However, this is why you see sheeple in China get hit with a car and the unaffected sheeple just walk by, sometimes looking, sometimes not. You can be lying on the road in a pool of blood and school girls will be snapping your picture with their omnipresent cell phones. I have even seen police standing watching brawls, they do not interfer, they just wait until it dwindles and then they safely intervene so they do not risk themselves.

Perhaps the most glaring example I saw was in Baoding, Hebei province. I stepped out of the hotel for my early morning walk and some guy is beating the living shit out of his wife. From the amount of blood, her shoes and clothing torn and lying along the sidewalk, I think it had gone on for several minutes. Although I was shocked that no one had intervened, I was more shocked that people walked right by them and did not even glance at them. Now I am Canadian, I am funny about stuff like this. I grabbed his collar and face fucked him with my fist. As I was wailing on his head, what does he say?, **But it is my wife**! I held him long enough for her to get her shoes and clothes and get on a bus.

So, later that day I called my female Chinese friend in Toronto to tell her what I had done and saw. Her response, **You must not interfer with Chinese society**! *It is the business of the husband and wife*!. That is (无为, **wúwéi, nothing do**). She was upset with me. Twice since that time I have stopped men beating their girl on the street, the next one said, "**But it is my wife**!, the third said, **But it is my girlfriend**! The fourth and last one I saw was in Chengdu, this time I did not interfer. The young man, maybe 22, grabbed his girlfriend by the head and hair and ran her into the men's washroom and smashed her head into the paper towel holder, visible from the outside, and proceded to start to beat her. Then there was a terrible commotion, I could hear the man screaming and crying like a bitch using broken English, begging his assailants to stop. There were distinct sounds of flesh on flesh. He was taking an ass kicking. Perhaps 30 seconds later my two sons emerge from the washroom dragging him with big smiles and the girl ran off to the bus stop. What does my one son say, *Dad, there are paper towel holders in the washroom and they have paper towels*. God I love Chengdu. They were coming into the big city for a weekend after spending months at a Chinese Gongfu school finessing their Japanese black belt karate skills, both of them felt that Chinese Gongfu was relatively useless.

(无, wú, nothingness, nothing, not)

(无, wú, without, not have, there is not)

(为, wéi, be, become) can be added to *Adjectives* to form *Adverbs*. In this construction (为, wéi, become) is attached to the *Adjective* for the **Hanyu Pinyin**.

大为	可贵
Dàwéi	**kěguì**.
Big become	**valuable**.
Extremely	**valuable**.

(大, dà, big, great)   (贵, guì, expensive, costly)

(可, kě, can, may, need)   (可贵, kěguì, valuable)

(为, wéi, be, become) can also be attached to *Adverbs* to act as an intensifier.

极为	可怕
Jíwéi	**kěpà**.
Extremely become	**afraid**.
Exceedingly	**afraid**.

(极, jí, extremely)   (可, kě, can)

(为, wéi, be, become)   (怕, pà, to fear)

(极为, jíwéi, extremely)   (可怕, kěpà, fearful)

Now, think of how clever a society is to make the most important virtue, not honesty, truth, kindess, compassion but taking care of your parents. **Filial Piety** is The virtue held above all else in **Confucian** ideals. The single character is (孝, **xiào**, **filial piety**). Note the character for son, (子, **zǐ**, **child**) at the bottom of this character. The top Radical is (**R#125'**, 耂, **lǎo**, **old**). This is one of the unusual situations in which there is some actual meaning in a character. As you may be learning by now there are all kinds of idioms in Chinese culture. Now what do you think of this translation? *Filial Piety is the most important of all virtues*. The book reference I used says this;

百善孝为先

Bǎi shàn xiào wéi xiān.

Filial Piety is the most important of all virtues.

百	善	孝	为	先
Bǎi	shàn	xiào	wéi	xiān.
100	kindness	filial	become	first.

(百, **bǎi**, **hundred**, **numerous**)   (为, **wéi**, **be**, **become**)

(善, **shàn**, **kindness**)   (先, **xiān**, **first**, **before**, **earlier**)

(孝, **xiào**, **filial piety**)

Now, again, nothing is clear and there are always stories and explanations to these idioms. Numbers are often used to indicate vague large amounts. 100, 1000, and 10,000 are all used to indicate vague large numbers. The expression means that of all the possible kind things that can be done, *Filial Piety* comes first. This is the basis of the social security network in China, the old age pension. Not only is it law to take care of your aged or infirm parents, it is also entrenched in their philosophical moral construct. Young adults leave their rural villages to go to the big city to find a job to send money home to their parents so that they can have a better life. Sound familiar?, probably not. Young adults in the west leave their family home and get a job to make their own life better.

So one of the more confusing things that occurred when I first went to China was young single girls of marriage age telling me that they had an older brother when I first meet them. It took me some time to figure this out. The eldest or only son is morally and legally obligated to take care of his parents. In a society crippled by the **One Child Policy** a girl that has no brother then has to care for her parents and becomes a liability for marriage as she has to take care of her parents and her husband may well have to contribute to this if not underake it in entirety. So by having a brother, it is easier for her to get married.

Here are a few more (为, **wéi**) words.

(作为, zuòwéi, deed)

(作为, zuòwéi, achievement)

(作为, zuòwéi, regard as)

(做为, zuòwéi, same as 作为)

(行为, xíngwéi, behavior)

(做, zuò, make, do)

(作, zuò, make, do)

(为首, wéishǒu, be headed by)

(为着, wèizhe, for, in order to)

(较, jiào, rather, quite, relatively)

(较为, jiàowei, rather)

(人为, rénwéi, man-made)

(这样, zhèyàng, this manner)
(这样, zhèyàng, like this)
(样, yàng, appearance, shape, form)
(样, yàng, manner)
(谁, shuí, shéi, who)
(为, wèi, for)
(因, yīn, cause)
(为, wèi, for)
(因为, yīnwèi, because)
(回, huí, return)
(家, jiā, home)
(回家, huíjiā, return home)
(没, méi, not)
(有, yǒu, have)
(没有, méiyǒu, not have)
(是, shì, is)
(所, suǒ, place)
(以, yǐ, using)
(快, kuài, fast, quick)
(黑, hēi, black)
(天, tiān, sky)
(走, zǒu, go forth)
(做, zuò, do, make)
(为什么, wèishénme, for what, why)

(为, wèi, for)
(什么, shénme, what)
(为什么, wèishénme, for what, why)
(说, shuō, speak)
(话, huà, a talk)
(说话, shuōhuà, converse, talk)
(前, qián, front)
(途, tú, road)
(前途, qiántú, future)
(而, ér, and)
(努, nǔ, put forth strength)
(力, lì, force)
(努力, nǔlì, work hard)
(认, rèn, recognize, know)
(想, xiǎng, think)
(觉得, juéde, think)
(以为, yǐwéi, think)
(想想, xiǎngxiang, think)
(怎, zěn, how)
(样, yàng, appear)
(怎样, zěnyàng, how)
(迷, mí, lost)
(路, lù, path)
(迷路, mílù, lose way, lost)

(以, yǐ, use, take)
(人, rén, person)
(们, men, pluralizer)
(人们, rénmen, people)
(以为, yǐwéi, think)
(梦, mèng, dream)
(想, xiǎng, think)
(梦想, mèngxiǎng, dream of)
(终, zhōng, end, finish)
(于, yú, in, at, to, from, out of, by)
(终于, zhōngyú, at last, finally)
(现, xiàn, present, current)
(现实, xiànshí, reality, actuality)
(实, shí, true, real)
(成, chéng, become, turn into)
(为, wéi, do)
(成为, chéngwéi, become, turn into)
(他, tā, he)
(为, wéi, do, accomplish)
(为, wéi, be, become)
(难, nán, difficult, disaster)
(难, nán, hard, troublesome)
(左, zuǒ, left)
(右, yòu, right)

(左右, zuǒ-yòu, left right)
(左右, zuǒ-yòu, repeatedly)
(左右, zuǒyòu, control, influence)
(他, tā, he)
(觉, jué, perceive)
(觉, jiào, sleep)
(觉得, juéde, feel, think)
(很, hěn, very)
(难为, nánwéi, difficult to become)
(情, qíng, feeling, emotion)
(情, qíng, sentiment, sensibility)
(难为情, nánwéiqíng, ashamed)
(难为情, nánwéiqíng, embarrassed)
(今, jīn, the present)
(天 tiān, day)
(今天, jīntiān, present day)
(工, gōng, work)
(作, zuò, make)
(工作, gōngzuò, work)
(就, jiù, just)
(到, dào, arrive)
(此, cǐ, this)
(为, wéi, become)
(止, zhǐ, stop, halt, arrive at)

(为止, wéizhǐ, become stop)

(为止, wéizhǐ, until)

(到此为止, dàocǐwéizhǐ, stop here)

(无, wú, nothingness, nothing, not)

(无, wú, without, not have)

(大, dà, big, great)

(可, kě, can, may, need)

(贵, guì, expensive, costly)

(可贵, kěguì, valuable)

(极, jí, extremely)

(为, wéi, be, become)

(极为, jíwéi, extremely)

(可, kě, can)

(怕, pà, to fear)

(可怕, kěpà, fearful)

(百, bǎi, hundred, numerous)

(善, shàn, kindness)

(孝, xiào, filial piety)

(为, wéi, be, become)

(先, xiān, first, before, earlier)

(作为, zuòwéi, deed)

(作为, zuòwéi, achievement)

(作为, zuòwéi, regard as)

(做为, zuòwéi, same as 作为)

(行为, xíngwéi, behavior)

(为首, wéishǒu, be headed by)

(为着, wèizhe, for, in order to)

(较, jiào, rather, quite, relatively)

(较为, jiàowei, rather)

(人为, rénwéi, man-made)

子

zǐ
son

Notes: Common Noun

(子, **zǐ**, **child**, **son**)

(子, **zi**, **noun suffix**)

亅 了 子

子 子 子 子 子 子 子 子 子

子	子	子	子	子	子	子	子	子	子
zǐ	zǐ	zǐ	zǐ	zǐ	zǐ	zǐ	zǐ	zǐ	zǐ
son	son	son	son	son	son	son	son	son	son
子	子	子	子	子	子	子	子	子	子
zǐ	zǐ	zǐ	zǐ	zǐ	zǐ	zǐ	zǐ	zǐ	zǐ
son	son	son	son	son	son	son	son	son	son
子	子	子	子	子	子	子	子	子	子
子	子	子	子	子	子	子	子	子	子
子	子	子	子	子	子	子	子	子	子
子	子	子	子	子	子	子	子	子	子
子	子	子	子	子	子	子	子	子	子
子	子	子	子	子	子	子	子	子	子
子	子	子	子	子	子	子	子	子	子

子

(子, **zǐ**, **child**) is a character that has many uses devoid of word meaning. In fact, the minority use is (子, **zǐ**, **child**). The most common use is to tack it onto the backside of nouns only to mark that they are nouns. As such is called a *Nominalizing Suffix*. Of the myriad word forms of child, both generic and sexed, many have (子, **zǐ**, **child**) stuck on the far side of them.

(女, **nǚ**, **female**)

(孩, **hái**, **child**)

(女孩, **nǚhái**, **girl**)

(女孩子, **nǚháizi**, **girl**)

(孩子, **háizi**, **child**)

(男, **nán**, **male**)

(男孩, **nánhái**, **son**)

(男孩子, **nánháizi**, **son**)

(小, **xiǎo**, **small**)

(小子, **xiǎozi**, **child**)

(孩子, **háizi**, **son, daughter**)

(儿子, **érzi**, **son**)

(嗣, **sì**, **heir**)

(子嗣, **zǐsì**, **male heir**)

(息, **xī**, **breath**)

(子息, **zǐxī**, **son**)

(孺, **rú**, **child**)

(孺子, **rúzǐ**, **child**)

(伢, **yá**, **child**)

(伢子, **yázi**, **child**)

(稚, **zhì**, **young**)

(稚子, **zhìzi**, **child**)

(弟, **dì**, **brother**)

(子弟, **zǐdì**, **child**)

(女, **nǚ**, **female**)

(子女, **zǐnǚ**, **daughter**)

Nouns, are the most predictable parts of Mandarin grammar. As such, you do not need to be a rocket scientist to place them in a sentence. If you want them to be the *Topic* of the sentence, you can put them in the *Sentence Initial* position. This allows a *Topic – Comment* sentence structure. It is additionally dramatic to add a rhetoric pause after the *Topic Noun*.

孩子们	差不多	老是	淘气
Háizimen,	chàbuduō	lǎoshi	táoqì.
Children	differ not much	old is	naughty energy.
Children	almost	always	naughty.
Topic	Comment		

(孩子, háizi, child) (老, lǎo, old)

(孩子们, háizimen, children) (是, shi, is)

(差, chà, differ) (老是, lǎoshi, always)

(不, bu, not) (淘, táo, naughty)

(多, duō, much) (气, qì, vital energy)

(差不多, chàbuduō, almost)

2. (样子, yàngzi, appearance) is often glossed as (样子, yàngzi, manner). In Chinese society your social appearance and behaviour is judged as your manner.

我	不	喜欢	他	的	那个	样子
Wǒ	bù	xǐhuan	tā	de	nàge	yàngzi.
Me	not	like	his		that	appearance.

(样, yàng, appearance) (喜欢, xǐhuan, like)

(喜, xǐ, like) (那, nà, that)

(欢, huān, happy) (样子, yàngzi, appearance)

看	样子	天	要	下雨
Kàn	yàngzi	tiān	yào	xiàyǔ.
Look at	appearance	sky	want	down rain.

(看, kàn, look at)   (下, xià, down)

(天, tiān, sky)   (雨, yǔ, rain)

(要, yào, want)   (下雨, xiàyǔ, down rain)

3.   Here is a stereotype of us (鬼子, guǐzi, foreign devil).

那	位	鬼子	有	大	肚子	巨大	鼻子	小	脑子
Nà	wèi	guǐzi	yǒu	dà	dùzi	jùdà	bízi	xiǎo	nǎozi.
That		devil	have	big	belly	huge	nose	small	brain.

(那, nà, that)   (肚子, dùzi, belly)

(位, wèi, CNI person)   (巨, jù, huge)

(鬼, guǐ, ghost)   (巨大, jùdà, huge)

(鬼子, guǐzi, foreign devil)   (鼻子, bízi, nose)

(有, yǒu, have)   (小, xiǎo, small)

(大, dà, big)   (脑子, nǎozi, brain)

4.   (名字, míngzi, name)

我	的	名字	叫	大	毛	猴子
Wǒ	de	míngzi	jiào	Dà	Máo	Hóuzi.
Me		name	call	Big	Hairy	Monkey.

(名子, míngzi, name)   (毛, máo, hair)

(叫, jiào, call)   (猴子, hóuzi, monkey)

5. (子, zǐ, **nominalizing suffix**) has no known pattern of use but is common. Here are four uses in one sentence. Slapping it onto the farside of a noun identifies it as a noun. Although this may sound pointless, it is relevant in spoken Mandarin but not necessary in **Hanzi**. As written, the characters without (子, zǐ) stand alone in identical meaning. Spoken, with (子, zǐ), it adds phonetic discrimination. This is relevant in a language that has only 409 distinct sounds times the number of tones for each sound. Strictly, it helps the listener get a closer approximation to the correct word.

走进	院子	房子	里面	桌子	上边	有	椅子
Zǒujìn	yuànzi,	fángzi	lǐmiàn,	zhuōzi	shàngbian	yǒu	yǐzi.
Enter	courtyard,	house	inside,	table	upon	have	chair.

(走进, zǒujìn, walk into) (桌子, zhuōzi, table)

(院子, yuànzi, courtyard) (上边, shàngbian, top)

(房子, fángzi, house) (有, yǒu, have)

(里面, lǐmiàn, inside) (椅子, yǐzi, chair)

他	弄	的	我	的	日子	不	好过
Tā	nòng	de	wǒ	de	rìzi	bù	hǎoguò.
He	make		my		life	not	easy.

(日, rì, sun, day) (好过, hǎoguò, easy)

(日子, rìzi, days, life) (弄, nòng, make, do)

6. (仔细, 子细, zǐxì, **careful, attentive**) has two character formulations. 仔细 is the more common compilation. (仔, zǐ,) is a character that represents the young of

domestic animals. You can see that it plays no role in the meaning of the character word. The below phrase glosses as ***think carefully***. (想想, xiǎngxiang, think) follows the rule of character duplication words having neutral tone for the second character phonetic.

子细　想想
Zǐxì　xiǎngxiang.
Careful　think.

(细, xì, careful)　　　　　　　　　(仔细, 子细, zǐxì, careful, attentive)

(仔, zǐ, domestic animal offspring)　(想想, xiǎngxiang, think)

Here are some more common (子, zǐ, **nominalizing suffix**) words.

(身子, shēnzi, body)　　　　　　　(小伙子, xiǎohuǒzi, young fellow)

(电子, diànzǐ, electronic)　　　　　(影子, yǐngzi, shadow)

(村子, cūnzi, village)　　　　　　(绳子, shéngzi, rope)

(叶子, yèzi, leaf)　　　　　　　　(虫子, chóngzi, insect)

(帽子, màozi, hat)　　　　　　　　(胡子, húzi, beard)

(猴子, hóuzi, monkey)　　　　　　(种子, zhǒngzi, seed)

(脖子, bózi, neck)　　　　　　　　(铺子, pùzi, shop, store)

(老头子, lǎotóuzi, old codger)　　(屋子, wūzi, room)

(一阵子, yīzhènzi, a burst of anger)　(院子, yuànzi, courtyard)

(子细, zǐxì, careful, attentive)　　(上边, shàngbian, top)

(一下子 yīxiàzi, one fell swoop)

7. Now here is something interesting. (子, **zǐ, first of the 12 Earthly Branches**) is an ancient method of reckoning time using astrological reference. Jupiter has a 11.86 year astrological orbit cycle. Somehow the Chinese rounded this off to 12 years and made it the basis of their calendar, 24 hour clock, seasons, months, directions, and zodiac like horoscope. The Chinese call Jupiter, from (岁, **suì, years of age**) and (星, **xīng, star**) forming (岁星, **Suìxīng, Year Star**). The twelve (地支, *dìzhī*, **earth branch**) are often referred to as simply the twelve branches.
(十二支, *shíèrzhī*, **twelve branch**)

The clock time was broken into 12 two hour cycles. When a time branch is used for a two hour interval in marks the entire two hour interval. (午, **wǔ, noon**) is the seventh branch and marks the time interval 11 a.m. to 1 p.m.. When used as an exact time, the middle of the interval is the marked time.

	Branch	Chinese	Zodiac	Direction	Season	Month	Double Hour
1	子	zǐ	Rat	0° N	winter	Month 11	11pm to 1am
2	丑	chǒu	Ox	30°	winter	Month 12	1am to 3am
3	寅	yín	Tiger	60°		Month 1	3am to 5am
4	卯	mǎo	Rabbit	90°E	spring	Month 2	5am to 7am
5	辰	chén	Dragon	120°		Month 3	7am to 9 am
6	巳	sì	Snake	150°		Month 4	9am to 11am
7	午	wǔ	Horse	180° S	summer	Month 5	11am to 1pm
8	未	wèi	Sheep	210°		Month 6	1pm to 3pm
9	申	shēn	Monkey	240°		Month 7	3pm to 5pm
10	酉	yǒu	Rooster	270° W	autumn	Month 8	5pm to 7pm
11	戌	xū	Dog	300°		Month 9	7pm to 9pm
12	亥	hài	Pig	330°	winter	Month 10	9pm to 11pm

(地, *dì*, **earth**)

(支, *zhī*, **branch**)

(地支, *dìzhī*, **earth branch**)

(岁, *suì*, **age**)

(星, *xīng*, **star**)

(岁星, *Suìxīng*, **Year Star**)

(十二, *shí'èr*, **twelve**)

(十二支, *shí'èrzhī*, **twelve branch**)

(中, *zhōng*, **middle**)

(午, *wǔ*, **noon**)

(中午, *zhōngwǔ*, **noon**)

Directions

The compass directions are broken into twelve additional divisions placing South at the top. There are also names for the four cardinal directions, (北 *běi*, **north**), (东, *dōng*, **east**), (南, *nán*, **south**), and (西, *xī*, **west**).

Chinese sailors, astronomers and astrologers preferred using the twelve directions of the *Earthly Branches*. This is somewhat similar to the modern-day practice of English speaking pilots using clock directions. Since twelve points were not accurate enough for sailing, twelve midpoints were added. Rather than combining two adjacent direction names, they assigned new names as follows.

For the four diagonal directions appropriate trigrams from the **I Ching** were used.

http://en.wikipedia.org/wiki/List_of_hexagrams_of_the_I_Ching

For the rest, the **Heavenly Stems** were used. I have no idea what these are but here is a link.

http://en.wikipedia.org/wiki/Celestial_stem

Please don't think I know anything about this, I am cutting and pasting from Wikipedia. This is just filler so that I can get the following table on this page without breaking it up.

Table of 24 Directions:

	Character	Chinese name	Direction
1	子	zǐ	0° (north)
2	癸	guǐ	15°
3	丑	chǒu	30°
4	艮	gèn	45° (northeast)
5	寅	yín	60°
6	甲	jiǎ	75°
7	卯	mǎo	90° (east)
8	乙	yǐ	105°
9	辰	chén	120°
10	巽	xùn	135° (southeast)
11	巳	sì	150°
12	丙	bǐng	165°
13	午	wǔ	180° (south)
14	丁	dīng	195°
15	未	wèi	210°
16	坤	kūn	225° (southwest)
17	申	shēn	240°
18	庚	gēng	255°
19	酉	yǒu	270° (west)
20	辛	xīn	285°
21	戌	xū	300°
22	乾	qián	315° (northwest)
23	亥	hài	330°
24	壬	rén	345°

The ten *Celestial* or *Heavenly Stems* (天干, tiāngān, Heaven Stem) are the elements of an ancient Chinese cyclic character numeral system. They were used for dates as early as the Shang Dynasty, and are now used with the twelve *Earthly Branches* in the Sexagenary cycle. They are associated with the concepts of **Yin** and **Yang** and the *Five Elements*.

	Celestial Stem	Hanyu Pinyin	Yin and Yang 阴阳	Wu Xing 五行	*Wu xing* correlations
1	甲	jiǎ	阳 yang	木 wood	東 East
2	乙	yǐ	阴 yin		
3	丙	bǐng	阳 yang	火 fire	南 South
4	丁	dīng	阴 yin		
5	戊	wù	阳 yang	土 earth	中 Middle
6	己	jǐ	阴 yin		
7	庚	gēng	阳 yang	金 metal	西 West
8	辛	xīn	阴 yin		
9	壬	rén	阳 yang	水 water	北 North
10	癸	guǐ	阴 yin		

Origins

The Shang people believed that there were ten suns, each of which appeared in order in a ten-day cycle (旬, xún). The *Heavenly Stems* were the names of the ten suns, which may have designated world ages. They were found in the given names of the kings of the Shang dynasty. Some historians think the ruling class of the Shang had ten clans, but it is not clear whether their society reflected the myth or vice versa. The associations with *Yin-Yang* and the *Five Elements* developed later, after the collapse of the Shang Dynasty. ***1766 BC to 1122 BC***

The literal meaning of the characters was roughly as follows.

Celestial Stem	Meaning	
	Original	Modern
甲	shell	helmet, armor, one, words related to beetles, crustaceans, methanol, fingernails, toenails
乙	fishguts	two, twist, words related to ethanol
丙	fishtail	bright, fire, fishtail (rare)
丁	nail	male adult, robust, T-shaped, to strike, a surname
戊	lance	(not used)
己	threads on a loom?	self, already, past
庚	evening star	age of person
辛	to offend superiors	bitter, piquant, toilsome
壬	burden, porter	to shoulder, to trust with office
癸	both feet	(not used)

Here are the Wikipedia references for whatever they are worth. Whether or not they are reliable is of minor importance as this stuff is of mythologic value only. Surely you do not believe in this crap?

http://en.wikipedia.org/wiki/List_of_hexagrams_of_the_I_Ching

http://en.wikipedia.org/wiki/Shang_Dynasty

http://en.wikipedia.org/wiki/Wu_Xing

http://en.wikipedia.org/wiki/Celestial_stem

http://en.wikipedia.org/wiki/Earthly_Branches

http://en.wikipedia.org/wiki/Yin_yang

(地, dì, earth)
(支, zhī, branch)
(地支, dìzhī, earth branch)
(岁, suì, age)
(星, xīng, star)
(岁星, Suìxīng, Year Star)
(十二, shíèr, twelve)
(十二支, shíèrzhī, twelve branch)
(中, zhōng, middle)
(午, wǔ, noon)
(中午, zhōngwǔ, noon)
(身子, shēnzi, body)
(电子, diànzǐ, electronic)
(村子, cūnzi, village)
(叶子, yèzi, leaf)
(帽子, màozi, hat)
(猴子, hóuzi, monkey)
(脖子, bózi, neck)
(老头子, lǎotóuzi, old codger)
(一阵子, yīzhènzi, a burst of anger)
(子细, zǐxì, careful, attentive)
(一下子 yīxiàzi, one fell swoop)
(小伙子, xiǎohuǒzi, young fellow)
(影子, yǐngzi, shadow)

(绳子, shéngzi, rope)
(虫子, chóngzi, insect)
(胡子, húzi, beard)
(种子, zhǒngzi, seed)
(铺子, pùzi, shop, store)
(屋子, wūzi, room)
(院子, yuànzi, courtyard)
(上边, shàngbian, top)
(细, xì, careful)
(仔, zǐ, domestic animal offspring)
(仔细, 子细, zǐxì, careful, attentive)
(想想, xiǎngxiang, think)
(日, rì, sun, day)
(日子, rìzi, days, life)
(好过, hǎoguò, easy)
(弄, nòng, make, do)
(走进, zǒujìn, walk into)
(院子, yuànzi, courtyard)
(房子, fángzi, house)
(里面, lǐmiàn, inside)
(桌子, zhuōzi, table)
(上边, shàngbian, top)
(有, yǒu, have)
(椅子, yǐzi, chair)

283

(名子, míngzi, name)
(叫, jiào, call)
(毛, máo, hair)
(猴子, hóuzi, monkey)
(那, nà, that)
(位, wèi, CNI person)
(鬼, guǐ, ghost)
(鬼子, guǐzi, foreign devil)
(有, yǒu, have)
(大, dà, big)
(肚子, dùzi, belly)
(巨, jù, huge)
(巨大, jùdà, huge)
(鼻子, bízi, nose)
(小, xiǎo, small)
(脑子, nǎozi, brain)
(看, kàn, look at)
(天, tiān, sky)
(要, yào, want)
(下, xià, down)
(雨, yǔ, rain)
(下雨, xiàyǔ, down rain)
(样, yàng, appearance)
(喜, xǐ, like)

(欢, huān, happy)
(喜欢, xǐhuan, like)
(那, nà, that)
(样子, yàngzi, appearance)
(孩子, háizi, child)
(孩子们, háizimen, children)
(差, chà, differ)
(不, bu, not)
(多, duō, much)
(差不多, chàbuduō, almost)
(老, lǎo, old)
(是, shi, is)
(老是, lǎoshi, always)
(淘, táo, naughty)
(气, qì, vital energy)
(女, nǔ, female)
(孩, hái, child)
(女孩, nǔhái, girl)
(女孩子, nǔháizi, girl)
(孩子, háizi, child)
(男, nán, male)
(男孩, nánhái, son)
(男孩子, nánháizi, son)
(小, xiǎo, small)

(小子, xiǎozi, child)

(孩子, háizi, son, daughter)

(儿子, érzi, son)

(嗣, sì, heir)

(子嗣, zǐsì, male heir)

(息, xī, breath)

(子息, zǐxī, son)

(孺, rú, child)

(孺子, rúzǐ, child)

(伢, yá, child)

(伢子, yázi, child)

(稚, zhì, young)

(稚子, zhìzi, child)

(弟, dì, brother)

(子弟, zǐdì, child)

(女, nǚ, female)

(子女, zǐnǚ, daughter)

和	Notes: Conjunction (和, **hé**, and) (和, **hé**, together, with, union, harmony) (和, **hé**, gentle, mild, kind, peace)
hé	
and	

丿 二 千 千 禾 和 和 和

和 和 和 和 和 和 和 和

和	和	和	和	和	和	和	和	和	和
hé	hé	hé	hé	hé	hé	hé	hé	hé	hé
and	and	and	and	and	and	and	and	and	and
和	和	和	和	和	和	和	和	和	和
hé	hé	hé	hé	hé	hé	hé	hé	hé	hé
and	and	and	and	and	and	and	and	and	and
和	和	和	和	和	和	和	和	和	和
和	和	和	和	和	和	和	和	和	和
和	和	和	和	和	和	和	和	和	和
和	和	和	和	和	和	和	和	和	和
和	和	和	和	和	和	和	和	和	和
和	和	和	和	和	和	和	和	和	和
和	和	和	和	和	和	和	和	和	和

和

(和, hé, and) primarily serves as a conjunction equivalent to the English conjunction *and*. It is primarily used for joining *Nouns* and *Pronouns*.

我	和	你	坐	火车	去	昆明
Wǒ	hé	nǐ	zuò	huǒchē	qù	Kūnmíng.
Me	and	you	sit	fire cart	go	Kunming.
Me	and	you	ride	train	go to	Kunming.

(和, hé, and) (火车, huǒchē, train)

(坐, zuò, sit) (去, qù, go)

(火, huǒ, fire) (明, míng, clear)

(车, chē, cart) (昆明, Kūnmíng, Kunming)

2. (和平, hépíng, peace)

我们	都	爱好	和平
Wǒmen	dōu	àihào	hépíng.
We	all	love	peace.

(我, wǒ, me) (好, hào, good)

(们, men, pluralizing suffix) (爱好, àihào, love)

(我们, wǒmen, we) (和, hé, harmonious)

(都, dōu, all) (平, píng, level)

(爱, ài, love) (和平, hépíng, peace)

大	冷	的	天	快	进	屋	来	暖和
Dà	lěng	de	tiān,	kuài	jìn	wū	lái	nuǎnhuo.
Big	cold		day,	quick	enter	house	come	warm up.

(大, dà, big) (进, jìn, enter)

(冷, lěng, cold) (屋, wū, house)

(的, de, subordination particle) (来, lái, come

(天, tiān, day) (暖, nuǎn, warm)

(快, kuài, fast) (暖和, nuǎnhuo, warm up)

3. (温和, wēnhé, mild)

他	的	父亲	说话	温和
Tā	de	fùqin	shuōhuà	wēnhé.
His		father	talk	mild.

(他, tā, he) (说, shuō, speak)

(的, de, possessive marker) (话, huà, talk)

(父, fù, father) (说话, shuōhuà, talk)

(亲, qīn, relatives) (温, wēn, warm)

(父亲, fùqin, father) (温和, wēnhé, mild)

4. (柔和, róuhé, gentle, mild)

我	喜欢	比较	柔和	的	音乐
Wǒ	xǐhuan	bǐjiào	róuhé	de	yīnyuè.
Me	like	relative	gentle		music.

(我, wǒ, me)

(喜, xǐ, like)

(欢, huān, happy)

(喜欢, xǐhuan, like)

(比, compared to)

(较, jiào, relatively)

(比较, bǐjiào, relatively)

(柔, róu, soft, supple)

(和, hé, harmonious)

(音, yīn, sound)

(乐, yuè, music)

(音乐, yīnyuè, music)

5. (和蔼, hé'ǎi, kindly, affable, amiable)

和蔼	的	笑容
Hé'ǎi	de	xiàoróng.
Kindly		smile.

(和, hé, harmonious)

(蔼, ǎi, amiable)

(和蔼, hé'ǎi, kindly)

(笑, xiào, smile, laugh)

(容, róng, contain)

(笑容, xiàoróng, smiling expression)

6. (和气, héqi, friendship)

别	伤	和气
Bié	shāngle	héqi.
Do not	wound	friendship.

(和气, héqi, friendship)

(伤, shāng, injure, wound)

(别, bié, do not)

(气, qì, vital energy)

7. (附和, fùhè, echo, chime in with)

他	就	会	一味	附和	老板
Tā	jiù	huì	yīwèi	fùhè	lǎobǎn.
He	just	able to	one flavour	echo	old board.
He	just	able to	blindly	echo	boss.

(他, tā, he)

(就, jiù, just)

(会, huì, meet)

(一, yī, one)

(味, wèi, flavour)

(附, fù, agree)

(老, lǎo, old)

(板, bǎn, board)

(老板, lǎobǎn, boss)

(一味, yīwèi, one flavour, blindly)

8. (缓和, huǎnhé, relax)

他	试图	缓和	紧张	的	气氛
Tā	shìtú	huǎnhé	jǐnzhāng	de	qìfēn.
He	try	relax	nervous		atmosphere.

(试, shì, try)

(图, tú, picture)

(试图, shìtú, attempt, try)

(缓, huǎn, slow)

(和, hé, harmonious)

(共和, gònghé, republic)

(缓和, huǎnhé, relax)

(紧张, jǐnzhāng, nervous)

(气, qì, vital energy)

(氛, fēn, ambience)

(气氛, qìfēn, atmosphere)

(和尚, héshang, Buddhist monk)

(乐乐和和, lèlehēhē, joyous, happy)

(傻傻和和, shǎshǎhuōhuō, silly)

(和平, hépíng, peace)

(和, hè, join in singing)

(和, huò, mix with water)

(和, hú, complete a set in mahjong)

(和, huó, knead)

(和, hē,)

(和, huō,)

(和蔼, hé'ǎi, kindly)

(和约, héyuē, peace treaty)

(媾和, gòuhé, make peace)

(和会, héhuì, peace conference)

(调和, tiáohé, mediate, reconcile)

(和, hé, and)

(坐, zuò, sit)

(火, huǒ, fire)

(车, chē, cart)

(火车, huǒchē, train)

(去, qù, go)

(明, míng, clear)

(昆明, Kūnmíng, Kunming)

(我, wǒ, me)

(们, men, pluralizing suffix)

(我们, wǒmen, we)

(都, dōu, all)

(爱, ài, love)

(好, hào, good)

(爱好, àihào, love)

(和, hé, harmonious)

(平, píng, level)

(和平, hépíng, peace)

(大, dà, big)

(冷, lěng, cold)

(的, de, subordination particle)

(天, tiān, day)

(快, kuài, fast)

(进, jìn, enter)

(屋, wū, house)

(来, lái, come

(暖, nuǎn, warm)

(暖和, nuǎnhuo, warm up)

(他, tā, he)

(的, de, possessive marker)

(父, fù, father)

(亲, qīn, relatives)

(父亲, fùqin, father)

(说, shuō, speak)

(话, huà, talk)
(说话, shuōhuà, talk)
(温, wēn, warm)
(温和, wēnhé, mild)
(我, wǒ, me)
(喜, xǐ, like)
(欢, huān, happy)
(喜欢, xǐhuan, like)
(比, compared to)
(较, jiào, relatively)
(比较, bǐjiào, relatively)
(柔, róu, soft, supple)
(和, hé, harmonious)
(音, yīn, sound)
(乐, yuè, music)
(音乐, yīnyuè, music)
(和, hé, harmonious)
(蔼, ǎi, amiable)
(和蔼, hé'ǎi, kindly)
(笑, xiào, smile, laugh)
(容, róng, contain)
(笑容, xiàoróng, smiling expression)

(和气, héqi, friendship)
(伤, shāng, injure, wound)
(别, bié, do not)
(气, qì, vital energy)
(他, tā, he)
(就, jiù, just)
(会, huì, meet)
(一, yī, one)
(味, wèi, flavour)
(附, fù, agree)
(老, lǎo, old)
(板, bǎn, board)
(老板, lǎobǎn, boss)
(一味, yīwèi, one flavour, blindly)
(试, shì, try)
(图, tú, picture)
(试图, shìtú, attempt, try)
(缓, huǎn, slow)
(和, hé, harmonious)
(缓和, huǎnhé, relax)
(紧张, jǐnzhāng, nervous)

你

nǐ
you

Notes: Second Person Singular Pronoun

(你, **nǐ**, you)

(你, **nǐ**, you) is the *Second Personal Singular Pronoun you* and is used the same as the English *you*.

丿 亻 亻 伫 伫 你 你

你

1. (你, nǐ, you) is the third **Personal Pronoun** in this book and it is manipulated just like (他, tā, he) and (我, wǒ, me / I). Grammatically, it is a **Second Person Pronoun** and functions exactly like its English equivalent. To make the plural collective *you* simply add (们, **men, pluralizing suffix**), which is used to make plural **Personal Nouns** and **Pronouns**.

你	干	你	的	我	干	我	的
Nǐ	gàn	nǐ	de,	wǒ	gàn	wǒ	de.
You	work	your,		me	work	mine.	

The gloss for this sentence was *You work in your way and I'll work in mine*.

2. (你们, nǐmen, you) *plural*

你们	不	喜欢	这个	吗
Nǐmen	bù	xǐhuan	zhèige	ma.
You	not	like	this one	?

3. To mark possessive forms of **Personal Nouns** and **Pronouns** (的, de, **possessive particle**) follows the character. (你的, nǐ de, your)

你的	老婆,	有	大	屁股	没有	牙齿
Nǐ de	lǎopo	yǒu	dà	pìgu	méiyǒu	yáchǐ.
Your	wife	have	big	ass	not have	teeth.

(老, lǎo, old)   (婆, pó, old woman)

(老婆, lǎopo, wife)

(没有, méiyǒu, not have)

(没, méi, not)

(大, dà, big)

(牙, yá, tooth)

(牙齿, yáchǐ, tooth)

(齿, chǐ, tooth)

(屁, pì, fart)

(股, gǔ, thigh)

(屁股, pìgu, buttocks)

4. (你们的, nǐmen de, your) *plural*

你	要	用	你们的	车	吗
Nǐ	yào	yòng	nǐmen de	chē	ma.
You	want	use	your	vehicle	?

(自, zì, self) and (己, jǐ, oneself) are combined to form (自己, zìjǐ, oneself). This is an example of **A+B=AB**. Characters are not always combined logically to make a word that is a product of the meaning of each individual character / word. Often when the combination is based on two words that have similar meaning, the second syllable is spoken in the neutral tone. Apparently not true in this case.

5. (你自己, nǐzìjǐ, you self)

这	件	事儿	你自己	能	做	好
Zhè	jiàn	shì'r	nǐzìjǐ	néng	zuò	hǎo.
This	CNI	matter	yourself	can	make	good.

(这, zhè, this)

(件, jiàn, item)

(事儿, shì'r, issue, matter)

(能, néng, can)

(做, zuò, do, make)

(好, hǎo, good)

6. I have touched on phonetic loans in which English sounding words are created to give Mandarin words that did not exist in the traditional lexicon. (你, nǐ, you) is the adopted phonetic to create words that have a *knee* sound. (迷, mí, to be lost) is combined with (你, nǐ, you) to form (迷你, mínǐ, mini) meaning small. Here are some of the phonetic loan words.

(迷你裙, mínǐqún, miniskirt) (电, diàn, electric)

(电脑, diànnǎo, computer) (脑, nǎo, brain)

(公, gōng, public) (电脑, diànnǎo, computer)

(园, yuán, garden) (裙, qún, skirt)

(公园, gōngyuán, park) (裙子, qúnzi, skirt)

(迷你电脑, mínǐ diànnǎo, minicomputer)

(迷你公园, mínǐ gōngyuán, minipark)

7. Idioms, metaphors, **Chengyu**, really, I think are to be avoided if you are just learning Mandarin. Mandarin is a language with thousands of idiotic idioms. The usual word to collectivize them is (成语, chéngyǔ, idiom). Many of them are four characters and four words. Remember that it is possible to have four characters making one word. Many of them have a story entrenched in history and the words out of context can appear meaningless. Worse, there is a website with over 30,000 (成语, chéngyǔ, idiom). The literal translation is;
(成语, chéngyǔ, become language).

(成, chéng, become) (成语, chéngyǔ, idiom)

(语, yǔ, language)

(成语, **chéngyǔ**, **idiom**) are used in Classical Chinese, a literary form used in the written language from antiquity until 1919, and are still commonly used in Vernacular writing today. Classical Chinese can be compared to the way Latin was used in the Western world in science until recently. According to the most stringent definition, there are about 5,000 (成语, **chéngyǔ**, **idiom**) in Mandarin, though some dictionaries list over 20,000.

(成语, **chéngyǔ**, **idiom**) are usually derived from ancient literature. The meaning of a (成语, **chéngyǔ**, **idiom**) usually surpasses the sum of the meanings carried by the individual characters. (成语, **chéngyǔ**, **idiom**) are often linked with a myth, story or historical fact from which they were derived. As such, (成语, **chéngyǔ**, **idiom**) do not follow the usual grammatical structure and syntax of the modern Mandarin spoken language, and are instead highly compact and novel.

(成语, **chéngyǔ**, **idiom**) in isolation are often unintelligible to readers of modern Chinese, and when students in China learn (成语, **chéngyǔ**, **idiom**) in school as part of the Classical curriculum, they also need to study the context from which the idiom was born. Often the four characters reflect the moral behind the story rather than the story itself. Here is a typical example.

(**破釜沉舟**, **pò fǔ chén zhōu**, **smash cauldron sink boat**)

The idiom is based on a historical account where ***General Xiang Yu*** ordered his troops to destroy all cooking utensils and boats after crossing a river into the enemy's territory. He won the battle because of this ***no-retreat*** policy. The phrase is used when one succeeds by pushing on to victory and creating no retreat. The English idiom *burning the bridge* would apply.

(破, pò, smash)   (沉, chén, to sink)

(釜, fǔ, cauldron)   (舟, zhōu, boat)

Another example is; (瓜田李下, guātián lǐxià, melon field plums below)

This idiom has a deeper meaning that implies suspicious situations. It is derived from a poem (君子行, jūnzǐ xíng) from the **Han Dynasty**. The poem contains two phrases;

瓜田	不	納	履
Gūatián	bú	nà	lǚ.
Melon field	not	sew	shoes.

李	下	不	整	冠
Lǐ	xià	bù	zhěng	guān.
Plum	under	not	neaten	hat.

So this roughly translates as; *don't repair your shoes in the melon field, don't tidy your hat under the plum trees*. This makes sense right? You are stuffing melons up your pant leg while faking sewing your shoes and neatening your hat while stuffing plums under it.

This idiom is a warning to avoid suspicion of stealing. The literal meaning of the idiom is impossible to understand without the background knowledge of the origin of the phrase. This becomes (瓜田李下, **guātián lǐxià**, **melon field plums below**). Ah yes, the inscrutable Chinese. Three pages to explain something that I am encouraging you not to study.

(瓜, **guā**, **melon**)

(田, **tián**, **field**)

(不, **bù**, **not**)

(納, **nà**, **sew**)

(履, **lǚ**, **shoes**)

(李, **lǐ**, **plum**)

(下, **xià**, **under**)

(下, **xià**, **under**)

(整, **zhěng**, **neaten**)

(冠, **guān**, **hat**)

(君子, **jūnzǐ**, **gentleman**)

(行, **xíng**, **walk**)

Ah, so where was this going, right, I have pretty well run out of (你, **nǐ**, **you**) words. So here are a few four character words that are a story unto themselves. These are in fact one word composed of four characters. Please remember this as I have split them up for ease of analysis.

你死我活

Nǐsǐwǒhuó

你	死	我	活
Nǐ	sǐ	wǒ	huó.
You	die	me	alive.

(死, **sǐ**, **die**)

(活, **huó**, **live**)

The meaning of this idiom is a ***fight to the death***. I guess this is what you yell out when you bust out some kick ass gongfu and strike up a **Praying Mantis Stance**.

You are probably wondering what to do with three third tones in one word that occur before a second tone. The rule is that the first two third tones convert to second tones and the third third tone is a fourth tone. So in other words, no third tones. Now if you want to write a letter to an idiot that tries to teach tone by assigning colours to them, write to;

Nathan Dummit,
Columbia Prepatory School
5 West 93rd Street
New York, New York
U.S.A.
10025

This guy wrote one of the most idiotic books on learning Chinese character writing. He assigns colours to each character so that rather than learn just the tone he wants you to learn a colour too. This system does not work as you can see, three of the four tones in this word morph to other tones, or in his world, the colours change.

Here is another one;

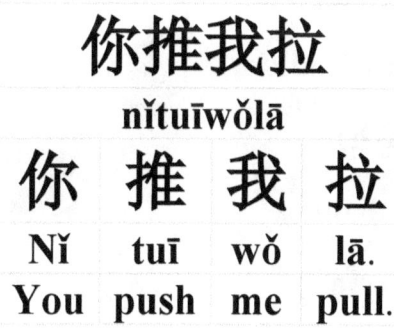

(推, tuī, push)　　　　　　　　　　　(拉, lā, pull)

If you can find a translation and a story e-mail me at **damaohouzi@yahoo.ca** and let me know. I could not find the originating story, if there is one, for the above.

(成, chéng, become)

(语, yǔ, language)

(成语, chéngyǔ, idiom)

(拉, lā, pull)

(你, nǐ, you)

(他, tā, he)

(我, wǒ, me / I)

(们, men, pluralizing suffix)

(你们, nǐmen, you) *plural*

(的, de, possessive particle)

(你的, nǐ de, your)

(老, lǎo, old)

(婆, pó, old woman)

(老婆, lǎopo, wife)

(没有, méiyǒu, not have)

(没, méi, not)

(大, dà, big)

(牙, yá, tooth)

(牙齿, yáchǐ, tooth)

(齿, chǐ, tooth)

(屁, pì, fart)

(股, gǔ, thigh)

(屁股, pìgu, buttocks)

(你们的, nǐmen de, your) *plural*

(你自己, nǐzìjǐ, you self)

(自, zì, self)

(己, jǐ, oneself)

(自己, zìjǐ, oneself)

(迷你裙, mínǐqún, miniskirt)

(电脑, diànnǎo, computer)

(公, gōng, public)

(园, yuán, garden)

(公园, gōngyuán, park)

(电, diàn, electric)

(脑, nǎo, brain)

(电脑, diànnǎo, computer)

(裙, qún, skirt)

(裙子, qúnzi, skirt)

(成, chéng, become)

(语, yǔ, language)

(成语, chéngyǔ, idiom)

(破, pò, smash)

(釜, fǔ, cauldron)

(沉, chén, to sink)

(舟, zhōu, boat)

(瓜, guā, melon)

(田, tián, field)

(不, bù, not)

(納, nà, sew)　　　　　　　　　　　(納, nà, sew)

(履, lǚ, shoes)　　　　　　　　　　(履, lǚ, shoes)

(李, lǐ, plum)　　　　　　　　　　 (李, lǐ, plum)

(下, xià, under)　　　　　　　　　 (下, xià, under)

(下, xià, under)　　　　　　　　　 (下, xià, under)

(整, zhěng, neaten)　　　　　　　 (整, zhěng, neaten)

(冠, guān, hat)　　　　　　　　　 (冠, guān, hat)

(君子, jūnzǐ, gentleman)　　　　　 (君子, jūnzǐ, gentleman)

(行, xíng, walk)　　　　　　　　　 (行, xíng, walk)

(破, pò, smash)　　　　　　　　　 (迷, mí, to be lost)

(釜, fǔ, cauldron)　　　　　　　　 (你, nǐ, you)

(沉, chén, to sink)　　　　　　　 (迷你, mínǐ, mini)

(舟, zhōu, boat)　　　　　　　　　 (成, chéng, become)

(瓜, guā, melon)　　　　　　　　　 (语, yǔ, language)

(田, tián, field)　　　　　　　　　(成语, chéngyǔ, idiom)

(不, bù, not)　　　　　　　　　　　(成语, chéngyǔ, become language)

(迷你电脑, mínǐ diànnǎo, minicomputer)

(迷你公园, mínǐ gōngyuán, minipark)

http://www.chinese-tools.com/chinese/chengyu/dictionary

Oops!, forgot the all important (你好, nǐhǎo, how are you). Hopefully you have come across this word before. This is the ubiquitous greeting in China. The real meaning is *you good*. (好, hǎo, good)

地 dì earth	Notes: Common Noun (地, de, **manner adverb forming particle, acts as -ly**) A common grammatical construction is to add 地 to an adjective to form a manner adverb. (地, dì, **earth, ground, dirt, soil, fields**) (地, dì, **place, position, distance**)

一 十 土 圵 坰 地

地 地 地 地 地 地 地 地 地

地	地	地	地	地	地	地	地	地	地
dì	dì	dì	dì	dì	dì	dì	dì	dì	dì
earth	earth	earth	earth	earth	earth	earth	earth	earth	earth
地	地	地	地	地	地	地	地	地	地
dì	dì	dì	dì	dì	dì	dì	dì	dì	dì
earth	earth	earth	earth	earth	earth	earth	earth	earth	earth
地	地	地	地	地	地	地	地	地	地
地	地	地	地	地	地	地	地	地	地
地	地	地	地	地	地	地	地	地	地
地	地	地	地	地	地	地	地	地	地
地	地	地	地	地	地	地	地	地	地
地	地	地	地	地	地	地	地	地	地
地	地	地	地	地	地	地	地	地	地

地

1. (地, dì, **earth**) can act both as a stand alone word variably glossed as; *the earth*, *land*, *soil*, *fields* and *ground*. It can also mark a place (地, dì, **place**, **position**).

2. (地, **de**, **adverb forming particle**), **AFP**, also acts as a grammatical suffix to change an adjective into an adverb, answering the question how, hence, it forms *Manner Adverbs*.

Manner Adverbs answer the question *how* and tell us how something happens. In English grammar they are usually placed after the *Main Verb* or after the *Object*. Often they have *–ly* added to the end of the parent *Adjective*. The *–ly* of Chinese grammar is (地, **de**, **manner adverb forming particle**, **acts as -ly**). However, (地, **de**, **AFP**) is not attached to the root adjective in **Hanyu Pinyin**. As usual this is not discriminated in the character string. (快, **kuài**, **quick**) (快地, **kuài de**, **quickly**)

她	很	快	地	开车
Tā	hěn	kuài	de	kāichē.
She	very	quick	-ly	drive vehicle.

(她, tā, she)

(很, hěn, very)

(快, kuài, quick)

(地, de, adverb forming particle)

(快地, kuài de, quickly)

(开, kāi, operate)

(车, chē, vehicle)

(开车, kāichē, operate vehicle)

Although the general rule is that modifiers come before the modified, it is also acceptable to write;

她	开车	很	快	地
Tā	kāichē	hěn	kuài	de.
She	drive vehicle	very	quick	-ly.

The first construction is most likely to act as a neutral statement and the second is most likely to be used as a warning. The most formal and correct construction is;

Adjective + (地, de, AVP) + Verb

天天	我们	努力	地	工作
Tiāntiān	wǒmen	nǔlì	de	gōngzuò.
Day day	we	exert force	-ly	work do.
Daily	we	energetically		work.

(天, tiān, daily)　　　　　　　　　　(工作, gōngzuò, work)

(天天, tiāntiān, daily)　　　　　　　(努, nǔ, put forth strength, exert)

(我们, wǒmen, we)　　　　　　　　(力, lì, force)

(工, gōng, work)　　　　　　　　　(努力, nǔlì, energetic)

(作, zuò, do, make)　　　　　　　　(地, de, AFP)

Another great word for energetic is (意气风发, yìqìfēngfā, energetic). It is an adjective and is modified thus. (意气风发地, yìqìfēngfā de, energetically).

(意, yì, meaning, idea)　　　　　　(风, fēng, wind)

(气, qì, vital energy)　　　　　　　(发, fā, emit)

Predictably, (地, **dì**, **earth, place**) plays a prominent role in forming words of location. I used to live and work in Nigeria in a hospital called the *Joe Jane Medical Center*. One of the greatest experiences in my life. I was in medical school doing a surgical elective. Then I returned, to work during an election / war. That could be a book on its own. Anyways, I learned to speak a little *Yoruba*, the regional coastal language. So I see this guy, obviously Nigerian in Chengdu so I greet him in *Yoruba*. Freaked him right out to see a white guy in China speaking Yoruba. Freaked me out to see a Nigerian in no wheres ville in Chengdu speaking Chengdu hua. Oddly, after we spoke in Yoruba a little, he started to speak Pidgin / Yoruba-English-Mandarin.

Una jus lan	这个	地方	吗
You just land	zhèige	dìfang	ma.
You just arrive	this	place	?

(这, **zhèi**, **this**)   (方, **fāng**, **place, position**)

(个, **ge**, **one of**)   (地, **dì**, **earth**)

(这个, **zhèige**, **this one**)   (地方, **dìfang**, **place**)

3.   (这个地方, **zhèige dìfang**, **this place**) is a great phrase to begin a sentence with. You will be asked in China to give an evaluation of your hotel, location, **KTV**, etc.

这个	地方	太	好	了
Zhèige	dìfang	tài	hǎo	le.
This	place	extreme	good	!

(太, **tài**, **extreme**)   (好, **hǎo**, **good**)

Addresses in China follow a very logical order, like time, they are arranged biggest to smallest. The kicker is that the closest your parcel gets is the local post office. Then you get a phone call that you have mail or a person rides around your village blasting out on a loud speaker megaphone at 6 a.m. that you have mail. So always put a phone number on any package you send. In bigger areas there is delivery to the door and in apartment buildings, to a collective mail box.

4. (地区, dìqū, district)

国家	省	城市	地区
guójiā	shěng	chéngshì	dìqū
country	province	city	district

A typical address in China goes like this.

国家	省	城市	地区
中国	河北省	保定市	新市区
Zhōngguó	Héběi shěng	Bǎodìng shì	Xīnshì Qū
Middle Kingdom	River North province	Protect Certain city	New City district

But that only gets you to the neighbourhood, a name you might be familiar with is prefecture. Which in a big city can be millions of people. There is a whole complex taxonomy of names for streets. Here are some that I have seen, I am sure there are more.

(街, jiē, street) (街道, jiēdào, street path)

(道, dào, path) (马路, mǎlù, horse road)

(街头, **jiētóu**, street head)

(长街, **chángjiē**, long street)

(路, **lù**, road)

(道路, **dàolù**, big road)

(公路, **gōnglù**, public road)

(胡同, **hútòng**, alley)

China loves patriotic names for streets, address continued.

人民南路	九	号
Rénmín nán lù	**jiǔ**	**hào**
People's South Road	nine	number

(人, **rén**, person)

(民, **mín**, people)

(人民, **rénmín**, people)

(南, **nán**, south)

(路, **lù**, road)

(九, **jiǔ**, nine)

(号, **hào**, number)

After you get to the street name, it can get complex after that. Many villages do not have street names, my wife's village has 1800 people, not a name on a street or an address number. Her address ends at the name of the village, which comes after the name of the closest city. But there is no mail delivery. An old lady drives a three wheeled bike around in the morning before the sun comes up yelling out who has mail, selling seeds, food, toilet paper, etc. Then you go to the post office, show your identity card, and get your mail.

There can be named buildings, or if a building complex the number of the building, floor level, suite or apartment number. Usually there is a spot on Chinese envelopes to put the (编码, **biānmǎ**, encoding) functionally the same as our postal code. I do not see any use of giving an example as there are so many options once the address gets to street level. Really, it is very logical, the last thing is the persons name and the title comes after the name.

(编, biān, to organize)

(码, mǎ, indicating number)

(编码, biānmǎ, encoding)

(中国, Zhōngguó, China)

(国家, guójiā, country)

(河北, héběi, river north)

(河北, Héběi, Hebei province)

(保, bǎo, protect)

(定, dìng, calm, stable)

(省, shěng, province)

(县, xiàn, county)

(镇, zhèn, town)

(村, cūn, village)

(城, chéng, wall)

(市, shì, city)

(城市, chéngshì, city)

5. (地, dì, distance)

我们	学校	离	这儿	有	三	站	地
Wǒmen	xuéxiào	lí	zhèr	yǒu	sān	zhàn	dì.
Our	school	separated	this place	have	three	stand	distance.

Although this sentence makes no mention of buses the gloss I borrowed was *Our school is three bus stops from here*. Always remember that *positions can possess* in Mandarin grammar. That explains the use of (有, yǒu, have). Inanimate objects and locations can possess qualities using (有, yǒu, have).

(校, xiào, school)

(学, xué, to learn)

(学校, xuéxiào, school)

(离, lí, separated)

(站, zhàn, stand)

(地, dì, distance)

6.   Here are some words describing all or some of the surface or material of the earth. Again, it is a list of nouns so their sentence position and use is predictable.

(球, qiú, ball) (形, xíng, form, shape)

(地球, dìqiú, the earth) (地形, dìxíng, topography, terrain)

(土, tǔ, soil, earth, clay) (大, dà, big)

(土地, tǔdì, soil) (大地, dàdì, earth)

(面, miàn, face, surface) (草, cǎo, grass)

(地面, dìmiàn, earth's surface) (草地, cǎodì, grassland)

7.   Rent day? So who is the guy that comes to collect the money? The **Dirt Master**. The (地主, **dìzhǔ, landlord**) is composed of (地, **dì, dirt**) and (主, **zhǔ, master**). In many villages, years ago, pre-Mao, the peasants would work for the village landlord (地主, **dìzhǔ, landlord**) who could own the entire village. Like medievel Europe, oppression and indentured servitude was the norm. They were oppressed their entire life by rent arrears and the costs of seed and supplies. So, Mao fixed that. The Red Guard Youth had free reign to butcher them. Millions were murdered to establish modern day China.

On 18 August 1966, Mao met a million Red Guards formally in an audience given in Tiananmen Square, when he donned a Red Guard armband to demonstrate his support for the movement and its objectives. It was this rally that signified the beginning of the Red Guards' involvement in implementing the aims of the Cultural Revolution.

The 11th Plenum, which was meeting in August, had ratified the 'Sixteen Articles', a document that stated the aims of the Cultural Revolution and highlighted the role students would be asked to play in the movement. After the August rally, the Cultural Revolution Group directed the Red Guards to attack the 'Four Olds' of Chinese society (old customs, old culture, old habits and old ideas). For the rest of the year, Red Guards marched across China in a campaign to eradicate the 'Four Olds'. Old books and art were destroyed, museums were ransacked, and streets were renamed with new revolutionary names and adorned with pictures and the sayings of Mao. Many famous temples, shrines, and other heritage sites in Beijing were attacked and, in total, 4,922 out of 6,843 were destroyed.

//en.wikipedia.org/wiki/Red_Guards_%28People%27s_Republic_of_China%29

So the more modern term for the guy who collects the rent is not dirt master but (房东, **fángdōng**, **room east**) from (房, **fáng**, **room**) and (东, **dōng**, **east**), makes sense right?

8. (地震, **dìzhèn**, **earthquake**) Remember that horrible earthquake in Sichuan province on May 12th 2008. 90,000 plus dead. A million housing units destroyed and 5 million people left homeless. I slept through it about 50 kilometres from the epicentre. 7,000 thousand schools collapsed killing 19,065 students. The contractors cheated the state and poured the concrete floors at half thickness and did not use proper reinforcing rod. At least 1,300 children and teachers died at Beichuan Middle School alone. Construction standards in China are abysmally inadequate in remote areas. Before the earthquake I watched contractors mixing concrete with half the necessary cement powder and using smooth steel wire instead of reinforcing rod. My family has been in the construction business for decades. I remember thinking **what would ever happen if there was a huge earthquake**.

China immediately cut all electronic communication and internet to control media, which, they always control the media. Please read the link below to read about how China deals with people speaking out against the corruption and graft that played a role in these catastrophies.

Due to China's one-child policy, many families lost their only child when schools in the region collapsed during the earthquake. Consequently, local officials in Sichuan province have lifted the restriction for families whose only child was either killed or severely injured in the disaster. So-called "illegal children" under 18 years of age may be registered as legal replacements for their dead siblings; if the dead child was illegal, no further outstanding fines would apply. Reimbursement would not, however, be offered for fines that were already levied.

On May 29, 2008, government officials began inspecting the ruins of thousands of schools that collapsed, searching for clues about why they crumbled. Thousands of parents around the province have accused local officials and builders of cutting corners in school construction, citing that after the quake other nearby buildings were little damaged. In the aftermath of the quake, many local governments promised to formally investigate the school collapses, but as of July 17, 2008 across Sichuan, parents of children lost in collapsed schools complained they had yet to receive any reports. Local officials urged them not to protest but the parents demonstrated and demanded an investigation. Furthermore, censors discouraged stories of poorly built schools from being published in the media and there was an incident where police drove the protestors away.

http://en.wikipedia.org/wiki/2008_Sichuan_earthquake

Did man contribute to this **natural catastrophe**? Of course they did. Earthquakes have occurred in response to mining and oil drilling all over the world. China was warned about the hazards of their massive hydroelectric dam projects. How many dams are in the area and got damaged?, **During the Richter magnitude 8 Wenchuan earthquake of 12 May 2008, 1803 concrete and embankment dams and reservoirs and 403 hydropower plants were damaged**. China had been warned about this risk but their scientists always know more than their international peers. The Three Gorges Dam project was so immense that it changed the rotation of the earth. China has over 20,000 dams higher than 15 metres. On April 26, 2008, Chinese geologist Geng Qingguo 耿庆国 who was also said to have predicted the 1976 Tangshan earthquake, predicted a 7+ magnitude earthquake to strike Ngawa Prefecture, Sichuan on May 8, 2008, ±10 days, and that this prediction was dismissed by mainstream seismologists.

http://en.wikipedia.org/wiki/2008_Sichuan_earthquake

What happened to the most outspoken activist against the shoddy schools, he has been jailed for 5 years for *inciting subversion of state power*.

http://chinadigitaltimes.net/2010/02/china-sentences-quake-activist-to-5-years-jail/

The Chinese government has promised *severe punishment* for any parties responsible for construction standards issues. What is *severe punishment* in China?, execution. China executes more people each year than all other countries in the world together. About 10,000 executions made it to the news in 2005 but most are family embarrassments and are done secretly. Some estimate 30,000 each year. Chengdu has the world's largest liver transplant program at Huaxi hospital, all from executed prisoners. China executes for tax fraud, corruption, killing panda bears, damaging national relics, 26 categories of crimes. 50 grams of heroin and you are dead. They even have mobile execution vans. So behave.

//en.wikipedia.org/wiki/Capital_punishment_in_the_People%27s_Republic_of_China

//en.wikipedia.org/wiki/Organ_transplantation_in_the_People%27s_Republic_of_China

//en.wikipedia.org/wiki/Three_Gorges_Dam

Here is an article from 1999 predicting earthquakes from the Three Gorges Dam.

http://www2.gi.alaska.edu/ScienceForum/ASF14/1465.html

Then there is this article predicting earthquakes in the exact area.

1) *The Three Gorges Dam is situated near six active fault lines and above 15 million people.*

2) *In fact, earthquakes between 6.0 and 6.5 are expected once the reservoir is filled in 2009*

3) Already major cracks have developed in the dam, and even after extensive repairs, they have reappeared.

http://katabasis.cementhorizon.com/archives/001604.html

And of course they built the dam 500 metres from the fault line.

The dam was built 500 meters from the earthquake's fault line. A research paper by a group of Chinese scientists concluded that the weight of collected water clearly affected seismic activity.

The government, and some Chinese scientists, have said there is no connection between the dam and the quake.

Scientists discovered 10 years after the Hoover Dam was built in 1935 that its reservoir was increasing seismic activity.

Along China's Three Gorges Dam, officials acknowledge that seismic activity has increased slightly since the 400-mile reservoir began filling eight years ago.

http://online.wsj.com/article/SB123391567210056475.html

Anyways, I am really getting off on a tangent. China does not like to take advice from outside sources. You speak out, you go to jail. But despite their growing resources, they never seem to do things quite right.

9. (地图, **dìtú**, **map**), maps, really, a sore topic with me. Very few English maps available in China. Very few Chinese people can read maps. Very few Chinese people know the cardinal directions. If you get a map, it will have the smallest fonts you can imagine. If you are in **Xi'an** airport, the official tour desk sells maps of **Xi'an** that say *free tourist map courtesy of Xi'an*. The Chinese ones are free. You should have heard me argue that one. Suddenly the fluent English tourist guides

could not speak English. And when clerks reach into their own purse for change you know you are being cheated. So I walked away with it. You definitely need magnifying glasses if you get a map. The over all best source of travel information are the **Lonely Planet** books. I used to laugh at recommendations to take a compass when you travel. That is so 1890-ish. But when the sun comes up in Guangzhou, it is like a frosted flourescent fixture. You know there is light but the source is ill defined.

So this is the way it played out in the **Xi'an** airport after a prolonged argument in which the Chinese tourists were getting handed free maps and the white guys were being asked to pay 20 kuai. The Chinese map also had the *free* message on it. The question arises of course that if I am so fucking smart, why did I need a map. My unnamed travel partner Bill, also known that day as shit head, left 5 bags of stuff in a hotel in Dingzhou, including all my maps, and my **Lonely Planet China**, unbeknownst to me. On his first trip to the Middle Kingdom he decided to unload about 10 kilograms of stuff I told him not to bring. While I was drinking in the hotel lounge in Dingzhou he was playing room cleanup bitch and he put some of my shit in plastic bags and checked them in at the front desk locker. Which was November and now it is mid January and according to relatives, the bags have been pilfered and of the 5 original, there is only my long underwear left and the pillow my mother in law knitted for me, yes, knitted. So this is how the conversation went at the tourist desk.

傻屄	给	我	张	地图	我	不	给	你	钱	肏	你
Shǎbī,	gěi	wǒ	zhāng	dìtú,	wǒ	bù	gěi	nǐ	qián	cào	nǐ.
Stupid cunt,	give	me	sheet	map,	me	not	give	you	money	fuck	you.

(傻屄, shǎbī, stupid cunt) (给, gěi, give)

(我, wǒ, I, me)   (地图, dìtú, map)

(张, zhāng, sheet of)   (钱, qián, money)

(你, nǐ, you)   (肏, cào, fuck)

(张, zhāng, sheet of) is the **CNI** for (地图, dìtú, map). A linguistic purist would use (一, yī, one) to precede the **CNI**. Incidently, this above sentence left the three employees speechless. You would love to travel with me. Nary a glitch or judiciary detention. Shock and awe, shock and awe. A crowd of sheeple were standing around listening. I should have a velcro patch on my pack so that I can take off my Canadian flag and put an American flag on when I act like that.

10. (地点, dìdiǎn, place, site) is used different than (地方, dìfang, place). The former refers to a small concise area and the latter to a larger more general area.

放	这个	东西	在	那个	地点
Fàng	zhèige	dōngxi	zài	nàge	dìdiǎn.
Put	this	thing	at	that	place.

(放, fàng, to put, to place)   (在, zài, at)

(这个, zhèige, this one, this)   (那个, nàge, that)

(东西, dōngxi, thing)   (地点, dìdiǎn, place, site)

Here are some more location type nouns.

(山, shān, mountain)   (工, gōng, work)

(山地, shāndì, mountain country)   (工地, gōngdì, building site)

(当, dāng, undertake, accept)   (陆, lù, land)

(当地, dāngdì, locality, the place) (陆地, lùdì, dry land)

(板, bǎn, plank)

(地板, dìbǎn, floor)

(场, chǎng, site)

(场地, chǎngdì, space, place, site)

(坟, fén, grave)

(坟地, féndì, graveyard)

(平, píng, level, flat)

(平地, píngdì, level flat ground)

(田地, tiándì, farmland)

(田, tián, field)

(理, lǐ, principle)

(地理, dìlǐ, geography)

(带, dài zone)

(地带, dìdài, district)

(毯, tǎn, blanket)

(地毯, dìtǎn, carpet)

11. (地道, dìdào, tunnel) is a word you will often see for underground tunnels leading to shopping malls, across a road, to a subway, etc. There are also train tunnels through mountains marked this way. Large areas of Southwest China is beautiful Karst topography. Train trips are punctuated by dark intervals where trains drive through the mountains. On my first train trip from Guangzhou to Chengdu a young Chinese couple would kiss each time the train went through a dark tunnel.

下	个	地道	我	想	要	接吻	你.
Xià	ge	dìdào	wǒ	xiǎng	yào	qīnwěn	nǐ.
Next		tunnel	me	think	want	kiss	you.

(下, xià, under)

(下个, xià ge, next)

(地道, dìdào, tunnel)

(想, xiǎng, think)

(要, yào, want)

(亲, qīn, kiss)

(吻, wěn, kiss)

(亲吻, qīnwěn, kiss)

12. (天地, tiāndì, heaven earth, realm, universe)

我们	要	开创	新	天地
Wǒmen	yào	kāichuàng	xīn	tiāndì.
We	want	initiate	new	realm.

This sentence was glossed as *We must expand to a new realm*.

(我们, wǒmen, we)

(要, yào, want)

(开, kāi, operate)

(创, chuàng, initiate)

(开创, kāichuàng, start, initiate)

(新, xīn, new)

(天, tiān, sky, heaven)

(天地, tiāndì, realm)

These five words below are *Locative Particles* (**LP**), thus they must be introduced with a *Prepositional Phrase* (**PP**) beginning with (在, zài, at).

(下, xià, under, below)

(地下, dìxià, on the ground)

(地下, dìxià, underground)

(内地, nèidì, inland, interior)

(外地, wàidì, outside ground)

An *Adverb* is a part of speech. It is any word that modifies any part of language other than a *Noun*. Modifiers of *Nouns* are primarily *Adjectives* and *Determiners*. *Adverbs* can modify *Verbs*, *Adjectives*, *Clauses*, *Sentences* and other *Adverbs*.

Adverbs typically answer questions such as *how?*, *in what way?*, *when?*, *where?*, and *to what extent?*. This function is called the *Adverbial Function*, and is realized not just by a single **Adverb** but by *Adverbial Phrases* and *Adverbial Clauses*. As such, (遍地, biàndì, everywhere) answers the question *where* and is an *Adverb*.

13. (遍地, biàndì, everywhere)

昨天	人们	从	公园	遍地	快地	骑	自行车	去	北京
Zuótiān	rénmen	cóng	gōngyuán	biàndì	kuài de	qí	zìxíngchē	qù	Běijīng.
Yesterday	people	from	park	everywhere	quickly	ride	bike	go to	Beijing.
When	Subject	Where		Where	How	Verb	I. Obj.	Verb	D. Obj.
Adverb	Subject	Preposition Phrase		Adverb	Adverb	Object	I. Obj.	Verb	D. Obj.

There is a formal correct word order for Mandarin. The above example includes as much formal grammar as I can get into one table. Mandarin, often called an **SVO** or **Subject Verb Object** grammar style, aptly demonstrates this in the above example. (人们去北京, **rénmen qù Běijīng, people go to Beijing**) is the root sentence which includes the *Main Verb* and the *Direct Object* upon which the *Subject* uses the *Main Verb* to enact the *Verb* action upon the *Direct Object*.

(昨天, **zuótiān, yesterday**) is a *Time Adverb* or *Temporal Adverb*. These are known as *Moveable Adverbs* in *Mandarin Grammar*. They can go either before the *Subject* or immediately after it, thus there are two acceptable ways to start the sentence. (昨天人们从, **zuótiān rénmen cóng, yesterday people from**) emphasizes the time and (人们昨天从, **rénmen zuótiān cóng, people yesterday from**) emphasizes the *Subject*, see below.

人们	昨天	从	公园	遍地	快地	骑	自行车	去	北京
Rénmen	zuótiān	cóng	gōngyuán	biàndì	kuài de	qí	zìxíngchē	qù	Běijīng.
People	yesterday	from	park	everywhere	quickly	ride	bike	go to	Beijing.
Subject	When	Where		Where	How	Verb	I. Obj.	Verb	D. Obj.
Subject	Adverb	Preposition Phrase		Adverb	Adverb	Object	I. Obj.	Verb	D. Obj.

The order after the **SVO** order is *when where how*. As you saw above, *When* is moveable about the *Subject*. *Where* is the *Locative Phrase*.

(昨天, zuótiān, yesterday) (自行车, zìxíngchē, bike)
(人们, rénmen, people) (去, qù, 走)
(从, cóng, from) (北京, Běijīng, Beijing)
(公园, gōngyuán, park) (遍, biàn, everywhere)
(遍地, biàndì, everywhere) (遍地, biàndì, everywhere)
(快, kuài, fast, sharp) (忽地, hū, suddenly)
(骑, qí, ride) (大为, dàwéi, greatly)

I have probably covered this but the overall format of Mandarin grammar is;

| When | Subject | Where | How | Verb | Indirect Object | Verb | Direct Object |

Vietnamese Beef Noodle Soup January 22nd 2011

Friday night my wife and I go out for Vietnamese soup, the beef noodle soup. She loves that stuff. Plus the place is full of Asians so she always has some Chinese people to chat with. Funny how it works, we get immediate service, table pampering, only because I have her on my arm. All the girls in the place are Asian and they admire her for marrying a white guy, the rumours are true.

So, I tell her about a story I read on a blog done by an American guy who lives in China. He has a friend visit from home and they go to a fish restaurant. The chef fetches the fish out of the tank, puts his finger through the mouth and gill, and winds up and smashed it on the sidewalk to stun it so he can weight it. You pay for your fish dinner by the pound in China so the diner is standing there to make sure he is not being cheated. The chef has a cigarette dangling from his mouth the whole time. I comment on how disgusting it was as the sidewalk is the surface that people spit on and kids piss and shit on. My wife's comment, *for sure he should have put the fish in a bag first*. The guy who was living in Beijing realized that he was becoming a little Chinese as it did not bother him at all but his visitor freaked at the cruelty to the fish.

The wife is unphased, so I move on to a story from when I worked in Guizhou province. I am walking down a very rural village dirt road and I round a corner and four men are holding a big pig down on its back in the middle of the street. A fifth man brandishes a knife and slits its throat and the blood flies everywhere. The pig is squelling, well, like a pig. I comment that they used the middle of the street, my wife's comment, *Ah my gawd, really, nobody collect the blood, so much the waste, the blood is very delicious and healthy for you, so much waste, Guizhou people very stupid*. One day I will understand. And damn those Guizhou people.

The Book to Date

So, this book has now covered, in a circuitous fashion, the first 25 characters. My goal was to keep the book under 350 pages but I think I am in trouble on that one. My goal was to take the first 10 characters and then do some grammar constructions but I think at 25 characters we can do this with some borrowed characters. Most of what you may have learned in other books is an inefficient way to learn. Phrase books can be a huge detriment to learning. Most have perverted the grammar and sentence construction in the translations so badly that you will not be able to intuitively make new sentences. So we will concentrate on literal translations.

While I was sitting at my laptop pounding out these drills on the next five pages,, my wife named them **Dumb Dumb Drills**. She simply cannot understand the difficulty us foreigners have with the Chinese language. When I was in university we used to joke about the Chinese foreign students getting 95% in sciences and barely passing English. My wife arrived in Canada 14 months ago, May 17th 2011. However, when asked, she points out that she has been here 13 months. She subtracts the 4 weeks we returned to China for Chinese New Years. She knew about 6 words of English when she arrived.

June 2010: So she is doing Grade 12 in Ontario. She was given 26 credits for her work in China. First she had to prove her ability in English and her grade 11 English mark was 70%. She took a few months of English literacy sponsored by the Canadian governement to do this, then to high school. Then she got 99% in math while barely speaking English, then she got 97% in chemistry. Now she has done grade 12 English and has 82%. This is higher than I got when I was in grade 12. Now she is doing Biology with *so many the crazy words*.

But Biology is more work for her. Note I did not say she is having difficulty with it. Chinese people have a slightly different perspective. She worked about 12 hours a day while doing English, then Math, then Chemistry. Now she is spending at least 16 hours per day on Biology. She has somehow found a network of Chinese students all over the world online who share information with her. She is negotiating with the school board to install Microsoft **Pinyin** on a school computer so that she can add Chinese character descriptions to the online course content. She has downloaded the entire course content and she and her network of friends all over the world are adding Chinese words to match the difficult English biology words. She goes to bed each night at 1a.m. or 2 a.m. so happy that she gets an opportunity to study for free. Does this sound like high school students you know?

So why can they do so well in sciences? The written Chinese language dissociates meaning from sound and shape. By the time a student gets to high school they know 3500 plus individual characters and ten's of thousands of words compiled as one, two, three or more characters. This is done mostly on memory. The language has no reliable phonetic or semantic clues, contrary to the crap you read in other books. Their ability to memorize independent of sounds or other clues is amazing. My wife can rewrite the periodic table or complex math equations but she cannot remember to use *a* and *the* in front of nouns.

This is typical of many Chinese that I studied with or knew socially. Her difficulty in Biology is the lack of symbols and equation like language that is found in math and chemistry. But she has found a solution, she is creating phonetic loan characters using Chinese characters constructed to sound like words used in Biology. Now she has symbols to represent meaning. She has ***Chinese-ified*** Biology words.

Addendum: I write this about two weeks later, she has finished her biology, her final mark was 96.89% which she was quick to point out is 97% using her new found math skills. Her final contribution to the course was to submit all her test and quiz questions that had been marked wrong but in fact were correct. She provided researched evidence. The department sent her a thank you letter, corrected their course ware and amended her marks, higher.

So, here are five pages of **Dumb Dumb Drills**. My wife explained grade 12 math to her new uncle **Fled** (**Fred**) and auntie **Rinda** (**Linda**) thus, "*similar to grade 6 math in China but with easier exam questions, no tlicks*". So fellow *foreigner*, muster up some racial pride and knock off these five pages, the rules of stroke order are indexed in the Contents page.

April 23rd 2011

My wife finished her first semester of Nursing yesterday and thanks to electronics received all of her marks by today. I started this book when she was taking English as a new immigrant in 2009. It has been an amazing adventure watching and helping her acquire a new language. Perhaps the best investment we made was an Apple iPhone. This is her dictionary, translator, word pronouncer, note taker, information transferer and of course phone and internet surfer. True to form, she got 91% in human biology as her highest mark in Nursing. She of course passed everything and endeared herself to the staff. One teacher wrote her a thank you card and noted how she would miss being called *teacher*. This last week I would be in my study working and she would be in her's 3 meters away, cramming for her exams I would hear her iPhone pronouncing words, ***ventricular systole***, ***mitral stenosis***, ***tricuspid valve***, ***endometrium***, ***estrogen***, ***follicle stimulating hormone***. Then there is a pause and she asks me a few questions for her human sexuality content. Then I hear ***fellatio***, a gasp, then, ***oh my gawh!***, ***the West girl so naughty***!

(日, rì, sun, day) (旧, jiù, old)
(白, bái, white) (但, dàn, but)
(百, bǎi, hundred) (早, zǎo, early)
(旦, dàn, dawn) (电, diàn, lightning, electricity)
(申, shēn, explain) (亘, gèn, extend)

日	白	百	旦	申	旧	但	早	电	亘
rì	bái	bǎi	dàn	shēn	jiù	dàn	zǎo	diàn	gèn
sun	white	100	dawn	explain	old	but	early	electric	extend
日	白	百	旦	申	旧	但	早	电	亘
rì	bái	bǎi	dàn	shēn	jiù	dàn	zǎo	diàn	gèn
sun	white	100	dawn	explain	old	but	early	electric	extend
日	白	百	旦	申	旧	但	早	电	亘
日	白	百	旦	申	旧	但	早	电	亘
日	白	百	旦	申	旧	但	早	电	亘
日	白	百	旦	申	旧	但	早	电	亘
日	白	百	旦	申	旧	但	早	电	亘
日	白	百	旦	申	旧	但	早	电	亘
日	白	百	旦	申	旧	但	早	电	亘
日	白	百	旦	申	旧	但	早	电	亘
日	白	百	旦	申	旧	但	早	电	亘
日	白	百	旦	申	旧	但	早	电	亘
日	白	百	旦	申	旧	但	早	电	亘
日	白	百	旦	申	旧	但	早	电	亘
rì	bái	bǎi	dàn	shēn	jiù	dàn	zǎo	diàn	gèn
sun	white	100	dawn	explain	old	but	early	electric	extend

(目, mù, eye)
(自, zì, self)
(泪, lèi, tear)
(苜, mù, alfalfa)
(直, zhí, straight)
(相, xiàng, looks, appearance)
(看, kàn, look at)
(着, zháo, to touch)
(想, xiǎng, think)
(眼, yǎn, eye)

目	自	泪	苜	直	相	看	着	想	眼
mù	zì	lèi	mù	zhí	xiàng	kàn	zháo	xiǎng	yǎn
eye	self	tear	alfalfa	straight	looks	look at	to touch	think	eye
目	自	泪	苜	直	相	看	着	想	眼
mù	zì	lèi	mù	zhí	xiàng	kàn	zháo	xiǎng	yǎn
eye	self	tear	alfalfa	straight	looks	look at	to touch	think	eye
目	自	泪	苜	直	相	看	着	想	眼
目	自	泪	苜	直	相	看	着	想	眼
目	自	泪	苜	直	相	看	着	想	眼
目	自	泪	苜	直	相	看	着	想	眼
目	自	泪	苜	直	相	看	着	想	眼
目	自	泪	苜	直	相	看	着	想	眼
目	自	泪	苜	直	相	看	着	想	眼
目	自	泪	苜	直	相	看	着	想	眼
目	自	泪	苜	直	相	看	着	想	眼
目	自	泪	苜	直	相	看	着	想	眼
目	自	泪	苜	直	相	看	着	想	眼
目	自	泪	苜	直	相	看	着	想	眼
mù	zì	lèi	mù	zhí	xiàng	kàn	zháo	xiǎng	yǎn
eye	self	tear	alfalfa	straight	looks	look at	to touch	think	eye

(大, dà, big)
(太, tài, too)
(犬, quǎn, dog)
(头, tóu, head)
(尖, jiān, point, tip of)

(天, tiān, day)
(夫, fū, man)
(夭, yāo, die young)
(矢, shǐ, arrow, swear, vow)
(夹, jiā, press, squeeze, clip)

大	太	犬	头	尖	天	夫	夭	矢	夹
dà	tài	quǎn	tóu	jiān	tiān	fū	yāo	shǐ	jiā
big	too	dog	head	tip	day	man	die	arrow	press
大	太	犬	头	尖	天	夫	夭	矢	夹
dà	tài	quǎn	tóu	jiān	tiān	fū	yāo	shǐ	jiā
big	too	dog	head	tip	day	man	die	arrow	press
大	太	犬	头	尖	天	夫	夭	矢	夹
大	太	犬	头	尖	天	夫	夭	矢	夹
大	太	犬	头	尖	天	夫	夭	矢	夹
大	太	犬	头	尖	天	夫	夭	矢	夹
大	太	犬	头	尖	天	夫	夭	矢	夹
大	太	犬	头	尖	天	夫	夭	矢	夹
大	太	犬	头	尖	天	夫	夭	矢	夹
大	太	犬	头	尖	天	夫	夭	矢	夹
dà	tài	quǎn	tóu	jiān	tiān	fū	yāo	shǐ	jiā
big	too	dog	head	tip	day	man	die	arrow	press

(木, mù, tree)
(术, shù, skill)
(本, běn, basis, book volume)
(禾, hé, grain)
(末, mò, end, minor details)

(未, wèi, have not, did not, not yet)
(耒, lěi, plough)
(朱, zhū, vermilion, bright red)
(米, mǐ, rice)
(来, lái, come)

木	术	本	禾	末	未	耒	朱	米	来
mù	shù	běn	hé	mò	wèi	lěi	zhū	mǐ	lái
tree	skill	basis	grain	end	did not	plough	red	rice	come
木	术	本	禾	末	未	耒	朱	米	来
mù	shù	běn	hé	mò	wèi	lěi	zhū	mǐ	lái
tree	skill	basis	grain	end	did not	plough	red	rice	come
木	术	本	禾	末	未	耒	朱	米	来
木	术	本	禾	末	未	耒	朱	米	来
木	术	本	禾	末	未	耒	朱	米	来
木	术	本	禾	末	未	耒	朱	米	来
木	术	本	禾	末	未	耒	朱	米	来
木	术	本	禾	末	未	耒	朱	米	来
木	术	本	禾	末	未	耒	朱	米	来
木	术	本	禾	末	未	耒	朱	米	来
木	术	本	禾	末	未	耒	朱	米	来
木	术	本	禾	末	未	耒	朱	米	来
木	术	本	禾	末	未	耒	朱	米	来
木	术	本	禾	末	未	耒	朱	米	来
mù	shù	běn	hé	mò	wèi	lěi	zhū	mǐ	lái
tree	skill	basis	grain	end	did not	plough	red	rice	come

(田, tián, field)	(界, jiè, boundary, border)
(里, lǐ, village)	(备, bèi, prepare)
(果, guǒ, fruit)	(画, huà, draw, picture)
(男, nán, male]	(鱼, yú, fish)
(思, sī, thought)	(甲, jiǎ, first)

田	里	果	男	思	界	备	画	鱼	甲
tián	lǐ	guǒ	nán	sī	jiè	bèi	huà	yú	jiǎ
field	village	fruit	male	thought	border	prepare	picture	fish	first
田	里	果	男	思	界	备	画	鱼	甲
tián	lǐ	guǒ	nán	sī	jiè	bèi	huà	yú	jiǎ
field	village	fruit	male	thought	border	prepare	picture	fish	first
田	里	果	男	思	界	备	画	鱼	甲
田	里	果	男	思	界	备	画	鱼	甲
田	里	果	男	思	界	备	画	鱼	甲
田	里	果	男	思	界	备	画	鱼	甲
田	里	果	男	思	界	备	画	鱼	甲
田	里	果	男	思	界	备	画	鱼	甲
田	里	果	男	思	界	备	画	鱼	甲
田	里	果	男	思	界	备	画	鱼	甲
田	里	果	男	思	界	备	画	鱼	甲
田	里	果	男	思	界	备	画	鱼	甲
		果			界				
tián	lǐ	guǒ	nán	sī	jiè	bèi	huà	yú	jiǎ
field	village	fruit	male	thought	border	prepare	picture	fish	first

(了, liào, observe, watch over)	(孔, kǒng, hole)
(子, zǐ, son)	(孕, yùn, pregnant)
(孑, jié, alone)	(存, cún, keep, to store)
(孓, jué, *has no meaning*)	(孖, zī, twins)
(字, zì, Han character)	(学, xué, study)

了	子	孑	孓	字	孔	孕	存	孖	学
liào	zǐ	jié	jué	zì	kǒng	yùn	cún	zī	xué
watch	son	alone		character	hole	pregnant	to keep	twins	study
了	子	孑	孓	字	孔	孕	存	孖	学
liào	zǐ	jié	jué	zì	kǒng	yùn	cún	zī	xué
watch	son	alone		character	hole	pregnant	to keep	twins	study
了	子	孑	孓	字	孔	孕	存	孖	学
了	子	孑	孓	字	孔	孕	存	孖	学
了	子	孑	孓	字	孔	孕	存	孖	学
了	子	孑	孓	字	孔	孕	存	孖	学
了	子	孑	孓	字	孔	孕	存	孖	学
了	子	孑	孓	字	孔	孕	存	孖	学
了	子	孑	孓	字	孔	孕	存	孖	学
了	子	孑	孓	字	孔	孕	存	孖	学
了	子	孑	孓	字	孔	孕	存	孖	学
了	子	孑	孓	字	孔	孕	存	孖	学
了	子	孑	孓	字	孔	孕	存	孖	学
liào	zǐ	jié	jué	zì	kǒng	yùn	cún	zī	xué
watch	son	alone	alfalfa	character	hole	pregnant	to keep	twins	study

Numbers

You would think that something as simple as numbers would be easy to work with in Chinese characters. Instead, there is a simple and common set of numbers and a more complex secure set for financial transactions to decrease the chance of fraud. Most transactions now use the common numbers.

Arabic	Common	Secure	Pinyin
0	零	零	líng
1	一	壹	yī
1	幺		yāo
2	二	贰	èr
2	两	俩	liǎng
3	三	叁	sān
4	四	肆	sì
5	五	伍	wǔ
6	六	陆	liù
7	七	柒	qī
8	八	捌	bā
9	九	玖	jiǔ
10	十	拾	shí

If your intent is to travel and experience China, I would not agonize over the numbers used for financial transactions. I have never seen them used in banks. Apparently they were used for handwritten notations and cheques to prevent people from changing the numbers to their advantage. Numbers, being what they are, must share common concrete values across cultures. **Hanzi** however has some subjective number characters, that is, separate characters for non-countable objects. While an apple is objective and countable, a telephone number is subjective and not countable. Both the numbers one and two have a subjective and objective character.

Number One

(一, **yī**, **one**, **1**) is used for countable numbering. It also has many uses in **Hanyu** grammar as an adverb. When using numbers in **Hanzi** / **Hanyu** a character is put after the number to signify that it is acting as a numeric counter of a noun. This character can be (个, **ge**, **non-specific measure word**). **Hanzi** / **Hanyu** uses many *Countable Noun Indicators*, **CNI's**, also called *measure words* and *classifiers*. Simplification has increased the use of (个, **ge**, **non-specific measure word**) as a **CNI**. It is useful to see this character in a character string as it identifies the next character as being a noun that is countable. (一个, **yī ge**, **one of**, **one piece**) fairly translates as *one of* or *one piece of*.

(幺, **yāo**, **one**, **1**) is the subjective number one. It is used for things like phone numbers and room numbers in hotels. A Chinese reader will read (幺, **yāo**, **one**, **1**) for the character written as (一, **yī**, **one**, **1**) in the correct context. For example, your hotel room number might be 111, it will be written 111 on the room door, the desk clerk will send you to **yāo yāo yāo** and it may be written 111 on the bill. You will never see the character (幺, **yāo**, **one**, **1**) on a room number plate. Simple right!

Number Two

(二, èr, two, 2) is the subjective number two for non-countable nouns. You do not use it with (个, ge, **non specific measure word**) in the market to ask for two apples. Again, it would be used for telephone numbers and room numbers and other non countable nouns.

(两, liǎng, two, 2) is the objective countable *two*. This is the number you use in the market place. (两个, liǎng ge, two of, two piece) is the correct construction. Room 211 becomes **èr yāo yāo**, any other combination of **liǎng** and **yī** would be met with vacant stares which is what many of the hotel girls have all of the time anyways.

Number Three

(三, sān, three, 3) is the common number three that acts for both countable and non countable usage. The less common more secure character is (仨, sān, three). Three is also used in grammar construction for words that signal repetition. An example is (再三, zàisān, repeatedly), from (再 zài, again) and (三, sān, three, 3).

Number Four

(四, 肆, sì, four, 4) is the common number four that acts for both countable and non countable usage. The less common more secure character is (肆, sì, four, 4).

Number Five

(五, wǔ, five) is the common number five that acts for both countable and non countable usage. The less common more secure character is (伍, wǔ, five).

Number Six

(六, **liù**, **six**) is the common number six that acts for both countable and non countable usage. The less common more secure character is (陆, **liù**, **six**).

Number Seven

(七, **qī**, **seven**) is the common number seven that acts for both countable and non countable usage. The less common more secure character is (柒, **qī**, **seven**).

Number Eight

(八, **bā**, **eight**) is the common number eight that acts for both countable and non countable usage. The less common more secure character is(捌, **bā**, **eight**).

Number Nine

(九, **jiǔ**, **nine**) is the common number nine that acts for both countable and non countable usage. The less common more secure character is (玖, **jiǔ**, **nine**).

Number Ten

(十, **shí**, **ten**) is the common number ten that acts for both countable and non countable usage. The less common more secure character is (拾, **shí**, **ten**).

Zero

(零, **líng**, **zero**) is the correct but now uncommon form of *zero*. The complexity of the character and difficulty writing it in small scale has made the *Arabic* **0** the standard. It is uncommon to see (零, **líng**, **zero**) written but you will often see written *0* pronounced as *líng*.

Eleven to Twenty

Assembly of numbers follows a simple format with the representative **Pinyin** simply being serially compiled. The character (十, **shí**, **ten**) comes first followed by the next appropriate character. These numbers can be written with the common numbers or the more secure numbers. You are not likely to ever see the secure teen numbers unless you read older documents.

Number	Common	**Pinyin**
11	十一	**shíyī**
12	十二	**shíèr**
13	十三	**shísān**
14	十四	**shísì**
15	十五	**shíwǔ**
16	十六	**shíliù**
17	十七	**shíqī**
18	十八	**shíbā**
19	十九	**shíjiǔ**
20	二十	**èrshí**
20	廿	**niàn**

As you can see there is a variant number for twenty. Arabic numbers are being used very commonly in China, the same numbers we use. The need for secure characters has diminished with electronic banking and computer usage. Cash is king in China and there are not many cheques and written financial documents.

Twenty to Thirty

The pattern of number increases is of course consistent within any category.

Number	Common	Pinyin
20	二十	èrshí
21	二十一	èrshíyī
22	二十二	èrshíèr
23	二十三	èrshísān
24	二十四	èrshísì
25	二十五	èrshíwǔ
26	二十六	èrshíliù
27	二十七	èrshíqī
28	二十八	èrshíbā
29	二十九	èrshíjiǔ
30	三十	sānshí

Twenty to One Hundred

Number	Common	Pinyin
20	二十	èrshí
20	廿	niàn
30	卅	sà
30	三十	sānshí
40	四十	sìshí
50	五十	wǔshí
60	六十	liùshí
70	七十	qīshí
80	八十	bāshí
90	九十	jiǔshí
100	百	bǎi
100	佰	bǎi

One Hundred and Beyond

I do not know how much money you are planning to take to China or whether you are renting a hotel room, a whore, buying a condominium, or a factory. For our numbers we use a system in which we put a place holder before the third zero. We write 1,000. China breaks their characters up at the fourth zero and they write 1000. Therefore we write 10,000 and they write 1,0000. This of course only becomes relevant when you are using large amounts of money. Always carefully check division and conversion of large numbers. Even my Chinese friends in Toronto have trouble with this after more than a decade in Canada. My friend Mao Bei kept insisting she bought a condominium in Shanghai for her parents for $10,000. She in fact paid $100,000. Her confusion occurred as she paid 十万, or ten ten thousand. She was confused about her monthly mortgage payments being ten times as much as expected. She was working at the time as a certified accountant for a branch of the provincial government of Ontario, scary.

English	Chinese Arabic	Arabic	Hanzi	Hanzi Secure	Pinyin
one	1	1	一	壹	yī
ten	10	10	十	拾	shí
hundred	100	100	百	佰	bǎi
thousand	1000	1,000	千	仟	qiān
10 thousand	1,0000	10,000	十千	拾仟	shíqiān
10 thousand	1,0000	10,000	万	萬	wàn
100 thousand	10,0000	100,000	十万	拾萬	shíwàn
one million	100,0000	1,000,000	百万	佰萬	bǎiwàn
ten million	1000,0000	10,000,000	千万	仟萬	qiānwàn
100 million	1,0000,0000	100,000,000	万万	萬萬	wànwàn
100 million	1,0000,0000	100,000,000	亿	億	yì
1 billion	10,0000,0000	1,000,000,000	十亿	拾億	shíyì

Special Case Counting Number Two 两 vs 二

In situations where this number two occurs before (百, **bǎi**, **100**), (千, **qiān**, **1,000**) or (万, **wàn**, **10,000**) you can use either (两, **liǎng**, **two**) or (二, 贰, **two**).

The Number Character 号

(号, **hào**, **number, name, mark**) is a suffix position character to indicate a position in a numbered sequence. For example, the 15th day of the month is indicated as (十五, **shíwǔ, 15**) plus (号, **hào, number, name, mark**) to form the date (十五号, **shíwǔ hào, fifteen number**).

Reading the Zero Position 零

(零, **líng, zero, 0**) when reading a number that has an empty hundreds or tens place you can read this position as (零, **líng, zero, 0**). The separation of **Hanyu Pinyin** follows the separation of units of tens. Compare;

647 (六百四十七, **liùbǎi sìshíqī**)
to
6,000 (六千, **liùqiān**)
to
6,007 (六千零七, **liùqiān ling qī**)
to
6,407 (六千四百零七, **liùqiān sìbǎi ling qī**)
to
6,470 (六千四百七, **liùqiān sìbǎi qī**)
to
6,047 (六千零四十七, **liùqiān ling sìshíqī**)
to
60,047 (六万零四十七, **liùwàn ling sìshíqī**)

Number	10,000's 万	1,000's 千	100's 百	10's 十	1's 一
647			六百 liùbǎi	四十 sìshí	七 qī
6,000		六千 liùqiān			
6,007		六千 liùqiān	零 líng		七 qī
6,407		六千 liùqiān	四百 sìbǎi	零 líng	七 qī
6,470		六千 liùqiān	四百 sìbǎi	七 qī	
6,047		六千 liùqiān	零 líng	四十 sìshí	七 qī
60,047	六万 liùwàn		零 líng	四十 sìshí	七 qī
60,007	六万 liùwàn		零 líng		七 qī
60,070	六万 liùwàn		零 líng	七十 qīshí	

(零, líng, zero, 0) is used as a placeholder in a column in which there is no representative number. For 6,407 the character string reads in translation *six thousands, four hundreds, zero tens, seven ones*. However, the *tens* is spoken as (零, líng, zero, 0) If the number ends in a zero or zeros, that last whole number counter is the final number. There does not have to be the appropriate multiple of ten place holder. If you fill in all the columns and do a long form it will take a native Chinese person a few seconds to figure it out but it is understandable.

Reading Phone Numbers

Phone numbers are read as serial non-countable numbers with place holder (零, líng, zero, 0) for *zero*. 2113-5007 is read **èr yāo yāo sān wǔ líng líng qī**. The use of the Arabic numbers 1 to 10 is universal in China now. If you recited that number to a Chinese person they would probably write it 2113-5007 or 二一一三五 00 七. The written use of (零, líng, zero, 0) is now uncommon. These rules for naming numbers are also used on addresses, passports, identity cards, licenses and other identification documents.

Special Number 250

250 or (二百五, èrbǎiwǔ, 250, idiot) has special significance in Chinese literature and conversation. There is a very old story of 4 men who stole 1000 pieces of gold. As the judge sentenced them to execution he stated that they were each ¼ of 1000, or 250. In modern vernacular spoken Mandarin it has come to mean *idiot*. If you use this number as a price, gift, weight or any reference, you are making an implication that someone is an idiot. So, as it is common during Chinese New Year to give gifts of money, do not up the usual ante of 200 ¥ to 250 ¥ or you may be running out the family compound and up the street.

Ordinal Number Character

(第, **dì**, **prefix marker of ordinal numerals**) is a character set before the number characters to mark ordinal numbers.

Number	Ordinal Number	Hanzi	Pinyin
1	1st	第一	dì yī
2	2nd	第二	dì èr
3	3rd	第三	dì sān
4	4th	第四	dì sì
5	5th	第五	dì wǔ
6	6th	第六	dì liù
7	7th	第七	dì qī
8	8th	第八	dì bā
9	9th	第九	dì jiǔ
10	10th	第十	dì shí
11	11th	第十一	dì shíyī
12	12th	第十二	dì shíèr
13	13th	第十三	dì shísān
14	14th	第十四	dì shísì
15	15th	第十五	dì shíwǔ
16	16th	第十六	dì shíliù
17	17th	第十七	dì shíqī
18	18th	第十八	dì shíbā
19	19th	第十九	dì shíjiǔ
20	20th	第二十	dì èrshí
100	100th	第一百	dì yìbǎi
1000	1000th	第一千	dì yìqiān

Multiplier Character

(次, cì, **occurrences**, **times**) is a character placed before the number characters to mark the number of times a number occurs.

Number	Ordinal Number	**Hanzi**	**Pinyin**
1	once	一次	yī cì
2	twice	二次	èr cì
3	thrice	三次	sān cì
4	4 times	四次	sì cì
5	5 times	五次	wǔ cì
6	6 times	六次	liù cì
7	7 times	七次	qī cì
8	8 times	八次	bā cì
9	9 times	九次	jiǔ cì
10	10 times	十次	shí cì
11	11 times	十一次	shíyī cì
12	12 times	十二次	shíèr cì
13	13 times	十三次	shísān cì
14	14 times	十四次	shísì cì
15	15 times	十五次	shíwǔ cì
16	16 times	十六次	shíliù cì
17	17 times	十七次	shíqī cì
18	18 times	十八次	shíbā cì
19	19 times	十九次	shíjiǔ cì
20	20 times	二十次	èrshí cì

Ordinal Number and Multiplier

Number	Ordinal Number	Hanzi	Pinyin
1	1st time	第一次	dì yī cì
2	2nd time	第二次	dì èr cì
3	3rd time	第三次	dì sān cì
4	4th time	第四次	dì sì cì
5	5th time	第五次	dì wǔ cì
6	6th time	第六次	dì liù cì
7	7th time	第七次	dì qī cì
8	8th time	第八次	dì bā cì
9	9th time	第九次	dì jiǔ cì
10	10th time	第十次	dì shí cì
11	11th time	第十一次	dì shíyī cì
12	12th time	第十二次	dì shíèr cì
13	13th time	第十三次	dì shísān cì
14	14th time	第十四次	dì shísì cì
15	15th time	第十五次	dì shíwǔ cì
16	16th time	第十六次	dì shíliù cì
17	17th time	第十七次	dì shíqī cì
18	18th time	第十八次	dì shíbā cì
19	19th time	第十九次	dì shíjiǔ cì
20	20th time	第二十次	dì èrshí cì
100	100th time	第一百次	dì yìbǎi cì
1000	1000th time	第一千次	dì yìqiān cì

Currency ¥

Contrary to the many different names in books, the currency of the **PRC** is the **RMB** or *Renminbi*. A lot of American written books call it the dollar. From;

(人, **rén, person**)

(民, **mín, citizen**)

(人民, **rénmín, people's**)

(币, **bì, currency**)

(人民币, **rénmínbì, peoples currency**)

The basic unit of currency is the (元, **yuán, Chinese monetary unit**) contrary to many American written books, it is not the *dollar*. Like all countable nouns in Mandarin, it has a *Countable Noun Indicator* which is (块, **kuài, piece, currency**). The abbreviated money symbol for (元, **yuán, Chinese monetary unit**) is ¥. The most correct grammatical constructions are;

Hanzi number + (块, **kuài, currency**) + (元, **yuán, monetary unit**)

Hanzi number + (块, **kuài, currency**) + (钱, **qián, money**)

So, for example, 一百块元 is (一百块元, **yībǎi kuài yuán, 100 kuai yuan**) **RMB**. However, just as Canadians use terms like *toonie* and *loonie* and Americans use *bucks*, the Chinese generally use (块, **kuài, currency**) only, after the number in spoken usage. Therefore (一百块, **yībǎi kuài**) is equivalent to 100 basic units of Chinese currency. It is uncommon but not grammatically incorrect to use (块元, **kuàiyuán, kuai yuan**). It is more likely to be written in long form rather than spoken in long form.

The smaller divisions of currency are the 1/10th (元, **yuán**, **Chinese money**) which is usually verbally called the (毛, **máo**, **1/10th 元**) and written as (角, **jiǎo**, **1/10th yuán**). (毛, **máo**, **1/10th 元**) is less formal. The smallest division of currency is the (分, **fēn**, **1/10th 毛, or 1/100th 块**) it is thus 1% of the basic monetary unit.

To summarize, the spoken usage is (块, **kuài**, **currency**), (毛, **máo**, **1/10th 块**) and (分, **fēn**, **1/100th 块**). The more formal written expression is (元, **yuán**, **Chinese monetary unit**), (角, **jiǎo**, **1/10th yuán**) and (分, **fēn**, **1/100th 元**). At current money exchange, there are 7 RMB to a Canadian dollar. So one ¥ is about 14 cents Canadian. This makes one (毛, **máo**, **1/10th 块**) about 1.4 cents. This makes one (分, **fēn**, **1/100th 块**) about 0.14 cents. You are not likely now to see (分, **fēn**, **1/100th 块**) used in an open produce market which is where most food is sold in China. You are not likely to see (分, **fēn**, **1/100th 块**) quoted as a division of a price in any market except in Western style stores where prices are listed with stickers. Most prices you will be quoted will be in (块, **kuài**, **currency**) and (毛, **máo**, **1/10th 块**). The balance beam scales used on the merchants finger are waved all over to make the scale display to his advantage does not have fine enough calibration to measure (分, **fēn**, **1/100th 块**). Plus, most prices are very negotiable.

When talking about money generically you can use the expression (钱, **qián**, **money**) and use the **CNI** (块, **kuài**, **currency**). Just as pennies, nickels, quarters are money, so are 元, 角 and 分. In market situations in which (分, **fēn**, **1/100th 块**) is not part of the price you may hear the price expressed in (元, **yuán**, **Chinese monetary**

unit) and (角, **jiǎo**, **1/10th yuán**) rather than (块, **kuài**, **currency**) and (毛, **máo**, **1/10th** 块).

Spoken Mandarin relies on sound signals to give clarity of information. In a market situation where there is an obvious intent that you want to buy something by your presence in the market. Adding (钱, **qián**, **money**) to the statement may not add further clarity and it is often omitted. (钱, **qián**, **money**) is generally not used for values of less than one **RMB ¥**. (钱, **qián**, **money**) becomes optional.

RMB ¥	块 kuài 1's	毛 máo 1/10's	分 fēn 1/100's	钱 qián money
0.75		七毛 qī máo	五分 wǔ fēn	钱 qián
0.11		一毛 yī máo	一分 yī fēn	钱 qián
0.47		四毛 sì máo	七分 qī fēn	钱 qián
15.32	十五块 shíwǔ kuài	三毛 sān máo	二分 èr fēn	钱 qián
1.45	一块 yī kuài	四毛 sì máo	五分 wǔ fēn	钱 qián

For prices that are whole numbers with no fractional monies, you are most likely to hear only (元, **yuán**, **Chinese monetary unit**) used. If the price has a fractional number divisible by 10 only and the whole number is less than one, you are most likely to hear only (角, **jiǎo**, **1/10th yuán**) used.

RMB ¥	元 yuán	角 jiǎo	钱 qián
.20		二角 èr jiǎo	钱 qián
.50		五角 wǔjiǎo	钱 qián
.80		八角 bājiǎo	钱 qián
1	一元 yīyuán		钱 qián
11	十一元 shíyī yuán		钱 qián
27	二十七元 èrshíqī yuán		钱 qián
87	八十七元 bāshíqī yuán		钱 qián

When the expression you are making is obviously financial, and there is the money classifier (块, **kuài**, **currency**) in your sentence, you can leave off the final currency classifiers (毛, **máo**, **1/10th** 块) and (分, **fēn**, **1/100th** 块) where applicable. (钱, **qián**, **money**) is always optional.

Please remember that at any time you can use the complex secure numbers for financial figures if you wish. As always, confusion is best resolved in China by writing. You may have trouble understanding directions and many other things from Chinese people. But I assure you, when it comes to money, they will make every effort to be understood. All merchants have a pen and paper and a desire to do business. They love that money.

零一二三四五六七八九十 - líng-yī-èr-sān-sì-wǔ-liù-qī-bā-jiǔ-shí

Calendar Dates

The **PRC** uses both a traditional lunar calendar and a Western calendar. The Western calendar date format follows the sentence construction ***Temporal Adverb*** construction of biggest to smallest. They list their dates in the format of year, month day, part of day, hour of day, minutes, and seconds. Their use of the Western calendar is to ease interaction with the west.

The traditional calendar starts at a variable date calculated on the lunar cycle. There are more complex names for the lunar months and a complex Chinese Horoscope that is very much an important part of planning business, engagements, and weddings. China enjoys mysticism about time, dates, and numbers. China reverts to their traditional calendar for all things Chinese. This remains a very important and revered part of their culture.

The character for year is (年, **nián**, **year**). The number of the year is not expressed as a whole number but rather is expressed as each number component of the total year number similar to a telephone number. As the date is not a countable noun the character (二, **èr**, **two, 2**) is usually used rather than (两, **liǎng**, **two, 2**).

The concept of month uses the character (月, **yuè**, **month, moon**). The number of the month comes before the character. China of course does not use the Roman names for months.

The number of the day can be expressed with the number of days into the month with a suffix (号, **hào**, **number**). You can also alternately use the character (日, **rì**, **sun**). As with most grammatical constructions in Standard Mandarin, the modifier precedes the modified except for the number of the day.

June 15th 2008	二零零八年	六月	十五号 or 十五日
	èrlínglíngbā nián	**liùyuè**	**shíwǔhào** or **shíwǔrì**
August 8th 2008	二零零八年	八月	八号 or 八日
	èrlínglíngbā nián	**bāyuè**	**bāhào** or **bārì**
May 19th 1919	一九一九年	五月	十九号 or 十九日
	yījiǔyījiǔ nián	**wǔyuè**	**shíjiǔhào** or **shíjiǔrì**

零一二三四五六七八九十 - líng-yī-èr-sān-sì-wǔ-liù-qī-bā-jiǔ-shí

One to One Hundred

一 yī 1	二 èr 2	三 sān 3	四 sì 4	五 wǔ 5	六 liù 6	七 qī 7	八 bā 8	九 jiǔ 9	十 shí 10
十一 shíyī 11	十二 shíèr 12	十三 shísān 13	十四 shísì 14	十五 shíwǔ 15	十六 shíliù 16	十七 shíqī 17	十八 shíbā 18	十九 shíjiǔ 19	二十 èrshí 20
二十一 èrshíyī 21	二十二 èrshíèr 22	二十三 èrshísān 23	二十四 èrshísì 24	二十五 èrshíwǔ 25	二十六 èrshíliù 26	二十七 èrshíqī 27	二十八 èrshíbā 28	二十九 èrshíjiǔ 29	三十 sānshí 30
三十一 sānshíyī 31	三十二 sānshíèr 32	三十三 sānshísān 33	三十四 sānshísì 34	三十五 sānshíwǔ 35	三十六 sānshíliù 36	三十七 sānshíqī 37	三十八 sānshíbā 38	三十九 sānshíjiǔ 39	四十 sìshí 40
四十一 sìshíyī 41	四十二 sìshíèr 42	四十三 sìshísān 43	四十四 sìshísì 44	四十五 sìshíwǔ 45	四十六 sìshíliù 46	四十七 sìshíqī 47	四十八 sìshíbā 48	四十九 sìshíjiǔ 49	五十 wǔshí 50
五十一 wǔshíyī 51	五十二 wǔshíèr 52	五十三 wǔshísān 53	五十四 wǔshísì 54	五十五 wǔshíwǔ 55	五十六 wǔshíliù 56	五十七 wǔshíqī 57	五十八 wǔshíbā 58	五十九 wǔshíjiǔ 59	六十 liùshí 60
六十一 liùshíyī 61	六十二 liùshíèr 62	六十三 liùshísān 63	六十四 liùshísì 64	六十五 liùshíwǔ 65	六十六 liùshíliù 66	六十七 liùshíqī 67	六十八 liùshíbā 68	六十九 liùshíjiǔ 69	七十 qīshí 70
七十一 qīshíyī 71	七十二 qīshíèr 72	七十三 qīshísān 73	七十四 qīshísì 74	七十五 qīshíwǔ 75	七十六 qīshíliù 76	七十七 qīshíqī 77	七十八 qīshíbā 78	七十九 qīshíjiǔ 79	八十 bāshí 80
八十一 bāshíyī 81	八十二 bāshíèr 82	八十三 bāshísān 83	八十四 bāshísì 84	八十五 bāshíwǔ 85	八十六 bāshíliù 86	八十七 bāshíqī 87	八十八 bāshíbā 88	八十九 bāshíjiǔ 89	九十 jiǔshí 90
九十一 jiǔshíyī 91	九十二 jiǔshíèr 92	九十三 jiǔshísān 93	九十四 jiǔshísì 94	九十五 jiǔshíwǔ 95	九十六 jiǔshíliù 96	九十七 jiǔshíqī 97	九十八 jiǔshíbā 98	九十九 jiǔshíjiǔ 99	一百 yībǎi 100

Cooking Lesson Number One

Rice

I know what you are thinking. You think that you already know how to cook rice. You probably go to your local supermarket and buy the no-name brand of white rice in the one kilogram bag, right? If you are American you probably don't eat rice or you buy it in one pound bags or you eat Rice-a-Roni. First rule, don't be cheap. There are many different kinds of rice and beyond having different flavours they also cook different and stick together differently. Read about different rices and how they are used.

One day I was busy trying to impress my mother in-law with my culinary skills when my wife asked me with a look of horror on her face, *how many time you make the rinse*? Rinsing rice is very important I found out. Pesticide use is unregulated in many countries, China has the worst record. Rinse the rice in cold water several times to remove dust, chemicals and other floaters. When I worked in West Africa we rinsed rice like panning for gold to get the rat and mouse shit and gravel out.

My wife was horrified to find out that I had been making rice for her family without rinsing it. Then we cooked it in a crusty pre-Mao era aluminum pot on an open coal fire in the unventilated kitchen.

Anyways, rice can be soaked over night. It cooks much faster and is not as mushy. Never use hot water from a hot water tank tap to rinse or cook the rice. Many hot water tanks are not glass lined or made from stainless steel and the hot water adds an odd taste to the rice.

Starch, a polymer of monosaccharides, my wife just taught me that, she learned it in chemistry, is what makes rice stick together. Now rinsing the rice with cold tap water will take away some of the starch and bran. Now I am sure the long skirt vegan Berkinstock wearing unshaved beaver crowd will balk at this, whatever.

Measure the amount of rice in a dry container. 250 ml makes a single serving. That is about a cup for you Yanks. Now, add exactly twice as much cold water as rice, for long grain rice. For short grain rice add an additional 10 mls of water per 250 ml of rice. Now secret number one, add 5 ml of vegetable oil and stir thoroughly. This goes a long way to preventing the rice from sticking. A pinch of sea salt per serving makes a difference to taste. Substituting sesame oil for vegetable oil gives a nice flavour.

Now is the time to add flavours. There are many dry flavourings, I like the dry chicken or beef soup bases. The first time I did this my mother-in-law was mystified. She had never seen or heard of this being done. God forbid you break a few thousand years of tradition. Be creative. Many people add soy sauce at this point. Remember it has salt in it and cancer causing *Aflatoxin*.

The faster you cook rice the worse the product. Rice cookers are fine, they are cheap to buy and reliable. Whether using a pot or an automated cooker, make sure you stir the rice several times so that the sticky stuff does not migrate down the pot with the disappearing water level and cause the bottom of the pot to stick and burn. If you are using a pot, control the rate of steam loss by keeping the lid on. Let the steam push the lid up, do not set the lid on so that it leaks. As the rice is getting close to finished, turn the heat down. When the water is gone, stir the rice and leave the lid off and turn the heat off. This will allow the rice to dry off without burning. The more you stir it, the dryer and less stuck together it will be.

So this is white rice ready for the bowl. The secret to great stir fries is to put the rice in the fridge when it cools and chill it. I often freeze cooked rice. But make sure it is dry before you put it in the fridge or freezer. This makes the rice in the stir fry easily separated with no sticky balls clumped together.

Proper manners for eating rice in China includes not leaving a single grain in the bowl. This is for respect for the farmers who toil their whole life to provide rice. There is actually a poem about this that all school children learn but I don't feel like translating it right now. Also, don't stick your chopsticks straight up in the bowl. This has something to do with burial customs. When people die in rural areas they mound dirt over the body and stick a white stick on top of the pile, vertically. China is big on parallel symbolism. The chopsticks straight-up symbolize the traditional burial mound.

Rice is generally served at the end of the meal. A traditional Chinese meal is composed of two components, the vegetables, (菜, **cài**, **vegetable**) and the carbohydrates, rice or noodles usually. (饭, **fàn**, **cooked cereals**) Note that there is no emphasis on a meat dish.

Anyway, it is two days later and here is the poem. Copying the efforts of other authors I will try and throw some cultural tidbits in. Really, the language is so complex that I would recommend ignoring culture initially, along with Chinese idioms and metaphors. China does not have one culture. Each ethnic group you meet will define culture by their own group. People who have attended school will relate to you the political construct of culture they were taught in school. Minus of course the atrocities of the last century. Concentrate on the language.

悯农
Mǐn Nóng
Pity Farmer

锄	禾	日	当	午
Chú	hé	rì	dāng	wǔ.
Hoe	grain	day	when	noon.

汗	滴	禾	下	土
Hàn	dī	hé	xià	tǔ.
Sweat	drip	grain	down	earth.

谁	知	盘	中	餐
Shuí	zhī	pán	zhōngcān.	
Who	know	plate	middle meal.	
			lunch	

粒	粒	皆	辛	苦
Lì	Lì	jiē	xīnkǔ.	
All rice		all	hard work.	

Now, the first two lines are workable. Some guy, lets call him Zhou Farmer, is out hoeing the rice in the hot midday sun. The sweat drips down onto the ground. Line three requires some work. (谁, **shuí**, **who**) references a collective group in this situation. Really, overall it means *all know lunch*. Then the final line, 粒粒 the duplicated character word is the **CNI** for grain. This construction is unusual but this is poetry.(粒, **lì**, **CNI for grain**) Duplication of nouns marks entirety. So this can translate as *all rice*. (皆, **jiē**, **all**) references people, so *everyone*. So, then comes

(辛苦, **xīnkǔ**, **work hard**) from (辛, **xīn**, **suffering**) and (苦, **kǔ**, **excessive**). *All rice everyone work hard*.

So the message is that all need to know that the rice on the plate comes from the suffering of the farmer. So you should eat it all. The author is(李 绅, **Lǐ Shēn**) He lived during the the *Tang Dynasty*.

Li Shen (李绅) (death July 29, 846), courtesy name **Gongchui (公垂)**, formally **Duke Wensu of Zhao (赵文肅公)**, was an official of the Chinese dynasty, *Tang Dynasty*, serving as a chancellor during the reign of *Emperor Wuzong*.

http://en.wikipedia.org/wiki/Li_Shen

(悯, **mǐn**, **pity, sympathize**)

(农, **nóng**, **farmer**)

(农民 **nóngmín**, **farmer**)

(锄, **chú**, **hoe**)

(禾, **hé**, **grain**)

(日, **rì**, **sun**)

(当, **dāng**, **when**)

(午, **wǔ**, **noon**)

(汗, **hàn**, **sweat**)

(滴, **dī**, **drip**)

(下, **xià**, **down**)

(土, **tǔ**, **earth**)

(谁, **shuí, shéi**, **who**)

(知, **zhī**, **know**)

(盘, **pán**, **plate**)

(中, **zhōng**, **middle**)

(餐, **cān**, **meal**)

(皆, **jiē**, **all, everyone**)

(粒, **lì**, **CNI rice**)

(辛, **xīn**, **suffering**)

(辛苦, **xīnkǔ**, **work hard**)

(苦, **kǔ**, **excessive**)

Locative Particles

Now, this table looks all very confusing but it really is not. However, the time I am finished typing this, the table immediately below may get pushed to the next page so that you will have no idea what I am talking about. There are three characters, (边, **biān**, **side**), (面, **miàn**, **face, surface**) and (头, **tóu**, **head**) that combine with location words to create *Locative Particles* (LP). The grammatical importance of these character words in forming *Preposition Phrases* (PP) will be explained when I do the chapter on (在, **zài**, **at**) which should be around page 124.

As you can see from the chart, the first character in the two character words stands alone in meaning to define generally what the sum of the two characters also mean. This initially appears repetitive but in fact it acts to mark the **Locative Phrase** as these single characters have other meanings and uses in grammar. (后, **hòu**) for example also means (后, **hòu, queen**). (上, **shàng**) also means (上, **shàng, to go to**).

Chapter 9, (在, **zài**, **at**), explains the construction and use of *Preposition Phrases*. I figured it would be easier to consolidate this all in one place rather than scatter it over numerous chapters. Besides, I copied it from an old book, it wasn't that difficult for me. Oddly this book is considered one of the classics of Mandarin grammar and there is not a single Chinese character in it. Li and Thompson 1981

As you can see, not all *Prepositions* take all combinations of combining characters. This group is easy to knock off and then below in a second table are a few that are atypical. (边, **biān, side**), (面, **miàn, face, surface**) and (头, **tóu, head**) are all spoke in the neutral tone when combined with the *Preposition*. You can see that the end result is a shit load of characters that have the same meaning.

Preposition	边 biān, side	面 miàn, surface	头 tóu, head	Meaning
(下, xià, under)	下边 xiàbian	下面 xiàmian	下头 xiàtou	below, under
(上, shàng, on)	上边 shàngbian	上面 shàngmian	上头 shàngtou	above, on
(里, lǐ, inside)	里边 lǐbian	里面 lǐmian	里头 lǐtou	in, inside
(外, wài, outside)	外边 wàibian	外面 wàimian	外头 wàitou	outside
(前, qián, front)	前边 qiánbian	前面 qiánmian	前头 qiántou	front
(后, hòu, behind)	后边 hòubian	后面 hòumian	后头 hòutou	behind
(右, yòu, right)	右边 yòubian	右面 yòumian		right side
(左, zuǒ, left)	左边 zuǒbian	左面 zuǒmian		left side
(这, zhè, this)	这边 zhèbian	这面 zhèmian		this side
(那, nà, that)	那边 nàbian	那面 nàmian		that side
(旁, páng, side)	旁边 pángbian			beside
(北, běi, north)	北边 běibian			north, north side
(南, nán, south)	南边 nánbian			south, south side
(西, xī, west)	西边 xībian			west, west side
(东, dōng, east)	东边 dōngbian			east, east side

(中, zhōng, middle)

(中央, zhōngyāng, middle)

(中间, zhōngjiān, middle)

(中部, zhōngbù, middle)

(当中, dāngzhōng, middle)

(半中腰, bànzhōngyāo, middle)

(当腰, dāngyāo, middle)

(当中间儿, dāngzhōngjiànr, middle)

(中间儿, zhōngjiànr, middle)

(边, biān, side)

(面, miàn, face, surface, aspect)

(头, tóu, head)

(部, bù, part, section)

(中, zhōng, middle)

(间, jiān, between)

(中部, zhōngbù, middle)

(中间, zhōngjiān, center, middle)

(当, dāng,)

(当中, dāngzhōng, middle, center)

(下, xià, under)

(上, shàng, on)

(里, lǐ, inside)

(外, wài, outside)

(前, qián, front)

(后, hòu, behind)

(后, hòu, queen)

(右, yòu, right)

(左, zuǒ, left)

(这, zhè, this)

(那, nà, that)

(旁, páng, side)

(北, běi, north)

(南, nán, south)

(西, xī, west)

(东, dōng, east)

(下边, xiàbian, under)

(下面, xiàmian, under)

(下头, xiàtou, under)

(上边, shàngbian, on)

(上面, shàngmian, on)

(上头, shàngtou, on)

(里边, lǐbian, inside)

(里面, lǐmian, inside)

(里头, lǐtou, inside)

(外边, wàibian, outside)

(外面, wàimian, outside)

(外头, wàitou, outside)

(前边, qiánbian, front)

(前面, qiánmian, front)

(前头, qiántou, front)

(后边, hòubian, behind)

(后面, hòumian, behind)

(右边, yòubian, right)

(右面, yòumian, right)

(左边, zuǒbian, left)

(左面, zuǒmian, left)

(这边, zhèbian, this side)

(这面, zhèmian, this side)

(那边, nàbian, that side)

(那面, nàmian, that side)

(旁边, pángbian, beside)

(北边, běibian, north)

(南边, nánbian, south)

(西边, xībian, west)

(东边, dōngbian, east)

Excellent Chinese Language Books

Beginner's Chinese by Yong Ho. 1977   ISBN 0-7818-0566-X

There are multitudes of introductory books on the market but this book has more useful methods to learn in this book of 174 pages than a huge pile of other books I have. I carried this book in China for a long time. The grammar is presented and vocabulary words are given to make new sentences. This is the way a book should be written.

Chinese Grammar by Claudia Ross. 2004   ISBN 0-07-137764-6

I have all the classic grammar texts, Chao, Li, etc. but this book has all the relevant grammar in it. If you master this book you do not need any other grammar to speak Mandarin. The book is structured in a very practical way. She writes several other books and all are excellent.

Chit-Chat Chinese by Rachel Meyer. 2010   ISBN 978-9576129063

This book is the best of the best. This book is a systematic and gradual progression of the most useful characters compiling the most useful grammatical constructions. Characters are introduced with pronunciation, Hanyu Pinyin, meaning and then simple useful sentences. There is no searching all over the book to chase the components of each character. Repetition is gently integrated without the psychosis of Pimsleur. The integration of pronouns, verbs, proper nouns, adverbs, and nouns is so well balanced that useful sentences compile at a comforting rate. The author effectively inserts anecdotes, cultural points, idioms and humour.

Useless Terrible Chinese Language Books

For every good book on Chinese language there are 10 useless ones and some of those are detrimental to your overall learning. I have distilled the useful ones from the useless spending about $10 for useless books for every $1 on good books.

Chinese Through Tone and Color (Worst idea)
ISBN 978-0-7818-1204-7
by Nathan Dummit

Chinese For Dummies (Worst book in the known universe)
ISBN 978-0471788973
by Wendy Abraham

1400+ Chinese Conversational Phrases (Worst translations)
ISBN 978-1-4196-6583-7
by Ju Brown

1880+ Chinese Business and Trade Phrases (Worst translations part II)
ISBN 1-4392-0247-8
by Ju Brown

The First 100 Chinese Characters (There is no quick and easy method)
"The Quick and Easy Method to Learn the 100 Most Basic Chinese Characters"
ISBN 978-0-8048-3830-6   by Alison and Lawrence Mathews

The Second 100 Chinese Characters (There is no quick and easy method)
ISBN 978-0-8048-3831-3   by Alison and Lawrence Matthews

Learning Chinese Characters (Using strategy of book is more effort than not)
A Revolutionary New Way to Learn and Remember the 800 Most Basic Chinese Characters
ISBN 978-0-8048-3816-0   by Alison and Lawrence Matthews

See comprehensive reviews at;

http://chineselanguagebookreview.blogspot.com/

Colours (色, sè, colour)

(红色, hóng sè, red)

(橙色, chéng sè, orange)

(黄色, huáng sè, yellow)

(绿色, lǜ sè, green)

(青色, qīng sè, teal)

(蓝色, lán sè, blue)

(紫色, zǐ sè, purple)

(浅绿色, qiǎnlǜ sè, aqua)

(银色, yín sè, silver)

(灰色, huī sè, grey)

(褐色, hè sè, brown)

(黑色, hēi sè, black)

(白色, bái sè, white)

(深红色, shēnhóng sè, crimson)

(靛蓝色, diànlán sè, indigo)

(淡紫色, dànzǐ sè, lavender)

Question of the Day

January 29th 2011

Me: So, were all of your classes taught in Mandarin?

Wife: Yes, of course!

Me: Even if the teachers were local and spoke the local language?

Wife: Always Mandarin.

Me: What about when you went out to play for recess?

Wife: What is recess?

Me: Free time to go outside and play during school, twice each day.

Wife: Really, the students not want to study? So soft and no discipline.

Me: Okay, did the students usually talk Mandarin at lunch and going to school?

Wife: Of course not, no one speak Mandarin.

Authors note: Reassuring right?, this is one hour from Beijiing.

Survival Swearing in China

Above is the traditional Chinese characters for the word *rotten egg* or *bad egg*. (坏蛋, **huàidàn, bad egg**).

China can challenge the most seasoned traveller. Kids shitting on the sidewalk, old ladies accidently spitting on your leg as they turn and hork, some guy the size of your little sister with bad garlic breath reaching over you to buy train tickets after you waited 2 hours. Add to that smoking in any no-smoking area; elevators, trains, your face, and then you bend over to look at your shoes and the head of some guys dick rubs your brown eye as you line up at KFC. Eventually you will want to strangle and murder a few of the rice chomping, karaoke singing, vertically challenged yellow skinned motherfuckers. China is the only country that I had to take a time out from and go to Thailand for a week as I thought I was going to murder the next person that cheated me. Cheated me on the bus, the train, the taxi, the hotel, the market, even the bank.

Chinese friends warned me never to say certain words in China as I would be immediately set upon and beat, yah right.

Did you ever watch George Carlin, what a great comedian.

"There are 400,000 words in the English language, and there are seven you can't say on television. What a ratio that is! 399,993 to 7. They must

really be baaaad. They must be OUTRAGEOUS to be separated from a group that large. "All of you words over here, you seven....baaaad words." That's what they told us, right? ...You know the seven, don't ya? That you can't say on TV? Shit, piss, fuck, cunt, cocksucker, motherfucker and tits."

http://blogzarro.com/2007/05/100-greatest-george-carlin-quotes/

I will hold him to expertice and will concentrate on these words and their derivatives. Study carefully, there will be a test at the end.

Cunt (kŭnt) *n*.

1. The female genital organs.
2. Portals of the gates to hell and poverty.

This is actually a proper anatomical word in the English language. But forget trying to argue that with any bitch you have used it on. The word appears several times in Chaucer's **Canterbury Tales** (c. 1390), but it does not appear to be considered obscene at this point. In the **Miller's Tale**;

"Pryvely he caught her by the queynte (cunt)."

Queynte, isn't that quaint!

The **Wife of Bath** also uses this term;

"For certeyn, olde dotard, by your leave. You shall have queynte right enough at eve. What aileth you to grouche thus and groan? Is it for yee would have my queynte alone?"

Imagine that medieval hairy twat. This is the only thing I remember from grade 12 English. The closest Mandarin term is (屄, **bī**, **cunt**). The most common word uses (傻, **shǎ**, **stupid**) to form (傻屄, **shǎbī**, **stupid cunt**). Complementing this is the word (二 **èr**, **two**) combining to form (二屄, **èrbī**, **double cunt**).

Remember those jokes about the blind man that walks past the fish market and says, "*hello girls*". (臭, **chòu**, **foul, stinking**) cums together with (屄, **bī**, **cunt**) to form (臭屄, **chòubī**, **stinking cunt**). Seems different cultures share similar problems. (骚, **sāo**, **lewd**) forms (骚屄, **sāobī**, **lewd cunt**) and (烂, **làn**, **rotten**) forms (烂屄, **lànbī**, **rotten cunt**).

***Ox cunt*?** (牛屄, **niú bī**, **ox cunt!**), hard to imagine the etymolgy of that one. Oxen are usually castrated male cattle. Not many *cunts* on male cattle. This can actually be a compliment. If you are highly skilled at something, this is a compliment.

他	真	他	妈的	牛	屄!
Tā	zhēn	tā	mā de	niú	bī!
He	real	he / his	mother's	ox	cunt!
He	really	is his	mother's	ox	cunt!

Now, for some actual grammar, (你个死屄, **Nǐ ge sǐ bī**, **Your dead cunt**) seems to be missing something. The most correct grammatical form would be;

你	的	一	个	死	屄
Nǐ	de	yī	ge	sǐ	bī.
Your		one	of	dead	cunt.

(一, **yī**, **one**) is often dropped in front of (个, **ge**, **of**). (的, **de**) can be dropped when it is forming a *Possessive Pronoun* that is *close and personal*.

我	肏	死	你	老	妈	的	臊	屄
Wǒ	cào	sǐ	nǐ	lǎo	mā	de	sāo	bī.
Me	fuck	dead	you	old	mother	's	fetid	cunt.

(臊, **sāo**, **fetid**)

Now, for you guys that don't want your balls kicked out your rice chewer or your eyes poked out with chopsticks, you might want to try something a little more neutral (桃花源, **táohuāyuán**, **peach flower source**). And trust me, Chinese girls do not like dirty talk in bed. They think us white guys are romantic so no whispering that you want to kiss their (臭屄, **chòubī**, **stinking cunt**).

(桃, **táo**, **peach**)　　　　　　　　　　(源, **yuán**, **source of a river**)

(花, **huā**, **flower**)

Fuck (fŭk)

Fuck is an English word that is generally considered profane which, in its most literal meaning, refers to the act of sexual intercourse. However, by extension it may be used to negatively characterize anything that can be dismissed, disdained, defiled, or destroyed. Fuck can be used as a verb, adverb, adjective, command, interjection, noun, and can logically be used as virtually any word in a sentence.

The Chinese character for fuck is elegant. But this took character simplification to actually give meaning to the components of the character. The original character is as meaningless as most Chinese characters, . The simplified character combines (入, rù, to enter) and (肉, ròu, meat) to form (肏, cào, to fuck). Get it?, *to enter the meat*. I think that committee members on the character simplification program had their drinking face on on that day with the opium bong loaded right up.

(肏你的妈妈的屄, **cào nǐde māma de bī**, **fuck your mother's cunt**)

You can see that there is **too many the de** in the above sentence. You can drop the first (的, **de**) and the second (吗, **mā**, **mother**) if you like.

If you are in a hurry, like say you are running from a group of angry Chinese men, (肏你的妈, **cào nǐde mā**, **fuck your mom**) is a little quicker. The most common form you will hear is a little hacked grammar, (肏你妈, **cào nǐ mā**, **fuck your mom**).

(祖宗, **zǔzōng**, **ancestor**) is formed from two characters that have the same meaning, (祖, **zǔ**, **ancestor**) and (宗, **zōng**, **ancestor**).

肏	你	祖宗	十八	代
Cào	nǐ	zǔzōng	shíbā	dài.
Fuck	you	ancestor	18	generation.

In China, ancestor worship is an important part of the culture. Confucianism mandates filial piety and respect for one's ancestors. Insulting one's ancestors is a sensitive issue and is generally confronting and definitely worth considering. I am not sure why they picked eighteen generations as the target.

Cock and Cocksucker

Vulgar terms for a man's external genitalia seem to be under represented in Mandarin. Most of the terms are cute and infantile. The most common term (小弟弟, **xiǎo dìdi**, **little brother**) oddly includes, **xiǎo**, **little**). Not something us white brothers would include in dick names. (鸡巴, **jībā**, **chicken tail**), another cute name. (鸡鸡, **jīji**, **chicken chicken**), duplication usually is an affectionate form of diminution, so *little chicken*. (龟头, **guītóu**, **turtle head**), no mention of the mighty shaft there. (屌, **diǎo**, **penis**), rather neutral. (胯下物, **kuàxià wù**, **hip under thing**), imagine that, *heh*! *Suck on my hip-under-thing*! I propose a new name;

单	眼睛	裤子	蛇
Dān	yǎnjing	kùzi	shé
Single	eye	trouser	snake

this gives a little dignity to the name.

Heh! (傻屄, **shǎbī**, **stupid cunt**), suck my;

(单眼睛裤子蛇, **dān yǎnjing kùzi shé**, **single eye trouser snake**!), good eh?

So what is Chinese foreplay? I found these terms under *Foreplay*. Actually, these were the only terms. The closest to fellatio is (口交, **kǒujiāo**, **mouth mate**) from (口, **kǒu**, **mouth**) and (交, **jiāo**, **to mate**). Then there is *blow service*.

(吹, **chuī**, **blow**) + (功, **gōng**, **service**) = (吹功, **chuīgōng**, **blow service**)

(口, **kǒu**, **mouth**)   (口交, **kǒujiāo**, **mouth mate**)

(交, **jiāo**, **mate**)   (吹, **chuī**, **blow**)

(功, gōng, service)   (吹功, chuīgōng, blow service)

Incidently, good luck talking a Chinese girl into the above *foreplay*. So I was going to write a story about love, Chinese girls and money, the real Chinese foreplay. My wife and I are watching a love story on television while I am writing this, **A Life Less Ordinary** with Cameron Diaz and Ewan McGregor. He kidnaps her, they fall in love, they extort a million dollars from her father. After the gun fight, a murder or two, and a car chase scene, the car plummets to the bottom of the gorge and the two lovers run off. What does my wife yell out as the vehicle gets wrecked and they run off barely surviving? Hell with true love and survival.

快	点儿	吧	钱	拿走
Kuài	diǎnr,	ba	qián	názǒu.
Quick	a little,		money	take go forth.

Quickly, take the money!

She is truly Chinese. Incidently, this is the (吧, *ba construction*). Note that there is no **Object** and that the **Verb** does not act on anything.

(吧, ba, expectation particle)

(钱, qián, money)

(快, kuài, fast)

(单, dān, single)

(只, zhī, one of a pair of things)

(眼睛, yǎnjing, eye)

(蛇, shé, snake)

(裤子, kùzi, trouser)

(祖宗, zǔzōng, ancestor)

(代, dài, generation)

(弟弟, dìdi, younger brother)

(胯下物, kuàxià wù, hip under thing)

(巴, bā, hope for, cling to, be near)

(鸡, jī, chicken)

(鸡巴, jībā, chicken)

(龟, guī, turtle)

(头, tóu, head)

(龟头, guītóu, turtle head)

(屌, diǎo, penis)

(胯, kuà, hip)

(下, xià, under)

(物, wù, thing)

(拿走, názǒu, take away)

(点儿, diǎnr, dot)

Breasts

Many things in China are petite. Breasts however come in three sizes, A, A- and A+. Again, like penis', breasts tend to take cute names. The cat's meow, that is, the noise the cat makes is (咪, mī, meow). Somehow (咪咪, mīmī, meow meow) became the most popular term. In my vaste experience, this is the term girls favour.

Several times in China I have almost died from eating the tasteless white doughy pastry called (馒头, mántou, steamed bun). The reason was that having drinks on hand during a meal is not so common. The stuff is like eating sponges. My esophagus does not seem to propulse it down so I need massive amounts of preferably beer to float it down the tube. The first time I was madly gesturing with the universal hand on my throat sign that I couldn't breath. However, it is not a sign that is nearly as universal as you might want to think. All the people in the restaurant seemed mystified. I ran through a door, thinking it was a washroom, where there is almost never water to drink, the toilet would have worked fine. I burst into another restaurant and puked on the floor, relieved. Anyways, another common term for breasts is (馒头, mántou, steamed bun). (馒, mán,) has no meaning on its own. Strange language, (头, tou, head). So a girl with a pair of (馒头, mántou, steamed bun) has a sizable set of knockers. The bun is fist sized, huge, Chinese style.

The approximately 250 million girls in China with almost no breasts have a (飞机场, fēijīchǎng, **fly machine site**) or (飞机场, fēijīchǎng, **airport**). Last time I heard that reference was grade 6. (波霸, bōbà, **boobs**) is a phonetic loan word. Characters chosen to sound like an English word where the meaning of each character does not add to the meaning of the word. (波, bō, **wave of water**) and (霸, bà, **tyrant**) form the word. I want to get my hands on your *undulating tyrants*. Kind of has an S&M theme to it. Imagine that, a tall thin Chinese girl with jet black hair down to her waist in black shiny leather and 6 inch spiked heels and a whip. Makes me want to get back to Chengdu.

(奶, nǎi, **milk**) is straight forward, two milks equal (奶奶, nǎinǎi, **breasts**).

(波, bō, **wave of water**)   (场, chǎng, **site, field**)
(霸, bà, **tyrant**)   (飞机场, fēijīchǎng, **fly machine site**)
(波霸, bōbà, **boobs**)   (咪, mī, **meow**)
(飞, fēi, **fly**)   (咪咪, mīmī, **meow meow**)
(机, jī, **machine**)   (奶, nǎi, **milk**)

Shit

I remember studying China in geography class in the mid seventies. ***Night soil*** was the euphamism for the human shit that they put on their field crops. What we didn't learn was that most households did not have a toilet, same today. They have a slit trench in the yard. Toilets are for the city dwellers. They are floor level squatters. In rural areas a family still collects shit for field crops. If they do not farm, they sell it to a neighbour, complete with sanitary napkins, cigarette butts, toilet paper, dead pets and any other thing that they throw in the open pit in their yard. How about another bowl of that the fresh salad? This helps explain the 100's of millions of people with various forms of hepatitis.

(屎, **shǐ**, **shit**) is the usual less than polite term. Interestingly, the stuff that collects in the corner of your eye, they call (眼屎, **yǎnshǐ**, **eye shit**). My wife put together *eye poo* for this one in English, cute. (便, **biàn**, **convenient**) forms the basis of #1 and #2. (大便, **dà biàn**, **big convenient**) is the family friendly name for laying the brown anaconda in the poo pit. (小便, **xiǎo biàn**, **little convenient**) is urinating.

One of the interesting things about the family poo pit is that other family members can look and comment on your shit and then prognosticate all your health concerns. Everyone thinks that they are a doctor in China so you hear all kinds of weird shit. In the winter in north China it freezes like a one metre tall shit-sicle and gets unnervingly close to the ol' cinammon eye. Like squatting over the Mater Horn in Switzerland. It can get a right proper pinnacle on it. Occassionally you have to push it into the pit with a stick or drink 8 beers so that you have enough hot piss to melt her down a few stools.

The squat toilet is actually a more normal position to take a crap from. I am always curious to know how amputees get it done in China.

(眼屎, **yǎnshǐ**, **eye shit**)   (便, **biàn**, **convenient**)

(眼, **yǎn**, **eye**)   (大便, **dà biàn**, **big convenient**)

(屎, **shǐ**, **shit**)   (小便, **xiǎo biàn**, **little convenient**)

The Chinese hate the Japanese like you cannot imagine. The flames of this are fanned by the media, books and the continual bantering between the countries. One of the favoured names for the asshole is (红日, **hóng rì**, **red sun**). This works in their hatred for the Japanese and smears shit on the Japanese flag. Then there is the insult to the plant kingdom, (菊花, **júhuā**, **chrysanthemum**, **asshole**).

So lets formulate a good curse;

Heh, stupid cunt, I want to stick my little chicken in your chrysanthemum!

Now farts, (放屁, **fàng pì**, **to fart**), the characters mean *release fart*. Shit, has some value as fertilizer whereas farts are useless and hence more of an insult. In fact the Chinese shit culture is based around fart insults. (屁话, **pìhuà**, **fart talk**) is like calling bullshit on someone. (话, **huà**, **talk**)

So my wife, who has had nothing to do with this chapter, just offered this one. She noted that this was ***man dirt talk***.

他	说的	都是	他	妈	的	屁话
Tā	shuō de	dōushì	tā	mā	de	pìhuà.
He / his	talk	all is	he / his	mother	's	fart talk.

(屁事, **pìshì**, **fart issue**) means a meaningless issue. (事, **shì**, **matter, issue**)

你	正在	讲	什么	屁话
Nǐ	zhēngzài	jiǎng	shénme	pìhuà.
You	straight at	talk	what	fart talk.
You	is	talk	what	fart talk.

(屁眼, **pìyǎn**, **fart eye**), not hard to figure out which orfice that is. (眼, **yǎn**, **eye**) Nothing worse than cursing someones children in China. Especially wishing they had an imperforate anus, see below.

叫	你	生	孩子	没有	屁股	眼
Jiào	nǐ	shēng	háizi	méiyǒu	pìgu	yǎn.
Call	you / your	born	child	not have	ass	eye.

Ass eye, that is so fucking funny!

(股, **gǔ**, **thigh**)

(屁股, **pìgu**, **ass**)

(叫, **jiào**, **call**)

(眼, **yǎn**, **eye**)

(说, **shuō**, **to speak**)

(吃屎, **chī shǐ**, **eat shit**)

(红日, **hóng rì**, **red sun**)

(菊花, **júhuā**, **chrysanthemum, asshole**)

(去吃大便, **qù chī dàbiàn**, **go eat shit**)

(放, **fàng**, **to put, to place, to release**)

(屁, **pì**, **fart**)

(放屁, **fàng pì**, **to fart**)

(事, **shì**, **matter, issue**)

(尻, **kāo**, **ass**)

(我尻, **wǒ kào**, **my ass**)

Bonus Filth Section

Turtles and Eggs

(王八, **wáng bā**, **Wang 8**) is the term that is usually written that means something like *son of a bitch*. (王, **Wáng**, **Wang**) (八, **bā**, **8**) The offspring of an unvirtuos woman is a (王八蛋, **wángbādàn**). (蛋, **dàn**, **egg**). Hence, the products of conception are *laid*. Another meaning of 王八 is (鳖, **biē**, **fresh-water turtle**). The turtles head re-emerging from hiding in the turtle's shell look like the head of a dick emerging from the foreskin, and turtles lay eggs. So a 王八 is a woman who has lost her virtue, and a 王八蛋 is the progeny of such a woman, a turtle product, but, figuratively, also a penis product.

This is high end insulting in China. A lot of insults flow from this thinking. The turtle becomes emblematic of the penis and of promiscuous intercourse. The tortoise is the close relative of the turtle. (龟, **guī**, **tortoise**) From this comes;

(龟孙子, **guī sūnzi**, **tortoise grandson**)

(龟儿子, **guī érzi**, **tortoise son**)

(混蛋, **hún dàn**, **confuse egg**) this one implies two men one woman.

(笨蛋, **bèndàn**, **stupid egg**)   (笨, **bèn**, **stupid**)

(蠢蛋, **chǔn dàn**, **stupid egg**)   (蠢, **chǔn**, **stupid**)

(倒蛋, **dǎodàn**, **topple egg**)   *to cause trouble*   (倒, **dǎo**, **topple**)

(滚蛋, **gǔndàn**, **roll up egg**)   *get out of sight*!   (滚, **gǔn**, **roll up**)

(坏蛋, **huàidàn**, **rotten egg**)   (坏, **huài**, **rotten**)

(孙子, sūnzi, grandson)

(儿子, érzi, son)

(龟, guī, tortoise)

(混, hùn, confuse)

(混蛋, hún dàn, confuse egg)

(蛋, dàn, egg)

(坏, huài, rotten)

(滚, gǔn, roll up)

(倒, dǎo, topple)

(龟孙子, guī sūnzi, tortoise grandson)

(鳖, biē, fresh-water turtle)

(王, Wáng, Wang)

(八, bā, 8)

(王八, wáng bā, Wang 8)

(王八蛋, wángbādàn)

(蛋, dàn, egg)

(蠢, chǔn, stupid)

(笨, bèn, stupid)

Another Biggie

(戴绿帽子, dài lǜmàozi, wear green hat) originates from male brothel workers in the *Tang Dynasty* that had to wear green hats. It is an insult that means some other guy is tapping your wife.

(戴, dài, wear)

(绿帽子, lǜmàozi, green hat)

www.insultmonger.com

The Cursing Exam

Now, here is the final cursing exam. Any words we have not covered are given, as usual. Fill in the translation in the empty table boxes. The correct answer is in the back of the book. This is a lame ass test but if I have drills like this I can submit this book to school boards for consideration.

咱们 今晚 吃 四川 菜 吧

你 个 死 屄

你 知道 我 不能 吃 那 种 恶心 的 东西

(今晚, jīnwǎn, this night)　　(吃, chī, eat)

(吧, ba, expectation particle)　　(你, nǐ, you)

(种, zhǒng, type)　　(个, ge, of)

(知道, zhīdao, know)　　(我, wǒ, me)

(菜, cài, dish)　　(死, sǐ, dead)

(恶心, èxīn, disgusting)　　(那, nà, that)

(四川, Sìchuān, Sichuan)　　(屄, bī, cunt)

(咱们, zánmen, we)　　(东西, dōngxi, thing)

(不能, bùnéng, not can)　　(的, de)

Language Lessons

Okay, time to take off the diapers and put on your big Chinaman pants. Actually, little kids in China have these cool quilted split-ass pants they wear. They are called (**开裆裤, kāidāngkù, open crotch pants**). You can see their rosey assed butt checks hanging out in winter. The pants are cool until you see some kid squat down in a store and lay a steaming brown chocolate smoothie at your feet. At our wedding, some little kid came out and laid one down right in front of us while we were being photographed. Try retouching that. I digress, back to *Chinese*.

Tone, especially third tone, varies with sentence position and neighbouring characters. Also read the chapter (一七八不, **yī, qī, bā, bù, one, seven, eight, not**). Each paragraph will be presented and then fulling parsed immediately after. Look at both and decide which way you want to do it, read first or look at analysis.

In the parsed section, under each sentence line there is a tone marker line. This shows the correct tone irrespective of **Hanyu Pinyin** tone marking. Comedians love to make jokes as do Americans about the choppy phonetics of Mandarin and more particularily Cantonese. This is because a near complete glottal stop should occur between words. Whereas English glides between words, Mandarin is a little choppy. This is one of the first things to go on the street slang and if you want to see correct spoken Mandarin, the best I have ever seen is on CCTV 9 on Chinese television. In order to keep their job they must speak perfect Mandarin and they get their pay penalized if they make tone errors. They love that money in China, hence perfect grammar.

At the back of the book there are cut out extra pages for phonetics and tones and should you be so motivated, the Kangxi Radicals.

王:	你好
张:	你好
王:	你的名字叫什么
张:	我的名字叫张,你呢
王:	我的名字叫王
张:	你是哪儿人
王:	我是加拿大人,你呢
张:	我是中国人
王:	啊好的
张:	我喜欢加拿大
王:	你去过加拿大吗
张:	我没有去过
王:	你要去吗
张:	当然我想要去
王:	你会说英语吗
张:	我不会说英语
王:	我懂英语太难了
张:	但是你会说汉语啊
王:	我会说一点汉语
张:	我觉得你非常好
王:	谢谢您
张:	你学习几年了
王:	我学习三年
张:	只学习三年吗

王: 对每天我学习
张: 每天啊太好了
王: 我在北京住了
张: 真的我来自北京
王: 太好了
张: 对不起我必须去
王: 明白我也必须去
张: 行行再见
王: 再见

So, how did you do? Language learning requires repetition. Reading quietly to yourself is of some benefit but linguists long ago determined that reading out loud is the most effective strategy. You will never learn Chinese characters by looking at them. You must practice writing them. If you break up sentences into the common occurring phrases, it is easier to learn them bit by bit. If you want to see a language learning Nazi take a look at this guy.

http://www.youtube.com/user/Glossika

(开, kāi, open, to operate)

(裆, dāng, crotch, seam)

(裤子, kùzi, pants)

(开裆裤, kāidāngkù, open crotch pants)

王	你 ↗ Nǐ You	好 √ hǎo! good!					(你, nǐ, you) (好, hǎo, good)
张	你 ↗ Nǐ You	好 √ hǎo! good!					(的, de, particle) (你的, nǐ de, your)
王	你的 ↘→ Nǐ de Your	名字 ↗→ míngzi name	叫 ↘ jiào call	什么 ↗→ shénme. what?			(名字, míngzi, name) (什么, shénme, what) (叫, jiào, call)
张	我的 ↘→ Wǒ de My	名字 ↗→ míngzi name	叫 ↘ jiào call	张, ↘ Zhāng, Zhang,	你 ↘ nǐ you	呢 → ne. ?	(我, wǒ, me) (我的, wǒ de, me) (张, Zhāng, Zhang)
王	我的 ↘→ Wǒ de My	名字 ↗→ míngzi name	叫 ↘ jiào call	王 ↗ Wáng. Wang.			(呢, ne, particle) (王, Wáng, king)
张	你 ↘ Nǐ You	是 ↘ shì is	哪儿 ↘→ nǎ'r where	人 ↗ rén. person?			(是, shì, is) (哪儿, nǎ'r, where) (人, rén, person)

王	我 ↘ Wǒ Me	是 ↘ shì is	加拿大 — ↗ ↘ Jiānádà Canada	人, ↗ rén, person,	你 ↘ nǐ you	呢 → ne. ?	(加拿大, Jiānádà, Canada) (加, jiā, add) (拿, ná, take)
张	我 ↘ Wǒ Me	是 ↘ shì is	中国 — ↗ Zhōngguó China	人 ↗ rén. person.			(中国, Zhōngguó, China) (是, shì, is) (大, dà, big)
王	啊 — Ā, Ah!,	好 ↘ hǎo good.	的 → de.				(啊, ā, elation particle) (好, hǎo, good)
张	我 ↗ Wǒ Me	喜欢 ↘ → xǐhuan like	加拿大 — ↗ ↘ Jiānádà. Canada.				(喜欢, xǐhuan, like) (喜, xǐ, like) (欢, huān, happy)
王	你 ↘ Nǐ You	去过 ↘ ↘ qù guò gone to	加拿大 — ↗ ↘ Jiānádà Canada	吗 → ma. ?			(去, qù, go) (过, guò, particle) (吗, ma, ?)
张	我 ↘ Wǒ Me	没有 ↗ ↘ méiyǒu not have	去过 ↘ ↘ qù guò. gone.				(没有, méiyǒu, not have) (没, méi, not) (有, yǒu, have)

王	你	要	去	吗		(要, yào, want)
	↘	↘	↘	→		(去, qù, go)
	Nǐ	yào	qù	ma.		(吗, ma, ?)
	You	want	go	?		

张	当然	我	想	要	去	(当然, dāngrán, of course)
	—↗	↗	↘	↘	↘	(想, xiǎng, desire)
	Dāngrán,	wǒ	xiǎng	yào	qù.	(当, dāng, accept)
	Of course,	me	desire	want	go.	(要, yào, want)

王	你	会	说	英语	吗	(然, rán, correct)
	↘	↘	—	—↘	→	(会, huì, able to)
	Nǐ	huì	shuō	Yīngyǔ	ma.	(说, shuō, speak)
	You	able to	speak	English	?	

张	我	不	会	说	英语	(英语, Yīngyǔ, English)
	↘	↗	↘	—	—↘	(不, bù, not)
	Wǒ	bú	huì	shuō	Yīngyǔ.	
	Me	not	able to	speak	English.	

王	我	懂	英语	太	难	了	(懂, dǒng, understand)
	↗	↘	—↘	↘	↗	→	(太, tài, extremely)
	Wǒ	dǒng,	Yīngyǔ	tài	nán	le.	(难, nán, difficult)
	Me	understand,	English	extreme	difficult.		

张	但是	你	会	说	汉语	啊	(汉语, Hànyǔ, Chinese)
	↘↘	↘	↘	—	↘↗	√	(啊, ǎ, puzzled surprise)
	Dànshì,	nǐ	huì	shuō	Hànyǔ	ǎ.	(但是, dànshì, but)
	But,	you	able to	speak	Chinese	ah!	

王	我 ↘ Wǒ Me	会 ↘ huì able to	说 → shuō speak	一点 ↘↘ yīdiǎn a little	汉语 ↘√ Hànyǔ. Chinese.	(一点, yīdiǎn, a little) (汉语, Hànyǔ, Chinese) (说, shuō, speak) (我, wǒ, me)
张	我 ↘ Wǒ Me	觉得 ↗→ juéde think	你 ↘ nǐ you	非常 —↗ fēicháng uncommon	好 √ hǎo. good.	(觉得, juéde, think) (非常, fēicháng, uncommon) (好, hǎo, good)
王	**谢谢** ↘→ Xièxie Thank	**您** ↗ nín. you.				(谢谢, xièxie, thank thank) (您, nín, you)
张	你 ↘ Nǐ You	学习 ↗↗ xuéxí study	几 ↘ jǐ how many	年 ↗ nián year?	了 → le?	(几, jǐ, how many) (学习, xuéxí, study) (年, nián, year)
王	我 ↘ Wǒ Me	学习 ↗↗ xuéxí study	三 — sān three	年 ↗ nián. year.		(三, sān, three) (学习, xuéxí, study)
张	只 ↘ Zhǐ	学习 ↗↗ xuéxí	三 — sān	年 ↗ nián	吗 → ma?	(只, zhǐ, only) (学习, xuéxí, study) (三, sān, three)

	Only	study	three	year	?	(年, nián, year)
王	对 ↘ Duì, Correct,	每天 ↘ — měitiān each day	我 ↘ wǒ me	学习 ↗ ↗ xuéxí. study.		(每天, měitiān, each day) (学习, xuéxí, study) (对, duì, correct)
张	每天 ↘ — Měitiān Each day	啊 — ā, ah!,	太 ↘ tài extreme	好 ↘ hǎo good.	了 → le?	(啊, ā, elation particle) (太, tài, great) (好, hǎo, good) (了, le, particle)
王	我 ↘ Wǒ Me	在 ↘ zài at	北京 ↘ — Běijīng Beijing	住了 ↘ → zhùle. lived.		(北京, Běijīng, Beijing) (在, zài, at) (住, zhù, live)
张	真的 — → Zhēn de, Really,	我 ↘ wǒ me	来自 ↗ ↘ láizì from	北京 ↘ — Běijīng. Beijing.		(真, zhēn, really) (真的, zhēn de really) (来自, láizì, from)
王	太 ↘ Tài Extreme	好 ↘ hǎo good	了 → le. !			(太, tài, extremely) (好, hǎo, good) (了, le)
张	对不起 ↘ →√ Duìbuqǐ, Sorry,	我 ↘ wǒ me	必须 ↘ bìxū must	去 ↘ — qù. go.		(对不起, duìbuqǐ, sorry) (必须, bìxū, must) (去, qù, go) (对, duì, correct)

王	明白	我	也	必须	去	(明白, míngbai, clear)
	↗ →	↘	↘	↘ —	↘	(也, yě, also)
	Míngbai,	wǒ	yě	bìxū	qù.	(必须, bìxū, must)
	Clear,	me	also	must	go.	(明, míng, clear)
						(白, bai, white)
张	行行	再见				(行, xíng, ok)
	↗ →	↘ ↘				(再见, zàijiàn, again see)
	Xíng xíng,	zàijiàn.				(再, zài, again)
	Okay,	again see.				(见, jiàn, see)
王	再见					(不起, bùqǐ, be very ill)
	↘ ↘					
	Zàijiàn.					
	Again.					

Conditional Sentences, Using *If*

Mandarin utilizes different words for *if* that are completely interchangable. Conditional sentences set a condition for an outcome. There are different grammatical categories of sentences but the constructions are all the same. There is no value to knowing the individual categories.

The five common words that mean *if* in Mandarin have no pattern of favourite usage. My favourite is (如果, **rúguǒ**, **to be like fruit**, **if**) You can pick a favourite and stick with it but you need to know all of them to understand others. Ah shit, here they are, the categories of sentences. ***To be like fruit***, now that is a good word.

1) Express specific fact or general truth
2) Express probable future result
3) Express imagined, impossible or unreal future situations
4) Express a regret about something that did not happen in the past

The two most common words for *if* are; (如果, **rúguǒ**, **if**) and (要是, **yàoshì**, **if**). These two words are used in common speech and common writing. (假如, **jiǎrú**, **if**) is used in both common and formal speech and writing. (若是, **ruòshì**, **if**) and (假使, **jiǎshǐ**, **if**) are seen in classical and formal writing. Less common are;

(倘若, **tǎngruò**, **if**)	(如其, **rúqí**, **if**)
(若是, **ruòshì**, **if**)	(设若, **shèruò**, **if**)
(如若, **rúruò**, **if**)	(设使, **shèshǐ**, **if**)
(假设, **jiǎshè**, **if**)	(倘或, **tǎnghuò**, **if**)
(倘使, **tǎngshǐ**, **if**)	(倘然, **tǎngrán**, **if**)

A) Express Specific Fact or General Truth

If you drink alcohol you become drunk.

假如	你	喝	很	多	白酒	你	就	会	醉
Jiǎrú	nǐ	hē	hěn	duō	báijiǔ	nǐ	jiù	huì	zuì.
If	you	drink	very	much	alcohol	you	just	able	drunk.

(假如, jiǎrú, if) (醉, zuì, drunk)

(喝, hē, drink) (就, jiù, just)

(喝, hē, drink) (会, huì, able to)

(白酒, báijiǔ, spirits) (多, duō, much)

(成为, chéngwéi, become) (很, hěn, very)

B) Express Probable Future Result

Example: *If you study Mandarin hard, your Mandarin will improve.* Incidently, the literal translation of the sentence below is *To be like fruit you know true study Han language your Han language just able to enter step*, that's not idiotic right?

如果	你	认真	学	汉语	你的	汉语	就	会	进步
Rúguǒ	nǐ	rènzhēn	xué	Hànyǔ	nǐ de	Hànyǔ	jiù	huì	jìnbù.
If	you	diligent	study	Chinese	your	Chinese	just	able	improve.

(如, rú, to be like) (真, zhēn, true, really)

(果, guǒ, fruit) (认真, rènzhēn, diligent)

(如果, rúguǒ, if) (学, xué, study)

(你, nǐ, you) (汉语, Hànyǔ, Chinese)

(认, rèn, recognize, know) (你的, nǐ de, your)

(就, jiù, just) (步, bù, step)
(会, huì, meet, can, able) (进步, jìnbù, progress, improve)
(进, jìn, enter)

C) Express Imagined, Impossible or Unreal Future Situations

Example: *If I were rich I would take you abroad.*

要是	我	很	有钱	我	就	带	你	出国
Yàoshì	wǒ	hěn	yǒuqián	wǒ	jiù	dài	nǐ	chūguó.
If	me	very	have money	me	just	take	you	exit country.

(要是, yàoshì, if) (就, jiù, just)

(我, wǒ, me) (带, dài, bring, take)

(很, hěn, very) (你, nǐ, you)

(有, yǒu, have) (出, chū, exit)

(钱, qián, money) (国, guó, country)

(有钱, yǒuqián, have money) (出国, chūguó, exit country)

D) Express Regret About Something That Did Not Happen

Example: *If you had not lied, I would not be so angry.*

假使	你	没有	撒谎	我	就	不会	那么	生气
Jiǎshǐ	nǐ	méiyǒu	sāhuǎng,	wǒ	jiù	búhuì	nàme	shēngqì.
If	you	not have	lied,	me	just	not able	so	angry.

(假使, jiǎshǐ, if) (没, méi, not)

(你, nǐ, you) (有, yǒu, have)

(没有, méiyǒu, not have) (会, huì, able to)

(撒, sā, let go, release) (不会, búhuì, not able to)

(谎, huǎng, lie, falsehood) (那, nà, that)

(撒谎, sāhuǎng, tell lies) (那么, nàme, like that, so)

(我, wǒ, me) (生, shēng, to bear, born)

(就, jiù, just) (气, qì, air, vapor, vital energy)

(不, bù, not) (生气, shēngqì, get angry)

http://www.peggyteacheschinese.com/latest/category/lessons?currentPage=2

(如果, rúguǒ, if) (假, jiǎ, false)

(要是, yàoshi, if) (使, shǐ, to make, cause to)

(假使, jiǎshǐ, if) (假如, jiǎrú, if)

(假如, jiǎrú, if) (若, ruò, seem, as if, if)

(若, ruòshì, if) (若是, ruòshì, if)

(如果, rúguǒ, if) (假使, jiǎshǐ, if)

(如, rú, to be like) (设, shè, to set up)

(果, guǒ, fruit) (借, jiè, borrow)

(要是, yàoshì, if) (脱, tuō, take off)

(要, yào, want) (倘 tǎng, if)

(是, shi, is) (其, qí, he, she, it)

Sentence Parsing 1

Exposure, practice and repetition are the only way you are going to ***get it right***. It is interesting to read about how the brain processes information. Apparently your brain is processing information further to the right in the character string than you are consciously aware of. However, when you begin, you need to look for logical divisions of the sentence. In the sentence below, you can pick out numbers, **CNI's** and compound character words. Numbers in Mandarin can be irritatingly long, especially dates.

This sentence is an example of a …(是, **shì, is**)… (的, **de**) sentence construction. In this example it is used to emphasize time or date. Simply, the first half of the sentence is stating a birthdate. To determine which is the *Subject* and which is the *Object* and *Indirect Object* there is a simple test. Grammatically, *Girlfriend of mine* works but *Mine of girlfriend* does not. For this sentence, *me* or *mine* is subordinate to *girlfriend* making *girlfriend* the *Subject* and *me / mine* an *Object*. The *Direct Object* is the target of the verb (是, **shì, is**) and is the the birth date.

我的女朋友是一九六七年五月二十八号出生的, 今年三十四岁, 这个星期天是她的生日.

我	的	女朋友	是
Wǒ	de	nǚpéngyou	shì…
Me	of	female friend	is…
My		girl friend	is…
		Subject	Verb

一九六七	年	五	月	二十八	号	出生	的
yījiǔliùqī	nián	wǔ	yuè	èrshíbā	hào	chūshēng	de,
1967	year	5	month	28	number	exit born,	

(出生, chūshēng, be born) (月, yuè, month)

(是, shì, is) (二, èr, two)

(的, de) (十, shí, ten)

(年, nián, year) (八, bā, eight)

(六, liù, six) (号, hào, number)

(七, qī, seven) (朋友, péngyou, friend)

(五, wǔ, five) (女朋友, nǚpéngyou, girl friend)

今年三十四岁,

今年	三十四	岁
Jīnnián	sānshísì	suì.
Current year	34	years age.

(今年, jīnnián, this year) (四, sì, four)

(三, sān, three) (岁, suì, years old)

这个星期天是她的生日.

这个	星期天	是	她	的	生日
Zhèige	Xīngqītiān	shì	tā	de	shēngri.
This one	star period day	is	she	of	born day.
This	Sunday	is	her		birthday.

(这个, zhège, this one)   (她, tā, she)
(星期天, Xīngqītiān, Sunday)   (生日, shēngri, birthday)
(是, shì, is)

So, it glosses like this; *My girlfriend is 1967 year 5 moon 28 number ē of, current year 34 years age. This Sunday is her birthday.*

我的 女朋友 是 一九六七 年 五月 二十八 号 出生 的, 今年 三十四 岁, 这个 星期天 是 她 的 生日.

Wǒ de nǔpéngyou shì yījiǔliùqī nián wǔ yuè èrshíbā hào chūshēng de, jīnnián sānshísì suì, zhèige Xīngqītiān shì tā de shēngri.

My girlfried is 1967 year 5 month 28 number born, current year 34 age, this Sunday is her birthday.

Comparative Grammatical Constructions

Direct Comparative

The construction of **Direct Comparative** sentences takes a standard pattern. The two compared **Subjects** are separated by (比, **bǐ**, **compare**). Of note, the **Adverb** used to quantify the comparison does not have to be (较, **jiào**, **relatively**, **quite**). This is used for example purposes but please look for the list at the end of this lesson. The comparison does not have to be positive. The Adverb can be negated.

An **Adverb** is a part of speech. It is any word that modifies any part of speech or other verbs other than a noun. **Adverbs** can modify verbs, adjectives, numbers, clauses, sentences and other adverbs. **Adverbs** typically answer questions such as *how?*, *in what way?*, *when?*, *where?*, and *to what extent?*.

A (比, **bǐ**, **compare**) B + (较, **jiào**, **quite**) + *Descriptive Adjective Phrase* (**DAP**)

Peggy	比	其他	的	中文	老师	较	漂亮
Peggy	bǐ	qítā	de	Zhōngwén	lǎoshī	jiào	piàoliang.
Peggy	compare	other		Chinese	teacher	quite	beautiful.
Subject₁	比			Subject₂		Adverb	DAP
A	比			B			DAP

(其, qí, he, she, it)   (亮, liàng, shine)

(他, tā, he)   (漂亮, piàoliang, beautiful)

(其他, qítā, others)   (比, bǐ, compare, than)

(老师, lǎoshī, teacher)   (比较, bǐjiào, relatively)

(漂, piāo, drift)   (较, jiào, relatively, quite)

Another *Comparative* construction is that which compares to an unidentified ideal or perfect situation. The general construction of this comparative structure is

Subject (比较, **bǐjiào**, **relatively**) **Verb + Object**.

我	比较	喜欢	Peggy	老师的	中文	课
Wǒ	bǐjiào	xǐhuan	Peggy	lǎoshī de	Zhōngwén	kè.
Me	relatively	like	Peggy	teacher's	Chinese	lesson.
Sbj.	Adverb	Verb		Object		

(喜, **xǐ**, **happiness**)   (老, **lǎo**, **old**)

(欢, **huān**, **happy**)   (师, **shī**, **teacher**)

(喜欢, **xǐhuan**, **like**)   (老师, **lǎoshī**, **teacher**)

(课, **kè**, **lesson**)

Again, (比较, **bǐjiào**, **relatively**) can be substituted for any reasonable and appropriate *Adverbial Phrase*, whether it is one word such as, (很, **hěn**, **very**) or a proper *Phrase* such as (很多, **hěn duō**, **very much**). The *Verb* can also be negated such as;

我	很	不	喜欢	………
Wǒ	hěn	bù	xǐhuan	…………..
Me	very	not	like	…………..
Sbj.	Adverbial Phrase		Verb	Object Phrase

Credits to Peggy, I copied it directly from her website.

http://www.peggyteacheschinese.com/

Superlative Comparative

In grammar, the *Superlative* of an *Adjective* or *Adverb* is the greatest form of the *Adjective* or *Adverb*. This indicates that something has at least one feature to a greater degree than anything it is being compared to in a given context.

The *Superlative* construction can be *Comparative* or *Absolute*. A *Comparative Superlative* implies that there is something, some quality or someone existing in a lesser state relative to the qualifying *Adjective* or *Adverb*.

The usual character word used to mark the *Comparative Superlative* (**CS**) in Mandarin grammar is (最, **zuì**, **most**). The typical (**CS**) grammatical construction is **Subject** + **Verb** (最, **zuì**, **most**) **Adjective** + **Object**. Okay Peggy, this is for you;

Peggy	是	最	可爱	的	中文	老师
Peggy	shì	zuì	kě'ài	de	Zhōngwén	lǎoshī.
Peggy	is	most	can love		Chinese	teacher.
Subject	Verb	Superlative	Adjective		Object	

(是, shì, to be)   (可爱, kě'ài, can love, lovable, cute)

(最, zuì, most)   (中文, Zhōngwén, Chinese)

(可, kě, can)   (老师, lǎoshī, teacher)

(爱, ài, love)   (师, shī, teacher)

The grammatical construction of an *Absolute Superlative* does not compare to a lesser entity but stands alone in its degree. The usual Mandarin word used to mark this is (非常, **fēicháng**, **not common**).

Peggy	是	最	可爱	的	中文	老师
Peggy	shì	fēicháng	kě'ài	de	Zhōngwén	lǎoshī.
Peggy	is	not common	can love		Chinese	teacher.
Peggy	is	uncommonly	cute		Chinese	teacher.
Subject	Verb	Superlative	Adjective			Object

(非, fēi, not)

(常, cháng, ordinary, common, normal, usual)

(非常, fēicháng, not usual, uncommon, unusually)

The above construction does not compare to another, it simply marks the highest level of the *Adjective*.

Again, thanks Peggy.

http://www.peggyteacheschinese.com/latest/category/lessons?currentPage=5

Sameness Comparative

To indicate that two *Noun Phrases* are similar or equal the construction is thus;

Noun Phrase₁ (和, hé, and) Noun Phrase₂ (一样, yīyàng, one same)

昨天	的	天气	和	今天	的	天气	一样
Zuótiān	de	tiānqi	hé	jīntiān	de	tiānqi	yīyàng.
Previous day	's	weather	and	current day	's	weather	one same.
Yesterday's		weather	and	today's		weather	the same.
Noun Phrase₁				**Noun Phrase₂**			

In this above construction, the second (天气, **tiānqi**, **weather**) is optional and its presence is more proper / formal. Without it there is left what I called the **hanging** (的, **de**) construction in the first character example at the front of the book.

To indicate that two *Adjective Phrases* are the same the construction is;

Noun Phrase₁ (和, **hé**, **and**) **Noun Phrase₂** (一样, **yīyàng**, **one same**) **Adjective**

我	妹妹	和	姐姐	一佯	呆笨
Wǒ	mèimei	hé	jiějie	yīyàng	dāibèn.
Me	young sister	and	elder sister	same	stupid.

(昨天, **zuótiān**, yesterday) (妹妹, **mèimei**, younger sister)

(天气, **tiānqi**, weather) (姐姐, **jiějie**, elder sister)

(今天, **jīntiān**, today) (和, **hé**, and)

(呆笨, **dāibèn**, stupid) (一样, **yīyàng**, one same)

Here is an alternate construction;

Noun Phrase₁ (像, **xiàng**, **resemble**) **Noun Phrase₂** (一样, **yīyàng**, **one same**)

这个	像	那个	一样
Zhèige	xiàng	nàge	yīyàng.
This one	resemble	that one	same.

(这个, **zhèige**, this one) (一样, **yīyàng**, one same)

(像, **xiàng**, resemble) (那个, **nàge**, that one)

Non Sameness Comparative

Either of the two *Similarity Comparative* constructions can be negated following the usual rules with (不, bù, not), (不一样, bù yīyàng, not same).

昨天	的	天气	和	今天	的	天气	不一样
Zuótiān	de	tiānqi	hé	jīntiān	de	tiānqi	bù yīyàng.
Previous day	's	weather	and	current day	's	weather	not same.
Yesterday's		weather	and	today's		weather	not same.
Noun Phrase₁				Noun Phrase₂			

Similarity Comparitive

To indicate that one Noun Phrase resembles another use (像, xiàng, resemble).

Noun Phrase₁ (像, xiàng, resemble) Noun Phrase₂

他的	脸	像	马	的	屁股
Tā de	liǎn	xiàng	mǎ	de	pìgu.
His	face	resemble	horse's		ass.
Noun Phrase₁			Noun Phrase₂		

他的	脸	和	马	的	屁股	很	像
Tā de	liǎn	hé	mǎ	de	pìgu	hěn	xiàng.
His	face	and	horse's		ass	very	resemble.
Noun Phrase₁			Noun Phrase₂				

(脸, liǎn, face)　　　　(马, mǎ, horse)

(屁股, pìgu, butt)　　　(像, xiàng, resemble)

Sentence Parsing 2

王先生是一位非常有经验的男老师. 在北京大学工作, 他专教留学生学习现代汉语和书法.

Now this is a good example of a very wordy *Object*. The beginning of the *Object Noun Phrase* is the **CNI**, (位, **wèi**, **CNI for people**) marking a noun that can be counted.

王	先生	是
Wáng	xiānsheng	shì…
Wang	Mr.	is…
Subject		Verb

一位非常有经验的男老师.

一	位	非常	有	经验	的	男	老师
…yī	wèi	fēicháng	yǒu	jīngyàn	de	nán	lǎoshī.
…one / a	CNI	not common	have	experience		male	teacher.
		Adjective Phrase					Direct Object

(一位老师, **yī wèi lǎoshī**, **one teacher**) is the most basic *Object* stripped of it's modifiers. (非常有经验, **fēicháng yǒu jīngyàn**, **not common have experience**) is an *Adjective Phrase* modifying the *Direct Object* (老师, **lǎoshī**, **teacher**). The use

403

of (的, **de**) is appropriate as it marks the preceding phrase as a modifier and marks the next characters as *Nouns*. There is no (的, **de**) between (男, **nán**, **male**) and the *Direct Object* (老师, **lǎoshī**, **teacher**) as (的, **de**) can be omitted between a *Noun* modifying another *Noun*.

(经验, jīngyàn, experience)

(王, wáng, King)

(先生, xiānsheng, teacher, mister)

(位, wèi, polite CNI for people)

(非常, fēicháng, not common)

(有, yǒu, have)

(男, nán, male)

(老师, lǎoshī, teacher)

在北京大学工作,

在	北京	大学	工作
zài	Běijīng	dàxué	gōngzuò.
at	Beijing	big school	work do.
at	Beijing	university	work.

(在, zài, at)

(北京, Běijīng, Beijing)

(大学, dàxué, university)

(工作, gōngzuò, work)

他专教留学生学习现代汉语和书法.

他	专	教	留学生	学习	现代	汉语	和	书法
Tā	zhuān	jiāo	liúxuéshēng	xuéxí	xiàndài	Hànyǔ	hé	shūfǎ.
He	special	teach	leave student	study	current times	Chinese	and	calligraphy.
He	special	teach	away student	study	modern	Chinese	and	calligraphy.

(书法, shūfǎ, calligraph)

(代, dài, time period)

(现代, xiàndài, current times)

(学习, xuéxí, study)

(留学生, liúxuéshēng, overseas student)

(专, zhuān, special)

(教, jiāo, teach)

(留, liú, stay)

(留, liú, to leave)

(汉语, Hànyǔ, Chinese)

(和, hé, and)

王 先生 是 一位 非常 有 经验 的 男 老师 在 北京 大学 工作, 他 专 教 留学生 学习 现代 汉语 和 书法.

Wáng xiānsheng shì yī wèi fēicháng yǒu jīngyàn de nán lǎoshī. Zài Běijīng dàxué gōngzuò. Tā zhuān jiāo liúxuéshēng xuéxí xiàndài Hànyǔ hé shūfǎ.

Wang Mr. is one not common have experience male teacher. At Beijing university work. He special teach away student study modern Han language and calligraphy.

The Subordinating Conjunctions

When and While

A ***Conjunction*** is a word that joins two thoughts, words, phrases, clauses or sentences. ***Subordinating Conjunctions*** (**SC**), also called ***Subordinators***, are conjunctions that introduce a ***Dependent Clause*** (**DC**). A clause is a sentence stuck after another sentence which depends on the first sentence, hence the term ***Dependent Clause***. The usual English ***Subordinators*** are; *after*, *although*, *as much as*, *as long as*, *as soon as*, *because*, *before*, *if*, *in order that*, *lest*, *since*, *so that*, *than*, *that*, *though*, *unless*, *until*, *when*, *whenever*, *where*, *wherever*, *whether*, and *while*.

The common character word that introduces this construction in Mandarin grammar is (当, **dāng, when, while**). The ***Dependent Clause*** is introduced with the phrase (的時候, **de shíhou, while, meanwhile**). On its own, (時候, **shíhou, time**) refers to a duration of time. As there are two phrases, clauses or sentences, they must each include all the components necessary to define themselves. Hence, a formula like approach can be applied. So you will often see this below or a similar expression in grammar books. These books also do a poor job explaining this.

As always, the ***Subject*** can be a ***Subject Phrase*** (**SP**) including more than one party. Usually it is a ***Pronoun*** or ***Pronoun Phrase*** or a ***Noun*** or ***Noun Phrase***. A ***Pronoun Phrase*** could be *he and she*. A ***Noun Phrase*** could be *Wang and Dong* or *cat and mouse*. Get the drift? You possibly think that you do not need to know all of these grammatical terms, but, it will ultimately speed your learning. It will allow you to apply a formula like approach to both analyzing and constructing sentences.

Mostly I wrote that last paragraph so that I could bump this graph onto this page, but it is true.

(当) +/- *Subject 1* + *Verb Phrase* (的時候) +/- *Subject 2* + *Verb Phrase 2*

当	他	洗澡	的時候	他	的	电话	响
Dāng	tā	xǐzǎo	de shíhou	tā	de	diànhuà	xiǎng.
When	she	shower	meanwhile	his		phone	ring.
SC	Sbj. 1	Verb 1	SC	Sbj. 2			Verb 2
Independent Clause				Dependent Clause			

(当, dāng, while) (澡, zǎo, bathe, bath)

(响, xiǎng, make a sound) (电话, diànhuà, telephone)

(洗澡, xǐzǎo, take a bath) (电, diàn, electric)

(洗, xǐ, wash, bathe) (话, huà, speech)

You can see that one phrase is happening *during* the other phrase hence it is a *Durative* construction. So, why is there no (了, le, CRS) marking the sentence you may ask. That is because this sentence is timeless, it is correct but has no placement in time. But you can add (了, le, CRS) to make the events in the past.

当	他	洗澡	的時候	他	的	电话	响	了
Dāng	tā	xǐzǎo	de shíhou	tā	de	diànhuà	xiǎng	le.
When	she	showered	meanwhile	his		phone	rang.	
	Sbj. 1	Verb 1	SC	Sbj. 2			Verb 2	
Independent Clause				Dependent Clause				

Now, (当, dāng, when, while) is a **Temporal Adverb** and as such can be substituted for other *time when* phrases or constructions. In this example below the use of (昨天, **zuótiān**, **yesterday**) marks it as an event in the past and therefore you can use (了, **le**, **CRS**) to mark the event as in the past.

昨天	他	洗澡	的時候	他	的	电话	响	了
Zuótiān	tā	xǐzǎo	de shíhou	tā	de	diànhuà	xiǎng	le.
Yesterday	she	showered	meanwhile	his		phone	rang.	
	Sbj. 1	Verb 1	SC	Sbj. 2			Verb 2	
Independent Clause				**Dependent Clause**				

Don't waste this space, practice some characters!

Sentence Parsing 3

如果你不知道咱们学校食堂和餐厅服务员叫什么名字, 就可以问她们: "小姐, 您贵姓?"

如果	你	不知道	咱们	学校	食堂	和	餐厅
Rúguǒ	nǐ	bùzhīdào	zánmen	xuéxiào	shítáng	hé	cāntīng...
If	you	not know	we	school	eat hall	and	meal hall...
If	you	not know	we	school	cafeteria	and	restaurant...

(咱们, **zánmen**, **we**) means *you and I*, it includes the speaker and those spoken too. That makes the **Subject**, (你, **nǐ**, **you**), a student at the school.

服务员 叫 什么 名字, 就 可以 问 她们:

...服务员	叫	什么	名字	就	可以	问	她们
...fúwùyuán	jiào	shénme	míngzi,	jiù	kěyǐ	wèn	tāmen:
server	called	what	name,	just	can	ask	them:

Really, it is not a good idea to pursue building sentences that are this big. Much safer to make shorter sentences. When you are working at building up your vocabulary, work on small common phrases. If I do not run out of space I will list some near the end of the book.

"小姐, 您 贵姓?"

小姐,	您	贵姓
Xiǎojie,	nín	guìxìng?
Miss,	you	honorably named?

如果 你 不知道 咱们 学校 食堂 和 餐厅 服务员 叫 什么 名字, 就 可以 问 她们:"小姐, 您 贵姓?"

If you not know we school cafeteria and restaurant server called what name, just ask them, Miss, you honorably named?

(如果, rúguǒ, if)

(你, nǐ, you)

(不知道, bùzhīdào, not know)

(咱们, zánmen, we)

(学校, xuéxiào, school)

(食堂, shítáng, eat hall)

(校, xiào, school)

(食, shí, eat)

(堂, táng, hall)

(和, hé, and)

(餐, cān, meal)

(厅, tīng, hall)

(餐厅, cāntīng, dining room)

(服务员, fúwùyuán, server)

(叫, jiào, called)

(什么, shénme, what)

(名字, míngzi, name)

(就, jiù, just)

(可以, kěyǐ, can)

(问, wèn, ask)

(她们, tāmen, they / them)

(小姐, xiǎojie, miss)

(您, nín, you)

(贵姓, guìxìng, honorably named)

The use of (咱们, zánmen, we) in the above sentence rather than a possesive form (咱们的, zánmen de, our) denotes a close relationship between the speaker and the university. It signals that he is either part of the student body, staff or support workers. (咱们, zánmen, we) is also the *Royal We* for you *Brits* or the inclusive *we* for the rest of us. That is, its use demonstrates that the speaker and those spoken to are an inclusive group.

Interestingly, Chinese universities often have a cafeteria style eating area and also a restaurant complete with wine, banquet sized platters and a fine menu. I always feel extremely awkward eating at these as they are often in full site of the cafeteria and it immediately brands you as special, wealthy or entitled which is exactly what it is supposed to do. It is probable that if you get invited, even by a student, you will eat in the (餐厅, **cāntīng**, **dining room**) not the (食堂, **shítáng**, **eat hall**).

So, use your best manners, gently argue that it is too expensive, but give in, and complement the hosts generousity. Either directly or indirectly, everyone in the cafeteria will look at you, judge your appearance, your use of chopsticks and how much you drink. I always impress my hosts by knocking back a bladder buster sized bottle of beer in one going. This can make you an instant legend.

Also, make a gentle argument to pay the bill. But it is not polite to win that argument if you are a foreign guest.

Current Progressive or Continuous Tense

There are a lot of old books that make Mandarin out to be some lame ass language of inferior construction. I actually have some old Mandarin grammar books that say this, calling it an *inferior language*. They were printed before the time of computerized fonts so there are no characters in them. Only variations of **Pinyin**. Amazing right? This is one of the reasons that the language was almost unlearnable to ol' Whitey. To make a character based book, the manuscript could not be typed in entirety. Each character would have to be typeset individually as a picture. Given the huge problem with homphones, some of these old books are hard to understand, which *zài*?

The *Verb Completion* (VC) compounds are easier to understand when you realize that some verbs exist in a *Current Continuous Tense* (CCT). Hence, to mark completion, you need to tack another character onto them to finish the action. (买, **mǎi**, **buying**) and (找, **zhǎo**, **looking for**) become (买了, **mǎile**, **bought**) and (找了, **zhǎole**, **looked for**). Note that (找了, **zhǎole**, **looked for**) does not mean *found*. There are different characters to mark successful verb action. (到, **dào**) is used to make (找到, **zhǎodào**, **look for achieve**).

(正在, **zhèngzài**, **straight at**) is used as a pre-verbal marker of ongoing *Verb Action*. Often it glosses very nicely as *is*.

他	正在	洗澡
Tā	zhèngzài	xǐzǎo.
She	straight at	shower.
She	is	showering.

I had a proper grammarian argue with me that (正在, **zhèngzài**, **straight at**) cannot mean *is* as (是, **shì**, **is**) holds this place. This is from a man who is an expert in a language that has 28 constructions for *if*. This can be simplified to;

他	在	洗澡
Tā	zài	xǐzǎo.
She	at	shower.
She	is	showering.

Or, it can be further complexed to; (着, **zhe**, **indicating continuing progress**), which can be placed after the **VOC** or after the *Verb*. (洗着澡, **xǐzhezǎo**)

他	正在	洗澡	着
Tā	zhèngzài	xǐzǎo	zhe.
She	straight at	shower	-ing.
She	is	showering.	

This is further often paired with (呢, **ne**, **indicating continued state or action**).

他	正在	洗澡	着	呢
Tā	zhèngzài	xǐzǎo	zhe	ne.
She	straight at	shower	-ing.	
She	is	showering.		

So if you use (呢, **ne**, **continued**) you must use (着, **zhe**, **continuing progress**), if you use (正, **zhèng**, **straight**) you must use (在, **zài**, **at**). If you use (在, **zài**, **at**) alone, you do not need to use any other characters. So do you remember the (**SC**) and the (当, **dāng**, **when**) ... (的時候, **de shíhou**, **meanwhile**) construction?

Subordinating Conjunctions (**SC**) can be used with ***Current Continuous Tense*** (**CCT**). What this means is that Verb Action can be modified in these combined constructions.

当	他	正在	洗澡	的時候	他	的	电话	响
Dāng	tā	zhèngzài	xǐzǎo	de shíhou	tā	de	diànhuà	xiǎng.
When	she	straight at	shower	meanwhile	his		phone	ring.
When	she	is	showering	meanwhile	his		phone	ring.
SC	Sbj. 1		Verb 1	SC	Sbj. 2			Verb 2
		Independent Clause				Dependent Clause		

In the above construction, the phone may have **rang once**. So, the first clause is an ongoing action. The **Dependent Clause** is ill defined. So to make it an ongoing action, the **Independent Clause** is unchanged but the **Dependent Clause** gets a marker of ongoing verb Action, (一直在, **yīzhí zài**, **is straight at**).

当	他	正在	洗澡	的時候
Dāng	tā	zhèngzài	xǐzǎo	de shíhou,
When	she	straight at	shower	meanwhile,
When	she	is	showering	meanwhile,
	Sbj. 1		Verb 1	SC
		Independent Clause		

他的	电话	一直	在	响
tā de	diànhuà	yīzhí	zài	xiǎng.
his	phone	straight	at	ring.
his	phone		is	ringing.
Sbj. 2				Verb 2
	Dependent Clause			

Note that (正在, **zhèngzài**, **straight at**) and (一直在, **yīzhí zài**, **straight at**) are the same meaning. Now, asking the resident expert if you can use the same one twice or use (一直在, **yīzhí zài**, **straight at**) in the first clause, she says that you must use (正在, **zhèngzài**, **straight at**) first and (一直在, **yīzhí zài**, **straight at**) second and that *the Chinese people do not like it any other way*.

(直, **zhí**, **straight**)

(正在, **action in progress**, **is**)

(一直在, **yīzhí zài**, **straight at**)

(正在, **zhèngzài**, **straight at**)

(一直, **yīzhí**, **straight**)

Sentence Parsing 4

在中国当熟悉的人见面打招呼和在街上遇见的时候不怎么爱说: "你好"! 最喜欢问: "你上哪去啊", "吃饭了吗", "怎么样"!

在	中国	当	熟悉	的	人	见面	打招呼	和
Zài	Zhōngguó,	dāng	shúxī	de	rén	jiànmiàn	dǎ zhāohu	hé…
At	China,	when	aware		person	meet	greet	and…
					Subject	Verb Phrase		

(熟悉, **shúxī**, **know something well**) comes from (熟, **shú**, **familiar**) and from (悉, **xī**, **complete**). *Knowledgeable* or *aware* or *in the know* would be a good gloss.

在	街上	遇见	的	时候	不怎么	爱	说	你好
zài	jiēshang	yùjiàn	de	shíhou	bùzěnme	ài	shuō;	nǐhǎo
at	street upon	meet		time	not how	love	say;	you good
on the street		meet		meanwhile	not very	love	say;	hello
Locative Phrase								

The overall message of the first phrase above is:

In China, when knowledgeable people meet greet and on the street meet meanwhile not very like to say hello,

Now you are wondering why the sentence uses (上, **shàng**, **on**) instead of one of the related structures such as (上边, **shàngbian**, **on the surface of**). That is because the road is more like a location than an object to mount.

最	喜欢	问;	你	上	哪	去	啊
Zuì	xǐhuan	wèn;	Nǐ	shàng	nǎli	qù	á?",
Most	like	ask;	You	toward	which place	go	?",

Note that there is no conjunction joining the three expressions. Whereas we would use (和, hé, and), using nothing is an option in Mandarin.

"吃饭了吗","怎么样".

吃饭	了	吗	怎么	样
"Chīfàn"	le	ma?",	"Zěnme	yàng?"
"Eat meal		?"	"How what	appear?"
Eaten?			How are things?	

在 中国 当 熟悉 的 人 见面 打 招呼 和在 街上 遇见 的 时候 不怎么 爱 说; "你好"! 最 喜欢 问; "你 上 哪里 去 啊", "吃饭 了 吗", "怎么样"!

Zài Zhōngguó, dāng shúxī de rén jiànmiàn dǎ zhāohu hé zài jiēshang yùjiàn de shíhou bùzěnme ài shuō; nǐhǎo! Zuì xǐhuan wèn; nǐ shàng nǎli qù á, chīfàn le ma, zěnme yàng?

In China, when knowledgeable people meet greet and on the street meet meanwhile not very like to say hello, most like ask; You toward which place go?, Eaten?, How appear?

(怎么, zěnme, how)
(样, yàng, appearance, manner)
(怎么样, zěnmeyàng, how appear)
(吃饭, chīfàn, eat meal)
(最, zuì, most)
(问, wèn, ask)
(你, nǐ, you)
(哪, nǎ, which)
(哪里, nǎli, which place, where)
(去, qù, go)
(啊, á, questioning)
(在, zài, at)
(中国, Zhōngguó, China)
(当, dāng, when)
(熟, shú, familiar)
(悉, xī, xī, know)
(熟悉, shúxī, know something well)
(见, jiàn, perceive, meet)
(面, miàn, side, aspect)

(见面, jiànmiàn, meet)
(打, dǎ, hit)
(悉, xī, complete)
(遇见, yùjiàn, meet)
(人, rén, person)
(街上, jiēshang, on the street)
(和, hé, and)
(上, shàng, on)
(上边, shàngbian, on the surface of)
(打招呼, dǎ zhāohu, greet)
(招呼, zhāohu, greet)
(街, jiē, street)
(遇, yù, meet)
(不怎么, bùzěnme, not very)
(爱, ài, love)
(说, shuō, say)
(你好, nǐhǎo, you good)
(时候, shíhou, time)
(喜欢, xǐhuan, to like)

Tips on Using 吃饭了吗

So, I am doing my usual typing away on this script, actually manifesto, it is getting huge, and my wife comes into my office and it is near dinner time and I say (吃饭了吗, **chīfàn le ma**, **eaten meal**?) And she says *O, velly goo dah, you Chinese velly goo dah, pah flect glamma*. I have used this term hundreds of times but I like praise. Then she peers over my shoulder and reads the last sentence exercise. Then she says;

Ima gunna tell you some Chinese custom, *If you have a bucket of pee*, *you never say* (吃饭了吗, **chīfàn le ma**, **eaten meal**?), *it is considered rude. So if you walk down the street*, *or greet your relative with the bucket of pee, do not chose this example* (吃饭了吗, **chīfàn le ma**, **eaten meal**?). *Chinese people gunna think you not very polite*.

So my natural response is; *What the frig would I have a bucket of pee for*? Her response, *Old custom*, *before Chinese people not have the toilet*, *so they take the pee away*. So I ask her, *well, what do I say then*? Her reply; *always you should say the greeting* (你好, **nǐhǎo**, **you good**) *when you have the bucket of pee*!

Did you get that? Near meal time, use (吃饭了吗, **chīfàn le ma**, **eaten meal**?) if you do not have a bucket of urine. If you do have a bucket of urine, you can use the ol' standard (你好, **nǐhǎo**, **you good**). Just a little cultural tip. I am afraid to ask the protocol for the crap bucket with the *night soil* in it.

Connecting Nouns and Pronouns with (和, hé, and)

Many books offer (和, **hé**, **and**) as the Mandarin equivalent of the English *and*. However, (和, **hé**, **and**) is only used to connect names, nouns and animate pronouns. In many situations in which it can be properly used, another option is to not use it at all.

1) Not using (和, **hé**, **and**) connecting *Person Nouns*.

他的	妈妈	爸爸	都	是	加拿大	人
Tā de	māma	bàba	dōu	shì	Jiānádà	rén.
His	mother	father	all	is	Canada	person.

2) Using (和, **hé**, **and**) connecting *Person Nouns*.

他的	妈妈	和	爸爸	都	是	加拿大	人
Tā de	māma	hé	bàba	dōu	shì	Jiānádà	rén.
His	mother	and	father	all	is	Canada	person.

The meaning is the same. With or without is a personal choice. However, like England, your perceived education depends largely how you speak. I would advise doing everything the long way before you go street level.

3) Using (和, **hé**, **and**) connecting *Proper Nouns*.

他	会	说	中文	和	英语
Tā	huì	shuō	Zhōngwén	hé	Yīngyǔ.
He	able to	speak	Chinese	and	English.

4) Using (和, **hé**, **and**) connecting *Common Nouns*.

他	喜欢	苹果	和	狗肉
Tā	xǐhuan	píngguǒ	hé	gǒuròu.
He	like	apple	and	dogmeat.

(苹果, **píngguǒ**, **apple**)

(狗肉, **gǒuròu**, **dog meat**)

(加拿大, **Jiānádà**, **Canada**)

(喜欢, **xǐhuan**, **like**)

(和, **hé**, **and**)

(中文, **Zhōngwén**, **Chinese language**)

5) **Connecting Phrases and Clauses not Using** (和, **hé**, **and**)

So you are eating on the street late at night at a barbeque pit. You pick out your favorite foods, hand them to the toothless old bag with disgusting dirty hands who is going to cook them for you then you spot some cold beer. You add it to your order, not with (和, **hé**, **and**) but with (还有, **háiyǒu**, **still have**, **in addition**). As mentioned above, *Pronouns* can be joined with (和, **hé**, **and**) hence (这个, **zhège**, **this one**) and (那个, **nàge**, **that one**) are joined with (和, **hé**, **and**).

给	我	这个	和	那个	还有	一	瓶	啤酒
Gěi	wǒ	zhège,	hé	nàge,	háiyǒu	yī	píng	píjiǔ.
Give	me	this one,	and	that one,	still have	one	bottle	beer.

(给, **gěi**, **give**, **give to**)

(瓶, **píng**, **bottle**)

(啤酒, **píjiǔ**, **beer**)

(还有, **háiyǒu**, **still have**)

A common word you can use in place of (还有, **háiyǒu**, **still have**) is (另外, **lìngwài**, **in addition**).

老包	给	我	一	串	蘑菇	另外	一	个	羊	睾丸
Lǎo bāo	gěi	wǒ	yī	chuàn	mógū	lìngwài	yī	ge	yáng	gāowán.
Old Bag	give	me	one	stick	mushroom	in addition	one	of	sheep	testicle.

(另, **lìng**, other)

(外, **wài**, outside)

(老, **lǎo**, old)

(包, **bāo**, bag)

(请问, **qǐngwèn**, please ask)

(给, **gěi**, give)

(蘑菇, **mógū**, mushroom)

(墨斗鱼, **mòdǒuyú**, cuttlefish)

(乌贼, **wūzéi**, crow thief, cuttlefish)

(贼, **zéi**, thief)

(乌, **wū**, crow)

(条, **tiáo**, a strip)

(羊, **yáng**, sheep)

(串, **chuàn**, string together)

(睾丸, **gāowán**, testicle)

6) **Using** (也, **yě**, **also**) to express *and*.

The word (也, **yě**, **also**) in Mandarin can be used like the English conjunction *and*. This should be done to connect **Verbs** and **Verb Phrases** only. Here are some examples:

他	不	懂	中文	也	不	懂	英文
Tā	bù	dǒng	Zhōngwén	yě	bù	dǒng	Yīngwén.
He	not	understand	Chinese	also	not	understand	English.
			Verb Phrase₁				**Verb Phrase₂**

7) Connecting Person Nouns and Pronouns with (跟, gēn, with)

The general format is;

(Noun/Pronoun) + (跟, gēn, with) + (Noun/Pronoun) + Verb + Object

我	跟	我	妹妹	去	吃饭
Wǒ	gēn	wǒ	mèimei	qù	chīfàn.
Me	with	me	sister	go	eat meal.
Pronoun			Pronoun	Verb	Object

(跟, gēn, with) is often used in conjunction with (一起, yìqǐ, one rise, together).

我	跟	我	妹妹	一起	去	吃饭
Wǒ	gēn	wǒ	mèimei	yìqǐ	qù	chīfàn.
Me	with	me	sister	together	go	eat meal.

8) Using a Sentence Pattern as a Connector

(又, yòu, again) **is** used in sentence constructions similar to the use of *and*. It is used to connect two *Adjectives* or *Verbs*. It is used to say *something* or *someone* is both one thing and another;

Subject + (又, yòu, again) + **Adj. / Verb** + (又, yòu, again) + **Adj. / Verb**

他	又	高	又	瘦
Tā	yòu	gāo	yòu	shòu.
He	again	tall	again	thin.
Subject	又	Adj.	又	Adj.

A more complex example is;

他	又	不	懂	中文	又	不	懂	英文
Tā	yòu	bù	dǒng	Zhōngwén	yòu	bù	dǒng	Yīngwén.
He	again	not	understand	Chinese	again	not	understand	English.
Sbj.	又		Verb Phrase₁		又		Verb Phrase₂	

(一边, yìbiān, one side) is the other sentence construction used similar to *and*. This construction is used to mark *doing something* while *doing something else*.

The general format of the sentence is thus;

Subject + (一边) + Verb + Object + (一边) + Verb + Object.

她	一边	吃饭	一边	看	电视
Tā	yìbiān	chīfàn	yìbiān	kàn	diànshì.
He	one side	eat meal	one side	look at	electric look at.
He	one side	eat meal	one side	look at	television.
Sbj.	一边	Verb Object	一边	Verb	Object

Handy Rules of Thumb

A) When in doubt just use nothing, you'll often be right.

B) If connecting *Nouns* and *Pronouns* at the beginning of a sentence use (和, hé, and).

C) When listing things or people use (还有, háiyǒu, still have).

D) When connecting *Verb Phrases* use (也, yě, also).

Sentence Parsing 5

从明天开始, 每天早上七点一刻我都要骑自行车到教室上课, 练习发音, 念课文, 记单词, 听写汉字, 回答问题.

从	明天	开始	每天	早上	七	点
Cóng	míngtiān	kāishǐ,	měitiān	zǎoshang	qī	diǎn...
From	clear day	open start,	each day	early before	7	dot...
From	next day	begin,	daily	morning seven o'clock...		

This is a great example of a sentence setting the scene by putting the *Time When* or *Temporal Adverb* at the beginning of the sentence. Time is always written from the biggest unit to the smallest. In this example (明天, **míngtiān**, **tomorrow**) is the biggest unit of time. *Temporal Adverbs* are movable immediately to the right or left of the *Subject*. So, before or after (我, **wǒ**, **I**, **me**).

(从, **cóng**, **from**)

(明, **míng**, **clear**, **next**)

(天, **tiān**, **day**, **sky**)

(明天, **míngtiān**, **tomorrow**)

(始, **shǐ**, **begin**, **start**)

(开, **kāi**, **open**, **operate**)

(每, **měi**, **every**, **each**)

(每天, **měitiān**, **every day**)

(早, **zǎo**, **morning**, **early**)

(早上, **zǎoshang**, **morning**)

(七, **qī**, **seven**)

(点, **diǎn**, **dot**, **a little**, **bit**)

(开始, **kāishǐ**, **begin**)

一刻	我	都	要	骑	自行车	到	教室	上课
…yī kè	wǒ	dōu	yào	qí	zìxíngchē	dào	jiàoshì	shàngkè,
…shortly	me	all	want	ride	bike	to	class	to lesson,

(刻, **kè**, **quarter hour**) is used to mark 15 minute intervals when giving clock time. It can also mark a short period of time. (刻, **kè**, **a moment of time**). As mentioned earlier in this book (一, **yī**, **one**) can also mark entirety of a noun or a short time period or small amount.

(刻, kè, quarter hour)

(一刻, yī kè, a short time)

(我, wǒ, I, me)

(都, dōu, all)

(要, yào, want)

(骑, qí, ride)

(自, zì, self)

(行, xíng, walk)

(车, chē, vehicle)

(自行车, zìxíngchē, bicycle)

(到, dào, towards)

(到, dào, arrive)

(教, jiào, teach)

(室, shì, room)

(教室, jiàoshì, schoolroom)

(上, shàng, attend, go to)

(课, kè, lesson)

(上课, shàngkè, attend class)

练习	发音	念	课文	记	单词
liànxí	fāyīn,	niàn	kèwén,	jì	dāncí,
practice	pronunciation,	read	text,	remember	word,

The words for memory associated acts have their own Mandarin psychosis.

(记, jì, remember) doesn't really commit to tense and can be used for an anticipated effort whereas (记得, jìde, remember) implies an act already completed. But you are wondering, why is (得, de) used in this way? In this situation it can mark the potential for verb action completion. So, if you have memorized something and then not been able to recall it, (记不得, jìbudé, remembered not achieve) is appropriate. The continuing act of remembering is (记着, jìzhe, remembering). If you have successfully remembered and recalled the issue, use (记住, jìzhu, remember). If you can remember some but not all (记不全, jìbuquán, remember not entire). But that is not all of them, see below.

(得, de, **potential complement**)

(记得, jìde, **remember**)

(记着, jìzhe, **remembering**)

(记住, jìzhu, **remembered**)

(住, zhù, **live at**)

(练习, liànxí, **practice**)

(记不得, jìbudé, **remembered not achieve**)

(记不牢, jìbuláo, **can't firmly memorize**)

(记不起来, jìbùqǐlai, **can't remember**)

(记不清, jìbuqīng, **remember not clear**)

(记不全, jìbuquán, **remember not entire**)

(记不住, jìbuzhù, **can't remember**)

(发音, fāyīn, **pronounce**)

(念, niàn, **read aloud**)

(课文, kèwén, **text**)

(记, jì, **remember**)

(单词, dāncí, **a word**)

(记岔, jìchà, remember incorrectly)

听写　汉字　回答　问题
tīngxiě　Hànzì　huídá　wèntí.
listen write　Hanzi　answer　question.

(听写, tīngxiě, dictation) refers to listening and writing a record or an act dependent on listening and writing, *dictation* is the usual gloss.

(听写, tīngxiě, dictation)　　　　　　(汉字, Hànzì, Chinese character)

(念书, niànshū, read book)　　　　　(回答, huídá, answer)

(听, tīng, listen to)　　　　　　　　(问题, wèntí, question, problem)

(写, xiě, write)

从 明天 开始, 每天 早上 七 点 一刻 我 都 要 骑 自行车 到 教室 上课, 练习 发音, 念 课文, 记 单词, 听写 汉字, 回答 问题.

Cóng míngtiān kāishǐ, měitiān zǎoshang qī diǎn yī kè wǒ dōu yào qí zìxíngchē dào jiàoshì shàngkè, liànxí fāyīn, niàn kèwén, jì dāncí, tīngxiě Hànzì, huídá wèntí.

From next day begin, each day morning seven o'clock one quarter me all want ride bicycle to classroom attend lesson, practice pronounce, read text, remember word, listen write character, answer question.

Acknowledge Previous Experience
(过, guò, in the past)

(过, guò, in the past) is used in a post-verb position to mark that the verb action has been experienced in the past. This character is often called the *experiential particle*. In keeping with the format for grammatical particles, verbs and the characters affixed to them as *Grammatical Particle Suffixes* such as (着, zhe), (了, le) and (过, guo) are written as one word. Of course, in the character string, this is indistinguishable. The general format is;

(有, yǒu, have) + (Verb) +(过, guò, in the past) + Object Phrase

你	有	看过	这	部	电影	吗
Nǐ	yǒu	kànguò	zhè	bù	diànyǐng	ma.
You	have	look at in the past	this	CNI	movie	?
You	have	looked at	this	CNI	movie	

(看, kàn, look at)   (电, diàn, electric)

(这, zhè, this)   (影, yǐng, shadow, image)

(部, bù, CNI films)   (电影, diànyǐng, film, movie)

你	有	听过	那	首	歌	吗
Nǐ	yǒu	tīngguò	nà	shǒu	gē	ma.
You	have	listen to in the past	that	CNI	song	?
You	have	listened to	that	CNI	song	

(首, shǒu, CNI songs)   (那, nà, that)

(听, tīng, listen)   (歌, gē, song)

(过, guò, in the past) can also exist as a *Verb* on it's own.

我	的	生日	已经	过	了
Wǒ	de	shēngri	yǐjing	guò	le.
My		birthday	already	in the past.	
My		birthday	already	passed.	

(生日, shēngri, birthday)   (已, yǐ, already)

(生, shēng, to birth, to bear)   (经, jīng, endure)

(日, rì, sun)   (已经, yǐjing, already)

现在	已经	过	了	八	点
Xiànzài	yǐjing	guò	le	bā	diǎn.
Present at	already endure	in the past		eight	dot.
Now	already	past		eight	o'clock.

(现, xiàn, present)   (已经, yǐjing, already)

(在, zài, at)   (八, bā, eight)

(现在, xiànzài, at present)   (点, diǎn, dot)

(过, guò, pass) can also refer to the act of *passing by* something or *crossing over* something.

过 马路

Guò mǎlù.
Cross over horse path.
Cross over road.

(过, guò, cross over) (路, lù, path, road)

(马, mǎ, horse) (马路, mǎlù, horse path, road)

过 两 个 红绿灯 再 右 转

Guò liǎng ge hóng-lǜdēng zài yòu zhuǎn.
Pass two of red-green light again right turn.
Pass two traffic light again right turn.

(两, liǎng, two) (红绿灯, hóng-lǜdēng, traffic light)

(红, hóng, red) (再, zài, again)

(绿, lǜ, green) (右, yòu, right)

(灯, dēng, light) (转, zhuǎn, turn)

http://www.peggyteacheschinese.com/

Parsing Sentences 6

后天下午差五分钟不到四点她也准备再跟班上的几个同学一起坐出租汽车和地铁去 "新世界" 商店买些生活用品.

后天	下午	差	五分钟	不到	四	点
Hòutiān	xiàwǔ	chà	wǔ fēnzhōng	búdào	sì	diǎn,
Behind day	below noon	differ	5 part time	not arrive	4	dot,
2 days hence	afternoon		5 minutes to 4,			

This sentence nicely demonstrates the front loaded *Temporal Adverb Phrase* or *Time When Phrase*. In fact the entire phrase is the *Temporal Adverbial*. This is certainly the long form of giving this time interval. (钟, **zhōng**, **clock**) is often omitted if the meaning otherwise is clear. If you omit the (差, **chà**, **differ**) the same time could be represented as;

三	点	五	十	五	分钟
sān	diǎn	wǔ	shí	wǔ	fēnzhōng,
three	dot	five	ten	five	parts of time,
	three o'clock 55 minutes,				

There are other time constructions using quarter hour intervals that can be marked as before or after the hour. (刻, **kè**, **quarter hour**)

她	也	准备	再	跟	班上的	几个	同学..
tā	yě	zhǔnbèi	zài	gēn	bān shàng de	jǐ gè	tóngxué
she	also	prepare	again	with	class attend	few	same study
she	also	prepare	again	with	class attend	few	school mate

Okay, (同学, **tóngxué**, **schoolmate**) means that the students are at the *same study*. This does not mean that they are in the same class, but likely the same school. (班上的, **bān shàng de**, **classs attend**) means that they are in the same class. Although (上, **shàng**) usually makes reference to a higher position, variably glossed as (上, **shàng**, **on**, **upon**, **on top of**, **over**) it can also mean (上, **shàng**, **attend**). (几个, **jǐ gè**, **how many**) is often a question asking marker, doing exactly what it suggests it does, which is ask *how many* in a question sentence. However, it can also gloss as *a few*. (几个, **jǐ gè**, **a few**, **several**) (班上的, **bān shàng de**) is marked with (的, **de**) which indicates that it modifies a noun and in this situation the *Head Noun* and its' **CNI** are (几个同学, **jǐ gè tóngxué**, **a few school mates**). This is a wordy way to note that *she* is *preparing with same school classmates*. This is an expression that exists and defies the usual common sense test.

一起	坐	出租	汽车	和	地铁	去
…yīqǐ	zuò	chūzū	qìchē	hé	dìtiě	qù…
…one rise	sit	exit rent	steam cart	and	dirt steel	go…
…together	ride		taxi	and	subway	go…

All of the compound words above are strange. (出, **chū**, **out go**, **exit**) compounded with (租, **zū**, **rent**) makes some sense *to rent something out*. The

(汽, **qì**, **steam**) of (汽车, **qìchē**, **vehicle**) arises from the era of steam powered cars. (地铁, **dìtiě**, **subway**) from (地, **dì**, **ground**) and (铁, **tiě**, **steel**) comes from the ***ribbons of steel*** era. You will often see ***Metro*** posted on the subways of China.

新世界	商店	买	些	生活	用品
…Xīn shìjiè	shāngdiàn	mǎi	xiē	shēnghuó	yòngpǐn.
…New World	merchant store	buy	some	life	use product.
…New World	shop	buy	some	life	product.

(新世界, **Xīn shìjiè**, **New World**) is a shopping district in Beijing. The character (商, **shāng**, **merchant**) is supposed to look like the face and hat of a merchant. (生, **shēng**, **to birth**) and (活, **huó**, **life**) combine to form ***life***. The *Verb* (用, **yòng**, **to use**) and the *Noun* (品, **pǐn**, **product**) forms a *Verb Object Compound* referring to products in daily use.

Again, I have never heard anyone use sentences this long in China. I stole these parsings from a poorly written book that is called ***Rapid Literacy in Chinese***. The concept of the book is that the author gives you 25 sentences of 30 words each and from that you are supposed to become literate in ***Chinese***, which, incidently is the written, not spoken language. There are several fatal flaws to the book. The major one is that you are supposed to become literate with no English translations of the 25 sentences. Brilliant right? There are pages entirely written in Chinese characters with no **Pinyin** or English. Then you will need a magnifying glass to read the English here and there. So, Zhang Pengpeng, I stole your shit and did it right, ***you got owned***! Credits to you and so on, ISBN 978-7-80052-695-4. Funny that there is a copyright claimer in the front cover, from the country that is famous for theft of intellectual property. I guess that they want the protection in the international market that they give no one else.

后天 下午 差 五 分 钟 不 到 四 点, 她 也 准备 再 跟 班 上的 几个 同学 一起 坐 出租汽车 和 地铁 去 "新世界" 商店 买些 生活 用品.

Hòutiān xiàwǔ chà wǔ fēnzhōng búdào sì diǎn, tā yě zhǔnbèi zài gēn bān shàng de jǐ gè tóngxué yīqǐ zuò chūzū qìchē hé dìtiě qù Xīn Shìjiè shāngdiàn mǎi xiē shēnghuó yòngpǐn.

Two days hence afternoon 3:55, she also prepare again with class attend a few same school mates together sit taxi and subway go New World shop buy a few life use products.

(活, huó, live)

(用品, yòngpǐn, to use)

(商店, shāngdiàn, shop)

(生活, shēnghuó, life)

(买, mǎi, buy)

(些, xiē, some)

(坐, zuò, sit)

(出租, chūzū, hire, let, rent)

(汽车, qìchē, vehicle)

(和, hé, and)

(上, shàng, attend)

(地铁, dìtiě, subway)

(去, qù, go)

(汽, qì, vapor, steam)

(她, tā, she)

(也, yě, also)

(准备, zhǔnbèi, prepare, get ready)

(再, zài, again)

(跟, gēn, heel, with)

(班, bān, class)

(上, shàng, attend)

(的, de)

(班上的, bān shàng de, ?)

(几个, jǐ gè, a few, several)

(几个, jǐ gè, how many)

(同学, tóngxué, schoolmate)

(一起, yīqǐ, together)

(坐, zuò, sit, take a seat)

(出租汽车, chūzū qìchē, taxi)

(上的, shàng de, upper, supra-)

(新世界, Xīn shìjiè, New World)

(汽车, qìchē, vehicle)

(后天, hòutiān, day after tomorrow)

(下午, xiàwǔ, afternoon)

(差, chà, differ)

(五, wǔ, five)

(分, fēn, part, portion of)

(钟, zhōng, clock)

(分钟, fēnzhōng, minute of time)

(不, bù, not)

(到, dào, to, towards, until)

(到, dào, arrive, reach)

(不到, búdào, not reach, not get to)

(四, sì, four)

(点, diǎn, dot, a little, bit)

(三, sān, three)

(刻, kè, quarter hour)

(后天, hòutiān, day after tomorrow)

(下午, xiàwǔ, afternoon)

(差, chà, differ)

(五, wǔ, five)

(分, fēn, part, portion of)

(钟, zhōng, clock)

(不, bù, not)

(到, dào, to, towards, until)

(到, dào, arrive, reach)

(四, sì, four)

(点, diǎn, dot, a little, bit)

(三, sān, three)

(点, diǎn, dot, a little, bit)

(十, shí, ten)

(五, wǔ, five)

Grammatical Vague-alities

All languages have expressions with vague meanings that can be used in multiple situations. Here are some of the common Mandarin examples.

1) (有事, **yǒu shì**, **have matter**) is the generic cover-up expression to avoid a situation or arrive late. In Nigeria they say *I was delaaaayed*. That expression can cover being a day or two late for an appointment with no other explanation.

对不起	我	不	能	来	因为	我	有事
Duìbùqǐ,	wǒ	bù	néng	lái	yīnwèi	wǒ	yǒushì.
Sorry,	me	not	can	come	because	me	have matter.

Or this lame ass excuse;

我	星期五	晚上	不	行	因为	我	有事
Wǒ	xīngqīwǔ	wǎnshàng	bù	xíng	yīnwèi	wǒ	yǒushì.
Me	star period five	evening	not	okay	because	me	have matter.
Me	Friday	evening	not	okay	because	me	have matter.

2) (这样, **zhèyàng**, **this appearance**) or (这样, **zhèyàng**, **this manner**) can also be used to as the verbal partner to showing someone how to do something.

你	可以	这样	做
Nǐ	kěyǐ	zhèyàng	zuò.
You	can	this manner	do.

It can also be used as an affirmation of an act demonstrated.

哦	原来	你	是	这样	做 的
O!,	yuánlái	nǐ	shì	zhèyàng	zuò de.
Oh!,	originally	you	is	this manner	do.
Oh!,	originally	you	is	this manner	do.
	Manner Adverb	Subject	Verb		

This is another (…是, shì, is)… (的, de) construction in which the *manner* is marked. I touched on *Manner Adverbs* (**Man. Adv.**) somewhere in this book. They are *moveable* about the Subject. This is why (原来, **yuánlái**, **originally**, **formerly**) is in front of the Subject.

这样	的	事情	真	让	人	生气
Zhèyàng	de	shìqing	zhēn	ràng	rén	shēngqì.
This manner	of	business	really	allow	person	angry.

如果	你	这样	做	就	不	够	我的	朋友
Rúguǒ	nǐ	zhèyàng	zuò	jiù	bú	gòu	wǒ de	péngyǒu.
If	you	this manner	do	just	not	enough	my	friend.

Conventionally, (我的, **wǒ de**, **my**) would be dropped in this sentence. Another gloss for (做, **zuò**, **do**, **make**) is *to act*. The expression has a close relative, which is (这样子, **zhèyàng zì**). It can be glossed as a reply to something someone said; "*oh, so that's the way it is, Oh I see, So it was like that, Ah that's what happened, So that's the way it is gonna be.*"

3) (那个, **nà ge**, **that one**) this is the most common irritating speech pattern in Mandarin. You can use it as a rhetoric stall or when you are stumbling on what to say next. If you repeat it more than twice you look like an illiterate moron. There is no fixed grammatical construction, it is ***bad Mandarin***. But if you want to look local and uneducated just say, (那个那个那个, **nàge nàge nàge**, **that, that, that**) while you are stumbling for something intelligent to say.

他	说	他	要	请	我	吃饭	然后	带	我	去
Tā	shuō	tā	yào	qǐng	wǒ	chīfàn,	ránhòu	dài	wǒ	qù…
He	say	he	want	invite	me	eat meal,	then	take	me	go…

那个	那个	那个	新	的	博物馆
…nàgè,	nàgè,	nàgè,	xīn	de	bówùguǎn.
…that one,	that one,	that one,	new		museum.

4) (怎么样, **zěnmeyàng**, **how appear**)

This is a generic query or statement of how things are. Common glosses are; ***How's it going?***, ***How'd it go?***, ***What's it like?***, ***What's happening?***, ***What's up?***, *etc*.

多伦多	怎么样
Duōlúnduō,	zěnmeyàng?
Toronto,	how appear?

天气	怎么样
Tiānqì,	zěnmeyàng?
Weather,	how appear?

5) (不好意思, bù hǎoyìsi, not good meaning) is used to ask to be excused from some action or oversight. The meaning above is literal. It can also be used as an interjection to request assistance, or an apology.

对不起	不好意思	你	能	告诉	我	地铁	在	哪儿
Duìbuqǐ,	bù hǎoyìsi,	nǐ	néng	gàosu	wǒ	dìtiě	zài	nǎr?
Correct not rise,	not good meaning,	you	can	tell	me	subway	at	where?
Sorry,	my apologies,	you	can	tell	me	subway	at	where?

Both of these phrases are hard to translate literally. (不起, bùqǐ, be very ill) is, on its own, a verb used to express serious illness. In compound characters, it is used to mark the inability to do the **Initial Verb**. (买不起, mǎibùqǐ, buy not rise) is somehow made to mean that you cannot afford the transaction. (对, duì) has a myriad of definitions. The most likely meaning in this situation is (对, duì, correct). As (对不起, duìbuqǐ, excuse me) is an apology, it is likely that the expression arose using (…不起, …bùqǐ, …unable) to mark the inability of an act to be *correct*, that is, you are apologizing for the incorrectness of the act.

(能, néng, can)

(告诉, gàosu, tell)

(地铁, dìtiě, subway)

(在, zài, at)

(哪儿, nǎ'r, where)

6) (随便, suíbiàn, follow convenient) or (随便你, suíbiàn nǐ, follow convenient) is often glossed as *It's up to you*, *You decide*, *Whatever you want*. Literally it means that you will comply to whatever is convenient. You can throw this one out at any situation that you don't really care or pretend to care about the course of events. One source says (随便, suíbiàn, casual, random, careless, wanton, willful).

我	穿	衣服	很	随便
Wǒ	chuān	yīfu	hěn	suíbiàn.
Me	wear	clothes	very	random.

(穿, chuān, wear)

(衣, yī, clothes)

(服, fu, serve)

(衣服, yīfu, clothes)

(随, suí, follow)

(便, biàn, convenient)

(随便, suíbiàn, casual)

7) (无所谓, wúsuǒwèi, It doesn't matter to me) (无, wú) is a *Negating Adverb*. It can be used to represent any variation of (**nothingness, not have, there is not, nothing, nil, no, not, without**). When characters are compiled together often a character is dropped. (所以, suǒyǐ, so) or *therefore* is implanted in the middle of this three character compound. (所以谓, suǒyǐ wèi) comes to mean *therefore called* or *so called*. This gets abbreviated to (所以谓, suǒwèi, so called). Roughly, the expression means *not so called* or *not therefore*. The expression is used to mark a lack of interest in an action.

他的	话	对	我	来说	无所谓
Tā de	hùa	duì	wǒ	láishuō	wúsuǒwèi.
His	speech	for	me	come speak	not so called.
His	speech	for	me	about	not important.

(来说, láishuō, concerning, about)

(对, duì, for)

(谓, wèi, call)

(所以, suǒyǐ, so)

(所谓, suǒwèi, so-called)

(所, suǒ, place)

(无, wú, without, not)

(谓, wèi, call)

(不起, bùqǐ, not rise, be very ill)

(样, yàng, manner)

(样, yàng, appearance, shape)

(随, suí, follow)

(事情, shìqing, affair, matter)

(情, qíng, sentiment)

(够, gòu, enough)

(就, jiù, just)

(多伦多, Duōlúnduō, Toronto)

(天气, tiānqì, weather)

(便, biàn, convenient)

(博物馆, bówùguǎn, museum)

The flavour of this above chapter was borrowed from;

http://chitchatchinese.blogspot.com/

Common Requests or Commands

Gloss	Hanzi	Pinyin	Literal	Notes
Come in	进来	jìn lái	enter come	movement
Go out	出去	chū qù	exit go	movement
Come up	上来	shàng lái	up come	movement
Come down	下来	xià lái	down come	movement
Go up	上去	shàng qù	up go	movement
Go down	下去	xià qù	down go	movement
Pick up	拿起来	ná qǐ lái	take come	Action
Put down	放下去	fàng xià qù	put down go	Action
Put on	穿上	chuān shàng	wear on	clothes
Take off	脱下	tuō xià	cast off down	clothes
Put in	放进去	fàng jìn qù	put enter go	Action
Take out	拿出来	ná chū lái	take exit come	Action
Get on	上车	shàng chē	on cart	vehicle
Get off	下车	xià chē	down cart	vehicle
Put on	戴上	dài shàng	wear on	accessories
Take off	脱下	tuō xià	cast off down	accessories
Come over	过来	guò lái	cross over come	movement
Go over	过去	guò qù	cross over go	movement
Get up	起来	qǐ lái	rise come	movement

Stand up	站起来	zhàn qǐ lái	stand rise come	movement
Sit down	坐下	zuò xià	sit down	movement
come back	回来	huí lái	return come	movement
go back	回去	huí qù	return go	movement
bring with	带来	dài lái	take come	movement
bring go	带去	dài qù	take go	movement
bring go	带走	dài zǒu	take go forward	movement
take back	带回去	dài huí qù	take return go	object
take from	带回来	dài huí lái	take return come	object

Adjectives in Mandarin Grammar

One of the great inventions of the Great White Man analyzing Mandarin grammar is the invention of the term *Adjectival Verb*. An *Adjective* is an *Adjective* and a *Verb* is a *Verb*. The fact that Mandarin may not use a *Verb* when equating with an *Adjective* does not mean that an *Adjective* is a *Verb*.

In grammar, an *Adjective* is a word whose main syntactic role is to qualify a noun or noun phrase, giving more information about the *Object* signified. *Adjectives* are one of the traditional eight English parts of speech.

http://en.wikipedia.org/wiki/Adjective

A *Verb*, from the Latin *Verbum* meaning *Word*, is a part of speech that in syntax conveys an action **bring**, **read**, **walk**, **run**, **learn**, or a state of being **be, exist, stand**.

http://en.wikipedia.org/wiki/Verb

Mandarin Adjectives usually need an *Adverb*. If no other *Adverb* is used, the unnegated *Adjective* is preceded with (很, **hěn**, **very**). In this situation, the grammatical value of (很, **hěn**, **very**) is diminished. Thus;

他	很	高
Tā	hěn	gāo.
He	very	tall.
Subject	Adverb	Adjective

comes close to meaning *he is tall*, the catch though is that Mandarin Grammar does not use (是, shì, is) to equate *Adjectives* in the absence of an *Object*.

To negate the above sentence there are two choices.

他	不	很	高
Tā	búshì	hěn	gāo.
He	not is	very	tall.

or,

他	不	高
Tā	bù	gāo.
He	not	tall.

This format is specific for using (很, hěn, very). Any other *Adjective* is negated thus;

他	太	高
Tā	tài	gāo.
He	extreme	tall.

(太, tài, extreme)

他	不	太	高
Tā	bú	tài	gāo.
He	not	extreme	tall.

The overall message is that you can use **Adjectives** in the absence of an **Object**. When you use an **Object** you use (是, **shì**, **is**).

他	太	高
Tā	tài	gāo.
He	extreme	tall.

versus,

他	是	一	个	很	高	的	人
Tā	shì	yì	ge	hěn	gāo	de	rén.
He	is	a		very	tall		person.
Subject	Verb			Adjective			Object

The usual question formats can be used with **Adjectives**.

他	是	不	很	高
Tā	shì	búshì	hěn	gāo?
He	is	not is	very	tall?

and,

他	很	高	吗
Tā	hěn	gāo	ma?
He	very	tall	?
Subject	Adverb	Adjective	

Really, there is no great magic to using **Adjectives**. Here are some simple common sentence constructions. Substitute, vocalize and practice.

Negating with (不, bù, not)

她	不	矮
Tā	bù	ǎi.
She	not	short.

Question Format with Demonstrative Pronoun

那个	很	大	吗
Nèigè	hěn	dà	ma?
That one	very	big	?

Negated Adjective Format

贵	不	贵
Guì	bú	guì?
Expensive	not	expensive?

Ten Most Common Adjectives

(高, gāo, tall)

(矮, ǎi, short)

(大, dà, big)

(小, xiǎo, small)

(便宜, piányí, cheap)

(贵, guì, expensive)

(瘦, shòu, thin, skinny)

(胖, pàng, fat)

(慢, màn, slow)

(快, kuài, fast)

Threateningly Big List of Adjectives

I took this off of Wikipedia, great chance for you to polish your skills at looking up words and learning characters. As you learn them check them off, there are close to 2000!

一切	不亦	不幸	不行
一如	不便	不当	不要脸
一定	不俗	不得了	不足
一应	不像话	不得人心	不足道
一样	不利	不忠	不透明
一流	不可能	不惜	不错
一点	不同	不成	不错
一点儿	不咋的	不敏	丑
一空	不备	不早	专门
一统	不大	不明	丛杂
一般	不好	不止	东南
一辈子	不好意思	不法	东方
丁字	不妙	不测	丢人
万国	不宁	不满	严寒
万幸	不安	不着调	严格
下	不定	不祥	严装
不一样	不宜	不第	严重
不世	不密	不臣	个人
不义	不对	不舒服	中华
不乐	不少	不良	中央
不二	不平	不薄	中年

中欧	五色	低音	光荣
中立	五陵	体面	免费
中西	交厚	何如	兢业
中间	产业	何足	全世界
中非	亲切	佚名	全副
丰富	亲爱	你娘的	全国
丰裕	人为	使得	全方位
临床	人均	便宜	全球
临行	人工	便当	全素食
主动	什锦	促销	全部
主要	仁慈	保守	全面
丽	从严	候补	八角
丽质	仔细	倭	公共
举凡	任何	值钱	公平
之类	任性	倾危	公开
乐意	休眠	健康	公正
乐观	众多	健美	公立
乱	优惠	偶然	公费
乱逆	优秀	傲慢	公道
了不起	优质	充分	共产
事济	伟大	充腴	共同
二十	伟懋	先是	兴奋
二手	传统	先行	其他
二流	伤心	先进	其它
互动	伤感	光学	其次
互动式	但有	光彩	具体
五彩	低速	光滑	典型

典雅	刚劲	单身	可信
内向	刚正	卫生	可口
冒牌	初步	危急	可怕
军用	初级	危险	可怜
冤枉	别扭	厉厉	可悲
决死	别的	厉害	可惜
凄惶	前怕狼后怕虎	厌倦	可憎
准时	剧毒	原来	可爱
准确	副高	原汁	可理解
凉快	加急	原生态	可疑
凋敝	动人	参差	可笑
凋零	动作	友善	可能
凛凛	动荡	友好	可见
凝重	势利眼	双语	可靠
凤仪	勇敢	反动	吃醋
凶暴	勇烈	发狂的	吃香
凸凹	勉强	发达	各种各样
凹	勤俭	受潮	合理
出众	化学的	变化多端	合适
出名	十全十美	变幻莫测	吉利
出色	千万	口语	同一个
分外	千百成群	古典	同心
分散	半盲	古板	同性
分明	半透明	古老	同性恋
分毫	半酣	另外	同时
划时代	华氏	可乐	同源
刚	单调	可以	同类

同质	困惑	多义	好
名誉	困窘	多大	好吃
名贵	困难	多少	好听
后	固执	多汁	好多
向日	国外	多重	好学
含情	国家	大	好极了
听话	国有	大不了	好玩
呟	国民	大众	好玩儿
周密	国营	大力	好用
命世	国际	大喜	好看
和	圆形	大妙	好走
和畅	圆环	大意	如是
和睦	土制	大方	如此
和解	地下	大肚子	如雨
和谐	地球外	大胆	妄作
哀伤	坚韧	天然	妖娆
哀戚	坦白	天生	妥当
哈哈	坦诚	天真	妩媚
响亮	基本	太阳	委婉
喜悦	基础	失望	娇气
喧闹	堂堂	失调	娴熟
嗡嗡	壮烈	失踪	婆婆妈妈
嗷嗷待哺	壮观	夺目	嫩
嚣张	备用	奇妙	字面
囊括	复杂	奇异	孤寂
团结	外向	奇怪	孤穷
困乏	外国	奋怒	宁静

守时	宽敞	巍然	广盛
安全	寂寞	左右	应用
安宁	富有	巨大	开心
安定	寒伧	巨富	开明
安稳	寒冷	差不多	开朗
安详	寒心	差得远	异常
安静	寒碜	已甚	异类
安顿	寒酸	帅呆	异质
完全	寓意	常用	弹性
完美	寡信	常规	强健
定向	对头	干净	强固
定性	对比	平和	强壮
定量	导向	平安	强弱
宛转	封建	平常	当地
宜家	小	平康	形象
宝贵	小心	平滑	彩色
实在	少	平生	彻底
实惠	就那么回事	平等	很多
实用	尿急	年幼	得力
实际	屌	年轻	得天独厚
审美	屡禁不止	年迈	得意
客气	屡禁难止	年青	得意扬扬
宫样	屡禁难绝	幸甚	得意洋洋
家贫	山梨	幸福	得时
容易	岌岌	幸运	得陇望蜀
容长	崇高	幽静	御用
宽和	巍巍	幽默	循环

微型	怏怏	惨澹	懒惰
微观	怕痒	惭愧	懦弱
德才兼备	怕老婆	惰慢	户均
心急如焚	怠慢	惶怖	所宜
心怯	急性	惶恐	所属
心羞	急躁	惶惶	所有
心狠	急迫	惶惶不安	所谓
心胸狭窄	性感	惶遽	手下
必修	怯弱	愉快	手提
必备	总会	意外	执着
必然	恍如	愕然	执著
必要	恍惚	愚	执行
忐	恐怖	愚昧	扰乱
忙	恐慌	愚笨	技术密集型
忠实	恢恢	愚蠢	投机
忠心	恼怒	感人	抖擞精神
忧愁	悲伤	愤怒	抱歉
忧虑	悲切	愤恨	抽象
忧郁	悲惨	愤恨不平	拘束
快乐	悲痛	慇勤	拥挤
快活	悲观	慌忙	拮据
快速	惊恐	慌急	挑剔
忻喜	惊惶	慢性	探囊
忿忿	惊慌	慢惰	搞笑
忿怒	惊耳	慢速	摄氏
怀愁	惊讶	慷慨	摩天
怎么样	惊骇	懂事	摩登

455

擎天	无常	无辜	最先
改革	无心	无限	最初
放浪	无忌	日中	最后
故意	无恙	日久	最好
救生	无情	时新	最终
散漫	无所谓	旷世	月报
敬爱	无指	昂扬	月白
数字	无政府	昂贵	有
数量	无敌	明亮	有了
整个	无数	明显	有些
整复	无机	明智	有口才
整齐	无比	明确	有名
斯拉夫	无毛	易怒	有害
斯文	无法	显然	有幸
新兴	无理	显达	有意思
新建	无用	普通	有戏
新颖	无疑	普遍	有效
新鲜	无益	暂时	有机
方便	无知	暖和	有用
方天	无端	暗喜	有病
旖旎	无罪	暗弱	有礼貌
无人	无耻	暗昧	有种
无偿	无聊	暗淡	有罪
无力	无能	暧昧	有营养
无后	无语	暴力	有说服力
无告	无谋	暴厉	有趣
无奈	无赖	曲折	有钱

有限	欢喜	汪洋	淫荡
望前	欣喜	沉着	深刻
朦胧	欣慰	沉重	深远
未几	正义	沉默	深重
未晚	正大	没心没肺	混一
本地	正好	没意思	混乱
本来	正式	没戏	混纺
本科	正比	没落	清一色
朱红	正确	没见过世面	清平
朴素	正统	沮丧	清晰
机关	正高	沿海	清楚
机变	歪斜	沿门	清爽
机智	殆尽	泌尿	清蒸
机械	殊胜	泰然	清醒
机谋不密	残余	洋洋	温厚
杰出	残废	活动	温暖
极端	残暴	活泼	温煦
枯燥	残破	活跃	渺茫
标准	残虐	流利	湿软
栩栩如生	殷勤	流行	滋润
根本	殷富	浅狭	滑溜
棘手	民主	浩大	满地
概括	水下	浪漫	满地荆棘
模棱两可	水平	浪费	满意
模糊	永昌	涉外	满眼
次要	永续	淘气	满足
欢乐	汪汪	淫秽	漂亮

漫山	牛	现实	白领
漫漫	牛	玲珑	百花
潜在	牛	理想	盖世
潺潺	牛叉	生气	直捷
激动	牛屄	生疏	直接
激烈	牛掰	生病	相与
火大	牛比	田园	相容
灰领	牛逼	电子	相对
灵活	牛鼻	男人	相应
灿烂	牵强	男性	相当
炎炎	特别	畸形	真实
炫耀	特殊	疑忌	真心
炭气	犹太	疑难	真的
烂银	狂热	疯狂	真诚
热	狠心	疯癫	着急
热心	狠毒	疲劳	矍铄
热情	狡猾	疲困	知人
热烈	独一无二	痒	知名
热络	独享	痛快	短促
热闹	独立	痛苦	短命
焦急	狭窄	瘸腿	短期
焦虑	狼戾	白	矮
熟娴	狼狈	白厉厉	确凿
爱乐	猖狂	白搭	确定
爱国	环保	白白	确实
爱理不理	环球	白花花	碍事
爽快	现代	白茫茫	碍口

碎	端正	紧张	罗马
碧绿	等于	紧急	美
神圣	等闲	紧迫	美丽
神妙	签证	累世	美好
神色不变	简便	累人	美妙
秀色可餐	简单	累坏	羞惭
私人	简朴	絮叨	群体性
私有	简直	繁忙	翻手之间
秋水	粉嫩	繁重	老
种种	粉领	纤	老不正经
科学	粗心	红	老不死
积极	精彩	约定俗成	老成
称心	精明	纯笃	老掉牙
称职	精湛	纳罕	老迈
移动	精灵	纳闷	老龄
稳妥	精确	细致	老龄化
稳定	精神	经典	耐心
稳当	精英	给力	耐用
稳重	精采	绝	联合
穷	精锐	绝版	联络
空想	糊涂	绰约	聪明
空洞	糜烂	绵绵	肠断
空白	糟糕	绿色	肥胖
空虚	糟透	绿领	肮脏
空闲	素著	缄默	肺腑
突出	紧	罕见	胆裂
童童	紧俏	罗曼蒂克	胎位不正

胖乎乎	艰难	蒸馏	诚恳
胡涂	色情	蓄意	该死
胶状	艳	蓝	详细
胶质	芬芳	蓝领	诧异
能干	花心	虎狼	说服力
能言	苏维埃	虎背	读书识字
脑残	苞桑	虚弱	调和
腐败	苟且	虚诞	调皮
卧底	若此	蜀锦	谦虚
自信	苦恼	融和	谦让
自动	英俊	衍生	豁达
自卑	英勇	裸体	贤惠
自发	茂盛	西倾	贤慧
自在	茫茫	西洋	质朴
自弃	草率	要紧	贪婪
自愧不如	草芥	要脸	贪得无厌
自我	荒乱	见效	贵不可言
自然	荒唐	见钱眼开	费力
自相矛盾	荒芜	规则	赖皮
自负	荒谬	规矩	赤脚
自足	荧煌	视觉空间	赤裸
臭美	莫大	认真	走红
至孝	菁英	认知	走运
舒服	萤光	讨厌	起劲
良好	萦纡	许多	趁钱
艰辛	萧索	试用	超常
艰险	著名	诚实	趿屉

跪下	透明	锐气	雄厚
踊跃	通畅	错乱	集体
轩昂	通行	错愕	雪片
轩豁	通顺	错杂	零星
轻佻	速成	错落	零碎
轻松	造次	锦绣	零落
轻舒	逸才	镀锌	雷动
轻蔑	遗憾	长期	雷鸣
辖下	遥远	长青	震怒
辛勤	郁卒	闪烁	震恐
辛苦	郁郁	闭塞	霜雪
辛辣	郁闷	闷热	霸道
辛酸	鄙俗	闻名	青涩
辣子	配套	防卫	青青
迅速	酒酣	阳明	非常
过分	酷	阴	非正式
过敏	酷毙	阿	非法
过时	醉	陈年	非营利
过火	重大	陌生	面善
远大	重感情	险峻	面熟
连续	重要	随便	顶好
追切	野蛮	随即	顺利
迷信	金贵	隔壁	顺天
迷惘	金领	隩	顺畅
迷漫	鉴识	难吃	顽劣
适用	铁青	难找	顽固
逆向	锋利	难看	频繁

风流	马虎	魁梧	齐心
风清	马马虎虎	鲜明	龙鳞
风趣	骁勇	麻木	龟毛
风骚	骄傲	麻烦	憨
飘渺	骄横	麻辣	黑
飘逸	高兴	黄金	默
飞快	高尚	黑暗	艳
饥寒交迫	高档	黑沉沉	黩
饥饿	高科技	黑漆漆	黠
饥馁	高级	黑色	矗
饮用	高速	黑领	画
饱和	高音	默然	
馋嘴	高高兴兴	鼎足	

The shì 是 ... de 的 Construction

This construction **shì 是 ... de 的** refers to a grammatical structure which focuses on *when*, *where* or *how* an action took place. It is used to seek or provide information about the *time*, *place*, *manner*, *agent*, or *target* of the action. This construction is used to add emphasis over usual constructions. Question forming words or question forming constructions can be used.

In this first example below, (什么时候, **shénme shíhou**, **what time**, **when**), the question forming word is used.

小	王	是	什么	时候	去	昆明	的
Xiǎo	Wáng	shì	shénme	shíhou	qù	Kūnmíng	de.
Little	Wang	is	what	time	go	Kunming	.

In this example below the question particle (吗, **ma**, ?) is used.

小	王	是	昨天	去	昆明	的	吗
Xiǎo	Wáng	shì	zuótiān	qù	Kūnmíng	de	ma.
Little	Wang	is	yesterday	go	Kunming		?

The answer reflects the question format.

小	王	是	昨天	去	昆明	的
Xiǎo	Wáng	shì	zuótiān	qù	Kūnmíng	de.
Little	Wang	is	yesterday	go	Kunming	.

(他, **tā**, **he**) can be substituted for (小王, **Xiǎo Wáng**, **Little Wang**).

(跟谁, **gēn shéi**, **with who**) asks the question *with who*? using the question forming word (谁, **shéi**, **who**).

小	王	是	跟	谁	去	昆明	的
Xiǎo	Wáng	shì	gēn	shéi	qù	Kūnmíng	de.
Little	Wang	is	with	who	go	Kunming	.

                    Preposition Phrase

(跟谁, **gēn shéi**, **with who**) is a *Preposition Phrase* and follows the rules of Mandarin grammar by being before the *Verb* of the sentence. The answer is constructed thus;

小	王	是	跟	他的	父亲	去	昆明	的
Xiǎo	Wáng	shì	gēn	tāde	fùqin	qù	Kūnmíng	de.
Little	Wang	is	with	his	father	go	Kunming	.

                    Preposition Phrase

(怎么, **zěnme**, **how**) is another question forming word.

小	王	是	怎么	去	昆明	的
Xiǎo	Wáng	shì	zěnme	qù	Kūnmíng	de.
Little	Wang	is	how	go	Kunming	.

小	王	是	开车	去	昆明	的
Xiǎo	Wáng	shì	kāichē	qù	Kūnmíng	de.
Little	Wang	is	operate vehicle	go	Kunming	.
Little	Wang	is	drive car	go	Kunming	.

In keeping with the general format of Mandarin grammar, question words can be substituted for a *Noun Phrase* to suggest or query an answer and the question particle (吗, **ma**, ?) is added.

小	王	是	开车	去	昆明	的	吗
Xiǎo	Wáng	shì	kāichē	qù	Kūnmíng	de	ma.
Little	Wang	is	operate vehicle	go	Kunming		?
Little	Wang	is	drive car	go	Kunming		?
			Noun Phrase				

Any appropriate *Noun Phrase* can be used to create an answer.

小	王	是	一个人	去	昆明	的	吗
Xiǎo	Wáng	shì	yī ge rén	qù	Kūnmíng	de	ma.
Little	Wang	is	one person	go	Kunming		?
Little	Wang	is	alone	go	Kunming		?
			Noun Phrase				

Answer,

不是,	小	王	是	跟	他的	父亲	去	昆明	的
Bú shì,	Xiǎo	Wáng	shì	gēn	tāde	fùqin	qù	Kūnmíng	de.
Not is,	Little	Wang	is	with	his	father	go	Kunming.	
				Preposition Phrase					

Or the question construction can be negated directly.

小	王	不	是	跟	他的	父亲	去	昆明	的
Xiǎo	Wáng	bú	shì	gēn	tāde	fùqin	qù	Kūnmíng	de.
Little	Wang	not	is	with	his	father	go	Kunming.	
				Preposition Phrase					

(不是, bù shì, not is)   (小王, Xiǎo Wáng, Little Wang)

(开车, kāichē, operate vehicle)   (王, wáng, king)

(怎么, zěnme, how)   (昆明, Kūnmíng, Kunming)

(跟, gēn, with)   (吗, ma, ?)

(谁, shéi, who)   (昨天, zuótiān, yesterday)

Expressing Distance With (离, lí, from)

The distance between two places can be expressed with a specific form of *from*. (离, lí, from) It is not used for movement, only distance or duration. To identify the starting point between two places you can use (从, cóng, from). The grammatical construction format is;

Location A (离, lí, from) Location B + distance / duration.

Distance can be expressed in conventional *units of distance*, *time intervals*, or *generalities*.

我的	家	离	火车站	很	近
Wǒ de	jiā	lí	huǒchēzhàn	hěn	jìn.
My	home	from	train station	very	close.
Location A		(离, lí, from)	Location B		Distance

学校	离	图书馆	很	远
Xuéxiào	lí	túshūguǎn	hěn	yuǎn.
School	from	library	very	far.
Location A		Location B		Distance

This can be made into a question very simply.

学校	离	图书馆	很	远	吗
Xuéxiào	lí	túshūguǎn	hěn	yuǎn	ma.
School	from	library	very	far	?
Location A		Location B		Distance	

To get a useful answer, well, to try and get a useful answer you can preload the question with the desired response units.

学校	离	图书馆	多少	公里
Xuéxiào	lí	túshūguǎn	duōshao	gōnglǐ?
School	from	library	much few	kilometres?
Location A		Location B		Distance?

It is near pointless on trains to try and establish distance so it is more relevant to ask distances in terms of time between stations by asking the time in hours or minutes. If you want to try the distance game substitute (多少, **duōshao**, **much few**) with (小时, **xiǎoshí**, **hour**). You would of course expect the anwser to be expressed in *hours*.

北京	西	站	离	成都	站	多	长	小时
Běijīng	xī	zhàn	lí	Chéngdū	zhàn	duō	cháng	xiǎoshí?
Beijing	west	stand	from	Chengdu	stand	much	long	hour.
Location A				Location B		Duration?		

Perhaps the epitomy of vagueness in question and expected answer would be this, pointing at a map. This would combine the Chinese inability to read maps, calculate distance and not admit lack of knowledge.

这个	地方	离	那个	地方	多少	公里
Zhège	dìfang	lí	nàge	dìfang	duōshao	gōnglǐ?
This	place	from	that	place	much few	kilometre?

(图, **tú**, picture)   (学, **xué**, study)

(书, **shū**, book)   (校, **xiào**, school)

(馆, **guǎn**, building)   (学校, **xuéxiào**, school)

(图书馆, **túshūguǎn**, library) (家, **jiā**, home, house, family)

(离, lí, from)   (不远, bù yuǎn, not far)
(从, cóng, from)   (不很近, bù hěn jìn, not very close?)
(这个, zhège, this one)   (很远吗, hěn yuǎn ma, very far?)
(多少, duōshao, much few)   (很近, hěn jìn, very close)
(小时, xiǎoshí, hour)   (很近吗, hěn jìn ma, very close?)
(地方, dìfang, place)   (远不远, yuǎn bù yuǎn, far not far?)
(那个, nàge, that one)   (多远, duō yuǎn, much far?)
(北京, Běijīng, Beijing)   (公里, gōnglǐ, kilometer)
(西, xī, west)   (里, lǐ, village)
(站, zhàn, stand)   (里, lǐ, lining, inside)
(离, lí, from)   (里, lǐ, internal, interior, inside)
(成都, Chéngdū, Chengdu)   (里, lǐ, neighborhood)
(多少, duōshao, much few?)   (里, lǐ, neighborhood)
(长, cháng, long?)   (里, lǐ, 1/2 kilometer)
(多长, duō cháng, much long?)   (里, lǐ, 1/3 mile)
(小时, xiǎoshí, hour)   (里, lǐ, 300 paces)

The Chinese Sense of Direction

I don't know if 1.5 billion Chinese people have the directional dyslexia gene or if they simply cannot say that they do not know to *save face*. I have never been given such misdirection as when I travel in China. Many people simply do not ever leave their immediate locale. Asking someone who has never ridden the subway as to where the entrance is is an exercise in futility. In my experience, direction, distance and location are all unreliable when given by street directions. But getting misdirected or lost can be its own fun. Really, I assure you, I don't really care. I have a worse sense of direction than any Chinaman I have meet.

There is also a myriad number of terms for distance in China that the locals have only a vague idea as to their relationship to other distances. The most common unit of distance in the villages is (里, **lǐ**) which is given as **1/2 kilometer, 1/3 mile** or **300 paces**. In the cities the most common distance used is (公里, **gōnglǐ, kilometre**). If you expect that they can convert to (英里, **yīnglǐ, mile**), good luck.

So, bring maps, do not expect to be able to buy one. Bring a compass as most intercity dwellers have no idea of the cardinal directions. Also, you can go weeks without seeing the sun due to smog. A GPS with waypoints is a great way to navigate and find your way home.

(米, mǐ, meter)
(里, lǐ, 300 paces)
(英里, yīnglǐ, mile)
(公里, gōnglǐ, kilometre)

Guizhou Veh lee Dangerous!

Fuck that, ***Guizhou veh-lee dangerous***, ***Guangzhou*** veh-lee dangerous. It all started out at a party, three rather wealthy Chinese families inToronto sponsoring a development in Guizhou province. They asked me if I wanted to contribute to the cause and being rather cheap I said, ***sure, I will go and work there***. Money they did not need, but someone brave enough to go to the poorest most dangerous province in China, they did. Now, I had no idea where Guizhou was and for sure they did not tell me about the dangerous and poor part. Having worked in many third world countries I have learned that danger often increases as poverty does.

The sponsors, in fact had not been to Guizhou except for one man's wife. And I was to learn later that this was his Canadian Chinese born wife, not the one in mainland China or Hong Kong. I was later to find out that this is common with wealthy Chinese men. His wife felt she was very lucky to have wealth and freedom, different right? Plus, she had a post graduate degree and this embarrassed him in front of his friends.

So in the due course of time I get a visa, a ticket and head to China. This was in fact not so easy. When the local government found out that a white guy was coming to the poorest most dangerous area in China, they did not want to issue a work permit as they were too embarrassed. God forbid if the outside world really finds out what China is about. So I got a tourist visa and thought I would apply for a work visa once I got there.

China, the emerging superpower and economic giant, not, has only a few points of entry. Beijing, Shanghai and Hong Kong. Now China would argue that Taiwan was an additional point of entry but Taiwan would politely tell them to go fuck themeselves. So I flew to Hong Kong, took the very confusing and unnecessarily complicated subway and walked to the Mainland and entered the Middle Kingdom. When I got off of the bus at Guangzhou train station, for the first time in my life I felt tall as I looked down on tens of thousands of black haired vertically challenged sheeple.

Having arrived late and thinking it was safest to take a taxi to a name brand hotel I lined up in an enormous taxi line-up that made Walt Disney line-ups look small time. About one hundred feet from the front of the line the men responsible for assigning people to cabs spotted me and came rushing and shoving and elbowing through the line-up and literally grabbed me and my bags.

As a traveller, stupid and inexperienced I am not. This is not from some great enlightment that I was gifted but from attempted scams in Africa, India, Central America, South America, and the Caribbean.

My first adventure travel was a trip to Nigeria to study with a renowned plastic surgeon at the Joe Jane Medical Center in Ondo State. A young university lad I arrived having researched books written 20 years before and I was niave beyond belief. Initially it was like a Humphrey Bogart movie. The airport had overhead fans, officers with gold braid and little canes tucked under their arms, and air conditioning. I was impressed, until I opened the front door of the airport and walked out into a blast furnace of heat and chaos.

I had three bags, I was to be there for a year. Within seconds I was swarmed by taxi drivers and my three bags were tore from me and each went into the back of a different hatch back taxi and the drivers started pushing and shoving each other trying to take my bags into one fare. And they pushed and shoved me when I tried to retrieve them.

At the time, I was very fit, I had recently held the Black Belt heavy weight full contact karate title for three years. Having my shit grabbed and detained by men wearing neck to ankle dresses and wearing Muslim lids was not an excuse for me to not use force to retrieve them. The first round house kick sent the guy with my biggest bag into the crowd and knocked him unconscious. The other two hit the ground within a second or two and suddenly the press of the crowd released. Then the police moved in with their truncheons and laid a stick beating on them.

I have never been successfully robbed, but not because it has not been attempted. The taxi agents in Guangzhou grabbed my bags from me forcibly and ran forward knocking people down and tossing them into the trunk of a dirty, oily taxi trunk. I strode forward and then grabbed my biggest bag in the trunk and the agent grabbed my arm and shoved me. Then the cry of *100 dollar!*, *100 dollar!* I could now see the hotel that I was going to walk to. I had read that meter fares were mandatory and that they would try and cheat me. Buddy was about 5'4" and 110 pounds. So I weighed twice as much as him, and had 5 inches on him. He was demonstrating bad judgement. The harder I tried to get my bags from the trunk the harder he pulled on my arm. He was trying to get two weeks pay in one fare. Jiu Jitsu is nasty, efficient and painful. I took his thumb, internally rotated his arm, brought him screaming to the ground, heard the crack of a broken bone and shoved him under that back of the taxi, held him with my foot and took out my bags.

Funny how I got respect after that from the taxi agents. I put my bags in a nice clean cab back seat that pulled up, got in the front and gave the taxi driver a print out for the hotel I had reserved, about 300 metres away. Getting there was not so direct, people swarming the street, divided roads and an on-ramp, elevated roads and 10 minutes later I was there. When we arrived, stage two started. Never argue with a taxi driver until you are out of the cab, the door or trunk is opened and you have your bags out. I asked the taxi driver for a receipt, pointed to the meter which he had not turned on. Why people in China have to yell I do not understand. He started into the ***50 dollar!, 50 dollar***! Rant. I pointed to the fare on the side of the taxi which said 10 kuai to get in the cab and this included a substantial distance. Taxi's in China are very cheap. 10 kuai is about $1.42. He wanted 35 times the correct price. He started to yell at the valet in front of the hotel who was dressed like an organ grinder's monkey.

So he shoved me, this guy was smaller than the last. He grabbed at my wallet which was in my front left pant pocket. This is attempted theft no matter how you look at it. He was trying to twist it from my pocket. Now there were hotel people yelling, three others cabbies yelling and coming toward me. I grabbed his wrist, brought my knee up and hyperextended and fractured his elbow. Taking care of ones self in an escalating situation is paramount to protecting oneself. The three taxi drivers who were coming toward me now rushed me. The hotel security dove in, and a melee was on. I stepped back and let the security lay a stick whooping on him and walked into the hotel to the reservation desk.

That was my first half hour in China departing the bus from Hong Kong. The girls at the check in desk looked at me like I was a super hero. Within minutes of going to my high end $30 a night room, the phone started to ring and, ***do you want sexy massage ee***? This went on until I unhooked the phone. At about 10 pm the knocks on the door started and the same ***do you want sexy massage ee***? Finally I went to the front desk and got them to stop giving my room number and phone number out to all the whores in town. In the morning, 6 business cards with scantily clad girls looking like 13 years old were under my door.

I walked to the train station, bought the ticket to Chengdu and then to Guizhou, Yuping. Now I had a day and a half to enjoy Guangzhou. Buying the ticket involved a mass crush of humanity and people pushing through the line, if there are 25 lines to buy tickets, some ignorant ass plus or minus his family will just traverse the line at a 90 degree angle pushing you out of the way, that is, until they meet me. I learned that if I left a foot in front of me, another person would walk up the line and just push their way in front of me. So I would grab their collar and pull they backwards over my knee and gently to the ground. In China, this makes them *lose face* and the man would go berserk on me, yelling in Cantonese 6 inches from my face spewing their garlic breath and spittle on me. So I would step on their foot, chest thrust them, and send them on their ass. I was having loads of fun.

But what intrigued me the most is that while I and thousands of people were lining up for over an hour, some guys with greasy hair, black clothes and an air of importance would walk right up to the front of the line and reach over the person buying their ticket, yell at the ticket sales person, pass their cash through and the girl would sell them their ticket. Not once did I see anyone complain. This would happen once every two or three minutes.

When I got to the ticket counter I asked in English for what I needed at the ticket wicket, which had a sign that said, **English Speaking Agent**. Everyone but me in the line was obviously Chinese. There was an audible noise of many people behind me upset that I was in the line for foreigners, speaking English. This is when it all went to hell. Several people then squeezed up the stainless steel cattle collector guard rail that organized the last short stretch of line up. They walked over or pushed over my day pack and reached over me and started yelling at the agent and passing money. The hole through the glass divider was small and about 4 feet off the ground so that you had to bend over to talk through it. This was difficult as everyone was pushing from behind. My wallet was on the counter, as was my passport, and about 1000 kuai cash which is about a months pay for a middle level job. There were now three people trying to push their hand and money through the hole and two reaching over my shoulder. Fuck, this was insane, I had been in this sweltering stink hole for over an hour. I brought my right arm down like a shear as hard as I could smashing the forearms of one girl and two young men who were humping my ass, putting their hands and arms over my wallet, money and passport. All of them had their hand in the hole and now their forearms were hammered onto the stone counter. There is an exit to the left, not wide enough to get through with a bag. I shoved all three of them through it falling on top of each other. Then I pushed off the counter with both arms as hard as I could and sent many people toppling over each other behind me. I seldom lose it, but I turned around and yelled *fuck you* as loud as I could and the people nearby just shrivelled. Five police came running, formed a wall around me. And the yelling of the crowd was overwhelming. Hundreds of sheeple gathered around like a herd of cows. Cell phone cameras snapping and others holding their cameras up to video the event.

I politely asked the girl for my tickets, paid for them and was escorted to the door, then the street by 5 policemen. They did not say a word. They called me a cab, I gave the police a hotel card, he said something to the taxi and I was returned to my hotel, for free.

I went to the very nice girls at the desk, asked where I could go for the day that was close and they wrote me instructions for the subway in Chinese to go to Beijing street, a high end local street market. The Guangzhou subway is awesome. It think it cost 3 kuai, 42 cents, and you can go huge distances on it. I got off several stops later and walked down through the shopping area. Within a minute a man grabbed my left arm, from behind. This is a really stupid thing to do. I lifted my arm high, rolled it backwards over his, brought it under his arm and brought my back fist up smashing his nose and fracturing his arm in one move. The screaming was intense, he rolled on the ground and all the fake Rolex watches from the inside of his coat were falling out on the ground. His nose was bleeding like a stuck pig. Three police came running, obviously they knew the **harass-the-tourist-scam** that the hustlers use. They grabbed him by both arms and tried to drag him and quickly realised his arm was injured and pulled him by his ankles through the street. They said not a word to me.

The street food was excellent. I have every vaccine known to man, plus good drugs. I eat near anything. I was grabbed by three other watch salesman and I just pushed them on their ass and walked on. Eventually I got to the Pearl River. The boardwalk was surprisingly empty. Beijing Street was jammed, this was wide open. The river was a disgusting cesspool as were the grounds. There was piles of shit in the bushes, piss stains and piss odours on the few benches. Like, why would you piss on a park bench?

I strolled on and was approached by an old man who was selling some odd fruit from wicker baskets. They were the size of bushel baskets and he carried them with a stick over his shoulder. I thought this was cool, he looked about 75 years old, so I took out my camera and got a picture, then it was the ***five dallah!, five dallah***! rant. I walked on and he eventually walked off. I found a place on the stone wall along the river that looked safe to sit and sat down and watched the river life. Not long after the same old man came along nicely offering me fruit to try. A Chinese couple came over and in perfect English told me that he was apologising and they asked me what had happened. I told them that I took a picture of him and they scolded him rather loudly, which is the usual tone in this province. They said he was offering each of the two fruits to try for free. I asked them the usual price for the fruit and they told me that the fruit was not tasty and very cheap, two for 1 kuai, 14 cents. I had had free sample scams done on me in many countries. I asked again for them to ask if the sample was free, they did, he nodded his head and wiped two fruits with a disgusting rag that he probably wiped his ass on and I took a bite.

The first fruit was bitter enough to pucker my asshole. I handed the second back and looked for a garbage can to toss it in. The closest was about a hundred yards away. I made a face of disgust and tossed it in the Pearl River. The couple had drifted off. I nodded my head in thanks and walked away, or so I thought. He came at me, set his baskets down and grabbed my arm and was right in my face. *20 kuai!*, *20 kuai!* he shreaked. What do you do to an old man? I pushed him away and started to walk away very quickly. He obviously did not want to abandon his fruit in his pursuit. He picked up his baskets and chased me. How fast can you go with two bushels baskets on a pole? At a slow walk I could keep him a few metres behind me while he was yelling at full steam. Really, it was funny. I walk a few hundred yards while he puffed and panted. He was gaining on me as the stone boardwalk started to slope down. The couple from before rushed toward me and asked what happened, I told them and they verbally chewed a new asshole for the old man. This didn't stop him, I think he figured that if he tried to make me *lose face*, I would pay him. This white nasty ass mother fucker don't care shit about the Asian concept of *face*.

In a few minutes the nice couple suggested I make him an offer of 10 kuai and shrugged their shoulders and walked off. I thanked them and started walking again with the old man screaming in pursuit. So then I got my Mandarin cursing phrase book out. So I asked him if his son had no asshole. This is apparently a massive insult in Mandarin, he understood it. He went nuts, his face reddened and spittle flew. Then I asked him if I could fuck his wife, if he liked to fuck his dog, and if he wore a green hat, which means that his wife is fucking other men. I referred to his mouth as his cocksucker, cursed 18 generations on his ancestors, and asked him if he had a cunt or a tiny penis. While I should have spent the months preceding this trip learning to talk to the hotel staff or how to get a bus, I learned to curse.

Just as I was to do the grand finale by calling him a turtle egg, he tripped. The fruits were the size of a tennis ball, several hundred in each basket, maybe a thousand all together. The down slopping path was cobbled stone, rough cobbled. The slope was hundreds of yards long and if you were on a bike, it would be a fast ride.

Within seconds the fruit was at terminal fruit velocity rolling and bouncing. The stones acted like those old pin ball machines, the stone deflectors sent the fruit in an increasing fan of fruit tsunami. He threw himself to the ground trying to trap the 1% that were having trouble getting up to speed. Then came the surprise. He was already screaming at full throttle. So he threw one at me. I was sitting on the stone wall along the river again. It missed but several more were already in flight. I caught one as he ran for others and I wheeled it at him, he was 10 feet away and I struck him square in the nuts as he wound up to throw another. Then I picked one up at my feet and threw it underhand. I had pitched fastball years before. A fast ball pitcher can throw faster than a major league pitcher. I used to clock at over 80 miles an hour. This one tore into his gut and he dropped to the ground.

Then I thought, ***what the fuck am I doing***? Here is some old man raging on me for three dollars that he thinks I owe him. He comes doubled over holding his nuts, screaming and walking about one mile a week. I stand up on the short stone wall, the water is about 10 feet below me and immediately behind me. Balance I have, I did gymnastics all through school and even while in medical school did varsity gymnastics. I was never good. I was about 50 pounds bigger than the team average and could not rotate quickly and I always landed like a huge sac of shit. So I stood on one leg and pretended I was teetering to fall in. I knew this would be like dangling shit in front of a fly, he came at me. Just as he neared me I jumped onto the pathway and grabbed him as he launched at me. People were starting to converge, I could see them on their cell phones. Several bicyclists were pulling up. A police car was racing down the huge wide path. Fisherman on the walkway were running, rods and creels in hand. So I pretended I was struggling and then pretended to fall and bumped him pushing him over the edge, holding on to his legs as he very slowly rolled over the edge, towards the water. I held onto him, he didn't weigh more than 80 pounds. Now the screams were terror, I was to learn later that to find someone in China who can swim is like finding a penny at a Polish picnic. This was timed perfectly so that the police saw him lounge at me and me hold onto him to stop him from falling in the disgusting river.

Just as the two police were only metres away I lifted him back and gently laid him on the ground, what a fucking hero. I stepped back and they surprisingly dove on him and detained and hand cuffed him. I felt bad when the old guy started to cry. Within a minute three more police arrived, one on a bike, two on motorcycles. A crowd of about 100 people now stood around filming and chattering. A police man came who spoke good English. He had the fancy black Audi. He told me that people had called about a crazy old man attacking a foreigner. Fuck, I hate that word, what is wrong with guest, tourist, visitor. A minivan came and they loaded the guy in. The police man explained that the old man had no permit and that there had been many complaints about him. He apologized and asked how long I had been in China. I told him less than a day. I thought he was going to cry. He continued apologizing and told me, **Chinese people velly honest**, he gave me his card, bowed to me, then he asked the critical question, *you want me get you taxi*? Yah, that's what I needed, another taxi ride. I told him *no thanks*, and returned to the subway and without troubles returned to the hotel.

Now I had to check out the night life of Guangzhou. I went online and found a bar called *Michael's*. What a great place. Turns out he is a Canadian. I had never seen so many beautiful Chinese girls in my life. Eventually I had to go to the washroom to flush the beer out. There are single stalls open along the bottom so that you can see the lower legs of the person squatting on the floor level toilet. In front of me is this stunning girl with a three tiered skirt on, long black boots and hair to her waist tied at four places. While I am falling in love the line is moving forward and the smell of shit and piss wafts to my nostrils. Then it is her turn, she goes in, starts to squat and closes the door as her panties are coming down. I am thinking, *damn, I should drink more beer and lineup here more often*. I see her skirt hit the floor which is covered in piss and I hear her ass eye blasting away. Then I think, *she is in backwards, the deep end and flush hole is at the other end*. The door opens, she smiles at me and walks out, in her wake is a huge brown coiler that she did not try to flush down. It was inconceivable that this came from one person but the consistency, colour and coilage indicated that it did. What the fuck? She shit in the wrong end, didn't flush it and walked away. This became a theme of public washrooms as I travelled around China.

Eventually I walked outside to leave, I had been invited to several after-hours parties but I had no desire. I decided to walk back to the hotel. It was about 10 kilometres. Less than a minute outside of the club I had an African guy bearing down on me. I was armed, I had a pair of stainless pointed chopsticks, these are not for eating. I had a kobuto baton and a can of pepper spray. I had a chain belt that comes off in seconds and is a vicious weapon. As he was about 10 feet from me I held up my hand and told him to stop. He launched into a west African English Pidgin and did not stop. His business, selling drugs. As he approached he offered me heroin, hash, cocaine, and Ectasy. The penalty for drugs in China includes execution. I told him three times that I did not want any, he persisted so I kicked him in the nuts as hard as I could and side kicked his knee inside to out and left him screaming on the ground. Running is not a good thing to do to avoid attention but I ran till I was out of sight.

Then came the whores. Street whores in China are uncommon. Two came at me laughing and staggering asking if I wanted *sexy massage ee*. I let them walk beside me for a few minutes, I had had a good amount of beer and pretended I was drunk. They took my arms and I thought this was harmless fun. Then came the third, she was loud, belligerent. After I made it clear that I was not buying her services she began to demand money for her and her friends time. I told her to *fuck off* and tried to shake off the arm whores and they tightened their grip and the third whore went straight for my wallet in my front pocket. My travel clothes are carefully chosen. The pockets are deep, cut horizontal on the top and tight to the pant, not easy to get into. But she continued to twist and pull on my wallet screaming for money as her friends held on to me, I was shocked, I was being jacket by three whores!

The last time I had knocked a girl unconscious was at a karate tournament in New York. I had again won the heavy weight match and she had won the girls title. She somehow thought we were best friends and on par. I told her that she was still a girl and fighting girls and that had no comparison to men. She challenged me. The gym was emptying out but we had both signed no liability waivers so I pointed to the ring and she entered. I offered to borrow some protective gear and she said not. The signal was made and she came at me and I right hooked her and knocked her unconscious. Easy.

So, the arm whores escalated their struggle as did the **Pocket Puller Whore**. I unloaded the **Right Arm Whore** first by smashing the back of whore number one's skull into an aluminum street standard. There was a scream and then a thud. **Left Arm Whore** then got a hair pull bringing her head down onto whore number three's head and then a closed fist strike to the cervical spine. This renders an electrical shock throughout the entire peripheral nervous system. It is terribly painful and instantly weakens the body. Whore number three got it worst. She was robbing me. I took her right hand with my left, externally rotating it and then kicked her in the right armpit. I took a step back and kicked her full force in the face with a heel kick.

All three whores were lying on the sidewalk. I ran ahead, waved down a cab and returned to the hotel.

Later the next day I got on a train 25 cars long, each was over a hundred feet. I was pointed to the far end of the train, I think my ticket was 25-1, but they sent me 2500 feet with three bags to the wrong end of the train. Half a mile away. It was too late to walk back so a stunning train attendant looking dressed as if it was 1944 called me onto the train as the final bell rang. Now I had to walk one half mile to my car with three bags, inside the train, with people packed in like sardines. I would say the cars that had a capacity of about 120 would have 400 people in them, standing obviously, for a 38 hour train ride.

Train capacity is a huge problem in China. There are four levels of seats, cattle car which is **hard seat**, lesser cattle car which is **soft seat**, which does not appear to be softer, but you usually get a seat, **hard sleeper** which is a tiny room with two triple bunks beds in it with the worst ladders in the world. Then there is soft sleeper, the elite, for the rich. Two double bunk beds, soft mattress, a door that closes, hot water in a disgusting thermos the size of a ICBM missile. And I had two tickets, each for the bottom bunk.

It took over an hour to get to my car. Three girls a third of my size carried my bags, they insisted, pencil skirts below the knees, high heels, hair in a bun with a pillow box hat. At times they pushed people aside as they would not move, they would just stand there and look away. I posed with babies, chatted with wanna be English speakers, had mothers hold their babies up so that they could see a white person. Had mothers pass their daughters phone number to me with a descriptive in Chinese characters. People posed for photos with me, phone videoed me, girls squelled. I thought, *fuck*, *I am Brad Pitt*.

Finally, I get to my room, there are people lying on my beds, clothes at the rail and reading. Fuck, here we go again. On each long trip train is a little desk, often in car 13, that will up sell you a better seat. So, I wasn't in my room, in first class soft sleeper they take your ticket, give you a special card, and come get you before your stop. So they sold my beds to someone else. The girls should have phoned first class I learned. But, they were still my beds, which was a problem on its own, they had never heard of someone buying two beds. The fat fuckers in my bed got all loud and the girls were pointing out the door so I knew they had to go. But they refused, looks like they would be getting a refund and their cheaper seat or bed probably got sold to someone else. I was getting tired of this shit. I stood there for about 15 minutes while everyone was arguing. Then buddy pulls out a cigarette, there is a no smoking sign entering the car, there is a no smoking sign on the room door, I was to learn that entitled men in China think that they can smoke anywhere. I pointed to the sign, tapped the hostess on the shoulder, pointed to the sign and the man laughed. And struck a match. I don't like smoking in my bedroom, I slapped the cigarette out of his mouth with a flick of my fingers hitting the match on the way in. He was shocked, his mouth dropped, he pulled out some sort of government ID card like he was Chairman fuckin Mao with a big grin on his face. He starts tapping it in the hostess's face and I slap flick it out of his hand, put my foot behind his lower leg as I stepped forward, pulled his leg forward and palm strike his opposite shoulder. He spins around. Long hair is uncommon on men in China, young faggy looking boys often have the gayest haircuts you can imagine, but not men. His hair was past his collar, this is what I wanted. I slid my splayed fingers of the left hand up through his hair, clenched it and rolled my wrist upward. The pain of this technique is beyond belief. This is why professional fighters, street fighters and tough guys in jail shave their heads. It will reduce the toughest guy to a crying, begging wimp. He was crying, I was pulling on thousands of hair cells with hundreds of pounds of force. Buddy, his buddy, came to his aid as I anticipated, you can't *lose face* with a white guy thrashing you. It is always best to leave you hammer hand free if fighting multiple targets. Buddy had a suit jacket on. It is very hard to punch someone with a suit jacket on, this is why gentlemen fighters take their jacket off. To get his arm lose, he had to lift it very high, he had his elbow above his shoulder, and in doing so he elbowed one of the girls in the mouth, split her lip and she screamed and started crying.

This didn't slow the Kungfu master down, he dropped his back leg into a Kungfu pose and punched at me. He was too far away, I just smiled as he came short. I dragged his buddy screaming into the hall, sheeple were rushing to the car and the girls were already at the car entrance pushing them back. The reason I dragged the first guy into the hall is that human behaviour is predictable, particularily when they panic and are in an unfamiliar situation. I knew that Kungfu dude would follow, that would leave my beds empty and I would enter my room, throw their shit out and all would be good.

Immediately in front of my room was a fold down table the size of a cafeteria tray. I thought that this would be a good place to split this guys forehead open so I reefed on his hair as hard as I could and sent him flying into the table with the desired result and dropped him to the ground bleeding. Suit jacket man was pushing the two girls in the tiny room aside and exiting the room close behind me. China has a lot of Hepatitis, A, B and C. There are many chronic carriers. 80% of people in China have been exposed to Hepatitis. An elbow to the mouth can cut the the elbow badly, been there, done that. So, I elbowed his throat, hard. If he had of shut his cock sucker and kept his tongue in he would not have near cut if off with his teeth. Now the train was pulling into the station and I could see police running beside my train car, fuck! Before the train stopped I was lying in my bed and I had tossed their shit into the hall. The seniors in the top bunk looked terrified. The seas parted as the police, about 30, blew their whistles and rushed the doors. I was sitting in my bed with my bags on my spare bed with my reading glasses on reading my Mandarin cursing book when 4 terrified police heads looked in. The girl with the split lips was crying up a storm and a police lady was comforting her. I did not understand anything they were saying. I just sat there pretending I was reading calmly.

Hundreds had gotten off their cars and were peering into the car. I waved like the Queen of England and smiled. A police van pulled up and I saw the two guys in hand cuffs get dragged out in front of my window. A police man looked at me, gave me a knod, and laid a slapping to both their heads. Within minutes a black Audi pulled up, a man in a very expensive suit came on, asked in perfect English if he could enter my room. I invited him in. Before he said another word I handed him a police flash and told him that I was a police officer in Canada and collected police badges from all over the world, actually a cop buddy of mine does and wanted me to get some Chinese ones so I had 20 local police sew-on-patches that I was supposed to trade for my buddy. The smile on his face was amazing, police all over the world trade and collect these patches, how fucking boring. Well, this guy was an avid collecter. I had local swat badges, specialty team badges, street badges, detective strips. The Chinese guy gets on his phone, an obvious new recruit appears seconds later and he tears the patch from his shirt and gives it to me. I hand him ten patches, but I am not done, I open my big bag, take out a brand new cop shirt, size small, which is large in China, I am a 5X in China, XL in Canada, and give it to him. He bows, thanks me three times and presses it to his forehead, fuck!!!!!!!! Then a detective comes in, reads the report from his pad to my new best friend and then I get the translation.

Seems the two guys were causing problems with the waitresses. They had tried to stop them from smoking near my room, no mention of them being in my bed was made. They got *trouble mood* and one punched the waitress in the mouth and then I stepped in to defend them. There was some bowing, some of the Buddhist stuff where they do the pray position thing with their hands to their foreheads and they backed out of the train. The two assailants were on the platform with their heads bowed handcuffed and about 15 cell phones are pressed to the glass recording the white demon. The train alarm rang and everyone bolted for their cars.

I got free food, free beer, one of the attendant girls came in late at night and giggled for a while, felt my biceps, then my shoulders, then chest, I clenched my ass checks and put her hand there and she squelled and laughed. She gave me a neck massage while I sat on the bed. I thought, **_I am not Brad Pitt, I am Jesus H Christ_**. For a day and a half I was treated like a prince, I would walk the train, 38 hours is a long time. Many girls in the train gasped, if they were with a guy the guy would glare at me. Lord knows how the story may have grown.

When I got off the train I had dozens of girls cell phone numbers, **_QQ_** addresses, home addresses, pictures of single girlfriends even pictures little kids drew for me. Now I was in Chengdu. Overall, this trip was the worst experience in my life. I had had many troubles in other countries but not this insanity, I had had five years of bullshit in less than 2 days. I seriously considered flying to Beijing and flying home. I tried to figure out if I was all wrong. A Chinese friend in Toronto had told me, **_even the Chinese do not like the Guangzhou people_**. Non-Han, non-Chinese. I made my way to a local hotel, on foot, and sat and pondered this trip for hours.

Not only had I repeatedly been cheated, I repeatedly had tiny little boy men get in my face and yell and threaten me. Old men, whores, taxi drivers, drug dealers, self entitled ticket buyers, men in my train bed, shit! I had heard that China was like this but I had not expected conflicts each day. I don't take bullshit. I have no problem knocking someone out but this was beyond random. I went to bed expecting to wake up with a better understanding.

But I had not yet got to **_veh-lee dangerous Guizhou_**, there a youth gang of 11, the biggest brawl of my life and a day in jail was waiting for me.

Descriptive Pairs

Adjectives Used in Pairs, Mandarin Stative Verbs

Stative Verbs (**SV**) denote states rather than actions. They have no duration or distinguished endpoint. Some *Verbs* that are *Stative* in one situation can be *Action Verbs* in another. Mandarin uses fixed constructions that parallel meaning in English constructions but use different words. In English, we call these words *Adjectives*. There is a lame ass explanation based on the fact that Mandarin does not always use the Verb *to be*, or (是, **shì**, **is**) to equate the *Subject* to the *Object* or *Attributive*.

Equivalent of;
Both...And ...

SUBJECT + (又, **yòu**, **again**) + **Adj.**$_1$ + (又, **yòu**, **again**) + **Adj.**$_2$

Whereas English uses *both* as in *The book is both interesting and informing*, Mandarin uses (又, **yòu**, **again**, **moreover**). The general construction is;

这	本	书	又	有趣	又	实用
Zhè	běn	shū	yòu	yǒuqù	yòu	shíyòng.
This	volume	book	again	interesting	again	practical.
Subject			又	Adj.$_1$	又	Adj.$_2$

(有, yǒu, have)   (实, shí, true, real)

(趣, qù, interest)   (用, yòng, to use)

(有趣, yǒuqù, interesting)   (实用, shíyòng, practical)

Equivalent of;
Neither...Nor ...

SUBJECT + (也不, yě bù, also not) + Adj.₁ + (也不, yě bù, also not) + Adj.₂

今天	也不	太	熱	也不	太	冷
Jīntiān	yě bù	tài	rè	yě bù	tài	lěng.
Today	also not	extreme	hot	also not	extreme	cold.
Subject		Adj.₁			Adj.₂	

(太, tài, extreme)　　　　　　　　　(也不, yě bù, also not)

(熱, rè, hot)　　　　　　　　　　　(冷, lěng, cold)

Equivalent of;
Has...Also Has ...

SUBJECT + (也有, yě yǒu, also have) + Adj.₁ + (也有, yě yǒu, also have) + Adj.₂

他	也有	钱	也有	聪明
Tā	yě yǒu	qián	yě yǒu	cōngmíng.
He	also have	money	also have	intelligence.

(钱, qián, money)　　　　　　　　　(明, míng, clear)

(聪, cōng, intelligent)　　　　　　　(聪明, cōngmíng, intelligence)

    Having money is so important in Chinese society that the words 有, yǒu, have) and (钱, qián, money) come together to create (有钱, yǒuqián, have money, rich). In these fixed constructions negation is always repeated but the non-negated constructions are variable with this and part of the second pairing can be dropped, always the *Verb*. Learn the most correct form. You can also see that Mandarin has

other named grammatical groups of words that can be substituted for *Adjectives*.
Verb Object Compounds (**VOC**) can often be substituted for *Adjectives*.

Equivalent of;
Not Only...But Also...

SUBJECT + (不但, **bú dàn**, **not only**) + **Adj.**$_1$ (也, **yě**, **also**) + **Adj.**$_2$

他	不但	有錢	也	大方
Tā	bú dàn	yǒuqián	yě	dàfāng.
He	not only	have money	also	generous.
Sbj.	Adverb	VOC		Adjective

In this example above you may want to put *is* between *also* and *generous*. However, as there is no *Direct Object* for the *Subject* you cannot do this except for *contrastive* or *emphatic* purposes or to *dispel disbelief*.

Here is a little help with the various meanings of (方, **fāng**, **side**, **place**). Try and figure out which one applies to (大方, **dàfang**, **generous**).

(不但, **bú dàn**, **not only**)　　　　　　(方, **fāng**, **math, involution, power**)

(方, **fāng**, **side, place, region**)　　　　(方, **fāng**, **ten thousand**)

(方, **fāng**, **a party of**)　　　　　　　　(方, **fāng**, **square**)

(方, **fāng**, **prescription, recipe**)　　　　(方, **fāng**, **upright, honest**)

(方, **fāng**, **method, way**)　　　　　　　(方, **fāng**, **just, only just**)

Lists of Common Countable Noun Indicators

The Mandarin Grammar literature has a confusing number of terms and descriptions of **Countable Noun Indicators (CNI)**. Some of the more common terms are *classifier* and *measure word*. Neither of these adequately describe the class as a whole.

The term *Classifier* is a derivation of *Nominal Classifier* which are **CNI's** that group by physical characteristics of the *Head Noun*. You will see from the table below that some of the relationships are a little bit of a reach and there are categories within the groups.

The meaning of the character as it would stand alone or used compounded with another character may have nothing to do with its meaning as a **CNI**. They can in fact have no identifiable meaning as a **CNI**.

Table of Nominal Classifier CNI's

CNI	Pinyin	Meaning	Main Uses
把	bǎ	handful	objects that can be held with handles, relatively long and flat objects, knives, scissors, swords, keys, chairs
本	běn	a volume	bound print matter, books, magazines
部	bù	part of, a section	novels, movies, TV dramas
册	cè	book,	books, dictionaries, tomes
层	céng	layers	stories of buildings, layers,
场	chǎng	a site	public spectacles, games, drama, films
处	chù	location	ruins, construction site
出	chū	exit	acts in a play, performances, plays, circus
道	dào	path, way, route	linear projections, light rays, orders given by an authority figure, courses of food, walls and doors, questions, number of times for certain procedures
顶	dǐng	a top, to carry on the head	objects with protruding tops, hats
栋	dòng	pillars	pillars
堵	dǔ	to block	walls and encompassing fixtures
朵	duǒ		flowers, clouds

发	fā	to send out	military projectiles, bullets, artillery shells, rockets, guided missiles
封	fēng	to seal	letters, mail, fax
幅	fú	width of cloth	works of art, paintings
个	ge, gè	individual	individual things, people, general catch-all measure word
根	gēn	roots	thin, slender objects, needles, pillars, strands
架	jià	to erect	aircraft, pianos, machines
间	jiān	room, between	rooms
件	jiàn	item	matters, clothing
届	jiè	session of	regularly scheduled sessions, meetings, year-groups in a school
卷	juǎn	roll of	scrolls, film, toilet paper
棵	kē		trees, plants
颗	kē	round things	small objects, hearts, pearls, teeth, diamonds, objects appearing to be small, distant stars, planets
口	kǒu	mouth, opening	people in villages, family members, wells, blades, mouthfuls
类	lèi	type, kind of, class	objects of the same type or category, affair, circumstance
粒	lì	a grain, pellet	small objects such as a grain of rice
辆	liàng		wheeled vehicles, automobiles, bicycles

列	liè	line up, column	trains
轮	lún	round of, wheel	competition, discussions
枚	méi		medals, coins, small flat things like stamps, banana peels, bomb shells, rings
门	mén	doorway	objects pertaining to academics, courses, academic majors, also for artillery pieces
面	miàn	surface, aspect	flat and smooth objects, mirrors, flags
名	míng	name	honorific, or persons with perceived higher social rank, doctors, lawyers, politicians, royalty, can also be used for any type of person
盘	pán	dish, tray	flat objects, video cassettes, dishes of food
泡	pào	soak, bubble	classifiers for liquids which need preparation, tea, urine
匹	pǐ		horses, and other mounts, rolls or bolts of cloth
篇	piān	sheet, piece of writing	written work, papers, articles, novels
片	piàn	slice	flat objects, cards, slices of bread
瓶	píng	bottle	drinks
扇	shàn	to fan, slap, a leaf of	doors, windows

首	shǒu	head of	songs, poems, music
艘	sōu		ships, boats
所	suǒ	place	for buildings whose purposes are explicitly stated, hospitals
台	tái	platform	heavy objects, machines, TV's, computers, performances
堂	táng	a hall	periods of classes, suites of furniture
趟	tàng	a trip	trips, scheduled transportation services, flights
题	tí	topic, problem	classifier for questions
条	tiáo	long, narrow things	long, narrow, flexible objects, fish, dogs, trousers, roads, rivers, pertaining to human lives, counter-measures
头	tóu	head	domesticated animals, pig, cows, hair
团	tuán	ball	rotund and round objects, balls of yarn
坨	tuó	lump	mud, feces
尾	wěi	tail	fish
位	wèi	place	polite classifier for people, people attached to positions, workers, director
项	xiàng	items	items, projects, initiatives, ordinances, statements
样	yàng	types, kinds of	general items of differing attributes

则	zé	rule	sections of text, notices, jokes, news
盏	zhǎn	small cup	light fixtures, lamps, pots of tea
张	zhāng	sheet	flat objects, paper, tables, faces, bows, paintings, tickets, constellations, blankets, bedsheets
支	zhī	branch	stick-like objects, pens, chopsticks, roses, rifles, fleets
枝	zhī	branch	rifles, flowers
种	zhǒng	type of, kind of	types or kinds of objects
株	zhū	stump, tree trunk	trees
注	zhù	pour	incense
尊	zūn	respect	statues
座	zuò	a seat	large structures, buildings, mountains

Table of Mass Grouping Classifiers

CNI	Pinyin	Meaning	Main Uses
班	bān	a shift	scheduled services, trains, group of people, a class of pupils
帮	bāng	a group	gang, bandits, children
包	bāo	to wrap	cookies, cigarettes
杯	bēi	cup	cups of liquids, tea, water
辈	bèi	generation	people
笔	bǐ	currency	large quantities of money, money, funds
串	chuàn	to string	sets of numbers, something that comes in a string, a string of numbers, pearl necklace, a bunch of grapes, objects on a skewer, stick, kebabs, satays
床	chuáng	bed	blankets, sheets
次	cì	times	opportunities, accidents
袋	dài	bag, pouch	sackfuls, pouchfuls, bagfuls, pocketfuls, flour
道	dào	way, path	linear projections, light rays, orders given by an authority figure, courses of food, walls, doors, questions, number of times for certain procedures
滴	dī	a drip	water, blood, fluids

点	diǎn	a drop	ideas, suggestions, courage
段	duàn	section	cables, roadways, a part in a drama, play
堆	duī	pile of	trash, sand
对	duì	pair of	people, earrings,
顿	dùn	pause	meals
份	fèn	portion of	newspapers, notarized document, contract
服	fú	serve	dose of Chinese medicine
副	fù	assist	objects which come in pairs, gloves, also for spectacles, glasses, a pack of cards, mahjong
股	gǔ	a strand	flows of air, fragrances, influences
管	guǎn	tube	toothpaste and things that comes in tubes
罐	guàn	can, jar	small to medium cans of soda, of juice, bottles of water, cans of food
行	háng	a row of	objects which form lines, words
盒	hé	boxes of	tape, foods
户	hù	door	households
壶	hú	pot	pot of tea, coffee
伙	huǒ	group of	derogatory classifier for bands of people, gangs, hoodlums

剂	jì	dose of	medicine
家	jiā	family	gathering of people, families, companies, establishments, shops, restaurants, hotels
件	jiàn	item	matters, affairs, clothing
节	jié	section of	bamboo, a class period at school, batteries
句	jù	sentence	lines of sentences, poems, music
块	kuài	piece of	land, stones, cake, bread
俩	liǎ	two of	sometimes used informally instead of (两个, liǎng ge, two of), to mean two things, people
缕	lǚ	strand	hair, smoke, wind
排	pái	row of	objects grouped in rows, chairs
批	pī	batch of	people, goods
期	qī	time period	issues of periodicals
群	qún	group	people, students, birds
仨	sā	three	three of anything
束	shù	to bunch, to bind	flowers, light
双	shuāng	pair of	chopsticks, shoes
套	tào	set of	books, magazines, collectibles, clothes

碗	wǎn	bowl	soup, rice, congee
些	xiē	a few	general massifier used in the form 一些, a few, some of
行	xíng	walk	trade commission, diplomats, foreign aids, almost only used in the form 一行人
匝	zā	go around	number of revolutions, times to go around
扎	zhā	jar	drinks such as beer, soda, juice,
阵	zhèn	gust, burst	events with short durations, lightning storms, gusts of wind, sex
只	zhī	only, pair	one of a pair, hands, legs, animals such as birds, cats
注	zhù	pour, bet	lottery
组	zǔ	sets, series	sets, rows, series, group of people, batteries, military

Table of Time Unit CNI's

CNI	Pinyin	Meaning
秒	miǎo	second
分	fēn	minute
刻	kè	15 minutes
天	tiān	day
日	rì	day
年	nián	year

Table of Mass and Volume CNI's

克	kè	gram
两	liǎng	*50 grams*, *1/10 jīn*
公斤	gōngjīn	kilogram
千克	qiānkè	kilogram
斤	jīn	catty, pound, *1/2 kilograms*
吨	dūn	ton
毫升	háoshēng	millilitre
公升	gōngshēng	litre
加仑	jiālùn	gallon

Table of Distance CNI's

公分	gōngfēn	centimetre
厘米	límǐ	centimetre
寸	cùn	about ⅓ of a decimetre
吋	cùn	British inch
尺	chǐ	⅓ of a metre
呎	chǐ	British foot
英尺	yīngchǐ	British foot
公尺	gōngchǐ	metre
米	mǐ	metre
里	lǐ	about 500 metres
哩	lǐ	British mile
英里	yīnglǐ	British mile
公里	gōnglǐ	kilometre
天文单位	tiānwéndānwèi	astronomical unit
光年	guāngnián	light year
秒差距	miǎochājù	parsec

Currency CNI's

元	yuán	¥, main unit of currency
块	kuài	slang for main unit of currency
角	jiǎo	1/10th of a ¥, main unit of currency
毛	máo	slang for 10th of a ¥, main unit of currency
分	fēn	1/100th of a ¥, main unit of currency

Sentence Building Constructions

Large numbers of basic sentences can be created with a small number of words. There is great merit to practicing these as they are useful and help you to understand basic grammar constructions. In most conversation, the **Subject** will be a **Person Noun**. *He*, *she*, *they* etc. So, I will list common **Subjects**, common **Verbs**, and then common **Objects** and common **Question Words**. These sentences are going to be idiotically simple and highly repetitive in construction. With this you can master tone, pronunciation and hopefully learn to recognize characters. You will **get it** quickly. This will be progressive in nature and initially incomplete sentences. Tone is very important, how it changes relative to other characters is important. Please review the chapter in the back of the book if you are unsure. This is how you really learn to speak Mandarin.

If you do not **get it**, you are a hopeless case, buy one of those faggy French caps and study French, that's a useful language. Remember that studying Chinese is studying the characters. **Pinyin** is to learn the phonetic. You will be sorrily confused if you arrive in China thinking that you are going to see **Hanyu Pinyin** or **English**.

So, I am going to cut down on the hand holding. At the end of each example is a cut out with the words on it. You can cut it out or photocopy it and use it as a guide. Pay attention to the tone changes, see the guide at the back of the book chapter called **Tones**. Get creative, cover the **Pinyin** and English lines with a ruler and figure it out.

Wang and Chang Meet

王	您	好			
	Nín	hǎo!			
	You	good!			

长	好	你	是	王	先生	吗
	Hǎo!	Nǐ	shì	Wáng	xiānsheng	ma?
	Good!	You	is	Wang	mister	ma?

王	是的	我	是	王	先生
	Shì de,	wǒ	shì	Wáng	xiānsheng.
	Is,	me	is	Wang	mister.

长	王	先生	好
	Wáng	xiānsheng	hǎo.
	Wang	mister	good.

王	你	叫	什么	名字
	Nǐ	jiào	shénme	míngzi?
	You	called	what	name?

长	我的	名字	叫	长		
	Wǒ de	míngzi	jiào	Cháng.		
	My	name	called	Chang.		

王	你	是	哪里	人		
	Nǐ	shì	nǎlǐ	rén.		
	You	is	where	person.		

长	我	是	北京	人	你	呢
	Wǒ	shì	Běijīng	rén,	Nǐ	ne?
	Me	is	Beijing	person,	you	?

王	我	是	成都	人		
	Wǒ	shì	Chéngdū	rén.		
	Me	is	Chengdu	person.		

长	你的	太太	也是	成都	人	吗
	Nǐ de	tàitai	yěshì	Chéngdū	rén	ma?
	Your	wife	is also	Chengdu	person	?

王	不		她		不是	
	Bù,		tā		bú shì	
	Not,		she		not is	

长	对不起
	Duìbuqǐ.
	Sorry.

王	没关系	她	是	上海	人
	Méi guānxi,	tā	shì	Shànghǎi	rén.
	Not matter,	she	is	Shanghai	person.

长	啊	上海	人	好
	Ā!	Shànghǎi	rén,	hǎo!
	Ah!	Shanghai	person,	good!

王	你的	太太	他	是	哪里	人
	Nǐ de	tàitai,	tā	shì	nǎlǐ	rén.
	Your	wife,	she	is	where	person.

长	她	是	广州	人		
	Tā	shì	Guǎngzhōu	rén.		
	She	is	Guangzhou	person.		

王	谢谢	认识	您	很	高兴	
	Xièxie,	rènshi	nín	hěn	gāoxìng.	
	Thank thank,	acquaint	you	very	happy.	

长	谢谢	您	我	也	很	高兴
	Xièxie	nín,	wǒ	yě	hěn	gāoxìng.
	Thank thank,	you,	me	also	hen	happy.

王	再见	长	先生			
	Zàijiàn	Cháng	xiānsheng.			
	Again see,	Chang	mister.			

长	回	头	见	王	先生	
	Huí	tóu	jiàn	Wáng	xiānsheng.	
	Return	head	meet	Wang	mister.	

Wang and Chang get Stupid about a Picture Book

王	这	是	谁的	书		
	Zhè	shì	shuí de	shū?		
	This	is	whose	book?		

长	这	是	我的	书		
	Zhè	shì	wǒ de	shū.		
	This	is	my	book.		

王	那	是	什么	书		
	Nà	shì	shénme	shū?		
	That	is	what	book?		

长	那	是	图画	书		
	Nà	shì	túhuà	shū.		
	That	is	picture	book.		

王	那	是	谁的	图画	书	
	Nà	shì	shuí de	túhuà	shū?	
	That	is	whose	picture	book?	

张	那	是	张的	图画	书
	Nà	shì	Zhāng de	túhuà	shū.
	That	is	Zhang's	picture	book.

王	这	是	杂志	吗	
	Zhè	shì	zázhì	ma?	
	This	is	magazine	?	

张	不	这	是	图画	书
	Bú,	zhè	shì	túhuà	shū.
	Not,	this	is	picture	book.

王	这	是	你的	书	吗	
	Zhè	shì	nǐ de	shū	ma.	
	This	is	your	book	?	

张	我	已经	告诉	你	是	张的
	Wǒ	yǐjing	gàosu	nǐ	shì	Zhāng de.
	Me	already	tell	you	is	Zhang's.

王	可能	我	有点	二百五	
	Kěnéng	wǒ	yǒudiǎn	èrbǎiwǔ.	
	Possible	me	a little	250.	(stupid)

长	你	只	觉得	你	有点	二百
	Nǐ	zhǐ	juéde	nǐ	yǒudiǎn	èrbǎiwǔ.
	You	only	think	you	a little	250.

王	什么	你	觉得	我	呆笨	吗
	Shénme!,	nǐ	juéde	wǒ	dāibèn	ma?
	What!,	you	think	me	stupid	?

长	当然	我	就是	这个	意思
	Dāngrán,	wǒ	jiùshì	zhèige	yìsi.
	Of course,	me	just is	this one	meaning.

王	那	是	什么	东西
	Nà	shì	shénme	dōngxi?
	That	is	what	thing?

长	那	是	报纸		
	Nà	shì	bàozhǐ.		
	That	is	newspaper.		

王	那	是	谁的	报纸		
	Nà	shì	shuí de	bàozhǐ.		
	That	is	whose	newspaper.		

长	我	不	知道			
	Wǒ	bù	zhīdao.			
	Me	not	know.			

王	呵	明白	你	要	这个	东西
	Ā!	Míngbai,	nǐ	yào	zhèige	dōngxi.
	Ah!	Clear,	you	want	this	thing.

长	不	我	不要	这个	东西	
	Bú,	wǒ	búyào	zhèige	dōngxi.	
	No,	me	not want	this	thing.	

王	谁	给	你	这	本	书
	Shuí	gěi	nǐ	zhè	běn	shū.
	Who	give	you	this	volume	book?

长	我的	老师	给	我的		
	Wǒ de	lǎoshī	gěile	wǒ de		
	My	teacher	gave	me.		

王	他的	名字	叫	什么		
	Tā de	míngzi	jiào	shénme.		
	His	name	called	what?		

长	我的	老师	叫	张		
	Wǒ de	lǎoshī	jiào	Zhāng.		
	My	teacher	call	Zhang.		

王	啊	张	我	认识	他	
	Ǎ!,	Zhāng,	wǒ	rènshi	tā.	
	Ah!,	Zhang,	me	acquaint	he.	

长	真的	啊	他	有	几个	学生
	Zhēn de	ǎ?	Tā	yǒu	jǐgè	xuésheng.
	Really	?	He	have	how many	student.

王	我	不知道	但是	他	很	有名
	Wǒ	bù zhīdao,	dànshi	tā	hěn	yǒumíng.
	Me	not know,	but	he	very	famous.

长	可能	有	一千	个	学生	吧
	Kěnéng	yǒu	yīqiān	ge	xuésheng	ba!
	Possible	have	1000	CNI	student	!

王	那么	多	啊
	Nàme	duō	ǎ?
	Like that	many	?

长	他	教	什么
	Tā	jiāo	shénme?
	He	teach	what?

王 他 教 英语
Tā jiāo Yīngyǔ.
He teach English.

长 谢谢 我 必须 得 走 了
Xièxie Wǒ bìxū děi zǒu le.
Thank thank Me must should go forth !

王 行 再见
Xíng, zàijiàn
Okay, again meet.

长 再见
Zàijiàn.

Wang and Chang Talk Shit About School

王	你 Nǐ You	是 shì is	不是 bú shì not is	学生 xuésheng. student.	
长	是 Shì, Is,	我 wǒ me	是 shì is	学生 xuésheng. student.	
王	你 Nǐ You	在 zài at	上 shàng attend	中学 zhōngxué middle school	吗 ma? ?
长	不 Bù, Not,	我 wǒ me	是 shì is	大学 dàxué big school	学生 xuésheng. student.
王	啊 Ǎ, Ah!	你 Nǐ You	在 zài at	哪个 zhèige which one	大学 dàxué. big school?
长	我 Wǒ Me	在 zài at	北京 Běijīng Beijing	大学 dàxué. big school.	

王	北京 Běijīng Beijing	大学 dàxué, big school,	啊 ǎ, ah!	挺好 tǐnghǎo very good.	的 de.
长	你的 Nǐ de Your	老师 lǎoshī teacher	是 shì is	谁 shuí? who?	
王	我的 Wǒ de My	老师 lǎoshī teacher	是 shì is	卢 Lu Lu	教授 jiàoshòu. professor.
长	啊 Ǎ, Ah!	卢 Lú Lu	教授 jiàoshòu. professor.		
王	你 Nǐ You	认识 rènshi acquaint	卢 Lú Lu	教授 jiàoshòu professor	吗 ma? ?
长	不 Bú Not	认识 rènshi, acquaint,	我 wǒ me	知道 zhīdao know of	卢 Lú. Lu.
王	听说 Tīngshuō Hear say	卢 Lú Lu	最 zuì most	好 hǎo. good.	

长	真的	他	很	有名	吗
	Zhēn de,	tā	hěn	yǒumíng	ma?
	Really,	he	very	have name famous	?

王	当然	他	有
	Dāngrán	tā	yǒu.
	Of course,	he	have.

长	你	很	幸运
	Nǐ	hěn	xìngyùn.
	You	very	lucky.

王	嗯	我	是.
	Ǹg,	wǒ	shì.
	Nng!,	me	is.

长	王	先生	我	必须	去.
	Wáng	xiānsheng,	wǒ	bìxū	qù.
	Wang	mister,	me	must	go.

王	明白	明白	我	懂
	Míngbai	míngbai	wǒ	dǒng.
	Clear	Clear	me	understand.

长 再见
   Zàijiàn.
   Again meet.

王 再见
   Zàijiàn.
   Again meet.

Wang Thinks Chang's Wife has a Big Ass
Chang Tells Him to go Fuck Himself

王	早上	好
	Zǎoshang	**hǎo.**
	Early upon	good.

长	你	早
	Nǐ	**zǎo!**
	You	early!

王	最近	怎么样
	Zuìjìn	**zěnmeyàng?**
	Recently	how appear?

长	挺好的	你	呢
	Tǐnghǎo de,	**nǐ**	**ne.**
	Very good,	you	?

王	不错
	Búcuò.
	Not bad.

长	昨天	我	看到	你的	老婆	了
	Zuótiān	**wǒ**	**kàndào**	**nǐ de**	**lǎopo**	**le.**
	Yesterday	me	looked at	your	old wife.	

王	啊	我	太太	非常	漂亮	吧
	Ā!,	wǒ	tàitai	fēicháng	piàoliang	ba.
	Ah!,	me	wife	not common	beautiful.	

长	什么	你	太太	太	丑	了
	Shénme?!,	nǐ	tàitai	tài	chǒu	le.
	What?,	your	wife	extreme	ugly	!

王	肏	你	给	我	口	交
	Cào	nǐ,	gěi	wǒ	kǒu	jiāo.
	Fuck	you,	give	me	mouth	sex.
						fellatio

长	哈哈	口交	你的	鸡巴	太	小了
	Hā hā!,	kǒu jiāo,	nǐ de	jība	tài	xiǎo le.
	Ha ha!,	mouth sex,	your	cock	extreme	small.

王	你	妹妹	喜欢	我的	鸡巴	
	Nǐ	mèimei	xǐhuan	wǒ de	jība.	
	You	sister	like	my	cock.	

长	你	生个	儿子	没有	屁股	眼
	Nǐ	shēng ge	érzi	méiyǒu	pìgu	yǎn.
	You	born	son	not have	ass	eye.

王	哈哈	我	喜欢	他的	妈妈	屁股
	Hā hā!,	wǒ	xǐhuan	nǐ de	māma	pìgu.
	Ha ha!,	me	like	your	mama	ass.

长	谁的	屁股				
	Shuí de	pìgu?				
	Whose	ass?				

王	你的	妈妈	昨晚	给	我	肏
	Nǐ de	māma,	zuówǎn	gěi	wǒ	cào.
	Your	mama,	last night	give	me	fuck.

长	我	不	知道	这个		
	Wǒ	bù	zhīdao	zhèige.		
	Me	not	know	this.		

王	为什么	她	记得	我		
	Wèishénme,	tā	jìde	wǒ.		
	Why,	she	remember	me.		

长	哈哈	记得	你	我	不	觉得
	Hā hā,	jìde	nǐ,	wǒ	bù	juéde.
	Ha ha,	remember	you,	me	not	think.

王	你的 Nǐ de Your	太太 tàitai wife	有 yǒu have	大 dà big	屁股 pìgu. ass.	
长	肏 Cào Fuck	你, nǐ, you,	我 wǒ me	别 bié do not	说了 shuō le. speak.	
王	好的, Hǎo de, Good,	现在 xiànzài now	我 wǒ me	去 qù go	肏 cào fuck	她. tā. her.

Wang and Chang go to a Gay Bar

王	早 Zǎo Early	王 Wáng Wang	先生 xiānsheng. mister!		
长	你 Nǐ You	也 yě also	早 zǎo. early.		
王	今天 Jīntiān Today	你 nǐ you	休息 xiūxi rest	吗 ma. ?	
长	我 Wǒ Me	不 bù not	休息 xiūxi. rest.		
王	今天 Jīntiān Today	你 nǐ you	要 yào want	干 gàn do	什么 shénme? what?
长	今天 Jīntiān Today	我 wǒ me	要 yào want	学习 xuéxí study	英语 Yīngyǔ. English.

王	我	要	去	动物园		
	Wǒ	yào	qù	dòngwùyuán.		
	Me	want	go	zoo.		

长	上个	星期	我	去过	那个	地方
	Shàngge	xīngqī	wǒ	qùquo	nàge	dìfang.
	Previous	week	me	gone	that	place.

王	我	还想	去	动物园		
	Wǒ	háixiǎng	qù	dòngwùyuán.		
	Me	still want	go	zoo.		

长	别	忘了	我	不要	去	
	Bié	wàngle,	wǒ	búyào	qù.	
	Do not	forget,	me	not want	go.	

王	不行	你	得	听	我的	
	Bùxíng,	nǐ	de	tīng	wǒde.	
	Not okay,	you	have to	listen	mine.	

长	好的	坐	地铁	怎么样		
	Hǎo de,	zuò	dìtiě	zěnmeyàng?		
	Good,	sit on	subway	how about?		

王	不要 Búyào, Not want,	太 tài extreme	单调 dāndiào boring	了 le	啊 ā!, ah!,
长	现在 Xiànzài Now	几 jǐ how many	点 diǎn? dot?	(o'clock)	
王	我 Wǒ Me	不 bù not	知道 zhīdao, know,	干嘛 gànmá? why?	
长	我们 Wǒmen We	能 néng can	去 qù go	北京 Běijīng. Beijing.	
王	你 Nǐ You	要 yào want	什么 shénme what	时候 shíhou time	去 qù? go?
长	不管 Bùguǎn, No matter,	什么 shénme what	时候 shíhou time	都 dōu all	行 xíng. ok.

王	我	有	个	主意		;
	Wǒ	yǒu	gè	zhǔyi.		
	Me	have	one	idea.		

长	主意	啊	是	什么
	Zhǔyi	ā!,	shì	shénme?
	Idea	ah!,	is	what?

王	我	要	去	上海
	Wǒ	yào	qù	Shànghǎi.
	Me	want	go	Shanghai.

长	为什么	呢
	Wèishénme	ne?
	Why	?

王	上海	有	很多	可爱	的	男人
	Shànghǎi	yǒu	hěn duō	kě'ài	de	nánrén.
	Shanghai	have	very many	cute		men.

长	什么	啊	你	喜欢	小	男孩
	Shénme	ā?,	nǐ	xǐhuan	xiǎo	nánhái?
	What	ah?,	you	like	little	boy?

王	一点儿	你	有	问题	吗
	Yīdiǎn'r,	nǐ	yǒu	wèntí	ma?
	A little,	you	have	problem	?

长	我 Wǒ Me	没有 méiyǒu not have	问题 wèntí, problem,	我 wǒ me	也 yě also	喜欢 xǐhuan. like.
王	好的 Hǎo de, Good,	我们 wǒmen we	必须 bìxū must	买 mǎi buy	票 piào. ticket.	
长	火车站 Huǒchēzhàn, Train station,	走 zǒu go forth	吧 ba! !			
王	今晚 Jīnwǎn Tonight	我们 wǒmen we	去 qù go	同性恋 tóngxìngliàn gay	酒吧 jiǔbā bar	吗 ma? ?
长	同性恋 Tóngxìngliàn Gay	酒吧 jiǔbā bar	啊 ā?, ah?,			
王	当然 Dāngrán, Of course,	我们 wǒmen we	都 dōu all	喜欢 xǐhuān like	小 xiǎo young	男孩 nánhái. boy.
长	以前 Yǐqián Before	我 wǒ me	没有 méiyǒu not have	去过 qùguo. gone.		

王	别	忘了,	大家	不	知道	我们.
	Bié	wánle,	dàjiā	bù	zhīdao	wǒmen.
	Do not	forget,	everyone	not	know	us.

长	啊,	上海	有	同性恋	的	男孩.
	Ǎ!	Shànghǎi	yǒu	tóngxìngliàn	de	nánháir.
	Ah!	Shanghai	have	homosexual		boy.

王	嗯,	上海	有	很	多	的.
	Ǹg,	Shànghǎi	yǒu	hěn	duō	de.
	Nggg,	Shanghai	have	very	many.	

长	当然,	上海	女孩儿	男孩儿	样子	一样.
	Dāngrán,	Shànghǎi	nǚhái'r	nánhái'r	yàngzi	yīyàng.
	Of course,	Shanghai	girl	boy	appearance	same.

王	现代	男孩	女孩的	发型	都一样.
	Xiàndài	nánhái	nǚhái de	lǐfà	dōuyīyàng.
	Modern	boy,	girl's	hair cut	all same.

长	真的	啊!	我	不	懂	这个.
	Zhēn de	ā!	Wǒ	bù	dǒng	zhèige.
	Really	!	Me	not	understand	this.

王	也	听说	像	美女	一样.
	Yě	tīngshuō	xiàng	měinǚ	yīyàng.
	Also	hear say	similar	beauty girl	same.

长	他们 Tāmen They	给 gěi give	中国 Zhōngguó China	添 tiān increase	耻辱 chǐrǔ. shame.	
王	我 Wǒ Me	认为 rènwéi think	他们 tāmen they	喜欢 xǐhuan like	吃 chī eat	豆腐 dòufu. tofu.
长	我 Wǒ Me	不 bù not	懂 dǒng. understand.			
王	中国 Zhōngguó Chinese	人 rén people	不 bù not	吃 chī eat	牛肉 niúròu. beef.	
长	我 Wǒ Me	明白 míngbai clear	点儿 diǎn'r a little,	接着 jiēzhe continue	说 shuō. say.	
王	豆腐 Dòufu Tofu	把 bǎ	男孩 nánhái male	成为 chéngwéi become	女孩 nǚhái. girl.	
长	哎呀 Āiyā! Ai ya!	我 wǒ me	也 yě also	很 hěn very	喜欢 xǐhuan like	豆腐 dòufu. tofu.

王	你 Nǐ You	看 kàn look at	你的 nǐ de your	鸡巴 jība cock.	吧 ba.	
长	哎呀 Āiyā! Ai ya!	太 tài Extreme	小 xiǎo small	了 le! !	太 Tài Too	晚了 wǎn. late!
王	是的 Shì de, Is,	可是 kěshì but	我 wǒ me	爱 ài love	你 nǐ. you.	
长	我 Wǒ Me	也 yě also	爱 ài love	你 nǐ. you.		
王	末了 Mòliǎo, Finally,	中国 Zhōngguó China	美国 Měiguó America	都 dōu all	一样 yīyàng. same.	
长	不对 Búduì Not true,	美国 Měiguó America	只有 zhǐyǒu only have	一点 yīdiǎn a little	同性恋 tóngxìngliàn. faggot.	
王	哪 Nèi Which	国 guó country	有 yǒu have	更多的 gèngduō de more	同性恋 tóngxìngliàn. faggot.	

长	法国	差不多	都	是	同性恋	
	Fǎguó	chàbuduō	dōu	shì	tóngxìngliàn.	
	France	almost	all	is	faggot.	

王	真的	啊
	Zhēn de	!
	Really	!

长	意大利	男人	也	喜欢	肏	屁股
	Yìdàlì	nánrén	yě	xǐhuan	cào	pìgu.
	Italy	men	also	like	fuck	ass.

王	对	中国	来说	太	好	了
	Duì	Zhōngguó	láishuō	tài	hǎo	le.
	For	China	about	extreme	good	!

长	当然	男孩	数量	比较	女孩	多
	Dāngrán,	nánrén	shùliàng	bǐjiào	nǚhái	duō.
	Of course,	men	quantity	compare	girls	more.

王	现在	男孩	都	有	对象
	Xiànzài	nánrén	dōu	yǒu	duìxiàng.
	Now	boys	all	have	mate.

长	中国	老是	有	解答
	Zhōngguó	lǎoshi	yǒu	jiědá.
	China	always	have	solution.

王	中国	很	伟大		
	Zhōngguó	hěn	wěidà.		
	China	very	great.		

长	现在	男人	爱	男人	
	Xiànzài	nánrén	ài	nánrén.	
	Now	boy	love	boy.	

王	没	问题	帮助	解决	人口
	Méi	wèntí,	bāngzhù	jiějué	rénkǒu.
	No	problem,	help	control	population.

Wang and Chang Compare Their Penises

王	老	长	看一看	这个		喜	不	喜欢
	Lǎo	Cháng,	kànyīkàn	zhèige,		xǐ	bù	xǐhuan.
	Old	Chang,	look look	this one,		like	not	like.

长	哎呀	你	给	我	看	你的	鸡巴
	Āiyā!	Nǐ	gěi	wǒ	kàn	nǐ de	jība.
	Ai ya!	You	give	me	look at	your	cock.

王	喜欢	吗
	Xǐhuan	ma?
	Like	?

长	不	喜欢	阿	你	疯了	吧
	Bù	xǐhuan	ǎ.	Nǐ	fēngle	ba!
	Not	like	ah!	You	crazy	!

王	我	鸡巴	像	黄瓜	一样
	Wǒ	jība	xiàng	huánggua	yīyàng.
	Me	cock	similar	cucumber	same.

长	吃	屎	你	鸡巴	像	手指	一样
	Chī	shǐ,	nǐ	jība	xiàng	shǒuzhǐ	yīyàng.
	Eat	shit,	you	cock	similar	finger	same.

王	哈哈	我	不	觉得
	Hā hā	Wǒ	bù	juéde.
	Haha!	Me	Not	think.

长	第一	你的	鸡巴	太	细	了
	Dì-yī	nǐ de	jība	tài	xì	le.
	First,	your	cock	extreme	thin	!

王	什么	不是	你的	前臂	怎么样	呢
	Shénme?	Bú shì,	nǐ de	qiánbì	zěnmeyàng	ne.
	What?	Not is,	your	forearm	how about	?

长	老天	帮	我,	脱	裤子	吧
	Lǎotiān	bāng	wǒ,	tuō	kùzi	ba!
	Heaven	help	me,	take off	trousers	!

王	啊	目前	你	要	摸	吗
	Ǎ!	Mùqián	nǐ	yào	mō	ma?
	Ah!	Now	you	want	touch	?

长	肏	你	啊	我	要	砍
	Cào	nǐ	ǎ!	Wǒ	yào	kǎn.
	Fuck	you	ah!	Me	want	cut off.

王	现在	你	脱	裤子	
	Xiànzài	nǐ	tuō	kùzi.	
	Now	you	take off	trousers.	

长	哎呀	你	要	给	我	口交	吗
	Āiyā!	Nǐ	yào	gěi	wǒ	kǒujiāo	ma?
	Ai ya!	You	want	give	me	blow job	?

王	可能 Kěnéng Perhaps	要 yào, want,	你 nǐ you	喜欢 xǐhuan like	口交 kǒujiāo blow job	吗 ma. ?	
长	当然 Dāngrán, Of course,	男人 nánrén male	都 dōu all	喜欢 xǐhuan like	口交 kǒujiāo. blow job.		
王	你的 Nǐ de Your	儿子 érzi son	不 bù not	喜欢 xǐhuan like	口交 kǒujiāo. blow job.		
长	肏 Cào Fuck	你 nǐ, you,	我 wǒ me	打死 dǎsǐ beat dead	你 nǐ. you.		
王	不 Bù Not	可能 kěnéng, possible,	我 Wǒ Me	招 zhāo provoke	你 nǐ you	了 le. !	
长	好的 Hǎo de! Good!	如果 Rúguǒ If	真的 zhēn de true	我 wǒ me	肏 cào fuck	你的 nǐ de your	屁股 pìgu. ass.
王	行 Xíng, Okay,	昨晚 zuówǎn last night	在 zài at	上海 Shànghǎi Shanghai	你 nǐ you	干 gàn do	了 le. !

长	什么 Shénme? What?	哎呀 Āiyā! Ai ya!	我 Wǒ Me	喝 hē drink	很 hěn very	多 duō much	白酒 báijiǔ. alcohol.
王	没事 Méishì Not matter	你的 nǐ de Your	屁股 pìgu, ass,	你的 nǐ de your	太太 tàitai wife	屁股 pìgu, ass,	一样 yīyàng. same.
长	哦 Ò! Oh!	你 Nǐ You	肏 cào fuck	我的 wǒ de my	太太的 tàitai de wife's	屁股 pìgu ass	吗 ma. ?
王	天天 Tiāntiān Daily,	为什么 wèishénme why	呢 ne? ?	你 Nǐ You	不会 bú huì not able	干 gàn do	这个 zhèige. this.
长	是 Shì Is	真 zhēn, true,	我的 wǒ de my	鸡巴 jība cock	差不多 chàbuduō almost	死了 sǐle. dead.	
王	可能 Kěnéng Perhaps	你 nǐ you	需要 xūyào need	中 zhōng Chinese	药 yào. medicine.		
长	不必 Búbì, Not need,	我 wǒ me	用 yòng use	伟哥 wěigē. Viagra.			

王	啊	蓝色	丸药
	Ā!	lánsè	wányào.
	Ah!	blue	pill.

长	对了	你	知道
	Duì le!	Nǐ	zhīdao.
	Correct!	You	know.

王	你	要	我	买	吗
	Nǐ	yào	wǒ	mǎi	ma?
	You	want	me	buy	?

长	你	要	给	我	口交	吗
	Nǐ	yào	gěi	wǒ	kǒujiāo	ma?
	You	want	give	me	blow job	?

王	我	要	行	现在	我	去	药店
	Wǒ	yào,	xíng,	xiànzài	wǒ	qù	yàodiàn.
	Me	want,	okay,	now	me	go	pharmacy.

长	今天	晚上	你	给	我	口交	吗
	Jīntiān	wǎnshang	nǐ	gěi	wǒ	kǒujiāo	ma?
	Today	night	you	give	me	blowjob	?

王	最后	我	给	你	吹	功
	Zuìhòu,	wǒ	gěi	nǐ	chuī	gōng.
	Finally,	me	give	you	blow	service.

长	大好	了			
	Dàhǎo	le.			
	Great	!			

王	现在	我们	比较	我们的	鸡巴
	Xiànzài	wǒmen	bǐjiào	wǒmen de	jība.
	Now,	we	compare	our	cock.

长	但是	我的	鸡巴	太	软	了
	Dànshì,	wǒ de	jība	tài	ruǎn	le.
	But,	my	cock	extreme	soft	!

王	我的	也	是	没事		
	Wǒ de	yě	shì,	méishì.		
	My	also	is,	not matter.		

长	哎呀	我的	鸡巴	比	你的	小
	Āiyā!	wǒ de	jība	bǐ	nǐ de,	xiǎo.
	Ai ya!	my	cock	compare	your,	small.

王	我	已经	告诉	你	这个	了吧
	Wǒ	yǐjing	gàosu	nǐ	zhèige	le ba!
	Me	already	tell	you	this	!

长	你的	鸡巴	差不多	二	英寸
	Nǐ de	jība	chàbuduō	èr	Yīngcùn.
	Your	cock	almost	two	inches.

王	我	知道	很	多	美女	也	知道
	Wǒ	zhīdao,	hěn	duō	měinǚ	yě	zhīdao.
	Me	know,	very	many	beauty girl	also	know.

长	真的	吗	你	很	幸运		
	Zhēn de	ma?	Nǐ	hěn	xìngyùn.		
	Really	?	You	very	lucky.		

王	今晚	你	也	很	幸运		
	Jīnwǎn	nǐ	yě	hěn	xìngyùn.		
	Tonight	you	also	very	lucky.		

长	为什么	呢					
	Wèishénme	ne?					
	Why	?					

王	今晚	第一	口交	然后	肏	你的	屁股
	Jīnwǎn	dì-yī	kǒujiāo	ránhòu	cào	nǐ de	pìgu.
	Tonight	first	blow job	then	fuck	your	ass.

长	太	好了	我	等	不急	啦	
	Tài	hǎo le!	Wǒ	děng	bùjí	lā!	
	Extreme	good!	Me	wait	not can	!	

Canadian Birds

My wife is convinced that Canadian birds are not very smart. Anything in reach of a broom, brick, net or projectile is dinner meat in China. She was shocked at the Canadian geese, deer, foxes, turkeys and pidgeons in my neighbourhood. So she has been scheming as to how to get a goose since she got here. Seeing how she dispensed of a live chicken soon after I meet her I have no doubt that she can kill, pluck and dress it. For general knowledge I have pointed out how they mate for life.

So today, April 23rd 2011, we are driving down an industrial street in Stoney Creek, Arvin Avenue, where some geese perennially live in the ditch and surrounding swamp. I point out a goose sitting on the gravel at the side of the road and point out another stupid non-migratory bird to her. Whenever she is in animal stalking and killing mode in my Safari van she whispers and crouches down in the passenger seat so that only her slanted eyes and hair could be seen through the window. Then she rolls the window down and does bizarre animal calls to try and lure deer, geese, turkeys or whatever to the truck. Now comes the Chinese, (慢点儿吧, **màn diǎn'r ba!, slow a little!**) which she whispers a few times then a few frantic (停车吧, **tíngchē ba, stop car!**) So we are stopped and she slowly roles the window down making Chinese versions of animal calls and doesn't the damn goose waddle over making goose noises which I point out to her as a more natural call, and she reaches to the seat pocket and pulls out a large cloth shopping bag and I think *oh shit, there is going to be a chase, a struggle and a beating*. Then the beautiful male sticks his neck above the ditch makes a few goose noises, and my wife says, *oh mah gawh, the boy is gunna be so lonely I kill his wife*. So then she reaches back for another cloth bag and says, *Ima gunna have tah killem both*. This is when I pushed the electric door lock and took off. I shouldn't encourage her.

Vocabulary for the Above Conversations

(啊, ā, ah!)
(啊, ǎ, surprise interjection)
(爱, ài, love)
(哎, āi, heh!)
(哎呀, āiyā, surprise interjection)
(白酒, báijiǔ, alcohol)
(帮, bāng, to help)
(帮助, bāngzhù, help)
(北京, Běijīng, Beijing)
(本, běn, volume)
(报纸, bàozhǐ, newspaper)
(比, bǐ, compare)
(别, bié, do not)
(比较, bǐjiào, compare)
(必须, bìxū, must)
(必要, bìyào, need)
(不必, búbì, not need)
(不, bù, bú, not)
(不错, búcuò, not bad)
(不对, búduì, not correct)
(不好, bù hǎo, not good)
(不能, bùnéng, not can)
(不是, bú shì, not is)
(不要, búyào, not want)
(肏, cào, fuck)
(长, cháng, long)
(差不多, chàbuduō, almost)

(长, Cháng, Chang)
(吃, chī, eat)
(吃了, chī le, ate)
(耻辱, chǐrǔ, shame)
(成都, Chéngdū, Chengdu)
(成为, chéngwéi, become)
(丑, chǒu, ugly)
(吹, chuī, blow)
(吹功, chuīgōng, blow service)
(大, dà, big)
(大好, dàhǎo, excellent)
(大家, dàjiā, everyone)
(单调, dāndiào, boring)
(当然, dāngrán, of course)
(但是, dànshì, but)
(打死, dǎsǐ, beat dead)
(等, děng, wait)
(点, diǎn, a little)
(地方, dìfang, place)
(地铁, dìtiě, subway)
(第一, dì-yī, first)
(东西, dōngxi, thing)
(懂, dǒng, understand)
(动物园, dòngwùyuán, zoo)
(都, dōu, all)
(豆腐, dòufu, tofu)
(对不起, duìbuqǐ, sorry)

(对了, duì le, correct)
(对象, duìxiàng, mate)
(多会儿, duōhuir, whatever)
(呆笨, dāibèn, stupid)
(当然, dāngrán, of course)
(单调, dāndiào, boring)
(东西, dōngxi, thing)
(多, duō, many, much)
(二, èr, two)
(二百五, èrbǎiwǔ, 250)
(儿子, érzi, son)
(方向, fāngxiàng, direction)
(法国, Fǎguó, France)
(非常, fēicháng, not common)
(干, gàn, do)
(告诉, gàosu, tell)
(高兴, gāoxìng, happy)
(给, gěi, give)
(给看, gěikàn, show)
(更多, gèngduō, more)
(狗屎, gǒushǐ, dog shit)
(管理, guǎnlǐ, manage)
(国, guó, country)
(过, guò, cross, pass)
(哈哈, hā hā, ha ha)
(好, hǎo, good)
(好的, hǎo de, good)
(还, hái, still)

(喝, hē, drink)
(很, hěn, very)
(黄瓜, huánggua, cucumber)
(回, huí, return)
(回答, huídá, answer)
(会, huì, able)
(火车站, huǒchēzhàn, train station)
(一样, yīyàng, same)
(见, jiàn, see)
(几, jǐ, how many)
(交, jiāo, mate)
(教, jiāo, teach)
(交, jiāo, intercourse)
(叫, jiào, call)
(教授, jiàoshòu, professor)
(鸡巴, jība, cock)
(记得, jìde, remember)
(解答, jiědá, answer)
(径直, jìngzhí, straight)
(今天, jīntiān, today)
(今晚, jīnwǎn, tonight)
(就, jiù, just)
(酒吧, jiǔbā, bar)
(就是说, jiùshìshuō, just is said)
(吉祥, jíxiáng, lucky)
(觉得, juéde, think)
(看, kàn, look at)
(看不见, kànbujiàn, not see)

(看到, kàndào, looked at)
(看到, kàndào, see)
(可爱, kě'ài, cute)
(可能, kěnéng, possible)
(可是, kěshì, but)
(口, kǒu, mouth)
(口交, kǒujiāo, mouth mate)
(裤子, kùzi, pants)
(来说, láishuō, concerning, about)
(蓝色, lánsè, blue)
(老婆, lǎopo, old wife)
(老师, lǎoshī, teacher)
(老是, lǎoshi, always)
(老天, lǎotiān, Heaven)
(理发, lǐfà, haircut)
(卢, Lú, Lu)
(买, mǎi, buy)
(马路, mǎlù, road)
妈妈, māma, mama)
(没关系, méi guānxi, not relate)
(没问题, méi wèntí, no problem)
(妹妹, mèimei, sister)
(美女, měinǚ, beauty girl)
(没事儿, méishìr, not matter)
(没有, méiyǒu, not have)
(美国, Měiguó, America)
(迷路, mílù, lost)
(明白, míngbai, clear

(名字, míngzi, name)
(末了, mòliǎo, finally)
(目前, mùqián, now)
(那, nà, nèi, that)
(哪里, náli, where)
(那么, nàme, that?)
(男孩儿, nánhái'r, boy)
(男人, nánrén, men)
(哪儿, nǎ'r, where)
(呢, ne, aspect particle)
(呢, ne, reflective?)
(能, néng, can)
(你, nǐ, you)
(你的, nǐ de, your)
(你们, nǐmen, you)
(你们的, nǐmen de, yours)
(您, nín, you)
(牛肉, niúròu, beef)
(农民, nóngmín, farmer)
(嗯, ǹg, agreement interjection)
(女孩儿, nǚháir, girl)
(哦, ò, understanding interjection)
(票, piào, ticket)
(漂亮, piàoliang, beautiful)
(屁股, pìgu, ass)
(去, qù, go)
(让, ràng, let, allow)
(然后, ránhòu, then)

(人, rén, person)
(人口, rénkǒu, population)
(人民, rénmín, people)
(认识, rènshi, know)
(认为, rénwéi, think)
(软, ruǎn, soft)
(如果, rúguǒ, if)
(上, shàng, above)
(上海, Shànghǎi, Shanghai)
(生, shēng, birth)
(是, shì, to be)
(是的, shì de, is)
(市场, shìchǎng, market)
(死, sǐ, die)
(添, tiān, increase)
(听说, tīngshuō, hear say)
(头, tóu, head)
(脱, tuō, take off)
(上, shàng, on)
(什么, shénme, what)
(数量, shùliàng, quantity)
(师父, shīfu, master)
(时候, shíhou, time)
(书, shū, book)
(谁, shuí, who)
(谁的, shuí de, whose)
(她, tā, she)
(她的, tā de, her)

(他们, tāmen, they)
(太, tài, extreme)
(太太, tàitai, wife)
(天天, tiāntiān, daily)
(挺, tǐng, very)
(挺好, tǐnghǎo, very good)
(听说, tīngshuō, hear say)
(同性恋, tóngxìngliàn, homosexual)
(同意, tóngyì, agree)
(完了, wánle, finished, done)
(王, wáng, king)
(王, Wáng, Wang)
(忘了, wàngle, forget)
(晚上, wǎnshang, evening)
(丸药, wányào, pill)
(位, wèi, CNI people)
(伟大, wěidà, great)
(伟哥, wěigē, Viagra)
(为什么, wèishénme, why)
(问, wèn, ask)
(问题, wèntí, question)
(我, wǒ, me)
(我的, wǒ de, my)
(我们, wǒmen, we, us)
(西, xī, west)
(细, xì, thin)
(下, xià, down)
(下去, xiàqu, continue)

546

(先生, xiānsheng, mister)
(现在, xiànzài, now)
(像, xiàng, resemble)
(香, xiāng, fragrance)
(现代, xiàndài, modern)
(小, xiǎo, small)
(小心, xiǎoxīn, careful)
(谢谢, xièxie, thank you)
(喜欢, xǐhuan, like)
(心, xīn, heart)
(星期, xīngqī, week)
(行, xíng, ok)
(幸运, xìngyùn, lucky)
(休息, xiūxi, to rest)
(学生, xuésheng, student)
(学习, xuéxí, study)
(学校, xuéxiào, school)
(呀, yā, surprise interjection)
(阳物, yángwù, penis)
(样子, yàngzi, appearance)
(要, yào, want)
(药, yào, drug)
(药店, yàodiàn, drugstore)
(眼, yǎn, eye)
(意大利, Yìdàlì, Italy)
(一点, yīdiǎn, a little)
(英寸, Yīngcùn, inch)
(英语, Yīngyǔ, English)

(以前, yǐqián, before)
(一样, yīyàng, same)
(也, yě, also)
(有, yǒu, have)
(右, yòu, right)
(有名, yǒumíng, have name)
(有名, yǒumíng, famous)
(一点, yīdiǎn, little)
(已经, yǐjing, already)
(英寸, yīngcùn, inch)
(英语, Yīngyǔ, English)
(在, zài, at)
(再见, zàijiàn, again meet)
(早, zǎo, early)
(早上, zǎoshang, early morning)
(怎么样, zěnmeyàng, how)
(总是, zǒngshì, always)
(张, zhāng, sheet)
(张, Zhāng, Zhang)
(招, zhāo, provoke)
(这个, zhè ge, zhèi ge, this one)
(这, zhè, zhèi, this)
(真实, zhēnshí, true)
(这儿, zhèr, here)
(这个, zhège, zhèige, this)
(真, zhēn, real)
(真的, zhēn de, really)
(这些, zhèxiē, these)

547

(知道, zhīdao, know)

(只有, zhǐyǒu, only have)

(中, zhōng, middle)

(中国, Zhōngguó, China)

(转, zhuǎn, turn)

(走, zǒu, go forth)

(走道, zǒudào, walk)

(最, zuì, most)

(最多, zuìduō, most)

(昨天, zuótiān, yesterday)

(昨晚, zuówǎn, last night)

Kangxi Radicals

Introduction

The functional building blocks, the alphabet as such, of the written Chinese language known as (汉字, **Hànzì**, **Hanzi**) are the 214 Kangxi Radicals. A Radical is a visual representation, a written image that represents a thought or meaning but variable phonetic information. It may not help to pronounce or verbally *put forth* the spoken character but rather may give the character obvious flavour or meaning, or it may not. The Radical can be used alone or in combination to assemble a character.

All characters have one spoken syllable, hence, they are *monosyllabic*. The character list dates from the year 1615. They were compiled in a dictionary called (字汇, **Zìhuì**, **Zihui**). This allowed for collection, indexing and compilation of characters in an organized fashion. In 1716, a dictionary, the (康熙字典, **Kāngxī Zìdiǎn**, **Kangxi dictionary**) was created organizing the characters using the Radicals as organizational section headers. This dictionary was commissioned by Emperor Kangxi (**1654-1722**) of China's Qing Dynasty. This dictionary has 47,035 characters. Chinese dictionaries are organized not phonetically, but by the Radical then the number of additional strokes in each character. Since then no new Radicals or characters have been added but many words have been.

Modern words are created by creating descriptive character strings. *Phone* for example is an obvious modern word and is described by ancient characters. The characters are (电, **diàn**, **lightening**) and (话, **huà**, **talk**) forming (电话, **diànhuà**, **lightening talk**) roughly, *electric talk*. This makes utilization for a *foreigner* difficult, as he has to reference a lexicon of unfamiliarity. To get to the train station you must ask for the (火车站, **huǒchēzhàn**, **fire cart stand**).

Learning to write Chinese characters is best achieved by mastering the fundamental graphic components, the *Kangxi Radicals*. Then you can learn which strokes and Radicals are used in particular characters and how they are combined. This allows for efficient memorization and production of **Hanzi**. This is much easier than learning to write each character as a sequence of memorized strokes. For example, one can remember how to write (義 **yì**, **right conduct**) by knowing that it consists of the character for (羊, **yáng**, **sheep**) above (我, **wǒ**, **me**).

There are a total of some 50,000 Chinese characters. A far smaller number, some 4,000 to 6,000, are in daily use. All characters no matter how complex can be decomposed into radicals and constituent strokes.

A character may have typically one to three Radicals in its composition. Some of the Radicals are pictographic and visually project meaning. (女, **nǔ**, **female**) has a crossed leg, booty sticking out the back look and is easy to remember as it has visually anchoring clues. The picture however does not give any suggestion to pronunciation and this is what differs from a roman type alphabet. It can stand alone as a Radical forming a character, (女, **nǔ**, **female**), or can be part of a multi-Radical character. The character for (好, **hǎo**, **good**) is the Radical (女, **nǔ**, **female**) plus the Radical for (子, **zǐ**, **child**). However, it is not pronounced **nǔzǐ**. Neither Radical gives phonetic clues. You can draw inference that it is good for a female to have a child. Hence, the character makes some sense visually and adds flavour to the interpretation. However, (女, **nǔ**, **female**) is used as part of many characters that do not have a feminine flavour.

(要, **yào**, **want**) combines the Radical for (西, **xī**, **west**), with the Radical of (女, **nǔ**, **female**) under it. Neither (西, **xī**, **west**), nor (女, **nǔ**, **female**), lend phonetic clues or meaning to the character (要, **yāo**, **want**) If you want to make up a little story about a Chinese man looking *west* and he *want* to find a *female*, more power to you if it helps you remember. However, remember, you will have about 50,000 little stories to make up to remember all the characters.

Radicals and Their Variants

In writing **Hanzi**, many Radicals are distorted or changed in form in order to fit into a character with other Radicals or characters. They may be narrowed, shortened, or may have different shapes entirely. Changes in shape, rather than simple distortion, may result in a reduction in the number of strokes used to write it. In some cases, these written forms may have several variants. The actual shape of the component when it is used in a character can depend on its placement with respect to the other elements in the character.

Although there are 214 Radicals, some of them have numerous variants that are only generally recognizable once the parent Radical is compared to it. Some variants are very common and some are very obscure. As with all facets of learning **Hanyu** and **Hanzi**, it is best to build on the most commonly occurring components and then to add the less common variants. In this book variants are marked with a (**V**), simplified Radicals with an (**S**) and Traditional Radicals with a (**T**).

The tables in this book list the most common variants. Given the huge historic number of characters, you may never see many of the variants in common usage.

Examples

1) (刀, **dāo**, **knife**) can be represented in its full form with the Radical in these positions, appearing on the top, bottom, left and right within a character.

切刖分办刅召刍

A common variant is (刂, **dāo**, **knife**).

刖刂刐刊刏切刋

A less common variant is (刁, **dāo**, **knife**).

叼书汈芀

2) (人, **rén**, **person**) can be represented in its full form with the Radical in these positions.

天似亼坐从以贝囚仄

(亻, **rén**, **standing person**) appears on the left side of characters.

似亿他你仨仔仠仕仜

(人, **rén**, **person**) become can also appear on the top of characters.

夂全弇会仐厶仓个

3) (R#61, 心, **xīn**, **heart**) the character, is the same as Radical.

必志忘忠忑忒炁忴忉

For characters with (#61', 忄, **xīn**, **standing heart**) the Radical always appears on the left side of the character.

快怖怪悟忆忛忏忏忉

4) (手, **shǒu**, **hand**) appears in varied positions, top, bottom, left and right.

乳拳挐拿弄劼杍

(扌, **shǒu**, **hand**) appears on the left side of characters.

扎打抛打扔扑扒

(才, **shǒu**, **hand**)

团财材闭财麻

(龵, **shǒu**, **hand**)

毛拜掰

(ナ, **shǒu**, **hand**)

在存

(ナ, **shǒu**, **hand**)

发

5) (水, **shuǐ**, **water**) occurs on the top, bottom, left and right of characters.

水汆沓怸永氺汆丞

(氵, **shuǐ**, **standing water**) appears on the left of characters. An alternate name for this Radical is (三点水, **sān diǎn shuǐ**, **three dot water**)

氵 汀汁汇氾清

(氺, **shuǐ**, **water**) is a less common variant. There are very few Radicals forming characters with this Radical. Examples: (录, **lù**, **to record**), (黍, **tiǎn**, **to shame**)

In learning (汉字, **Hànzì**, **Hanzi**) it is imperative to compare the precise meaning of the individual characters to the **Pinyin** to the literal translation. This learning strategy will allow you to see how the Radicals flavour the characters and how the characters are compiled to make sentences. A methodical learning of the Radicals is essential to learn the language. What seems tedious at first and counterproductive to learning will give you the most important tools to (汉字, **Hànzì**, **Hanzi**). A close analogy would be to try to learn English without knowing the alphabet. After you grind away at learning the Radicals, the language will suddenly open up to you. You will no longer need to remember 13 strokes for (想, **xiǎng**, **think**, **desire**) to write the character but only need to remember the individual Radicals that compose it, (木, **mù**, **tree**) *beside* (目, **mù**, **eye**) *over* (心, **xīn**, **heart**) *equal* (想, **xiǎng**, **think**).

This reduces your memory load from 13 to 3 visual images. Again, if you want to make up a little memory aid story about a *tree* with an *eye* on the top standing on a *heart* equal *think* that only leaves 49,998 more little stories. However, if you can remember the **Hanzi** character for (相, **xiāng**, **mutually**), you only need to remember two visual images. *Mutually* or *each other* over *heart* equals *think*.

It is not a matter of this language being complicated or not, it is only *how complicated* you want to make it. However, 2 billion people cannot be wrong. To further complicate the story, each Radical has a name, a category and an assigned number. In addition, the Radical name may be different and more complex than the character name when the Radical stands alone as a character.

Convention dictates that the (汉字, **Hànzì**, **Hanzi**) characters roughly fit into a square. This leads the Radicals to morph to fit the space allowed. They may elongate, widen, deepen or narrow to fit the space. Some Radicals even change in form from the right side to the left side to the top to bottom of a character. Throughout this book are examples of Radicals in characters and they are represented by the various physical mutations as they change position in a character.

There will come a time when you have no choice but to buy a very large amount of paper, I would recommend a case of 10 reams, a box of soft tipped fine marker pens, a cushion for your butt, and start to start copying out the Radicals, writing their name in **Pinyin**, their assigned number, chanting the phonetic and the semantic translation.

Learning **Hanzi** is more akin to art class than English class. The amount of practice you will need will depend on your innate ability and the complexity of the character. The Radicals are conveniently indexed by order of increasing complexity. You can build on the initial simple Radicals and strokes, and progress through the list. Please look forward to the Work Book and find characters you can overwrite with a plastic sheet or velum paper. There is no other way. This is the way that billions of Chinese students have done it over thousands of years. This is not like learning French, German, Italian or Spanish, with an alphabet with which you are familiar. This is more like learning to draw thousands of pictures and remembering their names, meaning, pronunciation and intonation.

The workbook is a workbook to learn stroke order and to write **Hanzi**. The characters are not chosen for their general utility. I have tried to find a progressive selection of characters that will build your writing skills. You will not find any two references that give the exact same stroke orders for the Kangxi Radicals. The goal is to make a visual representation and get the meaning of the character communicated. **Hanzi** is an art form. This must not be forgotten as the Western world rushes to digitalize and standardize the stroke order of characters and Radicals.

Once you arrive in China you will see scripts on signboards that the native Chinese struggle to interpret. Just as we print and write our language, there is a free form artistic *grass script* that will defy your most imaginative interpretation. Also there remains much Traditional **Hanzi** on old signs and in villages.

The correct stroke choice is that which you have to draw to reproduce or create a character. It varies from font to font and author to author. Further ahead in this book is a detailed chapter on the various strokes of **Hanzi**. As an example, there are many sources that say the 1st stroke for (月, **yuè**, **moon**) is (撇, **Piě**, 丿). **Piě** stroke is a near 45 degree angle right to left descending stroke. The correct stroke has little curvature. It is obvious on inspection that the first stroke in 月 is not entirely curved but is (竖撇, **Shù Piě, SP,** 丿). **SP** is vertical line with a finishing curve to the left.

There are countless examples of these variations. There is no *solution*. Once written with a brush and ink, **Hanzi** is an artistic expression. If the message of the character is preserved, it is difficult to assign *right* or *wrong* to an individual's efforts.

As another example, here are some of the various expressions of the Radical #45 (**R #45**, 屮, **chè**, **sprout**). 屮, 屮, 屮, 屮. Each example of this character in different fonts introduces questions as to which named strokes are most appropriate. But, the visual meaning is preserved. Although there are tens of thousands of characters, the meaning is readily preserved in these examples even though the strokes are not standardized.

List of the 214 Kangxi Radicals

The following is a list of all 214 Kangxi Radicals categorized under the number of strokes along with some examples of characters containing these Radicals. The accompanying numbers are the officially assigned numbers. Further on in this book are the rules of writing the Radicals. Stroke order, stroke direction and stroke choice become very important. Common variants of each character are displayed such as (**R#64**, 手, **shǒu, hand**) and (**R#64'**, 扌, **standing hand, shǒu**). Some of the Radicals have both Traditional (**T**) and Simplified (**S**) forms. The written official Chinese language, (汉字, **Hànzì, Hanzi**), when broken down to its constituent components, is a combination of the Radicals plus or minus additional strokes.

Knowing how to draw each character stroke and Radical ultimately simplifies learning to write characters. The characters no longer look like a confusing collection of lines but become a small collection of Radicals. There is no way to master this other than repetitive copying and recitation of the name with the correct tone. If you do not do this, you will find that your ability to learn (汉字, **Hànzì, Hanzi**) will dead-end when you reach the limits of your usual memory for volume and complexity. It is easy to remember how to draw characters with up to four or five strokes. Beyond that, you need a systematic approach. There is no need to belabour learning theory in this book.

However, the volume and complexity of learning to write (汉字, **Hànzì, Hanzi**) and (汉语, **Hànyǔ, Hanyu**) is such that you need to recruit every learning tool possible. Native English speakers are not used to a non-phonetic based language with no recognizable alphabet. There are few clues to recognize previously unseen words or characters. You will need lots of paper, many pens and lots of time and patience. Once you can draw every Radical, you can draw every character.

There are numerous variants of many of the Radicals. This book attempts to compile the most common Radicals used in the PRC. These Radicals are shared to a degree by China, Japan and Korea and are often referred to as the CJK Radicals.

There are several defined sets of organized Radicals ranging in number from 187 to 540 Radicals, plus their variants. There is no *correct* collection. Traditional Chinese sets and Radicals are predictably quantitatively greater in number and complexity than Simplified Radicals. The Radical set chosen for this book is the Chinese Japanese Korean (**CJK**) Radicals from the Kangxi dictionary published in 1716. The original set was of course all Traditional Chinese Radicals and characters.

This set uses the original number of Radicals with simplified variants substituted. I have also added the historic Traditional Radicals in the work sheets for comparison. China currently uses a simplified set with 187 Radicals. Although China created and embraced simplification, there is still Traditional Chinese Radicals and characters throughout China. I was once entrenched in not learning any Traditional characters. This changed when I came across very old historic sites with poems, stories and explanations set into stone, bronze and pottery.

China will set the stage for Asia for usage of Simplified characters and spoken Standard Mandarin as the Lingua Franca of Asia. I encourage you to concentrate on Simplified Radicals but to gradually assimilate some Traditional Radicals and characters.

1 Stroke

- 1. 一 (one) (yī) - 丁 七 丈 三
- 2. 丨 (line) (gǔn) - 中 丰 串 十
- 3. 丶 (dot) (zhǔ) - 丸 丹 主 丼
- 4. 丿 (slash) (piě) - 乂 乃 久 乎
- 5. 乙 (second) (yǐ) - 乞 乾 挖 氹
- 5'. 乚 (second) (yǐ) - 也 乳 亂 说
- 6. 亅 (hook) (jué) - 了 予 丁 乎

2 Strokes

- 7. 二 (two) (èr) - 于 五 井 些
- 8. 亠 (lid) (tóu) - 亡 交 亥 京
- 9. 人 (human) (rén) - 今 介 从 令
- 9'. 亻 (standing human) (rén) - 仁 仕 他 休
- 10. 儿 (legs) (ér) - 兄 兆 先 光
- 11. 入 (enter) (rù) - 汆 籴 痊 拴
- 12. 八 (eight) (bā) - 公 共 兵 具
- 13. 冂 (down box) (jiǒng) - 冉 再 同 囝
- 14. 冖 (cover) (mì) - 冗 冠 冢 冥
- 15. 冫 (ice) (bīng) - 冰 冶 冷 凍
- 16. 几 (table) (jī) - 凡 凭 凰 凳
- 17. 凵 (open box) (qǔ) - 凶 凸 凹 出
- 18. 刀 (knife) (dāo) - 刃 分 切 券

- 18'. 刂 (standing knife) (dāo) - 刈 刊 刑 列
- 19. 力 (power) (lì) - 功 劣 努 励
- 20. 勹 (wrap) (bāo) - 勺 勻 勾 包
- 21. 匕 (spoon) (bǐ) - 北 匙 老 能
- 22. 匚 (right open box) (fāng) - 匠 匡 匣 匪
- 23. 匸 (hiding enclosure) (xǐ) - 匹 医 臣 匿
- 24. 十 (ten) (shí) - 千 午 南 博
- 25. 卜 (divination) (bǔ) - 卞 占 卡 卦
- 26. 卩 (seal) (jié) - 卯 印 危 却
- 27. 厂 (cliff) (hàn) - 厄 厘 厚 原
- 28. 厶 (private) (sī) - 厷 去 厹 参
- 29. 又 (again) (yòu) - 叉 友 双 受

3 Strokes

- 30. 口 (mouth) (kǒu) - 史 名 君 吟
- 31. 囗 (enclosure) (wéi) - 囚 因 困 国
- 32. 土 (earth) (tǔ) - 地 均 坊 城
- 33. 士 (scholar) (shì) - 壬 壻 喜 声
- 34. 夂 (go) (zhǐ) - 夅 夆 逢 缝
- 35. 夊 (go slowly) (suī) - 夋 复 夎 夏
- 36. 夕 (evening) (xī) - 外 名 多 夜
- 37. 大 (big) (dà) - 天 太 夫 契
- 38. 女 (woman) (nǚ) - 好 妊 妹 姓

- 39. 子 (child) (zǐ) - 孔 字 孝 孟
- 40. 宀 (roof) (mián) - 宅 宇 宗 官
- 41. 寸 (inch) (cùn) - 寺 封 射 时
- 42. 小 (small) (xiǎo) - 少 尖 尔 尚
- 43. 尢 (lame) (wāng) - 尣 尤 尬 尪
- 44. 尸 (corpse) (shī) - 尺 尻 尾 局
- 45. 屮 (sprout) (chè) - 屯 纯 出 沌
- 46. 山 (mountain) (shān) - 屹 岳 峰 屺
- 47. 川 (river) (chuān) - 州 训 顺 酬
- 48. 工 (work) (gōng) - 左 巧 巫 差
- 49. 己 已 巳 (oneself) (jǐ) - 巴 卮 巷 巽
- 50. 巾 (turban) (jīn) - 市 布 帆 怖
- 51. 干 (dry) (gān) - 平 开 并 平
- 52. 幺 (tiny) (yāo) - 幻 幼 幻 幼
- 53. 广 (dotted cliff) (yǎn) - 床 底 店 府
- 54. 廴 (long stride) (yǐn) - 延 廷 建 廻
- 55. 廾 (two hands) (gǒng) - 弁 异 弃 弄
- 56. 弋 (shoot) (yì) - 式 弌 弐 式
- 57. 弓 (bow) (gōng) - 引 弟 弦 弱
- 58. 彑 (snout) (jì) - 互 彖 彘 彝
- 58. 彐 (snout) (jì) - 事 当 档 铛
- 59. 彡 (bristle) (shān) - 形 彦 彩 彬

- 60. 彳 (step) (chì) - 役 往 待 律

4 Strokes

- 61. 心 (heart) (xīn) - 必 志 忘 忠
- 61'. 忄 (standing heart) (xīn) - 忙 快 怖 怪
- 62. 戈 (halberd) (gē) - 戍 戎 成 我
- 63. 戶 (door) (hù) - 房 所 扁 扇
- 64. 手 (hand) (shǒu) - 拜 拳 掌 掣
- 64'. 扌 (standing hand) (shǒu) - 打 批 技 抱
- 65. 支 (branch) (zhī) - 赽 敋 邊 技
- 66. 攴 攵 (rap) (pū) - 改 放 政 故
- 67. 文 (script) (wén) - 孝 斌 斐 斑
- 68. 斗 (dipper) (dǒu) - 料 斛 斜 斟
- 69. 斤 (axe) (jīn) - 斥 斧 斬 新
- 70. 方 (square) (fāng) - 於 施 旁 旅
- 71. 旡 (not) (wú) - 既 氎 慨 暨
- 71. 无 (not) (wú) - 芜 庑 抚 芜
- 72. 日 (sun) (rì) - 旦 旱 明 星
- 73. 曰 (say) (yuē) - 晋 曷 書 曹
- 74. 月 (moon) (yuè) - 胐 腅 期 朦
- 75. 木 (tree) (mù) - 末 本 杉 林
- 76. 欠 (yawn) (qiàn) - 次 欣 欲 歌
- 77. 止 (stop) (zhǐ) - 此 步 武 歪

- 78. 歹 (death) (dǎi) - 死 殉 殊 殘
- 78. 歺 (death) (dǎi)- 歽 餐 璨 瀍
- 79. 殳 (weapon) (shū) - 段 殷 殺 殿
- 80. 毋 (do not) (wú) - 毐 每 盅 冊
- 80. 母 (do not) (wú) - 每 毑 毒 毐
- 81. 比 (compare) (bǐ) - 毕 毖 毘 毚
- 82. 毛 (fur) (máo) - 毫 毯 毯 毳
- 83. 氏 (clan) (shì) - 氏 民 氒 氓
- 84. 气 (steam) (qì) - 氛 氙 氣 氤
- 85. 水 (water) (shuǐ) - 汞 泉 淼 漿
- 85'. 氵 (standing water) (shuǐ) - 河 泣 洋 海
- 85". 氺 (water) (shuǐ) - 求 泰 滕 录
- 86. 火 (fire) (huǒ) - 灼 炊 炎 炒
- 86'. 灬 (fire) (huǒ) - 烈 烹 焦 然
- 87. 爪 (claw) (zhuǎ) - 爬 笊 抓 抓
- 87'. 爫 (claw) (zhuǎ) - 采 爭 爯 爱
- 88. 父 (father) (fù) - 爸 爹 爺 交
- 89. 爻 (double crosses) (yáo) - 爼 爾 希 网
- 90. 爿 (bed) (qiáng) - 牀 牁 牂 牒
- 90. 丬 (bed) (qiáng) - 将 状 壮 妆
- 91. 片 (slice) (piàn) - 版 牋 牌 牒
- 92. 牙 (fang) (yá) - 岈 穿 呀 芽

- 93. 牛 (cow) (niú) - 牧 物 牲 犀
- 94. 犬 (dog) (quǎn) - 狀 猋 猷 獸
- 94'. 犭 (standing dog) - 犯 狂 狗 狩

5 Strokes

- 95. 玄 (profound) (xuán) - 玅 玆 率 旎
- 96. 玉 (jade) (yù) - 瑩 璗 璧 璧
- 96'. 王 (jade) (yù) - 珍 珠 現 球
- 97. 瓜 (melon) (guā) - 瓟 瓞 瓠 瓢
- 98. 瓦 (earthenware) (wǎ) - 瓮 瓷 甄 甌
- 99. 甘 (sweet) (gān) - 甙 甚 甜 魅
- 100. 生 (life) (shēng) - 甡 產 甥 甦
- 101. 用 (use) (yòng) - 甩 甫 甬 甭
- 102. 田 (field) (tián) - 男 界 留 畦
- 103. 疋 (bolt of cloth) (pǐ) - 疌 疎 疏 疑
- 104. 疒 (sickness) (chuáng) - 疼 疾 病 痴
- 105. 癶 (dotted tent) (bō) - 癷 癸 發 登
- 106. 白 (white) (bái) - 的 皆 皇 皎
- 107. 皮 (skin) (pí) - 皰 皴 皸 皺
- 108. 皿 (dish) (mǐn) - 盂 盆 盒 盛
- 109. 目 (eye) (mù) - 盲 看 眺 眼
- 110. 矛 (halberd) (máo) - 矜 矝 矞 稂
- 111. 矢 (arrow) (shǐ) - 矣 知 矩 短

- 112. 石 (stone) (shí) - 砂 砥 砲 硬
- 113. 示 (spirit) (shì) - 祟 票 祭 禁
- 113'. 礻 (standing spirit) (shì) - 礼 社 祈 祝
- 114. 禸 (track) (róu) - 禹 禺 离 禽
- 115. 禾 (grain) (hé) - 秋 税 稔 稻
- 116. 穴 (cave) (xué) - 究 空 穿 突
- 117. 立 (stand) (lì) - 站 竝 章 竣

6 Strokes
- 118. 竹 (bamboo) (zhú) - 竿 笏 算 箱
- 119. 米 (rice) (mǐ) - 粒 粗 粟 精
- 120. 糸 (silk) (mì) - 系 紊 素 索
- 120'. 纟 (standing silk) (mì) - 紅 納 紙 細
- 121. 缶 (jar) (fǒu) - 缸 缺 罅 罐
- 122. 网 (net) (wǎng) - 罾
- 122'. 罒 (net) (wǎng) - 罠 罪 置 罰
- 123. 羊 (sheep) (yáng) - 着 美 群 羯
- 124. 羽 (feather) (yǔ) - 翁 翌 習 翔
- 125. 老 (old) (lǎo) - 耄 耆 耋 姥
- 125'. 耂 (old) (lǎo) - 考 者 耆
- 126. 而 (and) (ér) - 耍 耏 耐 耑
- 127. 耒 (plow) (lěi) - 耕 耗 耘 耙
- 128. 耳 (ear) (ěr) - 耽 聰 聲 聽

- 129. 聿 (brush) (yù) - 건 肄 肅 肇
- 130. 肉 (meat) (ròu) - 胔 胾 腐 臠
- 130. 月 (standing meat) (ròu) - 肌 肝 肥 肱
- 131. 臣 (minister) (chén) - 臤 臥 臦 臧
- 132. 自 (self) (zì) - 乿 臬 臭 臱
- 133. 至 (arrive) (zhì) - 致 銍 臷 臻
- 134. 臼 (mortar) (jiù) - 臾 舁 舂 與
- 135. 舌 (tongue) (shé) - 舍 舐 舒 舔
- 136. 舛 (oppose) (chuǎn) - 舜 舞 桀 嶙
- 137. 舟 (boat) (zhōu) - 航 舫 般 船
- 138. 艮 (stopping) (gèn) - 艱 很 恨 狠
- 139. 色 (color) (sè) - 艴 艳 艶 绝
- 140. 艸 (grass) (cǎo) - 茻 芻 舛 屮
- 140'. 艹 (grass) (cǎo) – 花 茶 草 菓 樊
- 141. 虍 (tiger) (hǔ) – 虎 虐 處 號
- 142. 虫 (insect) (chóng) – 蛇 蛙 蜜 蝶
- 143. 血 (blood) (xiě) – 衄 衅 衆 衉
- 144. 行 (walk enclosure) (xíng) – 衒 術 街 衝
- 145. 衣 (clothes) (yī) – 表 衰 袋 裔
- 145'. 衤 (standing clothes) (yī) – 袂 袖 裸 裾
- 146. 襾 覀 西 (west) (yà) – 西 覀 覂 覄

- 146. 襾 (west) (yà) – 覃 覆 霸 覈
- 146. 西 (west) (yà) – 洒 牺 晒 栖

7 Strokes

- 147. 见 (see) (jiàn) – 现 觉 观 视
- 148. 角 (horn) (jiǎo) – 觜 确 嘴 触
- 149. 言 (speech) (yán) – 詈 誓 謦 警
- 149'. 讠 (standing speech) (yán) – 证 记 认 训
- 150. 谷 (valley) (gǔ) – 容 裕 浴 峪
- 151. 豆 (bean) (dòu) – 豈 豉 豌 短
- 152. 豕 (pig) (shǐ) – 豚 象 豢 家
- 153. 豸 (badger) (zhì) – 豹 豺 貂 貌
- 154. 贝 (shell) (bèi) – 员 则 责 负
- 155. 赤 (red) (chì) – 赦 赧 赫 郝
- 156. 走 (run) (zǒu) – 赴 起 超 越
- 157. 足 (foot) (zú) – 距 跨 跪 路
- 158. 身 (body) (shēn) – 躬 躲 躺 射
- 159. 车 (car) (chē) – 军 转 连 较
- 160. 辛 (bitter) (xīn) – 辜 辟 辣 新
- 161. 辰 (morning) (chén) – 辱 晨 唇 震
- 162. 辵 (walk) (chuò) – 辵 迉 迈 迊
- 162'. 辶 (walk) (chuò) – 近 返 述 道
- 163. 邑 (city) (yì) – 扈 挹 悒 邕

- 163'. 阝 (city) (yì) – 那 邦 邸 郁
- 164. 酉 (wine) (yǒu) – 酋 配 酒 酸
- 165. 釆 (distinguish) (biàn) – 釉 釋 悉 奧
- 166. 里 (village) (lǐ) – 重 野 量 理

8 Strokes

- 167. 金 (metal) (jīn) – 釜 鏖 鏨 鑾
- 167'. 釒 (standing metal) (jīn) – 銀 銅 鋼 錫
- 167'. 钅 (standing metal) (jīn) – 钱 错 银 铁
- 168. 长 (long) (cháng) – 长 张 涨 帐
- 169. 门 (gate) (mén) – 间 们 闷 扪
- 170. 阜 (mound) (fù) – 阜 埠 頔 煊
- 170'. 阝 (standing mound) (fù) – 防 降 阴 階
- 171. 隶 (slave) (lì) – 逮 隸 康 逮
- 172. 隹 (small bird) (zhuī) – 隻 隼 雀 雄
- 173. 雨 (rain) (yǔ) – 雪 雲 零 雷
- 174. 青 靑 (blue) (qīng) – 靖 艳 靓 靛
- 175. 非 (wrong) (fēi) – 辈 靠 靡 悲

9 Strokes

- 176. 面 (face) (miàn) – 靤 靦 靧 靨
- 177. 革 (leather) (gé) – 勒 靴 鞋 鞍
- 178. 韦 (tanned leather) (wéi) – 韧 韍 韓 韃
- 179. 韭 (leek) (jiǔ) – 韮 韲 韱 韲

- 180. 音 (sound) (yīn) – 韴 韶 䪼 響
- 181. 页 (face) (yè) – 项 顶 顺 预
- 182. 风 (wind) (fēng) – 疯 枫 讽 砜
- 183. 飞 (fly) (fēi) – 飞 飝 飜 飝
- 184. 食 (eat) (shí) – 養 餐 饕 饗
- 184'. 饣 (standing eat) (shí) – 饰 蚀 饵 钚
- 185. 首 (head) (shǒu) – 馗 馘 道 渞
- 186. 香 (fragrant) (xiāng) – 馚 馞 馥 馨

10 Strokes

- 187. 马 (horse) (mǎ) – 吗 妈 骂 玛
- 188. 骨 (bone) (gǔ) – 骰 骸 髀 髓
- 189. 高 (tall) (gāo) – 髛 髜 髝 髞
- 190. 髟 (hair) (biāo) – 髦 髮 髯 鬆
- 191. 鬥 (fight) (dòu) – 鬧 鬨 鬩 鬪
- 192. 鬯 (sacrificial wine) (chàng) – 鬱 鬰 鬰 䅟
- 193. 鬲 (cauldron) (lì) – 鬴 鬸 鬹 鬻
- 194. 鬼 (ghost) (guǐ) – 魁 魂 魃 魅

11 Strokes

- 195. 鱼 (fish) (yú) – 渔 蘇 鲁 鱻
- 196. 鸟 (bird) (niǎo) – 莺 袅 岛 鸡
- 197. 卤 (alkaline) (lǔ) – 齡 齢 鹹 鹾
- 198. 鹿 (deer) (lù) – 麋 麒 麓 麗

- 199. 麦 (wheat) (mài) – 唛 麸 麵 陵
- 200. 麻 (hemp) (má) – 摩 魔 麽 䃺

12 Strokes

- 201. 黄 (yellow) (huáng) – 尣 黇 黉 黌
- 202. 黍 (millet) (shǔ) – 黎 黏 黐 漆
- 203. 黑 (black) (hēi) – 嘿 澤 黔 熏
- 204. 㡀 (needlework) (zhǐ) – 黺 黻 黼 黻

13 Strokes

- 205. 黾 (amphibian) (mǐn) – 黿 鼉 鼇 鱉
- 206. 鼎 (tripod) (dǐng) – 鼐 鼏 鼑 鼒
- 207. 鼓 (drum) (gǔ) – 鼕 鼖 鼘 鼙
- 208. 鼠 (rat) (shǔ) – 鼧 鼩 鼪 鼫

14 Strokes

- 209. 鼻 (nose) (bí) – 濞 劓 齈 鼾
- 210. 齐 (uniformly) (qí) – 剂 济 挤 侪

15 Strokes

- 211. 齿 (tooth) (chǐ) – 啮 龀 龅 龈

16 Strokes

- 212. 龙 (dragon) (lóng) – 笼 拢 陇 珑
- 213. 龟 (tortoise) (guī) – 阄 龟

17 Strokes

- 214 龠 (flute) (yuè) – 龡 龢 龣 龥

Written Variants

Orthography

The nature of Chinese characters makes it very easy to produce an allograph for any character. There have been many efforts at orthographical standardization throughout history. The widespread usage of the characters in different nations that do not see *eye to eye* has prevented any one system from becoming universally adopted. Consequently, the standard stroke order of any given character in Chinese usage may differ subtly from its standard shape in Japanese or Korean usage, even where no simplification has taken place. With inherent individuality in hand writing, there is significant difference between individuals. Even type fonts create a great number of variations.

Usually each **Hanzi** character takes up the same amount of space due to their block-like square nature. This is more true for electronic fonts than free hand writing. Some introductory books typically practice writing with a grid as a guide. In addition to strictness for the space that a character takes up, **Hanzi** characters are written with very precise rules. The three most important rules are the strokes employed, stroke placement, and the order in which they are written, stroke order. Most words can be written with just one stroke order. Some words also have variant stroke orders. This may occasionally result in different stroke counts. Certain characters are also written with different stroke orders in different countries.

Common Typefaces

There are two common typeface groups. These typefaces are based on the regular script for Chinese characters, which are akin to serif and sans serif fonts in the West.

The popular set for body text is a family of serif fonts called Song typeface (宋体), also known as Minchō (明朝) in Japan, and Ming typeface (明體) in Taiwan and Hong Kong. This typeface is similar to Western serif fonts such as Times New Roman in both appearance and function. These two fonts give strong clues to named stroke and stroke direction.

The other common group of fonts are called the black typeface, (黑体) in Chinese, and Gothic typeface. This group is characterized by straight lines of even thickness for each stroke, akin to sans-serif styles such as Arial and Helvetica in Western typography. This group of fonts, first introduced on newspaper headlines, is commonly used on headings, websites, signs and billboards.

The sans-serif style fonts take away the esthetic beauty and clues to stroke and stroke order. The lines of even thickness give the beginner writer little visual clue to stroke technique. Microsoft operating systems have numerous Asian fonts that are esthetically appealing and many more can be purchased online. I encourage you to learn to type in **Pinyin** and convert to **Hanzi** and to use a font that shows the esthetic beauty and stroke clues.

If I was to pick one font that encompasses the spirit of the artistic nature of **Hanzi**, I would chose (楷体, **Kai Ti**). This is embedded in the Microsoft Office 2007 Word program. This font makes clear the artistic nature and defined strokes of each character. It retains a flavour of hand printed script.

Below are examples of the characters for (汉字, **Hànzì, Hanzi**) written with different type faces and type fonts. You can see how the top six fonts preserve the shape and definition of the individual strokes while the bottom four do not.

汉字	Sim Sun
汉字	Kai Ti
汉字	MS Mincho
汉字	P Ming Li U
汉字	DF Kai-SB
汉字	Sim Hei
汉字	MS YaHei
汉字	Arial Unicode MS
汉字	Microsoft Jheng Hei

Stroke Order

(筆順, **bǐshùn**, **stroke order**) refers to the way in which **Hanzi** characters are written. A stroke is a movement of the writing instrument. In modern times, this is most commonly a pen, pencil or writing brush. Historically, a (毛笔, **máobǐ**, **hair-brush**) was held vertically in the right hand and dipped in ink and the strokes were made. *Stroke Order* can refer both to the numerical order in which the strokes of a given character are written and to the direction in which the writing instrument must move in producing a particular stroke.

A common misconception is that Chinese characters were originally engraved into wood. In fact, Chinese characters are believed to have originally been brush-written on perishable materials such as bamboo or on wood slats. These would then be bound together like Venetian blinds and rolled for storage. Examples of such books have been found dating to the late Zhou dynasty. (周朝, **Zhōu Cháo, 1122 BC to 256 BC**)

History has shown that it would take over a thousand years for uniform, defined forms for each character to appear. Now, as then, each character comprises a number of strokes, which must be written in a prescribed order.

The number of strokes per character for most characters is usually between one and thirty. However, the number of strokes in some obscure characters may reach as many as seventy strokes. In the twentieth century, simplification of **Hanzi** characters took place in mainland China. This greatly reduced the number of strokes in some characters. The basic rules of stroke order, however, remained the same.

Basic and Compound Strokes

There are six basic strokes, eight classic strokes and an overall total of about 55 distinct named strokes recognized in Chinese characters. Many of these are compound strokes, that is, sequential single strokes comprising more than one movement of the writing instrument. There are also variants of some strokes that can be named. In addition, with the advent of electronic fonts and digitalization of the written Chinese language, each named font type has its own variation of the written characters.

All of the simple strokes have more than one name in Chinese literature. This book uses the most current and common names. Many of the compound strokes have no agreed-upon name. They are thus named by an acronym compilation of their strokes. Digitalization of the fonts has taken much of the shape and *character* out of the strokes.

Each single stroke includes all the motions necessary to produce a given part of a character before lifting the writing instrument from the writing surface. Thus, a single setting down of the brush may use more than one *stroke* and may produce complex lines.

The character above for *eternity* has eight strokes, two of which, the second and third, are compound strokes. These are considered the eight *classic strokes*. All of the six *basic strokes* are used in this character.

Development of Stroke Order Rules

This is an outline of the character (永, **yǒng**, **forever**) This character, meaning *eternity*, contains 8 stroke shapes in 5 sequential strokes, 3 basic and 2 compound strokes, and is often used for practice by beginning calligraphers.

The rules for stroke order facilitate vertical character writing, to maximize ease of writing and reading and to further aid in producing uniform characters. A person who has learned the rules of stroke order can infer the stroke order of most characters. This eases the process of learning to write.

Many experienced writers may ignore or forget the normalized stroke order characters, or develop idiosyncratic ways of writing.

The author encourages using the exact stroke order as prescribed by rules. This eases and hastens learning. It also produces a more visually appealing character.

The Eight Principles of Yong (永字八法, **yǒngzì bā fǎ**, **Yong character 8 rules**) often uses the single character (永, **yǒng**, **eternity**) meaning *eternity*, to teach the eight most basic strokes. These rules will be presented graphically starting on page 289. I encourage you to photocopy the page 366 and get a brush and some ink and get to it. This is what billions of Chinese have done over thousands of years.

Modern Stroke Order

The Chinese government began to reform the **Hanzi** character set in 1956. They also reformed the number of strokes and the stroke order of some characters. An obvious notable innovation of this reformed stroke order was the conception of a horizontal writing stroke order. This facilitates horizontal writing. The history of written Chinese had included right to left, top to bottom and now left to right.

Basic Rules of Stroke Order

(左, **zuǒ, left**)

(右, **yòu, right**)

(上, **shàng, upper**)

(中, **zhōng, middle**)

(下, **xià, lower**)

(左-右, **zuǒ-yòu, left to right**)

(上-下, **shàng-xià, upper- lower**)

(字, **zì, character**)

(筆順, **bǐshùn, stroke order**)

(文, **wén, language**)

1. Left to Right on Horizontal Strokes 一

The first character to learn is the number one, (一, **yī, one**), which is written with a single horizontal line. This character has one simple stroke, which is written from left (左, **zuǒ, left**) to right (右, **yòu, right**). The name of the horizontal character stroke is (横, **héng, H, horizontal character stroke**). Throughout this book, it will be abbreviated as **H**.

2. Left to Right and Top to Bottom on Multiple Horizontal Strokes 二

As a rule, characters are written from the top to the bottom, (上, **shàng, upper**) to (下, **xià, lower**). If the components of the character are horizontally stacked and the lowermost is towards the left (左, **zuǒ**, **left**), yet under the upper strokes, the top to bottom priority is preserved.

The character for *two* has two strokes. (二, **èr**, **two**) In this case, both are written from (左, **zuǒ**, **left**) to (右, **yòu**, **right**) hence **héng, héng** or **H, H**. The top stroke is written first, hence (上, **shàng**, **upper**) to (下, **xià**, **lower**). The character for three has three strokes, (三, **sān**, **three**), hence, **héng, héng, héng**, or **H, H, H**. Hence each stroke is written from left to right, 左-右, starting of course with the uppermost stroke, (上, **shàng**, **upper**), then next (中, **zhōng**, **middle**), then the lower most stroke (下, **xià**, **under**). The structures thus take the form of the first three examples below.

1st 一 1st / 2nd 二 1st / 2nd / 3rd 三

The Chinese character for *person*, (人, **rén**, **person**), has two strokes. The first stroke is the compound accelerating curve downward to the left (弯撇, **Wān Piě**, **downwards left double curved stroke**). The second stroke is the down swooping stroke on the right side thickening at the base (捺, **nà**, **downwards-right curved stroke**). This preserves the stroke order of (上-下, **shàng-xià**, **upper-lower**) and the (左-右, **zuǒ-yòu**, **left to right**) stroke order.

This rule applies also to characters that are formed more complexly. Take for example, (相, **xiāng**, **each other**). The polymorphic character can be divided into two separate characters. (木, mù, tree) and (目, mù, eye). The leftmost side of the character, (木, mù, tree) is written first. The right side (目, mù, eye) is written second.

1st 2nd

There are some exceptions to this rule, mainly occurring when the right side of a character has an underscore originating from the left character. Take for example the character (这, zhè, this) In this case, the right side is written first, followed by the left side, and finally the lower underscore stroke. This can be further seen in the characters, (迷, mí, bewilder) and (过, guò, to live). In a multi component character such as (谜, mí, riddle), there are three components. The left component is first, the right component (米, mǐ, rice) is second and the middle component (R#162', 辶, chuò, walk) underlining the right component goes last. When there are upper and lower components, the upper components are written first, then the lower components, as in (旦, dàn, dawn) which is composed of the character for *day* or *sun*, (日, rì, day) plus (一, yī, one).

3. Top to Bottom on Single Vertical Strokes   丨

The general rule for single vertical strokes is that they are written from top to bottom. The name of the stroke is (竖, shù, **vertical down character stroke**).

4. Left to Right and Top to Bottom in Multiple Vertical Strokes. 川

In a simple character such as (川, chuān, river), the rules of stroke are readily apparent in the top to bottom and left to right order. Again, the rules are preserved, all three strokes are written top to bottom. The name of the first vertical character stroke is (竖撇, 丿, **shùpiě, SP, vertical down stroke left curve**). Hence, the order is **shùpiě, shù, shù** or **SP, S, S**. The left side vertical down stroke has a short left curve finish on it (撇, ノ, **piě, downwards-left curved character stroke**). The stroke order is thus numerically,

1ˢᵗ 2ⁿᵈ 3ʳᵈ

There is not a fixed consensus on compound stroke naming. The names I will use will be functional and may not agree with other sources but will adequately describe the stroke.

(儿, **ér, son**) is another example. This is formed from two compound strokes, (竖撇, ノ, **shùpiě, SP, vertical stroke left curve**) then the right side stroke is (竖折弯鉤, ㄥ, **shùzhéwāngōu, SZWG, vertical down stroke, break, hook**).

5. Top Left Side Vertical Stroke meets Top Left Side Horizontal Stroke.

There is not a simple unifying rule to clarify what happens on the top left part of a character or Radical. Ultimately one needs to simply memorize the Radicals that deal with this. The first category of the Radicals that fit into this designation can be divided into groups that have similar patterns. The first group are Radicals in which **S** and **HZ** meet together.

丨 ㄇ

For these closed box Radicals the stroke order is the same. The left side **S** is always first. This is observed in (口, **kǒu, mouth**), (囗, **wéi, enclosure**), (日, **rì, sun**), (曰, **yuē, speak**), (田, **tián, field**), (目, **mù, eye**) and (R#108 皿, **mǐn, dish**). All other characters that contain these Radicals within another Radical or character follow the initial stroke order **S-HZ**.

The second category of Radicals that fit into this designation are the Radicals in which **S** and **HZG** meet. For (**R#13, 冂, jiǒng, down box**) the stroke order is **S-HZG**.

丨 冂

However, for (**R#26, 卩, jié seal**) the stroke order becomes **HZG-S**. You can see that it is the scale that differs, for **R#26**, **S** is proportionately longer.

𠃌 卩

The third category are Radicals in which **SP / WP** and **HZWG** meet. For the Radical (**R#16, 几, jī, table**) the stroke order is **SP-HZWG**.

丿 几

The fourth category are Radicals in which **WP** and **HZG** meet or intersect. For (**R#18, 刀, dāo, knife**) the stroke order is **HZG-WP**. This stroke order is also preserved for (**R#19, 力, lì, power**) in which the stroke order is also **HZG-WP**.

𠃌 刀 and 𠃌 力

The fifth category of Radicals are those in which **SZ** and **H** meet. For both Radical (**R#22, 匚, fāng, right open box**) and (**R#23, 匸, xǐ, hiding enclosure**) the stroke order is **H-SZ** or **H-SW**. For Radical (**R#131, 臣, chén, minister**) **H** is written first, the other strokes are written and **SZ** is written last. This follows a pattern in which characters based on **R#22** and **R#23** have **H** written first.

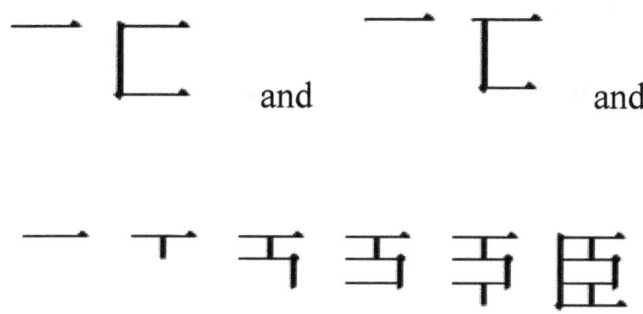

一 丅 王 丐 丏 臣

The sixth category are Radicals in which **SP** and **HZG** meet. The lone representative in this category is Radical (**R#74**, 月, **yuè**, **moon**). The stroke order is **SP-HZG**.

丿 刀

The seventh category are Radicals in which **SP** and **HZ** meet. The lone representative is Radical (**R#44**, 尸, **shī**, **corpse**). The stroke order is **HZ-(x)-SP**.

乛 ヨ 尸

The eighth category are Radicals and characters in which **SZ** and **HZG** meet. The lone Radical in this category is Radical (**R#80**, 毋 /母, **wú**, **do not**). The stroke order is **SZ-HZG**.

乚 口

The ninth category are characters and Radicals in which **H** and **S** meet. Radical (**R#99**, 甘, **gān**, **sweet**) and (**R#128**, 耳, **ěr**, **ear**) represent this category. The stroke order for both is **H-S**. A variant of **H-S** is (年, nián, year).

一 十 and 一 丁

The tenth category are characters and Radicals in which **ST** and **HZ** meet. The representative Radical is (**R#138**, 艮, **gèn**, **stopping**). In this Radical **HZ** comes before **ST**.

⁊ ⋺ ㅌ 𠃍

The eleventh category are characters and Radicals in which **SP** and **HG** meet. Radical (**R#107**, 皮, **pí**, **skin**) is the lone member of this category. The stroke order is **HG-SP**.

⼀ 厂 ナ 步 皮

The twelfth category are Radicals in which **H** and **SP** meet. This is seen in Radicals (**R#27**, 厂, **hàn**, **cliff**) and (**R#104**, 疒, **chuáng**, **sickness**). In both of these Radicals **H** precedes **SP**.

⼀ 厂   and   丶 ⼀ 广 疒 疒

6. Horizontal before Vertical 十

When **S** and **H** strokes cross, horizontal strokes are written before vertical strokes. The character for (十, **shí**, **ten**), has two strokes. The left to right horizontal stroke (横, **héng**, **H**, **horizontal stroke**) is written first. The top to bottom vertical stroke (竖, **shù**, **S**, **vertical down stroke**) is written second. Hence, the stroke order is **héng-shù** or **H-S**.

7. Bottom Horizontal Stroke Last 王

In situations where a horizontal stroke is on the bottom of a character and it is not crossed by the vertical stroke, but intersects with it, the vertical stroke is drawn before the last horizontal **H** stroke. Example, (王, **wáng**, **king**), the stroke order is **héng, héng, shù, héng** or **H, H, S, H**. This allows for a neater finish in which the horizontal stroke can neatly intersect the vertical line. This dates from the use of a hair brush and ink in which the descending hand would obscure the neat intersection of a horizontal line being drawn first. Further examples are (土, **tǔ**, **earth**), (工, **gōng**, **work**) and (主, **zhǔ**, **master**)

8. Vertical Cutting Strokes Last 中

Vertical strokes that cut through a character are written after the horizontal strokes that they cut through, as in (中, **zhōng**, **centre**). This rule applies when the vertical line starts above the top horizontal line and finishes below the bottom horizontal line. (中, **zhōng**, **center**) is such an example. The box is completed and then the vertical line is drawn through it.

9. Horizontal Cutting Strokes Last 母

Horizontal strokes that cut through a character are written last, as in 母 and 海. The usual strokes to cut through are **H** and **T**. Example (母, **mǔ**, **female**)

10. Right to Left down Sloping before Left to Right down Sloping 文

Right-to-left diagonals (丿) are written before left-to-right diagonals (㇏) such as in (文, **wén**, **language**), (这, **zhè**, **this**) and (友, **yǒu**, **friend**). The crossing strokes are typically **P, N** or **CD**.

11. Centre Verticals before Left and Right Strokes. 永

In characters that show a left to right symmetry with a central dividing vertical stroke, the central stroke is written first. Vertical centre strokes are written before vertical or diagonal outside strokes, left outside strokes are written before right outside strokes (水, **shuǐ**, **water**), (永, **yǒng**, **eternity**), (小, **xiǎo**, **small**).

12. Box Rules, Left Vertical First, Outside before Inside 回

All closed boxes are constructed the same. The left vertical edge is drawn first with the vertical downward stroke **S**. The top horizontal and right vertical strokes are written in one continuous stroke using (**HZ, héngzhé**). This is the left to right horizontal stroke with a down dropping vertical stroke. The box is left open at this time if it has contents inside. All inside contents are then finished. The bottom horizontal left to right box-closing stroke **H** is written last. If there is a box within a box, the inner box is closed first. Example, (回, **huí**, **turn around**). An easy order to remember is *make three sided down box*, *fill box*, *close box*.

This rule applies also to top enclosing characters that have no bottom stroke, such as 同 and 月. The outer structure is finished first, then the inside contents are added.

13. Bottom Enclosure Last (R#17, qǔ, 凵, Open Box)

Bottom box enclosures, (**R#17, qǔ, 凵, open box**) are always written last. The contents of the box are written first. Then the box encloses the contents. Examples are (画, **huà, draw**), (涵, **hán, contain**), (凶, **xiōng, fierce**). The box is made in two strokes, **SZ-S**. This follows the rule of underlining strokes being placed last.

14. Down Box Rules 冂

(**R#13, jiǒng, 冂, down box**) is made with **S-HZG**. If there is a Radical, stroke or character over top of (**R#13, jiǒng, 冂, down box**), as in (再, **zài, again**), it is made first. Next, (**R#13, jiǒng, 冂, down box**) is formed. Strokes dropping from above and entering the box, in this situation, **S**, are made after the open Down Box is formed. Strokes inside the box are made after the box is formed, (同, **tóng, same**).

15. Ride Side Open Box Rules 匚, 匚

(**R#22, fāng, 匚, right open box**) as a Radical, is formed with the strokes **H-SZ**. However, the stroke order is **H** plus whatever is under **H**, then **SZ** when a character is made. This follows the general rule of underlining and enclosing strokes occurring last. (匠, **jiàng, craftsman**) (匡, **kuāng, correct**) (匣, **xiá, box**).

(**R#23, xǐ, 匚, hiding enclosure**) as a Radical, is formed with the strokes **H-SW**. Again, any Radical or character is made under **H** then the enclosing-underlining stroke **SW** occurs last. This follows the general rule of underlining and enclosing strokes occurring last. (匹, **pī, mate**) (医, **yī, to treat**)

16. Bottom Underlining Strokes Last 这

Bottom underlining strokes are always written last. If the left hand Radical of a character has a bottom underlining stroke, it is written last. Examples are Radical (**R#162**', 辶, **chuò**, **walk**) and (这, **zhè**, **this**). This construction can even occur in the middle of a character composed of three radicals side by side. (谜, **mí**, **riddle**).

17. Dots and Minor Strokes Last 戈

Minor strokes are usually written last, as the small *dot* (点, **diǎn**, **dot**) in the following. (玉, **yù**, **jade**) In a character such as (国, **guó**, **country**), the **Box Rules** are preserved and the (玉, **yù**, **jade**) character is finished first then the box is closed. It must be remembered that **R#8**, (亠, **tóu**, **lid**) is a Radical and as it occurs at the top of a character (点, **diǎn**, **dot**) comes first.

18. 提, **Tí**, Stroke Rule ✓

(提, **Tí**, ✓) when it crosses another stroke is drawn after the stroke it crosses. Examples are (孑, **jié**, **alone**), (扌, **shǒu**, **hand**), (我, **wǒ**, **me**)

19. Not Withstanding Rule

There are apparent exceptions to many rules. However the apparent exceptions are often misinterpretations through choice of fonts or characters that have so many strokes that in a small sized font you cannot see the definition of the individual strokes. (**R#67**, 文, **wén**, **script**) appear to offend rule #**17**, **Dots and Minor Strokes Last**. It does follow the rule however of completion of radicals within a character and the first stroke (点, **diǎn**, **dot**) is part of the Radical (**R#8**, 亠, **tóu**, **lid**).

R#97, 瓜, **guā**, **melon** may appear to have a stroke selection of **H-P** or **H-WP** for the first two strokes. However, the first two strokes are not the **Radical R#27**, 厂, **hàn**, **cliff** but rather **PP-WP**. Despite trying four different fonts, 瓜 瓜 瓜 瓜, the proper strokes cannot be seen until you increase the size of the character.

(**R#26**, 卩, **jié**, **seal**) is another example of an apparent exception. On casual inspection it may look like **HZ-H-S**. The stroke order is in fact **HZG-S**. If one was to follow rule # **14. Down Box Rules**, it would be easy to assume that **S** is the first stroke. Again, font selection demonstrates the correct strokes. 卩 卩 卩 卩 In fact, some fonts make it look like Radical (**R# 13**, 冂, **jiǒng**, **down box**) 卩 卩 卩.

Hanzi characters are built up from basic strokes. The simplest characters have only one stroke while the more complex ones can have more than 60 strokes. You will find in the workbook below some **Hanzi** characters and the most common basic strokes in **Hanzi**. The strokes must be written in the right order and in the right direction. It is important to follow those rules. If you always write a character the same way you will develop a memorized pattern for how to write it. The character will also look much more symmetrical and be reproducible if you follow the rules. Proportions are very important so you have to have it in mind when you write.

Often a stroke can be altered to look more aesthetically pleasing in a character. If you look at the character for (学, **xué**, **study**), you find a character with a group of two (点, **diǎn**, **dot**) strokes on top and one **DP**. The two to the left are written angled from left to right while the last one is written angled from right to left. This is made to make the character more visually appealing.

学 学 学 学 学 学 学

The same occurs if you have many (横, 一, **héng**, **H, horizontal stroke**) in a character such as in the character (三, **sān**, **three**). In this example it is three **héng** and they are all different sizes.

However, in characters such as (士, **shì**, **scholar**) and (土, **tǔ**, **dirt**) the proportion of stroke length does have meaning. The upper (横, 一, **héng**, **H,**) stroke of (士, **shì**, **scholar**) is longer that the base **héng**. In the character (土, **tǔ**, **dirt**), the top most **héng** is shorter and this is what defines the difference between the two characters.

Certain strokes such as (折, **zhé**, **break**) and (钩, **gōu**, **left down hook**) never occur alone, but are components in compound strokes. Thus, they are not in themselves individual strokes. (折, **zhé**, **break**) is often described as a right angle turn but it often is not as in (也, **yě**, **also**) which has the compound character stroke (**横折鉤**, **Héng Zhé Gōu**, □) also seen as right-angled as in (刀, **Dāo**, **knife**). Other named components give *character* to names strokes by modifying their curvature or slope.

The Six Single Strokes

一   **横, Héng, H, Horizontal**, 一, is a horizontal or near horizontal stroke. It is drawn from the left to the right. As you can see with the character (三, **sān, three**) and angled in (七, **qī, seven**).

丨   **竖, Shù, S, Line**, 丨, is a vertical or near vertical top to bottom stroke. You can clearly see this is the character (中, **zhōng, middle**). However, in the character (五, **wǔ, five**) it is it is leaning to the right.

╱   **提, Tí, T, Flick**, ╱, is a left to right *flick* stroke at an upward and variable angle. It is drawn from the left to the right. As you can see in the example (玫, **méi, rose**) it rises slightly from the left to the right.

╲   **捺, Nà, N, Press Down**, ╲, is a left to right falling arc stroke at a 45 degree angle. It has a small concavity. In many electronic fonts it appears as a line and loses the brush stroke character.

丿   **撇, Piě, P, Slash**, 丿, is a right to left falling slash stroke at a 45 degree angle. It has a small concavity. In many electronic fonts it appears as a line and loses the brush stroke character.

丶   **点, Diǎn, D, Dot**, 丶, is a *dot* falling from the left to the right with a convexity. In many electronic fonts it appears as a line with no tear drop like character.

Stroke Variations and Additives

鉤, **Gōu**, **G** , **Hook**, ⌐ ↲, is a *hook* that is added to 6 other strokes to create the compound strokes, **HG, SG, PG, WG, XG, BXG**. It is not a named stroke by its self.

折, **Zhé**, **Z**, **Break**, ㄱ indicates a right angle or near angle change in direction. It is not a stroke but is used to describe the transition from (横, 一, **Héng**, **H**) to (横折, **Héng Zhé**, **HZ**, ㄱ).

折, **Zhé**, **Z**, **Break**, ㄴ indicates a right angle or near angle change in direction. It is not a stroke but is used as a descriptive to describe the transition from (竖, **Shù**, **S**) to (竖折, **Shù Zhé**, **SZ**).

短撇, **Duǎn Piě**, **DP**, **Short Slash**, ノ is a short variant of 撇, **Piě**. In this book, in a character with multiple variants of the stroke (撇, **Piě**, ノ), the shorter will be called **DP**.

平撇, **Píng Piě**, **PP**, **Flat Slash**, is a flattened stroke seen on the top of characters. It is a flattened version of 撇, **Piě**. It can be mistaken for (横, **Héng**) with some fonts.

右点, **Yòu Diǎn**, **YD**, **Right Dot**, is the most common variation of (点, **Diǎn**, **Dot**). It is not commonly referred to as (右点, **Yòu Diǎn**) but simply as (点, **Diǎn**, **Dot**).

左点, **Zuǒ Diǎn**, **ZD**, **Left Dot**, is a right to left falling concave dot. It is a mirror image inverse reflection of the right handed (右点, **Yòu Diǎn**, **right dot**).

长点, **Cháng Diǎn**, **CD**, **Long Dot** is the long dot seen as a long convex arc. It occurs in characters such as (这, **zhè**, **this**). As characters are scaled up **D** loses its dot shape and becomes **CD**

扁斜, **Biǎn Xié**, **BX**, is a curve flattening trait seen in one stroke (扁斜鉤, **Biǎn Xié Gōu**, ⌒). (扁, **biǎn**, **flat**) and (斜, **xié**, **slanting**) combine to form this trait.

直提, **Zhí Tí**, **ZT** is an upright version of (提, **Tí**).

点提, **Diǎn Tí**, **DT**, retains brush stroke character and is an alternative 提, **Tí**. It is formed by making (右点, **Yòu Diǎn**, **right dot**) then an uprising **T**.

短撇长点, **Duǎn Piě Cháng Diǎn**, **DPCD** is the same character stroke as (撇点, **Piě Diǎn**, **PD**). This alternate name is offered to provide a better sense of proportion.

弯, **Wān**, **W**, is a right to left falling slightly concave stroke.

Compound Strokes

亅   竪鉤, **Shù Gōu**, **SG**, 亅 is a vertical down stroke with a hook to the left.

乀   點捺, **Diǎn Nà**, **DN** is seen only in the character (入, **rù**, **to enter**) and its derivatives. It can be mistaken for (提捺, **Tí Nà**).

⌒   平捺, **Píng Nà**, **PN** is a left to right flattened falling stroke. It is a flattened version of 捺, Nà. It is seen as the underlining stroke in characters as above.

乁   提捺, **Tí Nà**, **TN** can be confused with 点捺, **Diǎn Nà** as in (入, **rù**, **enter**).

⌒   提平捺, **Tí Píng Nà**, **TPN** occurs as an under stroke as demonstrated. 氽

┐   橫折, **Héng Zhé**, **HZ** is a right angle or near right angle turn from (橫, **Héng**, **H**, **Horizontal**)

フ 横撇, **Héng Piě**, **HP** exists as a compound stroke and can be confused with **H-P**.

→ 横鈎, **Héng Gōu**, **HG** is often seen at the top of a character as **Diǎn - Héng Gōu**, ⌐.

L 竖折, **Shù Zhé**, **SZ** has a right angle turn and can be confused with 竖弯, **Shù Wān** which has a curved transition versus a right angle transition.

L 竖弯, **Shù Wān**, **SW** has a smooth turn and can be mistaken for (竖折, **Shù Zhé**, **SZ**).

レ 竖提, **Shù Tí**, **ST**. The (提, **Tí**, **T**, **Flick**, ✓) component can be proportionally different lengths compared to (竖, **Shù**, **S**, **Line**, │) component.

丿 竖折, **Shù Piě**, **SP** is a vertical down stroke with a 45 degree tail to the left.

丿 弯撇, **Wān Piě**, **WP** differs from (竖撇, **Shù Piě**) in the non-vertical initial stroke. Characters described as (撇, **Piě**, **P**) often are in fact (弯撇, **Wān Piě**, **WP**).

撇折, **Piě Zhé**, **PZ**, the (折, **Zhé**, **Z**) stroke is horizontal and longer than the stroke (提, **Tí**, **T**) in (竖提, **Shù Tí**, **ST**). ㄥ vs ㇑.

撇點, **Piě Diǎn**, **PD**

撇鉤, **Piě Gōu**, **PG** is a very rare stroke.

弯鉤, **Wān Gōu**, **WG** is characterized by the top portion of the stroke being to the left of the apex of the curve that occurs in the vertical plane.

斜鉤, **Xié Gōu**, **XG**

扁斜鉤, **Biǎn Xié Gōu**, **BXG** is the flattened character stroke (斜鉤, **Xié Gōu**, **XG**) as seen in (, **xīn**, **heart**) versus the stroke in (心, **xīn**, **heart**).

竖弯左, **Shù Wān Zuǒ**, **SWZ** differs from the compound stroke (竖折, **Shù Piě**, **SP**) in that the tail is not as acutely deviating from the vertical.

竖折折, **Shù Zhé Zhé**, **SZZ**

竖折撇, **Shù Zhé Piě**, **SZP**

竖折鈎, **Shù Zhé Gōu**, **SZG**

竖折弯鈎, **Shù Zhé Wān Gōu**, **SZWG** is a brush stroke variant of (竖折鈎, **Shù Zhé Gōu**, **SZG**).

横撇弯, **Héng Piě Wān**, **HPW**

横折折, **Héng Zhé Zhé**, **HZZ**

横折弯, **Héng Zhé Wān**, **HZW** differs from the compound stroke (横折折, **Héng Zhé Zhé**, **HZZ**) in that the transition from vertical to horizontal is curved versus a right angle.

横折提, **Héng Zhé Tí**, **HZT**

横折鈎, **Héng Zhé Gōu**, **HZG**

横折弯鈎, **Héng Zhé Wān Gōu**, **HZWG** is a brush stroke variant of (横折鈎, **Héng Zhé Gōu**, **HZG**).

横斜鈎, **Héng Xié Gōu**, **HXG**

横折折折, **Héng Zhé Zhé Zhé**, **HZZZ**

横折折撇, **Héng Zhé Zhé Piě**, **HZZP**

横折折弯鈎, **Héng Zhé Zhé Wān Gōu**, **HZZWG** is a variant of (**R#5**, 乙, **yǐ**, second).

横撇弯鉤, **Héng Piě Wān Gōu**, **HPWG**

竖折折鉤, **Shù Zhé Zhé Gōu**, **SZZG**

竖折折弯鉤, **Shù Zhé Zhé Wān Gōu**, **SZZWG** is a brush stroke variant of (竖折折鉤, **Shù Zhé Zhé Gōu**, **SZZG**).

横撇折弯鉤, **Héng Piě Zhé Wān Gōu**, **HPZWG** as a Radical is (**R#5**, 乙, **yǐ**, **second**). This stroke is often called **HZWG**.

横折折弯鉤, **Héng Zhé Zhé Wān Gōu**, **HZZWG**

圈, **Quān**, **Q** is an extraordinarily rare stroke not seen in the Chinese character set.

Exercise for Individual Strokes

This is the introduction to practical stroke and character writing in this book. Using the templates provided you can directly trace over the strokes. Alternately you can photocopy or use a clear acetate sheet and a wipe-off marker. Equally important is to recite the **Pinyin** word and tone. In the appendix you will find a section on pronunciation and tone.

Pick groups of five to ten sheets to practice by doing one character on each sheet and then going to the next. If you simply write over an entire page while watching television you may find that you flip the page over and do not remember any of it.

Once you have mastered the simple strokes and stroke additives, then it is time to move on to compound strokes. Try and stick to logical groups of strokes rather than randomly picking appealing strokes. For example, learn all the compound strokes that start with (横, **héng**, **H**, **horizontal**, 一) then move on to all the compound strokes with (竖, **shù**, **S**, **vertical line**, 丨).

The first 15 work sheets are the most important as the entire written language is built upon compounding and compiling these most basic units. Like all learning, set reasonable objectives. As your skills develop, you will see that more complex characters require balancing the proportions of different radicals to make the result esthetically pleasing.

Radicals are compilations of one or more strokes. The higher you go through the numbered Radical list the more the Radical is a composite of previous Radicals and additional strokes.

横

héng
H

Notes:

(横, héng, H, horizontal, 一)

héng	héng	héng	héng	héng	héng	héng	héng	héng	héng
H	H	H	H	H	H	H	H	H	H

héng	héng	héng	héng	héng	héng	héng	héng	héng	héng
H	H	H	H	H	H	H	H	H	H

竖

shù
S

Notes:

(竖, shù, S, vertical line, 丨)

shù	shù	shù	shù	shù	shù	shù	shù	shù	shù
S	S	S	S	S	S	S	S	S	S

shù	shù	shù	shù	shù	shù	shù	shù	shù	shù
S	S	S	S	S	S	S	S	S	S

提

tí / T

Notes:

(提, tí, T, flick, ✓)

撇

piě / P

Notes:
(撇, piě, P, slash, ノ)

捺

nà
N

Notes:

(捺, nà, N, press down, ㇏)

点

diǎn
D

Notes:

(点, diǎn, D, dot, 丶)

丶 丶 丶 丶 丶 丶 丶 丶 丶

丶	丶	丶	丶	丶	丶	丶	丶	丶	丶
diǎn	diǎn	diǎn	diǎn	diǎn	diǎn	diǎn	diǎn	diǎn	diǎn
D	D	D	D	D	D	D	D	D	D
丶	丶	丶	丶	丶	丶	丶	丶	丶	丶
diǎn	diǎn	diǎn	diǎn	diǎn	diǎn	diǎn	diǎn	diǎn	diǎn
D	D	D	D	D	D	D	D	D	D
丶	丶	丶	丶	丶	丶	丶	丶	丶	丶
丶	丶	丶	丶	丶	丶	丶	丶	丶	丶
丶	丶	丶	丶	丶	丶	丶	丶	丶	丶
丶	丶	丶	丶	丶	丶	丶	丶	丶	丶
丶	丶	丶	丶	丶	丶	丶	丶	丶	丶
丶	丶	丶	丶	丶	丶	丶	丶	丶	丶
丶	丶	丶	丶	丶	丶	丶	丶	丶	丶
丶	丶	丶	丶	丶	丶	丶	丶	丶	丶

鉤

gōu / **G**

Notes:

(鉤, **gōu**, **G**, **hook**) is added as an accessory to other strokes.

zhé

Z

Notes:

(折, **Zhé**, **Z**, **break**, ㄱ ㄴ) indicates a right angle or near right angle change in direction. It is not a stroke but is used as a descriptive to describe the transition from one linear stroke to another.

短	撇	Notes:
duǎn	piě	(短撇, **duǎn piě**, **DP**) The difference between this stroke and (撇, **piě**, **P**, slash, ノ) is only in scale proportionate to the character. In this book **DP** will be marked when it is ½ or less of the character height or unmatched to **N**.
D	P	

平	撇	Notes:
píng	piě	(平撇, **píng piě**, **PP**, **flat slash**) is a flattened version of (撇, **piě**) seen on the top of characters. It can be mistaken for (橫, **héng**, **H**) with some fonts.
P	P	

右	点	Notes:
yòu	diǎn	(右点, **yòu diǎn**, **right dot**, **YD**) is the most common variation of (点, **diǎn**, dot). It is not commonly referred to as (右点, **yòu diǎn**) but simply as (点, **diǎn, D**).
Y	D	

左	点	Notes:
zuǒ	diǎn	(左点, **zuǒ diǎn**, **left dot**, ZD) is a right to left falling concave dot.
Z	D	

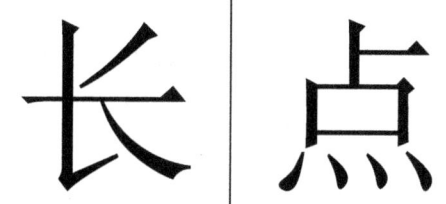

cháng	diǎn
C	D

Notes:

(长点, **cháng diǎn, long dot, CD**) is a elongated version of the (右点, **yòu diǎn, right dot, D**)

直	提	Notes:
zhí	tí	(直提, zhí tí, ZT) is an upright version of the stroke (提, Tí, T).
Z	T	

点	提	Notes:
diǎn	tí	(点提, **diǎn tí**, **DT**) retains brush stroke character and is an alternate (**提**, **Tí**).
D	T	

短	撇	长	点	Notes:
duǎn	piě	cháng	diǎn	
D	P	C	D	

く く く く く く く く く

く	く	く	く	く	く	く	く	く	く
DPCD	DPCD	DPCD	DPCD	DPCD	DPCD	DPCD	DPCD	DPCD	DPCD
く	く	く	く	く	く	く	く	く	く
DPCD	DPCD	DPCD	DPCD	DPCD	DPCD	DPCD	DPCD	DPCD	DPCD
く	く	く	く	く	く	く	く	く	く
く	く	く	く	く	く	く	く	く	く
く	く	く	く	く	く	く	く	く	く
く	く	く	く	く	く	く	く	く	く
く	く	く	く	く	く	く	く	く	く
く	く	く	く	く	く	く	く	く	く
く	く	く	く	く	く	く	く	く	く
く	く	く	く	く	く	く	く	く	く

竖	鉤	Notes: (竖鉤, shù gōu, SG, 亅)
shù S	gōu G	

亅 亅 亅 亅 亅 亅 亅 亅 亅

亅	亅	亅	亅	亅	亅	亅	亅	亅	亅
SG	SG	SG	SG	SG	SG	SG	SG	SG	SG
亅	亅	亅	亅	亅	亅	亅	亅	亅	亅
SG	SG	SG	SG	SG	SG	SG	SG	SG	SG

竖	撇	Notes:
shù	**piě**	(竖撇, **shù piě**, **SP**, 丿) has an initial vertical component to the stroke.
S	P	

丿 丿 丿 丿 丿 丿 丿 丿

丿	丿	丿	丿	丿	丿	丿	丿	丿	丿
SP	SP	SP	SP	SP	SP	SP	SP	SP	SP
丿	丿	丿	丿	丿	丿	丿	丿	丿	丿
SP	SP	SP	SP	SP	SP	SP	SP	SP	SP
丿	丿	丿	丿	丿	丿	丿	丿	丿	丿
丿	丿	丿	丿	丿	丿	丿	丿	丿	丿
丿	丿	丿	丿	丿	丿	丿	丿	丿	丿
丿	丿	丿	丿	丿	丿	丿	丿	丿	丿
丿	丿	丿	丿	丿	丿	丿	丿	丿	丿
丿	丿	丿	丿	丿	丿	丿	丿	丿	丿
丿	丿	丿	丿	丿	丿	丿	丿	丿	丿
丿	丿	丿	丿	丿	丿	丿	丿	丿	丿

平	捺	Notes:
píng	nà	(平捺, **píng nà**, **PN**) is a left to right flattened falling stroke. It is a flattened version of (捺, **nà**). It is seen as the underlining stroke in characters.
P	N	

提	捺	Notes: **(提捺, Tí Nà, TN)** is a rare stroke.
tí	nà	
T	N	

提	平	捺	Notes: (提平捺, Tí Píng Nà, TPN) occurs as an under stroke as demonstrated. 㔾
tí	píng	nà	
T	P	N	

点	捺
diǎn	nà
D	N

Notes:

(點捺, diǎn nà, DN) is a very rare stroke.

横	折	Notes: (横折, **Héng Zhé**, **HZ** is a right angle or near right angle turn from (横, **Héng**, **H**, **Horizontal**)
héng	zhé	
H	Z	

横	撇	Notes:
héng	piě	(横撇, Héng Piě, HP)
H	P	

フ フ フ フ フ フ フ フ フ フ

フ	フ	フ	フ	フ	フ	フ	フ	フ	フ
HP	HP	HP	HP	HP	HP	HP	HP	HP	HP
フ	フ	フ	フ	フ	フ	フ	フ	フ	フ
HP	HP	HP	HP	HP	HP	HP	HP	HP	HP

橫	鉤	Notes:
héng	gōu	(橫鉤, **Héng Gōu**, **HG**) is often seen at the top of a character as **Diǎn - Héng Gōu**, ⇁.
H	G	

→ → → → → → → → →

→	→	→	→	→	→	→	→	→	→
HG	HG	HG	HG	HG	HG	HG	HG	HG	HG
→	→	→	→	→	→	→	→	→	→
HG	HG	HG	HG	HG	HG	HG	HG	HG	HG
→	→	→	→	→	→	→	→	→	→
→	→	→	→	→	→	→	→	→	→
→	→	→	→	→	→	→	→	→	→
→	→	→	→	→	→	→	→	→	→
→	→	→	→	→	→	→	→	→	→
→	→	→	→	→	→	→	→	→	→
→	→	→	→	→	→	→	→	→	→
→	→	→	→	→	→	→	→	→	→

竖	折	Notes:
shù	zhé	(竖折, **Shù Zhé**, **SZ**) has a right angle turn and can be confused with **竖弯**, **Shù Wān** which has a curved transition versus a right angle transition.
S	Z	

竖	弯	Notes:
shù	wān	(竖弯, shù wān, SW) has a curved transition from the vertical stroke versus SZ which is a right angle.
S	W	

Practice: SW stroke (L shape)

竖提

(竖提, Shù Tí, ST)

shù	tí
S	T

撇	折	Notes: (撇折, Piě Zhé, PZ)
piě	zhé	
P	Z	

ㄥ ㄥ ㄥ ㄥ ㄥ ㄥ ㄥ ㄥ ㄥ

ㄥ	ㄥ	ㄥ	ㄥ	ㄥ	ㄥ	ㄥ	ㄥ	ㄥ	ㄥ
PZ	PZ	PZ	PZ	PZ	PZ	PZ	PZ	PZ	PZ
ㄥ	ㄥ	ㄥ	ㄥ	ㄥ	ㄥ	ㄥ	ㄥ	ㄥ	ㄥ
PZ	PZ	PZ	PZ	PZ	PZ	PZ	PZ	PZ	PZ

撇 点

piě P **diǎn** D

Notes:

(撇點, Piě Diǎn, PD)

撇	鈎	Notes: (撇鈎, **Piě Gōu**, **PG**) is a very rare stroke.
piě	gōu	
P	G	

弯	鉤	Notes:
wān	**gōu**	(弯鉤, **Wān Gōu**, **WG**) is characterized by the top portion of the stroke being to the left of the apex of the curve that occurs in the vertical plane.
W	**G**	

弯	撇	Notes:
wān	piě	(弯撇, **wān piě**, **WP**) differs from a similar stroke (竖撇, **shù piě**, **SP**, 丿) in that the initial stroke is non vertical. They are both used interchangeably in many characters without changing meaning.
W	**P**	

斜 鉤

xié / X
gōu / G

Notes:

(斜鉤, Xié Gōu, XG)

扁	斜	鉤	Notes:
biǎn	xié	gōu	(扁斜鉤, biǎn xié gōu, ⌣) is seen in (心, xīn, heart).
B	X	G	

竖	弯	左	Notes:
shù	wān	zuǒ	(竖弯左, **Shù Wān Zuǒ**) differs from (竖折, **Shù Piě**, SP) in that the tail is not as bent from the vertical.
S	W	Z	

竖折折

竖	折	折
shù	zhé	zhé
S	Z	Z

(竖折折, Shù Zhé Zhé, SZZ)

竖	折	撇	Notes: (竖折撇, Shù Zhé Piě, SZP)
shù	zhé	piě	
S	Z	P	

竖	折	鈎	Notes: (竖折鈎, Shù Zhé Gōu, SZG)
shù	zhé	gōu	
S	Z	G	

竖	折	弯	鉤
shù	zhé	wān	gōu
S	Z	W	G

横	折	折	Notes: (横折折, Héng Zhé Zhé, HZZ)
héng	zhé	zhé	
H	Z	Z	

横 折 弯

Notes: (横折弯, Héng Zhé Wān, HZW)

héng	zhé	wān
H	Z	W

横	折	提	Notes: (横折提, **Héng Zhé Tí, HZT**)
héng	zhé	tí	
H	Z	T	

橫	折	鉤	Notes: (橫折鉤, Héng Zhé Gōu, HZG)
héng	zhé	gōu	
H	Z	G	

橫	斜	鉤	Notes: (橫斜鉤, Héng Xié Gōu, HXG)
héng H	xié X	gōu G	

横	折	折	折	Notes:
héng	zhé	zhé	zhé	
H	Z	Z	Z	

横	折	折	撇
héng	zhé	zhé	piě
H	Z	Z	P

HZZP

橫 折 彎 鉤

héng - H
zhé - Z
wān - W
gōu - G

Notes:

横	撇	弯	鈎	Note:
héng	piě	wān	gōu	
H	P	W	G	

竖	折	折	鉤	Notes:
shù	zhé	zhé	gōu	
S	Z	Z	G	

竖	折	折	弯	鈎
shù	zhé	zhé	wān	gōu
S	Z	Z	W	G

乙 乙 乙 乙 乙 乙 乙 乙 乙

乙	乙	乙	乙	乙	乙	乙	乙	乙	乙
SZZWG	SZZWG	SZZWG	SZZWG	SZZWG	SZZWG	SZZWG	SZZWG	SZZWG	SZZWG
乙	乙	乙	乙	乙	乙	乙	乙	乙	乙
SZZWG	SZZWG	SZZWG	SZZWG	SZZWG	SZZWG	SZZWG	SZZWG	SZZWG	SZZWG

橫	撇	折	彎	鉤
héng	piě	zhé	wān	gōu
H	P	Z	W	G

乙乙乙乙乙乙乙乙

乙	乙	乙	乙	乙	乙	乙	乙	乙	乙
HPZWG	HPZWG	HPZWG	HPZWG	HPZWG	HPZWG	HPZWG	HPZWG	HPZWG	HPZWG
乙	乙	乙	乙	乙	乙	乙	乙	乙	乙
HPZWG	HPZWG	HPZWG	HPZWG	HPZWG	HPZWG	HPZWG	HPZWG	HPZWG	HPZWG

橫	折	折	彎	鉤
héng	zhé	zhé	wān	gōu
H	Z	Z	W	G

圈

quān
circle

Notes:

(**圈**, **quān**, **Q**) This is a very rare stroke. It is not seen in Chinese character sets.

Eight Principles of Yong

Yǒng

(永字八法, **Yǒngzì Bā Fǎ**, **Eternity Character Eight Method**)
There is a stream of explanation in classical Chinese literature that explains how to write the eight strokes common in Chinese characters. These strokes are all found in the one character (永, **yǒng**, **eternity**). It was believed that the frequent practice of these principles as a beginner calligrapher could ensure beauty in one's writing.

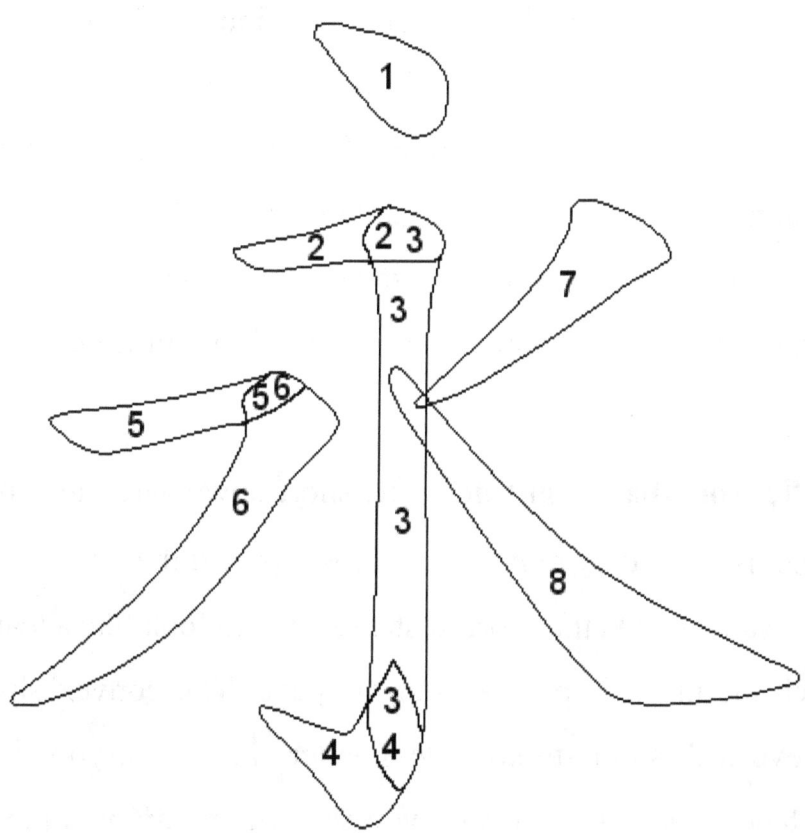

The direction and shape of these strokes originate from the use of a brush with soft hair bristles and black ink. The brush was held vertical between the first three fingers. Calligraphy is the art of drawing characters. Much can be learned from buying a bottle of ink and a brush. However, buy a large sheet of plastic to put under your work. I spent about two dollars in China for a large bottle of ink and a brush and did about $1,000.00 damage when I spilled it. There is a hotel owner in **Yuping** who is very angry. The ink will also penetrate most cheap paper so you may want to get a sheet of cardboard to put under your paper or a blotter sheet. If you can find a **Hero 99** pen or a refillable **Emporer Dragon 801**, they are excellent as they have a soft tapered synthetic tip. Also available but harder to find are fountain type pens with ink cartridges and similar soft tips that deform with pressure. They are mess free and the cartridges are inexpensive. Your Chinese friends may tell you to practice with a pencil. Forget it, they can alter the colour and the shape of the stroke by varying the pressure on the pencil or pen by moving it several thousandths of an inch. They have been doing it since they were infants, they have written millions of characters and they have better dexterity than you have.

1) (右点, **Yòu Diǎn, right dot**), the short downwards left to right convex stroke, is formed by drawing the brush toward the writer left to right in a downward arc. On the shortest strokes, it will look like a teardrop shape in which the brush is pushed into the page. The convex shape is hard to achieve with short strokes. On smaller characters, you simply push the brush down and pull it toward yourself with no draw of the tip.

2) (横, **Héng, horizontal**), the horizontal stroke is a varied stroke. The thickness is maintained by moving the wrist horizontally with no downward deflection. You will often see an ending flourish on various type fonts. This is a reflection of the history of **Hanzi** in which stamps

were carved in wood and the small notch at the end of the stroke kept the wooden block from splitting with repeated use.

3) (竖, **Shù**, **vertical**), the vertical down stroke, is a straight draw toward the writer. The thickness is varied by down pressure that comes at the beginning of the stroke. Any variations in down pressure result in uneven thickness of the line.

4) (鉤, **Gōu**, **hook**), the hook, exists as an addition to several strokes. It is formed by a flick of the writing instrument. The tip of the brush must be raised to get a sharp point. The direction of the stroke varies with the primary stroke it is attached to, either down or to the left.

5) (提, **Tí**, **to lift**), the left to right rising tapering stroke. This stroke is formed by a rising flick with a lift of the brush. This achieves the taper on the right tail of the stroke.

6) (弯, **Wān**, **bent**), describes a smooth curve. Although it is seen to exist standing alone in this classic character description, it is seldom seen in modern **Hanzi**. It is most often used to describe a curved transition.

7) (撇, **Piě**, **throw away**), the downwards right to left curved stroke is formed by drawing the brush initially down and to the left in a near flat rising arc at 45 degrees. A lift of the brush gives a tapered tail.

8) (捺, **Nà**, **press down firmly**), the downwards left to right up curved stroke is formed by drawing the brush toward and to the right of the writer. The brush follows a small flat rising arc to create a concave shape by pushing the brush away from the writer as it travels.

Guide to Pronunciation

If you become obsessed with the perfect pronunciation, grammar and tone of Standard Mandarin, your efforts will be in vain. You will be the only one in China and the world speaking it. A native English speaker from Hamilton, Ontario, where perfect English is spoken, can understand a man from England, Scotland, Australia, Newfoundland, East India and Nigeria. As long as you get close with Mandarin, an authentic Chinese friend can fine tune you. You will find that in China the pronunciation varies as much as the food and geography of China does. In fact you will find that as soon as you write a **Hanzi** character or speak Mandarin an enthusiastic smiling throng of proud Chinese will descend upon you to assist you. One of the more distressing things I have discovered is the inconsistency in different published books about the pronunciation of **Pinyin**.

Pinyin vowels are pronounced similarly to vowels in Roman alphabet languages and most consonants are similar to English. A pitfall for native English speakers is, however, the unusual pronunciation of *x*, *q*, *c*, *zh*, *sh* and *z* and sometimes *i* and the unvoiced portion of the pronunciation of *d*, *b*, *g*, and *j*. This will be detailed below.

The pronunciation of **Pinyin** is broken into Initials and Finals. Initials are initial consonants or vowels in a phoneme, while Finals are all possible combinations of consonants and vowels that form the ending of the word, hence the term *Finals*.

What Defines a Chinese Word?

Words used to describe English grammar do not entirely work for Chinese grammar. A word in **Hanzi** / **Hanyu** is not necessarily one character. Some characters do not have a distinct meaning and must be bound to one or more other characters to give them meaning. These are described as ***Bound Morphemes***.

Morpheme

In English, a morpheme is the smallest unit of meaning. For example, the *s* added to a noun to make it plural is a morpheme. It has meaning and is indivisible. If a Chinese character does not have meaning, it is not a morpheme. However, Chinese language is all characters. There are no *s* equivalents to add to a character. Adding another stroke to a character creates a different character. A morpheme in Chinese grammar is thus enough characters to give meaning and cannot be broken down to give a different meaning. But it can be more than one character.

With this definition, many characters stand alone as having meaning and are thus morphemes and also words. Some words then are minimally two characters. A Chinese word is one or more characters combined to have meaning.

Phoneme

Pinyin is a system of assigning sounds or phonemes written with the Roman English alphabet to assign a standardized sound to each character. The sounds however are not unique. Each character has a unique appearance, defined by the placement of strokes that are used to make it. Each **Pinyin** sound word is assigned to many characters. It is more like assigning part numbers to inventory than it is a language. Because **Pinyin** does not have uniqueness of meaning, it is not a language, you cannot effectively communicate in **Pinyin**. You can use it to study the pronunciation of Chinese characters.

The compilation of phonemes of **Pinyin** parallels the words of **Hanzi**. If two characters are put together to create a Chinese word, then two **Pinyin** phonemes are put together to create a **Pinyin** sound word. If four characters are put together to create a Chinese word, then the four corresponding sound words are put together to create a **Pinyin** sound word. However, as Chinese characters are currently written, there are no space breaks between characters. Reading the **Pinyin** can help you determine which Chinese characters are compiled together to create multi-character words.

It is always important to remember the mathematical difficulty of writing a sentence using **Pinyin**. If you have 4 sound words that each are assigned to 10 different characters, you have 10,000 possible character combinations. If you think that you can write in **Hanyu Pinyin** as a language I assure you I can write a sentence in which it is necessary to use a computer to plot the multitude of different translations. This is why you will read about the difference in written versus spoken grammar and sentence construction. The choice of words used to speak is much less than the choice of words used to write due to the confusion of homophones.

Homophones

A homophone is a sound that is unique yet has more than one meaning. In English, eight-ate, great-grate and lie-lye are all paired homophones. Each pairing sounds the same but has different meanings. There are about 70,000 Chinese characters. Yet there are only about 1500 unique sounds to represent them. This means that one sound can represent many characters, dozens sometimes. This has many implications. Mandarin is a spoken representation of Chinese characters. It is spoken differently than it is written. Writing gives much greater opportunity to use a broad range of characters that spoken would be confused with others. One does not have to worry about chose of words when writing.

Speaking is another matter. Every spoken sound has different meanings. The context of the conversation and what has been spoken before gives great assistance to the listener. Of necessity, the vocabulary of speaking is limited. It is possible to say something that written would be easy to understand but spoken would be indecipherable.

The advantage of this is that you can learn to communicate with a very small number of spoken words in Mandarin. The difficulty is understanding someone who has a greater vocabulary. The mythical Standard Mandarin is precise but you can create grammatically correct sentences that just are not commonly used. This is why the most common expression in China may be,

请写下来
Qǐng xiě xiàlái.
Please write down.

Initials

(声母, **shēng mǔ**, initial sound)

Pronunciation of Initials

Initials are the consonants that form the beginning of **Hanyu Pinyin** words. Fine tuning can only occur in a region specific context. The *she boo she* (是不是, **shì bù shì, is not is**) of Beijing becomes *see buh see* of Chengdu. While you are trying to get a Mandarin speaker to slow down you have to gauge their neutral tone, make adjustments for ethnic and geographic phonetic drift and figure out the dozens of meanings for each identical sounding word, good luck.

Just as an Englishman, an Australian and a Scotsman can understand each other, even though their accents vary, you will be able to adjust and understand various accents in **Hanyu**, eventually, maybe. In many books, you will find the Initial and Finals grouped according to where your tongue is in your mouth and whether you are leaking air up your nose. I encourage you to group the Initials as to how it makes most sense to you.

Pinyin	Explanation
b	As in English, un-aspirated *p*, as in *spit*, examples *b*ig, *b*ad, *b*one.
p	As in English, aspirated *p*, as in *pi*, examples *p*it, *p*athetic, *p*ortrait.
m	As in English, examples *m*an, *m*aw, *m*ow, *m*aul.
f	As in English, examples *f*ind, *f*eel, *f*ord.
d	As in English, examples *d*ig, *d*uffle, *d*oubt.
t	As in English, examples *t*ime, *t*empo, *t*art.
n	As in English, examples *n*o, *n*ight, *n*ever.
l	As in English, examples *l*eft, *l*ime, *l*over.
g	As in English, examples *g*ay, *g*ive, *g*ore.
k	As in English, examples *k*ill, *k*ick, *k*iss.
h	As in English, if followed by an *a*, otherwise, like the *ch* in *loch*.
j	As in English, almost, this exact sound is not used in English, the closest match is the *j* in *ajar*, examples *j*ing, *j*ittery, *J*esus.

q   Like the *ch* in *ch*urch, examples *ch*urch, *ch*ess, *ch*est.

x   Like the *sh* in *sh*y, examples *sh*ower, *sh*ade, *sh*iver.

zh   As in English, with no aspiration, the tongue is curled back on the roof of the mouth, retroflexed. Examples *fudge*, *judge*, *grudge*.

ch   As in English as in *ch*in, but with the tongue curled back on the roof of the mouth. Very similar to the *tu* of nur*tu*re but strongly aspirated.

sh   As in English, as in *sh*inbone, but with the tongue curled back on the roof of the mouth, retroflexed, very similar to under*sh*irt.

r   As in English as in *r*ank, but with the lips spread and with the tongue curled back on the roof of the mouth, retroflexed. Examples, plea*r*ure, t*r*easure.

z   As in the English, examples, su*ds*, bu*ds*, du*ds*.

c   As in English ca*ts*, examples ma*ts*, ba*ts*, ra*ts*.

s   As in English, examples *s*un, *s*ow, *s*ung, *s*ong.

w   As in English, examples *w*ay, *w*hy, *w*ind.

y   As in English, examples *y*es, *y*ellow, *y*et. Exception *yi* as *ēē*.

The only two-consonant Initials are *zh*, *sh* and *ch*. There are 11 **Pinyin** with no Initial consonant. They are *a*, *ai*, *ao*, *an*, *ang*, *o*, *ou*, *e*, *ei*, *en*, and *er*. Please note that none of these start with *i*, *u*, or *ü*. There are special and unnecessary rules for these.

In this table above I have put 23 Initials. Many books would disagree with this and would not include *w* and *y*. Some books say there are 21 Initials and a *zero* Initial. The *zero* Initial is put in front of phonemes that begin with an *i*, *u* or *ü*. So you are to pretend that there is a silent and invisible letter in front of the phoneme because some anal linguist cannot stand the thought of a consonant and vowel having the same sound.

The almighty and great reference Li and Thompson (1981) says that there are 22 Initials yet their table shows 21 so they must attribute an invisible and silent consonant in absentia. Hopefully one day someone will logically reference the great and mighty (大毛猴子, **Dà Máo Hóuzi, Big Hairy Monkey**) and point out that there are 23.

Finals

(韵母, yùn mǔ, final sound)

Pronunciation of Finals

Finals are the vowels and vowel consonant combinations that are the ending of **Pinyin** phonemes. Several of these sounds do not correspond directly to sounds in English. If you agonize over a perfect pronunciation, you will find it varies immensely in China. The assumption is that you speak a neutral tone English such as would be spoken in the province of Ontario in Canada. If you have a highland Scottish brogue, are a Hungarian who speaks English as a second language, or are from East India, good luck with your background accent.

The only parts of *Finals* that are purely consonants in standard **Hanyu** are *n* and *ng*. (儿化, érhuà, erhua) is a phonetic regional window dressing with no meaning so I will avoid it here. The *Finals* take the form of,

single Vowel only (V),

two vowels (VV),

three vowels (VVV),

one vowel and a consonant (VC),

one vowel and two consonants (VCC),

two vowels and a consonant (VVC),

and two vowels and two consonants (VVCC).

In all these situations the single (C) is the letter *n* and the (CC) is always *ng*.

This is important to know as many *words* in **Pinyin** are composed from more than one character and the **Pinyin** is thus compiled together similarly. Knowing which combinations cannot go together helps you know where the break in a phoneme string or word is.

To find a given final, remove the initial consonant. For *zh*, *ch*, *sh*, both letters should be removed. They are the only Initial consonants spelled with two letters.

Many books show Finals beginning with *i as* a standalone **Pinyin** beginning with *y*. Example, *-ian* as *yan*. I do not see the utility of this confusion. This language is already confusing enough. These statements result from the conversionof older styles of Romanization such as Wade Gillis. The rule is simple, the **Pinyin** *y* is silent before the **Pinyin** *i*. In all other situations it is pronounced as the English letter *y*. When you see a character represented with *yan* there is no value to trying to remember it as really being represented as *–ian* with the letter *y* acting as a silent place holder.

Many books show Finals beginning with *u* as a standalone **Pinyin** beginning with *w*. Example, *-ua* as *wa*. The rule is simple, the **Pinyin** *u* is pronounced *w* when the Final stands alone. Same argument as above.

Many books show Finals beginning with *ü as* a standalone **Pinyin** beginning with *y*. Example, *- ün* as *yun*. Same argument as above.

Pinyin is not a language, it is a system that assigns a sound to each Chinese character.

This is the reason that many books do not show *w* and *y* as Initial consonants. This language is already confusing enough. There are in fact very few **Pinyin** that begin with a vowel as an Initial. The 11 combinations are *a*, *ai*, *ao*, *an*, *ang*, *o*, *ou*, *e*, *ei*, *en*, and *er*. I see little reason to learn complex rules about stand alone Finals as they never stand alone. Learn the combined sounds of the Initials and Finals and forget the *i-y*, *u-w* and, *ü-y*.

Learning from a chart, you will never get it right as there is no right. Race, height, age, alcohol, tobacco, many things affect your voice. There is so much variation in China that there is no perfect sounds. The other variable is that the transition from one phoneme to another affects the sound. Even within individual words the tone can have a great effect on the sound as you glide from one vowel to another.

(儿化, **érhuà**, **erhua**) adds another variable. Added to the neutral and first tone it is a continuation. Added to the second, third and fourth tone it can be an awkward addition.

Some books say that *zhi*, *chi*, *shi*, *ri*, *zi*, *ci* or *si* are pure consonant only sounds and that the *i* acts as a phonetic silent neutral place holder. Other books say that the *i* is sounded as a prolonged **zzzzzz**. The **zzzzzz** theory is definitely wrong. Mandarin is usually spoken so fast there are no prolonged sounds. Some lackey with a Master's degree trying to get his Ph.D. must have some Chinese undergrads wired up to an phonetic oscilloscope in a laboratory. The *i* theory is a little more credible but try making any of the pure consonant sounds and ending them just as they started.

If you take any sound and isolate it phonetically and analyze it it bears little resemblance to how it is used dynamically. I have great fun in China playing my language learning DVD's to my relatives and watch them howl with laughter as some guy sounds out each **Pinyin** in a slow dramatic fashion with gigantic ranges of tone. The third tone is particularly impressive under scrutiny. The phonemes are stretched to about 5 times their length and 3 times their tonal range.

Pinyin	Explanation
-i	Displayed as an *i* after: *zh*, *ch*, *sh*, *r*, *z*, *c* or *s*. The consonant is very dominant with very little sound effect from the *i*.
-i	After all other consonants it sounds as Ē.
-a	As in *father*, examples *saw*, *raw*, *law*.
-o	Occurring only in **bo**, **po**, **mo**, **wo**, and **fo**, it has a *wahw* like sound.
-e	Similar to the English *uh*, but not as open, *nut*, *mutt*, *but*.
-ê	As in *bet*. This is only used in certain interjections.
-ai	As in English *eye*, *sty*, *my*, *fly*, *die*.
-ei	As in English alphabetic Ā as in *lay*, *day*, *stay*, *bay*.
-ao	As in English in *cow*.
-ou	As in English *oh* or the long alphabetic Ō, examples *so*, *tow*, *mow*.
-an	As in English **l**awn, *sawn*, *pawn*.

-en	As in English *-un*, as in *fun*, *done*, *run*.
-ang	As in English *angst*.
-eng	As in English *–ung*, *bung*, *sung*, *stung*.
er	As in English *are*. This word stands alone with no Initial.
-ia	As in English alphabetic *Ē* + **awh**, **ēēē-ahhh**.
-io	As in English alphabetic *Ē* + *Ō*.
-ie	As in English alphabetic *Ē* + **yuh**, but is short. The *yuh* is pronounced longer and carries the main stress. **Ē-yyyuh**
-iao	As in English alphabetic *Ē* + **yao**, as in English in **cow**.
-iu	As in English alphabetic *Ē* + **yoe**, as in English *knee-yoe*.
-ian	As in English alphabetic *Ē* + *yawn*.
-in	As in English *–ēēn*, *bean*, *seen*, *mean*.
-iang	As in English alphabetic *Ē* + **yawn-ggg**.
-ing	As in English *ing*, examples are *sing*, *bring*, and *sting*.

669

-u   As in English *ewe*, examples are *stew*, *do*, *crew*, *moo*.

-ua   As in English *w* plus the *a* in *father*, examples w*a*sh, p*o*sh.

-uo   As in English *woe* or *wah*, **w**ore, **w**orn.

-uai   As in English *why*.

-ui   As in English *way*.

-uan   As in English **wan**der, l**awn**, s**awn**.

-un   As in English **un**, *f*un, *d*one, *s*un.

-uang   As in English *wăng*.

-ong   Starts with the vowel sound in b'**oo**k and ends with the nasal sound in si**ng**, ŏŏ**ng**.

-ü   As in German *ü*ber or French *l*une.

-ue   As ü + ê, the *ü* is short and light as in **üüuh**

-üan   As ü + *on*.

-ün   As ü + **n**.

-iong   As Ē + ŏŏ**ng**.

Explanations and Exceptions to General Rules

1) *ü* is written as *u* after *j*, *q*, *x*, and *y*. *ü* is written as *u* when there is no ambiguity such as *j-u*, *q-u*, and *x-u*. These combinations of Initials and Finals do not phonetically exist. It is written as *ü* when there are corresponding Initial- *ü* syllables such as *lü* and *nü*) In such situations where there are corresponding *ü* syllables, it is often replaced with *v* on computer created correspondence, making it easier to type on a standard keyboard.

2) *uo* is written as *o* after *b*, *p*, *m*, *w*, or *f*. **Hanyu Pinyin** that are actually pronounced as *buo*, *puo*, *muo*, *wuo*, and *fuo* are given a separate written representation as *bo*, *po*, *mo*, *wo*, and *fo*. The pronunciation remains as *buo*, *puo*, *muo*, and *fuo*.

3) The Finals that would be phonetically arranged as, *iou*, *uei*, and *uen* are simplified as *iu*, *ui*, and *un*. This allows the following phonetic changes.

   -iu is pronounced as in English alphabetic *Ē* plus *ewe*. As in English *knee-yoe*.

   -ui is pronounced as in English *way*.

   -ün as **ü** + **n** similar to phonetic *nyun*.

Tones

To counter the effect of having so few combinations of *Initials* and *Finals*, **Hanyu** has distinct tones to give meaning to phonemes. Each *Initial Final* combination has a total of five possible tones. This has the effect of giving five times more distinct phonemes. What appears to be a small number of phonemes is amplified. However, each Initial Final combination does not always have all five tones.

The **Pinyin** system also incorporates markers to represent the four tones of **Hanyu**. Each tone is indicated by a mark above a non-medial vowel. Many books printed in China mix type fonts. This creates vowels with tone marks rendered in a different font than the surrounding text. This a practice that tends to give such **Pinyin** texts a typographically awkward appearance. This style originates from the limitations of the fonts made available to type setters printing literature. These limitations are overcome with electronic type fonts.

Fifth Tone / Zero Tone / Neutral Tone

轻声
Qīngshēng
Light tone

The tone that is neutral to a voice effort is called the *Fifth Tone*, *Zero Tone* or *Neutral Tone*. It is sometimes thought of incorrectly as a lack of tone. The *Neutral Tone* is particularly difficult for non-native speakers to master correctly because of its uncharacteristically large number of contours. The level of its pitch depends almost entirely on the tone carried by the syllable preceding it. It is not possible to end one phoneme without the effect of the *Final* influencing the neutral tone initiation of the next *Initial*. In the transition from one tone to another, there is in fact four short varied tones created that are not the named tones.

The only way to get around this is when you are learning to speak **Hanyu**, you can speak very slowly. This allows you to finish a word completely before you start the next word. This prevents the effect of the previous Final from influencing the coming Initial. This is not an efficient way to speak as it is so slow. However, you will learn to naturally acquire an understandable tone transition.

The learning curve will occur very naturally this way.

First Tone

阴平
Yīnpíng
High-level tone

The first tone is the ***High Level Tone***. It is represented by a macron marker (¯) added to the **Pinyin** vowel or by adding a #1 at the end of the phoneme. To create this tone the speaker lifts his voice to a comfortable reproducible level.

Second Tone

阳平,
Yángpíng
High rising

The second tone is the ***Rising Tone***. It is denoted by an French linguistic acute accent marker (´) or by adding a **#2** at the end of the phoneme. Second tone, or rising tone is a sound that rises from mid-level tone to high. Many books describe the tone raise as being similar to a hearing impaired person saying ***What***? This tone rises from the neutral position to the ***First Tone*** position.

Third Tone

上声
Shàngshēng
Up tone

The third tone is the ***Falling-Rising Tone***. It is symbolized by a grammatical marker caron (ˇ) or a **#3** added to the end of the phoneme. It has a mid-low to low descent, if at the end of a sentence or before a pause. It is then followed by a rising pitch. This tone is created by dropping the pitch from the Neutral Tone to a comfortable, reproducible and distinguishable lower tone.

Fourth Tone

去声
Qùshēng
Away tone

The fourth tone is the ***Falling Tone***. It is represented by a French grammatical grave accent (`) or by adding a **#4** at the end of the phoneme. Fourth tone or falling tone features a sharp downward accent dipping from high to low. It has a short sharp duration. Many books compare the sound to barking the command ***Stop***! This tone is created by quickly dropping the pitch from neutral tone to a tone near the depth of the downward deflection on the third tone.

Loud Tone

China has 1.5 billion people. You will seldom find yourself alone. With hundreds of people on any given bus or train conversation can get very loud. There is a tendency for cell phones to be ringing, music to be blasting and karaoke to being sung. At times like this it is very hard to discriminate tone. As a foreigner, you may find the volume uncomfortably loud. The context of the situation guides the listener as to what is being said. Usually in situations like this the topic is obvious and you will adjust to determine the tones, eventually. It is also difficult to whisper in tones.

Numbers in Place of Tone Marks

I totally cut and pasted and stole this page and table from the internet. So if you did not *get it* from the above discussion, read this. Numbers are useful in typing as the conversion to tone markers is often complex and requires more than one program on your computer. In the appendix I will include a chapter on modifying your computer to make in more useful for Chinese writing. Here is the paragraph I borrowed.

Since most computer fonts do not contain the accents, a common convention is to add a digit representing the tone to the end of individual syllables. For example, *tóng* is written *tong2*. The number used for each tone is as in the table below.

If you have Office 2007 with Word 2007 you can make your computer type **Pinyin** with tone markers if you have the patience. You must add all the variations of **Pinyin** with the tone numbers into your dictionary as equivalents to the **Pinyin** with tone markers. The you set your document to auto correct. That way, when you type **Pinyin** with numbers you can auto correct to **Pinyin** with tone markers. You will find a document to help you with this on the included CD or at the website.

Tone	Tone Mark	Number added to end of syllable in place of tone mark	Example using tone mark	Example using number
First	(ˉ)	1	mā	ma1
Second	(´)	2	má	ma2
Third	(ˇ)	3	mǎ	ma3
Fourth	(`)	4	mà	ma4
Neutral or Fifth	No mark	*no number* *five* *or 0*	ma	ma ma5 ma0

Table above was borrowed from the internet without permission. (stolen)

Rules for Placing the Tone Mark

Tone markings always go above the Final. The rules for determining on which vowel the tone mark appears are as follows.

1. If there is one vowel the tone marker goes above this vowel.

2. If there is more than one vowel and the first vowel is *i*, *u*, or *ü*, then the tone mark appears on the second vowel.

3. In all other cases, the tone mark appears on the first vowel

The reasoning behind these rules is in the case of Finals of more than one vowel, the first vowel may be preserved for pronunciation of the Initial consonant. That is, in phoneme words such as (犬, **quǎn**, **dog**) the correct pronunciation is a two part syllable, similar to *chew on* not *chwan*. The tone change begins with the *ǎn* and the *qu* is preserved in the neutral tone.

There is another algorithm for determining the vowel on which the tone mark appears is as follows:

1. First, look for an *a* or an *e* If either vowel appears, it takes the tone mark. There are no possible **Pinyin** syllables that contain both an *a* and an *e*.
2. If there is no *a* or *e* look for an *ou*. If *ou* appears, then the *o* takes the tone mark.
3. If none of the above cases hold, then the last vowel in the syllable takes the tone mark.

Umlaut

An *umlaut* is placed over the letter *u* when it occurs after the initials *l* and *n* in order to represent the sound *you*. This distinguishes the *you* sound from the *ŏŏ* sound as in *boo*!

Examples:

(驴, **lü**, **donkey**)

versus

(炉, **lú**, **oven**)

Tonal markers can be added on top of the umlaut, as in *lǘ*. However, the *ü* is not used in other contexts where it represents a front high rounded vowel, namely after the letters *j*, *q*, *x* and *y*. For example, the sound of the word (鱼, *yú*, **fish**) is transcribed in **Pinyin** simply as *yú*, not as *yǘ*. Genuine ambiguities only happen with *nu* / *nü* and *lu* / *lü*, which are then distinguished by an umlaut diacritic marker.

Many fonts or input output methods do not support an umlaut for *ü* or cannot place tone marks on top of *ü*. Likewise, using *ü* in input methods is difficult because it is not present as a simple key on many keyboard layouts. Although a computer can be configured to type the umlaut, most do not know how to do it. For these reasons *v* is sometimes typed instead of *ü*.

Tonal Shift Patterns, or Tone Sandhi

As if learning tone is not complicated enough, there are addition rules and patterns of tone shift depending on the surrounding tones. The basis of tonal shift is that the preceding tone affects the following tone. These changes are of course not reflected in writing Chinese characters, the characters are unchanged. Neither are these changes reflected in **Hanyu Pinyin**. The diacritic tone markers remain unchanged. It is only the spoken presentation that changes. Many books alter the official rules to try and make it easier to understand. This is confusing, especially in books that do not provide written characters.

Sequential 1st Tone Rule

Sequential first tones are unchanged.
Example:

Sequential 2nd Tone Rule

Sequential second tones are unchanged.
Example:

Sequential 4th tone Rule

Sequential fourth tones are unchanged.
Example:

Sequential 3rd Tone Rule

A single syllable third tone word preceding a single syllable third tone word changes to a second tone. If there are more than two 3rd tone words of a single syllable, the rules are more complex and not clear. If the sentence has a rhetoric pause between third tones, the first third tone is preserved. This is where a clear understanding of *word* becomes important.

Example: 老鼠, **lǎoshǔ**, becomes **lao2shu4**

Example: 我很好, **wǒ hěn hǎo**, is spoken **wo2 hen2 hao3**

In a character string with a polysyllabic word composed of two characters, each with a third tone, preceding a single syllable third tone word, the first two syllables become 2nd tones, the third syllable retains the 3rd tone.
Example: 保管好, **bǎoguǎn hǎo** is spoken **bao2guan2 hao3**

If the first word is one syllable, and the second word is two syllables, the first syllable becomes a 4th tone, the second syllable becomes 2nd tone, and the last syllable stays 3rd tone.
Example: 老保管, **lǎo bǎoguǎn** is spoken **lao4 bao2guan3**

Tone Changes After the Third Tone

When a character that is assigned a 3rd tone and it is followed by a neutral, first, second or fourth tone, it usually becomes a 4th tone. This tone is oft described as a ***half-third tone*** in that it descends but does not rise. However, it does not fall as far as a full 4th tone. Variably, it may be described as a ***low flat tone***, in that it does not descend but mirrors the first tone in tone profile. You will find dialectal and regional variations to these patterns. The speed of a conversation also affects these changes. There is no convention for assigning numbers or diacritic tone markers for this.

Example: 美妙, **měimiào** becomes **mei4miao4**

Rules for (一, yī, one)

(一, **yī, one**) has special rules which do not apply to other Chinese characters. When in front of a 4th tone syllable, (一, **yī, one**) becomes 2nd tone.

Example: (一定, **yīdìng, certainly**) becomes **yi2ding4**

When (一, **yī, one**) is in front of a 1st, 2nd, or 3rd tone syllable, (一, **yī, one**) becomes 4th tone.

Example: 1st tone (一天, **yītiān**) becomes **yi4 tian1**

Example: 2nd tone (一年, **yīnián**) becomes **yi4 nian2**

Example: 3rd tone (一起, **yīqǐ**) becomes **yi4 qi3**

When (一, **yī, one**) falls between two words, it becomes neutral tone.

Example: 不一样, **bù yī yáng** is spoken **bu4 yi yang2**

When used for numeric counting, and for all other situations, (一, **yī, one**) retains its value of 1st tone.

Rules for (不, bù, not)

(不, **bù, not**) has special rules which do not apply to other Chinese characters. (不, **bù, not**) becomes 2nd tone when followed by a 4th tone syllable.

Example: 不是, **bùshì** becomes **bu2shi4**

When (不, **bù**, **not**) comes between two words, it becomes neutral in tone.

Example: 是不是, **shìbùshì** becomes **shi4 bushi4**

Funny Stuff

Many books available to the learning student are written by people with numerous university degrees in language related fields. They use graphic pictures of human heads cut in cross section showing the position of the tongue inside the mouth. This is supposed to give you an idea as to how you are forming the sounds of **Hanyu**. If you just happen to have access to a human anatomy lab where you can look at heads cut in half, maybe this will help you, somehow. You will find it quicker and more useful if you just slosh your tongue around until the correct sound issues forth. Or buy a recording device to practice.

There is also a ton of words unique to those with Ph.D.'s that are specific to language sciences. Plosives, fricatives, labials, dental alveolars, bilabials, nasal something or another's. This is all just a barrier to learning how to speak. Toss them. Some guy even assigned numbers to the tone contours. Here they are, 55, 35, 214, 51. I have no idea what to do with them or what they mean. When I show this stuff to Chinese people they laugh heartily. The range of tones is variable on the situation. An MC in front of a crowd will make dramatic tonal ranges. An angry taxi driver will speak so fast that tone is near lost. There are many angry taxi drivers in China.

The most important hurdle to learning to speak is the acquisition of a Chinese friend. This is far better than books, tapes, MP3 players or DVD's. If you do not live in an area where there is a large Chinese population, say Antarctica, go to the local Chinese restaurant, Laundromat or computer science department at a local university and put up a sign that says,

我	教	你	英文	你	教	我	汉语
Wǒ	jiāo	nǐ	Yīngwén,	nǐ	jiāo	Wǒ	**Hànyǔ**.
Me	teach	you	English,	you	teach	me	**Hanyu**.

汉语 拼音
Hànyǔ Pīnyīn
Hanyu Pinyin

Pinyin, more formally *Hanyu Pinyin*, is the most commonly used system to assign standardized sounds to Chinese characters. From an English speakers perspective this may sound unusual. However, The Chinese characters represent a written language, not a spoken language. In fact, over the history of the many ethnic groups and regions that eventually became China, over two hundred spoken variants of the written language emerged.

History

The formation of the People's Republic of China (**PRC**) in 1948 lead to educational reforms to increase literacy. The people of the country were largely uneducated with 80% being illiterate. 57 ethnic groups spoke over 200 languages. In 1954, the Ministry of Education of the PRC struck a Committee for the Reform of the Chinese Written Language. This committee developed a unified system of sounds so that each Chinese character could be expressed the same throughout the different ethnic groups and regions of China.

This system was named **Hanyu Pinyin**. The (汉, **Hàn**, **Han**) are the ethnic majority group of China. **Hanyu** means the Han language from (汉, **Hàn**, **Han**) and (语, **yǔ**, **language**). **Pinyin** is formed from (拼, **pīn**, **spell**) and (音, **yīn**, **sound**).

Together, the characters (汉语 拼音, **Hànyǔ Pīnyīn**, **Hanyu Pinyin**) identify the language of the ethnic Han majority and the phonetics used to standardize it.

The pivotal work behind **Hanyu Pinyin** was done by Professor Zhou Youguang. Zhou was an American working in the New York banking system. With the end of the civil war in China in 1948, he decided to return to China to help rebuild the country. He became an economics professor in Shanghai. The government assigned him to help the development of a new Romanization system.

The Cultural Revolution began in 1957. Chairman Mao oversaw the execution of millions of literate Chinese. Doctors, lawyers, teachers, and the educated were all suspect. American trained economists were high on the list, however, Zhou was spared. The switch to language and writing largely saved him from the wrath of the Cultural Revolution of Mao Zedong.

The first draft was published on February 12, 1956. The first edition of ***Hanyu Pinyin*** was approved and adopted at the Fifth Session of the 1st National People's Congress on February 11, 1958. It was introduced to primary schools as a way to teach Standard Mandarin pronunciation. This made a major impact on literacy.

Romanization versus Anglisization

The Chinese characters are not phonetically driven. That is, you cannot determine the pronunciation from looking at the character, generally. This allowed different ethnic groups that adopted the written language to assign their own sounds to the characters. With the unification of China and increased migration within the country, this caused a biblical Babel.

Many efforts were made by the West to use the Roman based alphabet to assign sounds to the Chinese characters. Several systems evolved. The goal of **Hanyu Pinyin** was to forever create a standardized system developed by China that made use of the previous systems such as Wade and Wade-Gillis. Thus the rules and system of **Hanyu Pinyin** were struck.

Romanization refers to a method in which the English speaking world takes a non-alphabetic language that is composed of non-phonetically driven symbols or logograms and assign sounds using the Roman alphabet. The phonetics of **Hanyu Pinyin** generally follow the phonetics of the English alphabet, with some exceptions. **Hanyu Pinyin** is thus Romanized yet only partially Anglisized.

Pinyin replaced older Romanization systems such as Wade-Giles which was developed in 1859, modified Wade-Gillis in 1892 and the Chinese Postal Map system of Romanization.

The International Organization for Standardization (ISO) adopted **Hanyu Pinyin** as the standard Romanization for modern Chinese in 1982 as ISO 7098. This was superseded by ISO 7098 in 1991. The United Nations adopted it as an official and standardized Mandarin Romanization system in 1986. It has also been accepted by the government of Singapore, the Library of Congress, the American Library Association, and many other international institutions.

Hanyu Pinyin will also be the official ISO Romanization system in the Taiwan Republic of China starting in 2009.

In 2001, the Chinese Government issued the *National Common Language Law*, providing a legal basis for applying **Hanyu Pinyin**.

Rules of Pinyin

Pinyin differs from other Romanizations in several aspects. However, since we are not studying the other systems such as Wade Giles, it does not matter. This is not a history of Romanization but rather the modern state of affairs. Many books take great freedom in including their own altered rules of **Pinyin**, usually at the beginning of the book. Since **Pinyin** was fabricated recently, it was put together by committees, not history and time. Thus, there are rules. This book will follow the rules.

Use of the Apostrophe

In a situation in which two characters form one word, the two **Hanyu Pinyin** are joined together. However, this can create a situation in which a **Hanyu Pinyin** ending in a vowel and a **Hanyu Pinyin** beginning with a vowel appear as another single **Hanyu Pinyin**. The apostrophe marker ' is thus used before *a*, *o*, and *e* to separate syllables in a word where ambiguity could arise.

Examples:
(皮袄, **pí'ǎo, fur quilted jacket**) versus (票, **piào, ticket**)
(西安, *Xī'ān*, **Xian**) versus (先, *xiān*, **before, first**)

Word Formation

Ambiguity can exist in partitioning words. Each character is a single syllable sound. However, many words, being composed of two or more characters hence form polysyllabic **Hanyu Pinyin** words. Spacing between words is based on separating **Hanyu Pinyin** words, not single syllables. Generally, the separation is based on taking character compilations that form words and separating them as distinct **Hanyu Pinyin**. Simply, words, not characters, stand alone. If the world could get China to do the same with characters, that is, separating words with a space, learning and identifying compound character words would be much easier.

However, there are often ambiguities in partitioning a word due to the alphabetic structure of **Hanyu Pinyin**. Orthographic rules were put into effect in 1988 by the,

National Educational Commission of China
(State Education Commission)
国家教育委员会
Guójiā Jiàoyù Wěiyuánhuì

and the

National Language Commission of China
(National Language Writing Working Committee)
国家语言文字工作委员会
Guójiā Yǔyán Wénzì Gōngzuo Wěiyuánhuì

These above committee titles demonstrate the uninterrupted strings of Chinese characters, the **Hanyu Pinyin** words, and the literal versus common translation. Please note that in the first title, the word China does not appear in the character string but it appears in the translation. This is a good example of the randomness of some translations.

Single Meaning

Words that are created from **Hanyu Pinyin** that in combination or alone have a single meaning and are distinct recognizable combinations are written as one word and not capitalized.

Examples:

rén, 人, **person**

pǎo, 跑, **run**

hǎo, 好, **good**

hé, 和, **and**

hěn, 很, **very**

fúróng, 芙蓉, **cotton rose**

qiǎokèlì, 巧克力, **chocolate**

péngyou, 朋友, **friend**

diànhuà, 电话, **telephone**

yuèdú, 阅读, **reading**

dìzhèn, 地震, **earth quake**

niánqīng, 年轻, **young**

zhòngshì, 重视, **takes**

wǎnhuì, 晚会, **party**

qiānmíng, 签名, **signature**

shìwēi, 示威, **demonstration**

niǔzhuǎn, 扭转, **reverse**

chuánzhī, 船只, **ship**

dànshì, 但是, **but**

fēicháng, 非常, **extremely**

diànshìjī, 电视机, **television**

túshūguǎn, 图书馆, **library**

These above **Hanyu Pinyin** do not occur in the compiled format with the given tones for any other commonly spoken words.

Combined Meaning

Two And Three Character Words

Words created by combining two words or three words to have one meaning are written together.

Examples:

gāngtiě, 钢铁, **steel and iron**

wèndá, 问答, **question and answer**

hǎifēng, 海风, **sea breeze**

hóngqí, 红旗, **Red Flag**

dàhuì, 大会, **congress**

quánguó, 全国, **nation**

zhòngtián, 种田, **farms**

kāihuì, 开会, **holds a meeting**

dǎpò, 打破, **to break**

zǒulái, 走来, **walks**

húshuō, 胡说, **nonsense**

dǎnxiǎo, 胆小, **timidly**

qiūhǎitáng, 秋海棠, **begonia**

duìbuqǐ, 对不起, **sorry**

chīdexiāo, 吃得消, **able to endure**

àiniǎozhōu, 爱鸟周, **to like bird week**

Four Character Words

Words created by combining 4 or more characters are split up into constituent words with identified meaning. This rule is also used for compilations of more than 4 characters. **Hanyu Pinyin** words created by more than one character are separated in whole word units.

Examples:

wúfèng gāngguǎn, 无缝钢管, seamless steel-tube,

huánjìng bǎohù guīhuà, 环境保护规划, environmental protection planning,

jīngtǐguǎn gōnglǜ fàngdàqì, 晶体管功率放大器, Transistor power amplifier

Zhōnghuá Rénmín Gònghéguó, 中华人民共和国, People's Republic of China

Yánjiūshēngyuàn, 研究生院, graduate school

Hóngshízìhuì, 红十字会, Red Cross

Yúxīngcǎosù, 鱼腥草素, cordate houttuynia element

Gǔshēngwùxuéjiā, 古生物学家, paleontologist

Zhōngguó Shèhuì Kēxuéyuàn,
中国社会科学院,
China Academy Social Sciences

Duplicated Characters AA, AABB and ABAB

AA

When words are formed from characters that are duplicated in the form AA, they are written together.

Examples:

rénrén, 人人, **everybody**　　　　**gègè**, 个个, **each one**

kànkàn, 看看, **to have a look**　　**dàda**, 大大, **big**

niánnián, 年年, **yearly**　　　　　**shuōshuo**, 说说, **to say**

tiāntiān, 天天, **everyday**　　　　**hónghóng de**, 红红的, **red**

ABAB

When two characters are duplicated in the form ABAB they are separated into two AB words repeated.

Examples:

yánjiū yánjiū, 研究研究, **to study, to research**

xuěbái xuěbáide, 雪白雪白的, **snow-white**

chángshì chángshì, 尝试尝试, **attempts**

tōnghóng tōnghóngde, 通红通红的, **very red**

AABB

A hyphen is used with the schema AABB. The words are duplicated and separated with a hyphen.

Examples:

láilái-wǎngwǎng, 来来往往, **go back and forth**

qiānqiān-wànwàn, 千千万万, **numerous**

qīqī-bābā, 七七八八, **miscellaneous**

qīngqīng-chǔchǔ, 清清楚楚, **clear**

jiājiā-hùhù, 家家户户, **all families, each and every family**

shuōshuo-xiàoxiào, 说说笑笑, **chats**

wānwān-qūqū, 弯弯曲曲, **curving**

Abbreviations

For for ease of reading and understanding, the hyphen is used in certain situations. Words that are easily understood may be eliminated.

Examples:

huán-bǎo, 环保, versus **huánjìng bǎohù**, 环境保护, environmental protection

bā-jiǔ tiān, 八九天, versus 八十九天, eighty-nine days

rén-jī duìhuà, 人机对话, versus 人和机器的对话, man-machine dialog

lù-hǎi-kōngjūn, 陆海空军, land-sea-air armed forces

gōng-guān, 公关, versus **gōnggòng guānxì**, 公共关系, public relations

shíqī-bā suì, 十七八岁, versus **shíqī shíbā suì**, 十七十八岁, 17-18 years

zhōng-xiǎoxué, 中小学, versus **zhōngxué-xiǎoxué**, 中学小学, middle school-junior school

Common Nouns and People Nouns

Common Nouns formed from multiple characters are written as one **Hanyu Pinyin** word.

Examples:

zhuōzi, 桌子, **table**

mùtou, 木头, **wood**

fùbùzhǎng, 副部长, **vice minister**

chéngwùyuán, 乘务员, **conductor**

háizimen, 孩子们, **children**

fēijīnshǔ, 非金属, **nonmetallic**

chāoshēngbō, 超声波, **ultrasonic wave**

zǒnggōngchéngshī, 总工程师, **chief engineer**

fēiyèwù rényuán, 非业务人员, **non-servicers**

fǎndàndào dǎodàn, 反弹道导弹, **antimissile missile**

chéngwùyuán, 乘务员, **train attendant**

kēxuéxìng, 科学性, **scientific nature**

yìshùjiā, 艺术家, **artist**

xiàndàihuà, 现代化, **modernization**

tuōlājīshǒu, 拖拉机手, **tractor driver**

Words of Position

Words of position acting as prepositions forming locative phrases are separated. Although standard Mandarin grammar is very similar to English, locative phrases are composed with the locative particle in the sentence final position.

Examples:

mén wàimiàn, 门 外面, **door outside, outdoors,**

hé lǐmiàn, 河里面, **river inside, in the river**

huǒchē shàngmiàn, 火车上面, **train upon, on the train**

Huáng Hé yǐnán, 黄河以南, **Yellow River by south, south of Yellow River**

shān shàngmiàn, 山上面, **mountain upon, on mountain**

Yǒngdìng Hé shàng, 永定河上, **Yongding river on, on Yongdong River**

shù xià, 树下, **tree under, under the tree**

xuéxiào pángbiān, 学校旁边, **school nearby**

Exceptions

Words traditionally connected continue to be connected in **Hanyu Pinyin**.

Examples:

tiānshàng, 天上, **at the sky**

dìxià, 地下, **floor on, on the floor**

kōngzhōng, 空中, **in the air**

hǎiwài, 海外, **sea away, overseas**

Chinese Personal Names

Family names are separated from the given name. If the given name consists of two syllables, they should be written together. All proper person names are capitalized.

Examples:

Lú XuéFèng, 卢学凤

Lǐ Huá, 李花

Lǔ Xùn, 鲁迅

Zhāng Sān, 张三

Name Titles

Titles names follow the Proper name. The title is separated and not capitalized.

Examples:

Wáng bùzhǎng, 王部长, **Wang minister**

Lǐ xiānshēng, 李先生, **Li Mister**

Tián zhǔrèn, 田主任, **Tian director**

Zhào tóngzhì, 赵同志, **Zhao comrade**

The honorific and respectful forms of addressing people with *Lǎo*, *Xiǎo*, *Dà* and *A* are capitalized: These forms of address come after the Proper Name.

Xiǎo Liú, 小刘, **young Liu**

Dà Lǐ, 大李, **elder Li**

A Sān, 阿三, **honourable San**

Lǎo Wú, 老吴, **senior Wu**

Lǎo Qián, 老钱, **elder Qian**

Exceptions are:

Kǒngzǐ, 孔子, **Master Confucius**

Bāogōng, 包公, **Bao Judge**

Xīshī, 西施, **Xishi, a historical person**

Mèngchángjūn, 孟尝君, **Mèngchángjūn, a historical person**

Geographical Names of China

Proper Noun location names are compounded together and any other designation is separated. Proper Nouns are capitalized as in English.

Examples:

Běijīng Shì, 北京市, **Beijing City**

Yālù Jiāng, 鸭绿江, **Yalu Stream**

Héběi Shěng, 河北省, **Hebei Province**

Tài Shān, 泰山, **Tai Mountain**

Dòngtíng Hú, 洞庭湖, **Donting Lake**

Táiwān Hǎixiá, 台湾海峡, **Taiwan Strait**

When a Proper Noun has additional characters that further define the location, each noun phrase is kept together as a single **Hanyu Pinyin**. Precision in location always works and thus locative words become entrenched into the Proper name.

Examples:

Xīliáo Hé, 西辽河, **Xiliao River**

Jǐngshān Hòujiē, 景山后街, **Jingshan Backstreet**

Cháoyángménnèi Nánxiǎojiē, 朝阳门内南小街, **Chaoyang Gate Inside, South Alley**

Many villages, towns and features are written as one **Hanyu Pinyin** with the usual capitalized geographic name joined to the location feature name.

Examples:

Wángcūn, 王村, **Wang Village**

Sāntányìnyuè, 三潭印月, **three pools reflecting the moon**

Jiǔxiānqiáo, 酒仙桥, **Jiuxian bridge**

Zhōukǒudiàn, 周口店, **Zhōukǒu store**

Non-Chinese Proper Nouns and Names

There is great creativity and confusion with the methodology in which the Chinese translate non-Chinese names into **Hanyu Pinyin** and **Hanzi**. Some **Hanyu Pinyin** are attempts to phonetically mirror the sounds of the non-Chinese Proper Nouns.

Examples:

Marx, 马克思, **Mǎkèsī**

Newton, 牛顿, **Niúdùn**

Washington, 华盛顿, **Huáshèngdùn**

London, 伦敦, **Lúndūn**

Others provide descriptives from a Chinese perspective.

Examples:

Dōngnányà, 东南亚, **east south Asia (South East Asia)**

Měiguó, 美国, **beautiful country (America)**

Dōngjīng, 东京, **east capital (Tokyo)**

Nánměi, 南美, **south beautiful (South America)**

The remainder are somewhat mystifying.

Examples:

Paris, 巴黎, **Bālí**

Akutagawa Ryunosuke, 芥川龙之介, **jiè chuān lóng zhī jiè**

Seypidin, 赛福鼎, **Sàifúdǐng**

Fēizhōu, 非洲, **evil continent (Africa)**

Déguó, 德国, **morality country (Germany)**

Verbs
Dòngcí
动词

Verbs and the characters affixed to them as grammatical particle suffixes such as (着, **zhe**), (了, **le**) and (过, **guo**) are written as one word.

(着, **zhe, durative grammatical particle**) is added to a verb to indicate and ongoing process. Functionally, it acts as *–ing* added to an English verb.

(了, **le, completed verb action particle**) is added to a verb to indicate the completion of the verb action.

(过, **guo, experiential verb particle**) is added to a verb to indicate initial exposure to an action.

Examples:

kànzhe, 看着, **seeing, looking**　　**jìnxíngzhe**, 进行着, **to attempting**

kànle, 看了, **saw, looked**　　**jìnxíngle**, 进行了, **attempted**

kànguo, 看过, **seeing**　　**jìnxíngguo**, 进行过, **attempt**

The sentence final particle 了, **le**, indicating a new state or immediacy, is written separately.

Example:

Huǒchē dào le, 火车到了, **train arrived**

Verbs Object Compounds

Verbs and their objects are separated:

Examples:

kàn xìn, 看信, **read letter**

chī yú, 吃鱼, **eat fish**

kāi wánxiào, 开玩笑, **to be joking**

jiāoliú jīngyàn, 交流经验, **exchange experience**

In situations in which a Verb Object phrase word has numeric qualifiers, the quantitative adjectival phrase is inserted within the verb phrase following the appropriate rules.

Examples:

jūle gōng, 鞠了躬, **bowed body**

jūle yī gè gōng, 鞠了一个躬, bowed one body

lǐguo fà, 理过发, manages sent

lǐguo sān cì fà, 理过三次发, manages three times has sent

Verb Compliment Compounds

If one verb and it's complement verb are both monosyllabic and form a compound, they are written as one **Hanyu Pinyin**

Examples:

gǎohuài, 搞坏, causes to break down

jiànchéng, 建成, completes (such as a project)

shútòu, 熟透, thoroughly ripe

huàwéi, 化为, changes into

dǎsǐ, 打死, beat kill

If the verb or the compliment are polysyllabic they are written separately and two or more distinct **Hanyu Pinyin** are formed.

Examples:

zǒu jìnlái, 走进来, go forth enter come / go forth into

zhěnglǐ hǎo, 整理好, reorganizes well

jiànshè chéng, 建设成, construction becoming, constructs, builds

gǎixiě wéi, 改写为, rewrite for

Adjectives
Xíngróngcí
形容词

A one syllable adjective and its duplication are written as one and the complement is added to it to form one continuous **Hanyu Pinyin**.

Example:

mēngmēngliàng, 蒙蒙亮, **cover cover light, dim, dawn**

liàngtāngtāng, 亮堂堂, **shining bright**

Complement of Size or Degree Adjectives

Complements of size or degree are written separated from the word they qualify. They are written after the involved verb. Duplication acts to increase the quality of the duplicated adjective. Duplicates are written continuously.

Example:

Yīdiǎndiǎnr, 一点点儿, is less than **yīdiǎnr**, 一点儿.

Examples:

xiē 些, **few, some**

yīxiē, 一些, **a few**

diǎnr, 点儿, **little**

yīdiǎnr, 一点儿, **a little**

yīdiǎndiǎnr, 一点点儿, **a little**

dà xiē, 大些, **big some**,

dà yīxiē, 大一些, **big a little**

kuài yīdiǎnr, 快一点儿, **fast a little**

kuài diǎnr, 快点儿, **fast a little**

Pronouns
Dàicí
代词

Personal Pronouns

(们, **men, plural suffix for pronouns and human nouns**), the plural suffix is compounded with the root noun or pronoun to form a compound **Hanyu Pinyin** word written continuously.

Examples:

wǒmen, 我们, we / us

tāmen, 他们, they

nǐmen, 你们, you (plural)

zánmen, 咱们, we / us

háizimen, 孩子们, children

lǎoshīmen, 老师们, teachers

nánshìmen, 男士们, gentlemen

nǚshìmen, 女士们, ladies

Demonstrative Pronouns
指示代词
Zhǐshì Dàicí

Demonstrative pronouns acting as definite articles are written separately from the target subject or object of a sentence. The grammatical affixes 些, 里, 儿, 边, and 个 are added continuously with the demonstrative pronouns.

zhè / zhèi, 这, this
zhèxiē, 这些, these
zhèr, 这儿, here
nà / nèi, 那, that
nàxiē, 那些, those
nàli, 那里, there
gāi, 该, this

zhèli, 这里, here
zhèbian, 这边, this side / here
zhège / zheige, 这个, this one
nèige, 那个, that one / that piece
nàr, 那儿, there
běn, 本市, this

Examples:

zhè rén, 这人, this person
zhèxiē rén, 这些人, these person
dào zhèr lái, 到这儿来, to here come
dào nàr qù, 到那儿去, to there go
tā yào nàgè, 他要那个, he want that one
wǒ yào zhègè, 我要这个, I want this one

běn bùmén, 本部门, this department
nà cì huìyì, 那次会议, that conference
gāi kān, 该刊, this publication
gāi gōngsī, 该公司, this company
nàxiē cì huìyì, 那些次会议, those conference

Quantitative Adjectives

Modifers of nouns that add a quantitative adjectival quality are written separate from the target noun. As these can modify countable nouns, the **Countable Noun Indicator** is also written separately.

gè, 各, **each**

měi, 每, **each**

mǒu, 某, **some, a certain**

Examples:

gè gè, 各个, **each**

gè guó, 各国, **each country**

měi nián, 每年, **every year**

mǒu rén, 某人, **somebody**

měi cì, 每次, **each time**

gè rén, 各人, **each person**

gè xuékē, 各学科, **various disciplines**

Numbers

For numbers between eleven and one hundred, write them continuously.

Examples:

shíyī, 十一, **eleven**
shíwǔ, 十五, **fifteen**
sānshísān, 三十三, **thirty three**
jiǔshíjiǔ, 九十九, **ninety nine**

For one hundred, one thousand, ten thousand, and one hundred million, the number in the first position is continuous with the larger number.

Examples:

jiǔbǎi, 九百, **900**

sānqiān, 三千, **3000**

liùwàn, 六万, **60,000**

sìyì, 四亿, **400,000,000**

Ordinal numbers are separated with a hyphen.

Examples:

dì-yī, 第一, **first**

dì-èrshíbā, 第二十八, **28th**

dì-shísān, 第十三, **13th**

dì-sānbǎi wǔshíliù, 第三百五十六, **356th**

Number, Countable Noun Indicator and Target Noun

Countable Nouns (**CN**) are preceded by a *Quantitative Adjective* (**QA**) and a *Countable Noun Indicator* (**CNI**). **CNI**'s are variably called measure words or classifiers. The **QA**, **CNI** and **CN** are all separated. The **QA** can be an absolute number such as (两, **liǎng, two**) or can be a relative numeric indicator such as (多, **duō, many**), (几, **jǐ, several**) and (些, **xiē, a few**).

Examples:

liǎng gè rén, 两个人, two people

liǎng jiān bàn wūzi, 两间半屋子, two-and-a-half rooms

yī dà wǎn fàn, 一大碗饭, a large bowl food

wǔshísān réncì, 五十三人次, 53 people

yībǎi duō gè, 一百多个, 100 more, more than one hundred, 100 plus

jǐ jiā rén, 几家人, several family members

shí lái wàn rén, 十来万人, ten come ten thousand people

jǐ tiān gōngfu, 几天工夫, several day of free time

jǐshí, 几十, several dozen

shíjǐ gè rén, 十几个人, several people

jǐshí gēn gāngguǎn, 几十根钢管, several dozens steel pipes

Adverbs
副词
Fùcí

Adverbs are written separately from other words.
Examples:

hěn hǎo, 很好, **very good**

bù lái, 不来, **not come**

zuì dà, 最大, **most big**

fēicháng kuài, 非常快, **very quick**

dōu lái, 都来, **always comes**

gèng měi, 更美, **more beautiful**

Prepositions
介词
Jiècí

Prepositions are written separately.
Examples:

zài qiánmiàn, 在前面, **at frontside**

wèi rénmín fúwù, 为人民服务, **for people serves**

shēng yú 1940 nián, 生于1940年, **born in 1940 year**

xiàng dōngbiān qù, 向东边去, **toward eastside go**

cóng zuótiān qǐ, 从昨天起, **from yesterday**

guānyú zhègè wèntí, 于这个问题, **about this question**

Conjunctions
连词
Liáncí

Conjunctions are always written separately.

Examples:

gōngrén hé nóngmín, 工人和农民, worker and farmer

guāngróng ér jiānjù, 光荣而艰巨, honorable and arduous

bùdàn kuài érqiě hǎo, 不但快而且好, not only quick moreover good

Nǐ lái háishi bù lái, 你来还是不来, you come or not come

Structural Auxiliaries
结构助词
Jiégōu Zhùcí

的, **de**, possessive, modifying, or descriptive particle, of

地, **de**, subordinate particle adverbial, -ly

得, **dé**, adverbial particle

之, **zhī**, literary equivalent of 的 as a subordinate particle

Examples:

dàdì de nǚ' ér, 大地的女儿, earth daughter

zhè shì wǒ de shū, 这是我的书, this is my book

wǒmen guòzhe xìngfú de shēnghuó, 我们过着幸福的生活, we happy life

mài qīngcài luóbo de, 卖青菜萝卜的, sells green vegetables radish

tā mànman de zǒu, 他慢慢地走, he walk slowly

tǎnbái de gàosù nǐ ba, 坦白地告诉你吧, tells you honestly

dǎsǎo de gānjìng, 打扫得干净, cleans cleanly

hóng de hěn, 红得很, red very

xiě de bù hǎo, 写得不好, writes not good

lěng de fādǒu, 冷得发抖, is cold trembles

shàonián zhī jiā, 少年之家, children's club

zuì fādá de guójiā zhī yī, 最发达的国家之一, one of most developed national

Modal Particles
语气助词
Yǔqì Zhùcí

Particles indicating moods are written separately.

Examples:

Nǐ zhīdào ma?, 你知道吗, **You know?**

Zěnme hái bù lái a?, 怎么还不来啊, **How yet not come?**

Kuài qù ba!, 快去吧!, **Quick go!**

Tā shì bù huì lái de. 他是不会来的, **He is not able to come.**

Interjectives
叹词
Tàncí

Examples:

A! Zhēn měi!, 啊!真美, **Ah!, Really beautiful!**

Nnng, nǐ shuō shénme?, 嗯,你说什么, **You say what?**

Hmmph!, zǒuzhe qiáo ba!, 哼走着瞧吧, **Humph!, wait and see!**

Onomatopoeia
拟声词
Nǐshēngcí

pā!, 啪, **pa!**

jīji-zhāzhā, 叽叽喳喳, **chirp chirp**

huá huá, 哗哗, **whish whish**

hōnglōng yī shēng, 轰隆一声, **bang!, One time**

Dà gōngjī wō-wō-tí., 大公鸡喔喔啼, **Big cockerel wo-wo cries.**

Dū, qìdí xiǎng le. 嘟,汽笛响了, *"du"*, **the steam whistle made a sound.**

Idioms
成语
Chéngyǔ

Four word idioms are divided into two double syllables interpersed with a hyphen.

céngchū-bùqióng, 层出不穷, **emerges one after another incessantly**

àizēng-fēnmíng, 爱憎分明, **is clear about what to love and what to hate**

yángyáng-dàguān, 洋洋大观, **spectacular**

guāngmíng-lěiluò, 光明磊落, **frank**

fēngpíng-làngjìng, 风平浪静, **uneventful**

píngfēn-qiūsè, 平分秋色, **shares half and half**

diānsān-dǎosì, 颠三倒四, **disorderly**

There are four word idioms which are written continuously.

bùyìlèhū, 不亦乐乎, **delight**

àimònéngzhù, 爱莫能助, **wants to help but not be able**

húlihútu, 糊里糊涂, **bewildered**

diàoerlángdāng, 吊儿郎当, **careless**

zǒngéryánzhī, 总而言之, **in brief**

yīyīdàishuǐ, 一衣带水, **close**

hēibuliūqiū, 黑不溜秋, **swarthy**

Capital Letters
大写
Dàxiě

The first word in sentences and poetry each begin with a capital letter. Proper Nouns each begin with a capital letter.

Examples:

Běijīng, 北京, **Beijing**

Chángchéng, 长城, **Great Wall (long wall)**

Qīngmíng, 清明, **Pure Brightness (a city)**

For a Proper Noun which is composed of several words, each words first letter has a capital letter.

Examples:

Guójì Shūdiàn, 国际书店, **International Bookstore**

Guāngmíng Rìbào, 光明日报, **Guangming Daily**

Hépíng Bīnguǎn, 和平宾馆, **Peaceful Guesthouse**

When a Proper Noun forms a word with a Common Noun the word is written continuously. The Proper Noun is capitalized and the common noun is not.

Examples:

Zhōngguórén, 中国人, **Chinese person**

Míngshǐ, 明史, **Ming Dynasty history (Ming Dynasty is** 明朝, **Míng cháo)**

Guǎngdōnghuà, 广东话, **Cantonese (the spoken language of Guangdong province)**

There are some words that through common use have changed into common nouns. The first letter is therefore a small letter.

Examples:

guǎnggān, 广柑, **sweet orange**

zhōngshānfú, 中山服, **Chinese tunic**

chuānxiōng, 川芎, **rhizome of Ligusticum wallichii**

zàngqīngguǒ, 藏青果, **terminalia**

Dividing and Hyphenating Words

Dividing and hyphenating words to carry on to the next sentence must be done at the completion of a syllable. A hyphen is used between the two syllables.

Example:
(光明, **guāngmíng**, **bright**, **promising**)

Guāngmíng is split between the syllables forming the compound word, **guāng-míng**. The format **gu-āngmíng** cannot be used.

Tone Marker Placement

1. First, look for an *a* or an *e*. If either vowel appears, it takes the tone mark. There are no possible **Pinyin** syllables that contain both an *a* and an *e*.
2. If there is no *a* or *e*, look for an *ou*. If *ou* appears, then the *o* takes the tone mark.
3. If none of the above cases hold, then the last vowel in the syllable takes the tone mark.

The reasoning behind these rules is in the case of diphthongs and triphthongs, *i*, *u*, and *ü* are considered medial glides rather than part of the syllable nucleus in Chinese phonology. The rules ensure that the tone mark always appears on the nucleus of a syllable.

Another way to find the vowel for a tone mark is to apply the tone mark in the following order: *a*, *e*, *o*, *i*, *u*, except for *iu*, in which case *u* takes the tone mark.

The Character Ü

An umlaut is placed over the letter *u* when it occurs after the initials *l* and *n*. This is necessary in order to distinguish the front high rounded vowel in *lü* from the back high rounded vowel in *lu*. Tonal markers are added on top of the umlaut, as in *lǘ*.

However, the *ü* is *not* used in other contexts where it represents a front high rounded vowel, namely after the letters *j*, *q*, *x* and *y*. Genuine ambiguities only happen with *nu / nü* and *lu / lü*, which are then distinguished by an umlaut diacritic.

Chinese Learning Websites

Cautionary Statement, Internet Rules

1) That which is on the internet today may not be there tomorrow.

2) The internet is the final resting ground for opinion, errors and misdirection.

3) Wikipedia is particularly unreliable as any enthusiast can edit it.

4) Self declared experts with grammar and spell check can seem very authoritative.

5) Some sites offering audio clips of **Pinyin** phonemes are particularly unreliable and entertaining.

6) University sites seem more reliable but less visually interesting.

7) It is far easier to find fee sites than free sites.

8) Much of what you need is there for free if you can find it but it is scattered across many sites.

9) Most sites you sign up for do not offer a simple cancellation, they will keep auto debiting your credit card.

10) The web site with pictures of me in a brothel with three girls in Chengdu was an interview I was doing.

How to Find the Ultimate Tools

There are many poor quality books, tapes, CD's, DVD's and flashcards on the market, many that I have bought. Learn from my mistakes. Some rules.

1) If it can fit in your pocket it is not good because the font is too small to read.

2) If it does not have English, **Pinyin** and Characters it is relatively useless.

3) If it gets too creative with translations it will impede your understanding of grammar.

4) If it is made of that super thin onion skin paper it makes excellent toilet paper. Which, when you go to China, you will always find a shortage of.

5) If you buy a character book and it does not have the characters for rice, eat, train and middle, the writer has never been to China and the book may be useless.

6) Nobody has cassette tape players anymore, why buy cassettes?

7) Big multi-coloured boxes can have surprisingly little in them. Open and inspect.

8) Eight CD sets often have enough information to be all fit onto one CD, with lots of room left over.

9) Do not assume that a position at a university or a Ph.D. makes the book better. The worst grammar books I have are written by grammar professors. Even my Chinese friends do not understand some of the grammar constructions.

10) Books written by Cantonese Chinese may have slightly different sentence constructions.

11) Introductory character writing or grammar books with sentences with more than five words or characters are too advanced for a beginner.

My Personal Favorite Web Sites

www.SpeakandWriteChinese.com

This is my website. It is in the building phase. I am going to try and gradually introduce everything that you will need. I am working on building a database that anyone can add to to add words, sentences and phrases. Ultimately I will write a program to write English, **Hanzi** and **Pinyin** at the same time. It will also have a review for books, CDs, DVDs, websites and other learning resources. You will be able to order any of my books, flash cards and CD's from this site. First I have to learn to use a computer. At this date it is invaded with bots and I cannot access it!

www.mandarintools.com

This is hands down the best web site for character information in a dictionary format and it is free. Everything you need is there, dictionary, conversion utilities, the CEDICT database. There is even some useful grammar and sentence structure. The interface is a little awkward and unrevealing. If you delve into it and open everything it is a treasure of information and programs. They accept contributions. You can download their great stand alone program *DimSum* for free. You can also download the CEDICT database.

www.zhongwen.com

This is a great website for researching the Radicals and etymology of characters. The interface is easy to use. It also links to the Ocrat database, sometimes. The interface makes it easy to navigate quickly. The site is a no charge site. I feel that this is the best site for research and it shows the learner a fascinating look at how characters within a group evolved.

http://lost-theory.org/ocrat

This site has an easy to use interface and provides animated stroke order access. This side has common family names, P.R.C. provinces and other difficult to find but interesting characters. This site is a no charge site. Personally, I do not feel a great need to watch the stroke order of every character. I feel it is better to learn the rules of stroke order.

www.sexybeijing.tv

This website details the adventures of Su Fei, a girl from California who goes around creating adventure in Beijing. She takes her name from a brand name product line of women's sanitary pads. She is so funny and it is a great place to learn conversational Mandarin. Her videos are easiest to access at www.sexybeijing.tv. These videos give you a nice exposure to the real life for citizens of a big Chinese city. I think she has gone home now, no more new videos.

www.chinesesavvy.com

This site has a nice profile of everything you need to learn to function in China. It is expensive and in some of the paid features the native Beijingers talk so fast it is hardly an introduction to spoken Mandarin. There is little English translation of these conversations.They have a great forum for discussing any issues in China. However, the moderator edits out any issues that are controversial in China.

www.chineselearner.com

This is a great website and is rapidly getting bigger and better. It is being updated often so sometimes is does not fire up immediately. The moderators are friendly and they respond to e-mails quickly. Most of what they offer is currently free. Oddly there are lessons offered in the **Hanyu Pinyin** section that are not translated from **Hanzi**.

http://www.csulb.edu/~txie/**Pinyin/Pinyin**.htm

This is a great website that has all you need to get your computer to type **Pinyin** and convert to **Hanzi**, in fact, it is more useful than the Microsoft embedded utility. If you have a bootleg Windows and cannot access Microsoft free downloads, this is the solution. I carry it on my USB wherever I go.

http://www.globechinese.com/

Chinese Character Bible or **Hanzi** Explorer 9.2 is an animated character writing program with pronunciation. It is a free shareware download. It has a colourful interface and is easy to use. Oddly, it does not show **Pinyin** when it demonstrates a character. So you are left to try and figure out the **Pinyin** or plug it into another program.

http://babelfish.yahoo.com/

This is a translator program that can interconvert **Hanzi** and English. Like all such programs the **Hanzi** to English and English to **Hanzi** is somewhat speculative.

http://xenomachina.com/toys/Pinyin2Hanzi.html

This site has a program that takes **Pinyin** and converts it to **Hanzi** to give you choices of characters.

http://technology.chtsai.org/

This is a great website for statistics of word frequency and links to useful word lists. There is also a hard to find list of Chinese names. These lists can save you hundreds of hours if you are writing a book. This is a must have site for the committed learner.

http://www.Pinyin.info/

This website is full of useful tools for manipulating **Pinyin**. It has all the official rules of **Pinyin** along with conversion tools, spell checker and how to set up your computer for Chinese usage. There is also a comparison of the different Romanisation systems, which is very comprehensive

http://www.uni.edu/becker/chinese2.html

This website offers links to multitudes of other Chinese learning websites. The interface is easy and very colourful.

http://www.rci.rutgers.edu/~rsimmon/chingram/

This site has a good section on Mandarin Grammar but it lacks explanation. It appears to be a slide presentation that served as highlights to the speaker. It does cover all the relevant areas of Mandarin Chinese grammar.

http://www.askbenny.cn

Benny, the self professed *world's most famous Chinese teacher*, is a great site that introduces very useful sentence constructions and vocabulary. He is very personable and has more energy than is possible. This site is was free!!!! I would rank this site near the top in ease of access, utility and fun for a speaking tool. *was free* Benny has now sold out to capitalism. See ChinesewithMike below.

http://www.chinese-tools.com/

This website has a good dictionary and a translator that converts characters to **Hanyu Pinyin** with tone markers. There is also a idiom dictionary with 30,000 idioms.

http://chinesepod.com/

This website is a audio video site based on progressive learning of Standard Mandarin. There are various levels of membership and the price is very reasonable at the beginner level. The higher priced long winded explanations are too complex for learners. Some of the speakers speak far too fast to make it a learning experience. However, the transcripts in English and **Hanyu Pinyin** available with the sound files are excellent. The moderator **Ken** gives some very incorrect grammatical translations, plus he talks like he has a carrot up his ass. He can be a huge barrier to learning Mandarin Grammar as he mixes up both word order and word usage.

http://www.chinesewithmike.com/

Mike seems to be quickly making the only well organised and well planned site on the internet. He is both on Youtube and has his own site. Perhaps one of the better features is that he has extensive text downloads to supplement his teaching, *free*!. In an online Mandarin world where uncreativity is the hallmark, Mike is funny, presents Mandarin in a logical format and has a down-to-earth genius in teaching methodology. While Chinese born on-line personalities are teaching idioms, culture and strange choices of language, Mike from Chicago has the nuts and bolts of the language that will allow you to survive and learn in a progressive environment.

http://www.peggyteacheschinese.com/

Peggy has a great website and adds to it regularily. She is very personable and funny. I have never seen a Chinese person gesticulate with hands as much as she does. She dramatically slashes all the tones in the air, which is actually very effective for learners. She is very animated and entertaining. She is a student in Taiwan and does great videos and one on one teaching to support her studies. She offers one-on-one tutoring via Skype.com. Irrespective of how entertaining and eternally happy she is, her lessons are very relevant and useful. And guys, if you want to see why us foreign men fall for Chinese girls, it takes about three minutes to fall in love with Peggy. **http://www.youtube.com/user/PeggyTeachesChinese**

http://www.yoyochinese.com/index.html

Cheng Yangyang is another great online resource. Her Youtube name is Sloppy Cheng, I should comment on names? The lessons she provides for free are a great kickstart to learning. She also does teaching English lessons to Chinese students. The great thing about this is that once you are more advanced you can listen to her conversational English to Chinese people, ultimately, listening skills are what will slow you down. Writing and speaking seem like huge barriers at first, but ultimately you will need to adjust your listening to multitudes of personal expressions. Now perhaps this is not a professional way to promote her but my lord, she is one smoking hot babe. **http://www.youtube.com/user/sloppycheng**

Using a Computer in China

Using a computer in China at an internet café is full of risk. First, they are common sites for thieves and I have had young boys crawl on their hands and knees and try and unplug my USB, take by backpack, wallet, passport etc. Often the computers are set up with keystroke copy programs and will copy your credit card, bank account and e-mail passwords. I have had bank accounts emptied twice and charge cards charged up twice.

If you bring your own computer it is a target for thieves and you cannot fall asleep on a bus or train without risk. To safely prepare a computer for use is no short or simple task. I always carry a USB with **CCleaner** on it from **www.ccleaner.com**, a free registry cleaner. I clean the registry both before and after I use the computer.

I also carry the free download **Counter Spy** from **www.sunbelt-software.com** and I run the program to find viruses and spyware. Chinese computers can be very slow and it can take from 20 minutes to 2 hours to make a computer safe. Many Chinese chat programs open the IP address and will take whatever information you have to steal. **QQ** is the most popular chat program in China. Chinese people do not realize that the purpose of the program is to take your information for marketing purposes and sell it to advertisers. The chat utility is a cover. So I remove it. Programs such as **Windows Password Reset** will allow you to bypass security functions and remove malicious programs. I always remove **QQ** and the entire **Tencent** family of programs. I install my registry cleaner and spyware program and sometimes take out dozens of Trojans and viruses. I have found that most computers in China are not secured and they have no administrator passwords anyhow.

It is very important to have **Skype** on your USB, a headset and a **Skype** account. Calling out of China can be a real challenge in remote areas. **www.Skype.com**

How to Spend Your Money Wisely

1) My books, CD's and website. www.SpeakandWriteChinese.com

2) **Beginner's Chinese** by Yong Ho 1977   ISBN 0-7818-0566-X

There are multitudes of introductory books on the market but this book has more useful methods to learn in this book of 174 pages than a huge pile of other books I have. I carried this book in China for a long time.

3) **Chinese Grammar** by Claudia Ross. 2004   ISBN 0-07-137764-6

I have all the classic grammar texts, Chao, Li, etc. but this book has all the relevant grammar in it. If you master this book you do not need any other grammar to speak Mandarin. The book is structured in a very practical way.

4) Wenlin DVD available at www.wenlin.com

Of the multitude of Chinese learning DVD's I have, this replaces them all. You can learn everything here in an easy interface, stroke order, Radicals, Words versus characters. You can search specific Radicals within characters and words. For the beginner or researcher this is the best bang for the buck. Rather than randomly buy 10 different tools, buy this one.

5) e-Stroke available at www.eon.com

This program allows you to cut, paste, and drop a character into their tool and it gives you an animated stroke order, **Pinyin** and definition. It is indispensible for identifying obscure characters.

6) **Chit-Chat Chinese** by Rachel Meyer. 2010   ISBN 978-9576129063

This book is the best of the best. This book is a systematic and gradual progression of the most useful characters compiling the most useful grammatical constructions. Characters are introduced with pronunciation, Hanyu Pinyin, meaning and then simple useful sentences. There is no searching all over the book to chase the components of each character. Repetition is gently integrated without the psychosis of Pimsleur. The integration of pronouns, verbs, proper nouns, adverbs, and nouns is so well balanced that useful sentences compile at a comforting rate. The author effectively inserts anecdotes, cultural points, idioms and humour.

Finding a Chinese Language Partner

Cut these out or photocopy them and put your phone number in the columns and get these babies plastered all over China Town or the Faculty of Computer Science at your local university.

我	教	你	英文	你	教	我	汉语
Wǒ	jiāo	nǐ	Yīngwén,	nǐ	jiāo	Wǒ	Hànyǔ.
Me	teach	you	English,	you	teach	me	**Hanyu**.

我	教	你	英文	你	教	我	汉语
Wǒ	jiāo	nǐ	Yīngwén,	nǐ	jiāo	Wǒ	Hànyǔ.
Me	teach	you	English,	you	teach	me	**Hanyu**.

Version of Original Stroke Order Rules

1. From top to bottom (从上到下) 三

2. From left to right (从左到右) 川

3. First horizontal afterwards vertical (先横后竖) 十

4. First (撇, piě, throw) afterwards (捺, nà, press down) (先撇后捺) 文

5. From outside to inside (从外到内) 回

6. From inside toward outside (从内到外)

7. First inside afterwards seal (先里头后封口) 日

8. First middle afterwards two sides (先中间后两边) 小

9. Intersect stroke afterward write (相交笔画后写) 我

10. First left (竖, shù, vertical) afterward seal (先左竖后封口) 目

11. Dot at top side or left top first write (点在上边或左上先写) 头

12. Dot at right top or inside afterwards write (点在右上或里边后写) 我 国

(从, cóng, from)　　　　　　　(竖, shù, vertical)

(上, shàng, top)　　　　　　　(撇, piě, throw)

(到, dào, to)　　　　　　　　(捺, nà, press down)

(下, xià, under)　　　　　　　(外, wài, outside)

(左, zuǒ, left)　　　　　　　　(内, nèi, inside)

(右, yòu, righ)　　　　　　　(里头, lǐtou, inside)

(横, héng, horizontal)　　　　(封口, fēngkǒu, seal)

(后, hòu, after)　　　　　　　(两边, liǎngbiān, both sides)

(相, xiāng, each other) (在, zài, at)

(交, jiāo, join) (边, biān, side]

(相交, xiāngjiāo, intersect) (或, huò, or)

(笔画, bǐhuà, stroke) (里边, lǐbian, inside)

(写, xiě, write) (先, xiān, first)

(点, diǎn, dot) (中间, zhōngjiān, middle)

Ending this Book

As I never really had a thorough plan as to how I was going to do this book, I also did not have a plan as to how I was going to finish it. I hit all the most common grammar structures and my goal was to make this book heavy on examples versus the books that are out there. I started in 2009 just before my wife came from China. Today is May 1st 2011 and we celebrate her arrival two years ago on May 17th. Getting this book done has been slowed by tutoring grade 12 subjects and now Nursing courses. In this time I have made several trips to China and worked in Haiti after the earthquake and then Dominican Republic. In entirity my life has been enriched incredibly by meeting, marrying her and bringing her to Canada.

I have a very vague idea for 2 more grammar books. The plan is to make them progressively more complex, that is, the first is simple grammar and the next will use slightly more complex grammar.

So, this more or less finishes the book, my wife is in the kitchen singing some Chinese pop tune to the internet radio and chopping onions at super sonic speed to make (包子, **bāozi, steamed stuffed bun**), steamed dumplings with little treats inside. She has all of her seeds ready that she smuggled from China to plant her Chinese garden, again. She has already made the phone call to the old country to get an auspicious date for planting from her father. Not that he has any idea of Canadian weather.

So if you have any questions, ideas, comments, criticism, let me know. damaohouzi@yahoo.ca

Erratum?, Errors?, I don't think so!, Ideas?

My wife pointed out that I should end the book with an auspicious number with an eight so this is chapter 108. I really don't have anything to say here. So, given that I have great fun finding errors in others books, I am sure that there some in my books. In fact, I intentionally made an error for you to find so that you can send the corrections to me and I will email you some practice work sheets.

Let me now what you would like in future books. Oddly, I am the worlds most published author in Chinese character language books. Not that I am bragging. Now I can have a respite on book writing and try and figure out how to make a functional website. My plan on my website is to have a progressive series of videos and downloadable work lessons.

The best bang for your buck for ease of access, no cost and entertainment are these three sites below. And don't be afraid to go to China, if you are an initiate adventurer, arrive and then book an organized trip. A friend of mine recently did a ten day trip for $700.00, that's Canadian. This included in-country flights, trains, taxis, buses, boat cruises , hotels and food.

http://www.chinesewithmike.com/

http://www.peggyteacheschinese.com/

http://www.yoyochinese.com/index.html

大毛猴子

DaMaoHouzi@yahoo.ca

www.ingramcontent.com/pod-product-compliance
Lightning Source LLC
Chambersburg PA
CBHW080326170426
43194CB00014B/2481